On Black Psychology Today:

Perspectives, Theory, and Research

Patricia Heisser Metoyer, Ph.D. Editor

Printed in the United States of America

ISBN: ISBN-13: 978-1541384965

ISBN-10: 1541384962

Cover image courtesy of The African American Natural History Museum

Contents

Prologue   1

The History and Visions of African American Psychology Multiple Pathways to Place,
Space, and Authority Bertha Garrett Holliday   7

Racial Microagressions Against Black Americans Implications for Counseling   41

  Derald Wing et al.

A Contemporary History of the Church, Hip Hop and Technology   57

Their Influence on African American Youth Development Marybeth Gasman and Edward M. Epstein

Examining Race/Ethnicity and Fears of Children and Adolescents in the United
States   71

Differences Between White, African American, and Hispanic Populations Joy J. Burnham and Richard G.
Lomax

Advancing the Africentric Paradigm Shift Discourse Building toward Evidence-Based
Africentric Interventions in Social Work Practice with African Americans   81

  Dorie J. Gilbert et al.

Building on Strengths Intergenerational Practice with African American Families Cheryl Waites   94

Parental Infl uence, School Readiness and Early Academic Achievement of African
American Boys   108

  Emanique M. Joe and James Earl Davis

Perceptions of Teacher Expectations by African American High School Students 127

  Beverly E. Pringle, James E. Lyons and Keonya C. Booker

Operationalizing StyleQuantifying the Use of Style Shift in the Speech of African American Adolescents Jennifer Renn and J. Michael Terry   137

Cultural Considerations in the Development of School-Based Interventions for African American   156

Low-Income African American Male Youth with ADHD Symptoms in the United States

Recommendations for Clinical Mental Health Counselors Catherine Tucker and Andrea L. Dixon   170

What African American Male Adolescents Are Telling Us about HIV Infection   181
among Their Peers

Cultural Approaches for HIV Prevention Dexter R. Voisin and Jason D. P. Bird

Eating Disorders in African American GirlsImplications for Counselors Regine M. Tallyrand 193

Differences between European Americans and African Americans in the   ~203
Association between Child Obesity and Disrupted Parenting

Leslie Gordon Simons et al.

Racial and Ethnic-Related Stressors as Predictors of Perceived Stress and Academic Performance for African American Students at a Historically Black College and University   223

Tawanda M. Greer

Prologue

"It is a peculiar sensation, this double consciousness, this sense of always looking at one's self through the eyes of others, of measuring one's soul by the tape of a world that looks on in amused contempt and pity. One ever feels his(her) two-ness,—an American, a Negro: two souls, two thoughts, two unreconciled strivings; two warring ideals in one dark body, whose dogged strength alone keeps it from being torn asunder."

W.E.B. DuBois, *Th e Souls of Black Folks*, 1903, p. 3

For cultural invasion to succeed, it is essential that those invaded become convinced of their intrinsic inferiority. Since everything has its opposite, if those who are invaded consider themselves inferior; they must necessarily recognize the superiority of the invaders. Th e values of the latter thereby become the patterns for the former. Th e invasion is accentuated and those invaded are alienated from the spirit of their own culture and from themselves, the more the latter want to be like the invaders: to walk like them, dress like them, talk like them.

Unlike other immigrants, the African American experience in the United States is distinct. Th e African civilization of the 16th and 17th centuries was as advanced as that of the Europeans during that same period (Zinn, 2003, p. 26). Yet slavery in the United States interrupted the continuity of this legacy and has created a unique set of psychological dynamics that must be explored. *African American Psychology* provides students with the opportunity to delve into the complex historical, cultural, and linguistic realities of clients of African American descent.

African American Psychology focuses on the social I of the African American, which is formed in the socio-cultural relations of the American structure, and therefore refl ects the duality of experience in America. Th is duality, as W.E.B. DuBois explains, is why African-Americans, at a certain moment of their existential experience, almost 'adhere' to American 'values.' Cultural invasion is only one instrument of domination, and on the other, the result of domination. Th is book includes topics that represent the quintessential American cultural product that refl ects the experience of cultural domination and duality. Most important, from this journey has grown collaboration in the fi eld of psychology to assist those in the helping professions in understanding their experiences, rich narratives, spiritual development and in respecting their perceptions of themselves not only as individuals but also as members of a larger community.

Th e aesthetic of a nation defi nes its culture and shapes its history. Th e African American experience contains the history of this country, subtlety interrogating the offi cial historiography of the nation. It is a testament to and a voice of those who were offi cially rendered voiceless. Far from wallowing in sentimentality or anger, its achievement is triumph over adversity with elegance and exemplifi es many of the best ideals held sacred by Americans. Regardless of what Black people ultimately decide about the questions of separation, integration, segregation, revolution, or reform, it is vitally important that we develop, out of the authentic experience of Black people in this country. (White, 2004, p. 5)

Patricia Heisser Metoyer, Ph.D.

REFERENCES

DuBois, W.E.B. (1994), *Th e Souls of Black Folks*, New York, Dover Publications, Inc.

White, J. (2004) Towards a Black Psychology. In R. Jones (Ed.). *Black Psychology* (4th ed.) Hampton, VA. Cobb & Henry Press.

The History and Visions of African American Psychology

Multiple Pathways to Place, Space, and Authority

Bertha Garrett Holliday

Th e author describes the multiple pathways of events and strategies that served to nurture African American psychology in the United States. Special attention is given to strategies for inclusion and empowerment used in 4 psychological professional and scholarly associations: the American Counseling Association, the American Psychological Association, the Association of Black Psychologists, and the Society for Research in Child Development. In addition, the author describes 4 major intellectual traditions that informed not only the strategies of inclusion but also the theoretical, research, and intervention perspectives and other professional and academic eff-orts of African American psychologists. Th-ose perspectives are the Afrocentric/African-centered tradition derived from longstanding nationalist/ Pan-African and culturally centered traditions within African American communities; the social contextual/multidisciplinary research tradition of the University of Chicago School of Social Science; the empirical social science research tradition of the University of Michigan; and the Black scholar/activist tradition of Howard University. Th-is article also presents a chronological timeline of major events in the history of African American psychology.

Th-e attempt to defi-ne a black aesthetic based on the black experience, to fi-nd a particular black idiom both for artistic and political purposes, and to reform historical interpretation so that the black will be liberated from the subordinate position assigned him in most Western historical accounts—these are all aspects of the search or research for collective identity and, derivatively, for distinctive personality.

> —Raymond Betts (1971, p. 1), Introduction, *Th e Ideology of Blackness*

African American psychologist Algea Harrison-Hale has observed that there are certain minimum requirements for building a professional and scholarly tradition within an area of interest. Th-ese include mentors; colleagues who share common professional or research interests; and fi-nancial, administrative, and institutional support (Harrison-Hale, 2006, pp. 168–169). Until the 1960s, due in part to their small numbers, there was little possibility of developing such a tradition among African American psychologists. Indeed, prior to that time, there were distinct and harsh barriers to African

American participation in psychology, including restricted training opportunities, extremely limited occupational opportunities, and widely held assumptions among European American psychologists of the intellectual and social "defi-cits" of African Americans, which promoted a disciplinary consensus of the impossibility, diffi-culty, or lack of necessity of identifying "qualifi-ed" African American graduate students and professionals (Holliday, 1999). Consequently, as recently as the late 1960s, major universities such as UCLA, Cornell, Harvard, Illinois, Yale, Stanford, and Iowa had not granted a single doctorate in psychology to an African American (Wispe et al., 1969).

Such assumptions and restrictions were severely challenged by the Civil Rights era of the 1950s through 1970s, which served to dismantle the legal bases of racial segregation and its associated social conventions. Consequently, institutions of higher education began to seek students of color, and the number of African American students admitted to psychology graduate programs in the 1970s and 1980s was suffi-ciently large to constitute a cohort. Th-is fi-rst cohort of signifi-cant size of African American psychologists, in the absence of a prior tradition, was confronted with the challenges of establishing a place in psychology's occupational and organizational structures and collegial networks, securing an intellectual space within psychology, and acquiring suffi-cient authority to make a diff-erence.

It is my premise here that U.S. social-political history and unique professional and scholarly organizational histories and cultures, coupled with the infl-uences of varying extant broader intellectual traditions served to promote multiple pathways for addressing issues of place, space, and authority and fostered the rich diversity that now characterizes African American psychology.

Social and Historical Contexts

The 19th Century and the First Half of the 20th Century: Enslavement, Oppression, and Jim Crowism

Th-e participation of African Americans in psychology can only be fully understood against the background of U.S. history. For example, 19th-century U.S. history is to a great extent defi-ned by colonialism and national expansion that was marked not only by vast land acquisitions, but also by the conquest, oppression, and exploitation of peoples of color—including institutionalized strategies for the management of the U.S.'s enslaved African American population. Slavery and the southern plantation economy it supported were among the major factors precipitating the Civil War. As a result of the war, African Americans were emancipated, but shortly thereaft-er, an apartheid-like Jim Crow system of social and economic relations was established, especially in the South (Franklin & Moss, 2000).

Emancipation and Reconstruction after the Civil War, however, did bring some benefits that are of enduring significance—for example, the establishment of colleges for African Americans. Some of these colleges were financially supported by African American church denominations and their congregations of newly emancipated slaves. During the first quarter of the 20th century, the push of Jim Crow and the pull of northern industrialization resulted in the Great Migration of 500,000 to 1 million African Americans from the rural South to the urban northern areas (Great Migration, 1999, pp. 869–872). Simultaneously, the legacy of the ethos of slavery, the institutional patterns sanctioned by the Black Codes (which legally sanctioned segregation and subordinate Black social and political status), and the attitudes underpinning the behavioral patterns of Jim Crowism promoted within the fledgling discipline of psychology a type of scientific racism wherein the behavior of White Americans was interpreted as appropriate and normative, whereas African American behavior was interpreted as inferior and nonnormative. More troubling, such inferiority and nonnormativeness were typically viewed as genetically based and not modifiable (Richards, 1997).

During the first half of the 20th century, prior to the eradication of legally sanctioned social segregation and Jim Crowism, African American colleges provided the major institutional base for African American psychologists, who often viewed their teaching and research as opportunities to challenge scientific racism's assumptions and public policy implications, especially those related to the capabilities and education of African American children and youth (cf. Guthrie, 1998; Holliday & Holmes, 2003; Richards, 1997, chap. 2–5).

The Great Depression of the 1930s and the New Deal strategy of President Franklin D. Roosevelt's administration were especially significant for psychology in general and the nation's small number of African American psychologists. During the Depression, about 40% of members of the American Psychological Association (APA) were unemployed (Miller, 1986, p. 127). This, coupled with the Depression's scope of human misery, caused many psychologists to recognize that social-economic factors affect behavior, and that social issues, problems, and attitudes should be subjects of psychological theory and research, including prejudice and purported racial differences (Finison, 1986; Harris, 1986; Miller, 1986; Morawski, 1986; Sitkoff, 1978, pp. 194–201). In turn, such assumptions supported the emergence of a distinct "antiracism" perspective in psychology that emphasized such themes as the attribution of racial differences to environmental differences and race as a social construct. This perspective marked a formal (and progressive) challenge of the scientific racism perspective in psychology of innate racial differences (Richards, 1997, chap. 4). However, over time, this "antiracism" research, which most frequently involved racial comparative research paradigms that subtly promoted assumptions of White superiority, resulted in equally troubling alternative explanations of the behavior of people of color, characterized by emphases on "damage," "deficiency," and "deprivation" that were often portrayed as irreparable (cf. Katz, 1969; Pearl, 1970; Rainwater, 1970; Valentine, 1971).

The Depression's economic devastation of African American communities with their relatively small leadership class caused some private foundations (e.g., the Rosenwald Fund, the General Education Board) along with various New Deal programs to provide both higher educational opportunities and jobs for a small but growing number of social scientists of color, including psychologists (Holliday, 1989, 1999). This served to help strengthen an emerging institutional base for African Americans in psychology. According to Canady (1939, as reported by Guthrie, 1998, pp. 126–129), by 1936 Black colleges had a total of 88 psychology faculty—although most of these were European Americans. At the 1938 meeting of the all-Black American Teachers Association (ATA), a division was organized for ATA members interested in "the teaching and application of the science of psychology and related fi-elds, particularly in Negro institutions" (Guthrie, 1998, pp. 142–145).

The Post-World War II and Civil Rights Era Years

Aft-er World War II, psychological research was enriched and transformed by the establishment of the National Institute of Mental Health (NIMH) in 1946 and the National Science Foundation in 1950 (Holliday, 1999; Holliday & Holmes, 2003, pp. 26–27). Simultaneously, psychology continued to fl - ourish at the African American colleges when these institutions were strengthened by the infl-ux of former Black soldiers using their GI education benefi-ts. By 1950, 32 African Americans had received a PhD or EdD in psychology or educational psychology (Guthrie, 1998, chap. 7). Th-ese psychologists continued to confront a racially segregated social order and highly restricted professional opportunities. Most were employed at Black colleges; some were able to fi-nd employment in public school systems and government. Consequently, the professional eff-orts of nearly all of these psychologists focused on the needs and education of African American children and youth and gravitated to psychological issues with practical applications (Guthrie, 1998, p. 123; Slaughter-Defoe, 2006b).

However, the progressive racial integration of U.S. social institutions served both to transform social discourse about the place, capabilities, and social roles of African Americans, and to expand the occupational and advocacy opportunities of Black psychologists. By Executive Orders 9980 and 9981 (President Truman), the U.S. civil service and military services, respectively, were integrated in 1948. In 1954, the U.S. Supreme Court ruled in favor of the plaintiff in *Brown v. Topeka Board of Education.* Th-is decision resulted in dismantling the nation's legally sanctioned segregated public education systems "with all deliberate speed." Th-is decision also was notable for two other reasons: (a) It was the fi-rst Supreme Court decision to involve the citation of psychological data, and (b) the primary architect in the compilation and use of those data was an African American psychologist—Kenneth B. Clark, PhD (Benjamin & Crouse, 2002; J. P. Jackson, 2006; Pickren & Tomes, 2002).

Th-e *Brown* decision can be viewed as the beginning of the "Civil Rights era," which lasted for nearly a quarter of a century and primarily involved various social-legal tactics and challenges for both securing protections guaranteed by the 14th and 15th constitutional amendments and for eliminating racially diff-erential, legally sanctioned practices (Jim Crowism) that existed throughout U.S. society (cf. Sullivan, 1999). Th-e success of these eff-orts served to increase both the Civil Rights movement's self- consciousness and its concern with group solidarity and self-reliance. It also has been argued that the era resulted in four relatively sudden and major transformations within African American individuals and communities: social-economic (i.e., the distribution of valued social goods and services), ecological (i.e., spatial confi-gurations and environmental features or "behavioral settings" of group and family life), historical imperatives (i.e., guides to future action rooted in the past such as intergenerational and intergroup relations), and cultural imperatives (i.e., subjective interpretations of and responses to the social world as guided by values, beliefs, personal identity, and group ideology; Holliday, 1986).

African American psychologists were not immune from such changes and transformations, which they experienced both personally and professionally. Buttressed by a signifi-cant increase in the number of African American psychology graduate students and psychologists, and informed by a history of discipline- and organization-building at Black colleges and in other Black community settings, as well as by the indigenous community-based social change strategies of the Civil Rights movement, African American psychologists assumed leadership during the 1970s of ethnic minority psychologists' search for place, space, and authority.

Much of African American psychologists' eff-orts to ensure their place in psychology's occupational and organizational structures and collegial networks were enacted in the contexts of professional and scientifi-c associations and societies. Th-e following are limited overviews of African American psychologists' progressive strategic eff-orts and associated outcomes in four psychological associations and societies: the Association of Black Psychologists (ABPsi), the APA, the American Counseling Association (ACA), and the Society for Research in Child Development (SRCD). Th-is discussion of organizational contexts describes major challenges, strategies, initiatives, and outcomes of African American psychologists' quest for participation, inclusion, and policy change within the associations and societies of concern.

Additional detail of such eff-orts is provided in Table 1. (next page)

A more comprehensive analysis would include reviews of the history of African American participation in the Association for Psychological Science (formerly the American Psychological Society), in more of psychology's scientifi-c societies (which are characterized by collegial networks among persons in defi-ned specialty areas in psychology), as well as in multidisciplinary associations and societies that include concern for psychological issues (such as the American Orthopsychiatry Association and the Society for Neuroscience). Th-e four associations discussed here were selected because of the availability of documentation of African Americans' participatory experiences and the current relatively high visibility of Black psychologists in these associations. Across the associations and societies reviewed, one will note similarities and diff-erences in strategies used by Black psychologists to increase their participation and infl-uence, which are posited as responses primarily to variations in the associations' and societies' values, culture, mission, and size. It is also noteworthy that it was (and is) not uncommon for Black leadership to rotate among these associations and societies. Th-us, this rotation or expansion of leadership emerges as a strategy unto itself for bringing the experiences of and strategies for African American inclusion and participation to multiple association contexts while simultaneously broadening the experiences, capabilities, and collegial networks of Black leadership in psychology.

ABPsi

ABPsi was established in 1968 in San Francisco at the annual convention of the APA in protest to APA's lack of responsiveness to the interests and needs of African American psychologists and the communities they serve. Nearly all of the national ethnic minority psychological associations and Black caucuses within psychological associations and societies point to ABPsi as the inspiration and model for their establishment. As noted in a press release announcing its establishment, ABPsi was founded as an ethnocentric and community-centered organization and in reaction to the insensitivity of APA:

> Members of the Association have pledged themselves to the realization that they are Black people fi-rst and psychologists second. ... Th-e membership assumes primary responsibility for engaging in critical thinking about the relationships between Black people and the society in which they live ... we are pledged to eff-ect change in those areas in which the American Psychological Association has been insensitive, ineff-ectual, and insincere. (Williams, 1974, pp. 11–12)

At the 1968 APA convention, ABPsi presented the APA a petition of concerns. Th-is petition addressed the three major issues that would serve as organizing principles for future professional organization activities of persons of color in psychology. Th-ese issues were (a) the low numbers of Black psychologists and Black graduate students in psychology, (b) APA's failure both to direct its scientifi-c and professional energies toward the solution of permanent social concerns—particularly those of poverty and racism—and to address social problems of concern to communities of color (e.g., the Kerner Report on Civil Disorders; IQ testing), and (c) the inadequate representation of Blacks in the APA governance structure (Baker, 2003; Pickren & Tomes, 2002; Williams, 1974, 2008). Th-e petition included specifi-c proposals for addressing these issues (Williams, 1974, 2008). Th-e petition would guide many of ABPsi's activities for nearly a decade.

Th-e next year, in 1969, approximately 85 students at the Western Psychological Association meeting in Vancouver, British Columbia, established the Black Students Psychological Association (BSPA). Later, at the 1969 APA convention, BSPA students interrupted the APA presidential address and made a brief presentation of their concerns followed by a request to meet with the APA Council of Representatives for more detailed discussions. Th-e students were informed that they would be able to speak to the council the next day—and the APA president was then allowed to present his address uninterrupted. Th-e next day, BSPA President Gary Simkins presented a 5-point program to the council related to increasing ethnic minority recruitment and retention. In response, the APA's council and board immediately took action in support of BSPA's concerns (Williams, 1974).

Table 1

Timeline of the History of African Americans in U.S. Psychology

Year	Event
1869	Major General Canby, military commander of Union forces occupying Virginia, authorizes the establishment of the first U.S. institution for the exclusive care of African American mental patients. Howard's Grove Asylum, later name Central State Hospital, was opened April 1885 near Petersburg (Street, 1994, p. 42).
1892	The American Psychological Association (APA) is founded by 26 [White] men (Street, 1994).
1899	Howard University offers its first psychology course, "Psychology: The Brief Course" (Hopkins, Ross, & Hicks, 1994).
1917	U.S. War Department adopts the Army Alpha and Army Beta tests developed by psychologist Robert Yerkes (Street, 1994).
1920	Francis C. Sumner is the first African American awarded the PhD in psychology from a U.S. institution (Clark University); dissertation title: *Psychoanalysis of Freud and Adler* (Guthrie, 1994; Street, 1994).
	J. Henry Alston is first African American to publish a research article ("Psychophysics of the Spatial Condition of the Fusion of Warmth and Cold in Heat") in an exclusively psychological journal, *The American Journal of Psychology* (Cadwallader, as cited by Benimoff, 1995).
1928	Psychology department is established at Howard University chaired by Francis C. Sumner (Hopkins, Ross, & Hicks, 1994).
1930s	Four Historically Black Colleges and Universities (HBCUs) offer psychology as an undergraduate major (Evans, 1999; Guthrie, 1998).
1933	Inez B. Prosser is first African American woman awarded a doctorate (EdD) in psychology from a U.S. institution (University of Cincinnati; dissertation title: *Non-academic Development of Negro Children in Mixed and Segregated Schools*; Benjamin, Henry, & McMahon, 2005; Guthrie, 1976).
1934	The *Journal of Negro Education* (published by Howard University) develops a special issue of 14 papers that challenge the functions and findings of racial differences research.
1937	Alberta Banner Turner is first African American woman awarded a PhD in psychology from a U.S. institution (Ohio State University; Cadwallader, as cited by Benimoff, 1995; Guthrie, 1976).
1938	The first ethnic minority psychological association is established as Division 6, the Department of Psychology, at the meeting of the all-Black American Teachers Association (ATA) for ATA members interested in "the teaching and application of the science of psychology and related fields, particularly in Negro institutions," with Herman Canady, psychologist at West Virginia State College, elected as its chairman (Guthrie, 1998).
1942	Kenneth B. Clark becomes the first African American faculty hired at City College of New York (J. P. Jackson, Jr., 2006).
1947	Mamie and Kenneth B. Clark publish doll studies that demonstrate Black children's preference for White dolls, which the Clarks

[Handwritten margin notes: "1. Failure to address poverty & racism 2. Inadequate representation of Blacks within Governance structure"; "APA's ↓"; "ABPsi"; "ABPsi"]

interpreted as indicating the development of racial concepts and conflict in the children's ego structure (J. P. Jackson, Jr., 2006).

1951   The NAACP Legal Defense and Education Fund enlists the assistance of Kenneth B. Clark to (a) be a witness in *Brown v. Topeka Board of Education*, (b) enlist other social scientists, and (c) work directly with NAACP lawyers in going over the briefs that deal with social science material, such as racial differences in intelligence, psychological damage derived from segregation, and prejudice/intergroup contact, and how these might affect the process of desegregation (J. P. Jackson, Jr., 2006).

1954   U.S. Supreme Court rules on *Brown v. Topeka Board of Education,* and requires the dismantling of racially segregated systems of education "with all deliberate speed." Decision in part relied on psychological and social science data on the effects of segregation that were prepared by a committee of the Society for the Psychological Study of Social Issues (SPSSI—APA Division 9) that included Kenneth B. Clark, PhD, Isidor Chein, PhD, and Stuart Cook, PhD (Benjamin & Crouse, 2002).

1955   Publication of *Prejudice and Your Child* by African American psychologist Kenneth B. Clark.

1958   Publication of Audrey Shuey's *The Testing of Negro Intelligence*, which argues the existence of native [innate] racial IQ differences of 13 to 15 points (Richards, 1997).

1963   The APA ad hoc Committee on Equality of Opportunity in Psychology is established by the APA Board of Directors in response to a

proposal from Division 9 (SPSSI) relative to the training and employment of Negroes *sic*. The committee is charged "to explore" the possible problems encountered in training and employment in psychology as a consequence of race . . . " (APA, 1963; ComasDiaz, 1990; Wispe et al., 1969).

1965   Kenneth B. Clark, in his book *Dark Ghetto: Dilemmas of Social Power,* is one of the first scholars to describe U.S. race relations through use of the colonial metaphor by portraying Harlem as an internal colony of the White United States that had been systematically looted by the White power, which had profited from its social isolation (J. P. Jackson, Jr., 2006).

1967   Dr. Martin Luther King, at the invitation of Milton Rokeach, PhD, and the SPSSI (APA Division 9) Council, presents an address "The Role of the Social Scientist in the Civil Rights Movement" at the annual APA convention. African American psychologist Robert L.
Green, PhD, was pivotal in securing King's attendance and in providing assistance with the drafting of his presentation. Correspondence files also indicate that APA was unwilling to contribute to assist SPSSI in defraying King's associated travel expenses (personal correspondence, Joseph White to Bertha Holliday, February 6, 2007; Milton Rokeach correspondence files at the Archives of the History of American Psychology, University of Akron).

1968   The Association of Black Psychologists (ABPsi) is established at the APA convention in San Francisco, with Charles L. Thomas, PhD, and Robert L. Green, PhD, elected as co-chairs on September 2 (Street, 1994; Williams, 1974).
ABPsi Co-chair Charles L. Thomas presents a petition of concerns to the APA Council of Representatives that addresses three major issues: (a) the extremely limited number of Black psychologists and Black graduate and undergraduate students in psychology, (b) APA's failure to address social problems such as poverty and racism, and (c) the inadequate representation of Blacks in the APA governance structure (Baker, 2003; Guzman et al., 1992; Williams, 1974).
Howard University, a HBCU, establishes a PhD program in psychology (Hopkins, Ross, & Hicks, 1994).

1969   The Black Students Psychological Association (BSPA) is established at the Western Psychological Association meeting in Vancouver, BC (Williams, 1974).
BSPA President Gary Simpkins presents demands to APA related to the recruitment, retention, and training of Black students and faculty (Figueroa-Garcia, 1994; Guzman et al., 1992; Street, 1994; Williams, 1974).

(table continues)

Table 1 (*continued*)

Year	Event
1970	APA establishes the Commission for Accelerating Black Participation in Psychology (CABPP) composed of representatives of BSPA, ABPsi, and APA, and charges CABPP to address BSPA's concerns (Blau, 1970; Williams, 1974). ABPsi provides all graduate departments of psychology its 10-point program for increasing the representation of Blacks in psychology; 35 departments agree to immediately implement the entire program (Williams, 1974). ABPsi and APA develop a 3-year Black visiting scientist program to HBCUs (Williams, 1974). BSPA opens offices in the APA building in Washington, DC, with APA providing 3 years of funding; Ernestine Thomas is the office's director and BSPA national coordinator (Figueroa-Garcia, 1994; Williams, 1974). Kenneth B. Clark, an African American who previously served as the first Black on the APA Board of Directors, becomes the first person of color to become APA president (Pickren & Tomes, 2002; Street, 1994).
1971	In response to demands of the Black Psychiatrists of America, the National Institute of Mental Health (NIMH) Center for Minority Group Mental Health Programs is established with a focus on (a) funding investigator-initiated studies on the mental health concerns of ethnic minorities; (b) establishing and administering six research and development

centers, each of which focuses on mental health needs of a particular racial/cultural group; and (c) initiating the Minority Fellowship Program, which provides funding to five professional associations including APA to administer minority fellowships for research and clinical training in psychiatry, psychology, psychiatric nursing, psychiatric social work, and sociology (Guzman et al., 1992; Parron, 1990).

1972	Publication of the first edition of *Black Psychology* edited by Reginald L. Jones, PhD, which heralds a proactive perspective of the psychology of African Americans.
	The Bay Area chapter of the Association of Black Psychologists issues a position statement on use of IQ and ability tests, which demands that the California State Department of Education declare a moratorium on these tests' use in assessing Black children (Richards, 1997).
	The Association of Non-White Concerns in Personnel and Guidance is founded as a division of the American Personnel and Guidance Association (APGA) with voting rights in both APGA's Senate and on its Board of Directors.
1973	As a result of a vote of the APA membership, the APA Board for Social and Ethical Responsibility for Psychology is established with a mandate that includes issues related to minority participation in psychology (Pickren & Tomes, 2002).
	Joseph Hodges, Ura Jean Oyemade, Graham Matthews, and others convene the first meeting of African Americans interested in child development research (BICD)—the forerunner of the Society for Research in Child Development (SRCD) Black Caucus—with goals related to professional networking and support, linkage with other groups with similar interests in Black children, development of a position paper on its relationship with SRCD, and promotion of research and discussions on issues of significant for Black researchers and Black children. BICD renamed itself the Black Caucus of the SRCD in 1975, and Jean Carew became its first official chairperson in 1977 (Slaughter-Defoe, 2006a).
	Diana Slaughter on behalf of the SRCD Black Caucus prepares the first directory of some Black Americans interested in child development research, which lists 68 names.
1974	The APA Minority Fellowship Program is established, with funding provided by NIMH and Dalmas Taylor, PhD, as director (ComasDiaz, 1990; Guzman et al., 1992).
	ABPsi publishes the first issue of the *Journal of Black Psychology* edited by William David Smith, PhD (Street, 1994).
	ABPsi issues *Psychological Testing of Black People: A Position Paper* (B. Holliday's personal files).
1975	As a result of the California Supreme Court's decision in *Larry P. v. Wilson Riles* that use of intelligence tests results in racial bias in the placement of students into programs for the educable mentally retarded, the California Board of Education declares a moratorium on the uses of such tests for such purposes. African American psychologist Asa G. Hilliard III served as principal architect and lead expert witness of this challenge of the use of IQ tests (Bowser, 1996; Street, 1994).
1977	SRCD establishes the Committee on Minority Participation (COMP) with Algea Harrison as its appointed chair and with the goal of diversifying SRCD. In its 1978 initial report to the SRCD Governing Council, COMP recommended strategies for increasing minority participation relative to governance, professional socialization (including increasing Black participation in the SRCD publication process), and professional integration. Later, COMP becomes a SRCD standing committee (in 1985) and is renamed the Committee on Ethnic and Racial Issues (Garrett et al., 2006, pp. 197, 200; McLoyd, 2006, p. 137).
1978	With the leadership of Dalmas Taylor, the Dulles Conference is convened by the APA Board of Directors, the APA Board of Social and Ethical Responsibility, and NIMH on the topic of expanding the roles of culturally diverse peoples in the profession of psychology and recommends the establishment of an APA Office and Board on Ethnic Minority Affairs (Comas-Diaz, 1990; Guzman et al., 1992; Street, 1994; S. Sue, 1994).
	Kenneth B. Clark receives the first APA Award for Distinguished Contributions to Psychology in the Public Interest (Street, 1994).
	The APA ad hoc Committee on Minority Affairs is established, and later notes that major areas of ethnic minority concern include (a) psychological and educational testing, (b) APA accreditation criteria and procedures, (c) ethnic minority curriculum issues, (d) licensure/certification issues, (e) publication/editorial activities, (f) underrepresentation of ethnic minorities in APA's governance structure, and (g) APA's involvement in court and legislative advocacy (Comas-Diaz, 1990; Holliday, 1992).
	ABPsi declines to attend the Dulles Conference because of "numerous attempts by ABPsi to work out strategies with APA which met with nonresponsiveness in addition to an apparent "hidden agenda" to program the conference to deliver a recommendation for a Minority Division of APA" (ABPsi, 1978, p. 7).
1979	The APA Office of Ethnic Minority Affairs (OEMA) is established, with Estaban Olmedo, PhD, as its director (Comas-Dias, 1990). U.S. District Court rules that in regards to *Larry P. v. Wilson Riles*, California's use of standardized intelligence testing in schools for purposes of placing children in special education was discriminatory and therefore illegal (Guthrie, 1998; Hilliard, 1983; Street, 1994).
	ABPsi publishes *Sourcebook on the Teaching of Black Psychology* (two volumes) edited by Reginald L. Jones. Volume I (640 pages) provided undergraduate and graduate course outlines, and Volume II (320 pages) provided instructional materials such as films, activities, exercises , case studies, tests, group discussion topics, questionnaires, audiovisual materials, bibliographies, etc. (ABPsi, 1979).

(table continues)

Table 1 (*continued*)

Year	Event
	Unable to gain election of a person of color to the SRCD Governing Council, the council appoints African American Harriette McAdoo, PhD, to the council (Garrett et al., 2006, p. 197).
1980	By vote of the APA membership, the APA Board of Ethnic Minority Affairs (BEMA) is established; Henry Tomes, PhD, is elected chair.
	John McAdoo, PhD, becomes the first African American appointed to the editorial board of SRCD's journal, *Child Development* (Garrett et al., 2006, p. 198).
	Black Caucus of SRCD issues first issue of its newsletter (Garrett et al., 2006).
1981	BEMA establishes a task force on minority education and training.
	Diana Slaughter becomes the first person of color elected to the Governing Council of SRCD (Slaughter-Defoe, 2006a).
	William Hall, PhD, becomes first African American to serve as program chair for the biennial SRCD meeting (Garrett et al., 2006, p. 198). John McAdoo in *Black Families* publishes probably one of the first studies on the topic of involvement of fathers in the socialization of Black children.
1982	Initial multicultural competencies are authored by Derald Sue and others and published in *The Counseling Psychologist.*
1983	Na'im Akbar, PhD, and Wade W. Nobles, PhD, author ABPsi's *Ethical Standards of Black Psychologists,* which addresses the eight standards of responsibility, restraint, respect, reciprocity, commitment, cooperativeness, courage, and accountability, and notes, "only persons of African Descent and who are completely committed to no less than the absolute liberation of the Black mind shall be recognized as legitimate Black Psychologists" Association of Black Psychologists, 2006.
1984	BEMA establishes a task force on communication with minority constituents, which is charged to (a) identify and increase ethnic minority membership in divisions and state associations, (b) help divisions and state associations establish ethnic minority-oriented committees, and (c) increase ethnic minority participation in APA governance (Comas-Diaz, 1990).
1985	BEMA with the approval of the APA Council of Representatives establishes the BEMA Committee on Ethnic Minority Human Resources Development (CEMHRD) to address ethnic minority student and faculty recruitment and retention, and development of ethnic minority education and training resources, and appoints Martha Bernal, PhD, as CEMHRD's chair.
	NIMH is reorganized; ethnic minority research is "mainstreamed": All of NIMH's three research divisions assume responsibility for funding ethnic minority-focused research and ethnic minority investigators The Center for Minority Group Mental Health Programs is discontinued (Parron, 1990).
	Publication of *Beginnings: The Social and Affective Development of Black Children* edited by M. B. Spencer, G. K. Brookins, and W. Allen , which was the product of the first SRCD study group focused on Black children and families (Garrett et al., 2006, p. 200).
	ABPsi issues *Position Paper on Apartheid*, authored by Bertha G. Holliday, PhD, Dorothy Granberry-Stewart, PhD, and Sylvester Turner, MA (personal files of B. Holliday).
	The Association of Non-White Concerns changes its name to the Association of Multicultural Counseling and Development.
1986	The Society for the Psychological Study of Ethnic Minority Issues (APA's Division 45) is established (Comas-Diaz, 1990; Street, 1994).
	The Society for the Clinical Psychology of Ethnic Minorities is established as Section VI of APA's Division 12 (Clinical Psychology; M. Jenkins, 1994).
1987	In response to significant financial losses associated with the APA's purchase and operation of *Psychology Today*, the APA central office is streamlined and reorganized into four major directorates.
	The BEMA/Board of Social and Ethical Responsibility for Psychology (BSERP) Task Force on the Status of Black Men and Its Impact on Families and Communities is established (Comas-Diaz, 1990).
	The BEMA Task Force on the Delivery of Services to Ethnic Minority Populations is established and later issues APA councilapproved *Guidelines for Providers of Psychological Services to Ethnic, Linguistic, and Culturally Diverse Populations*, under the chairship of Joseph Pine, PhD (Comas-Diaz, 1990).
1990	APA's governance structure is realigned with its directorate structure. As a result, BSERP and BEMA are merged into a single Board for the Advancement of Psychology in the Public Interest, and a Committee on Ethnic Minority Affairs is established.
1991	SRCD Black Caucus explicitly opens its membership to persons who are not of African American descent (Garrett et al., 2006, p. 203).

Henry Tomes, PhD, former president of ABPsi and former commissioner of mental health in Massachusetts, is the first African American to serve as executive director of an APA directorate (Public Interest).

African American William Hall, PhD, chairs the SRCD Publications Committee, which formally reaffirms its commitment to diversity in the content of its publications and the make-up of its editorial boards, and initiates three strategies for facilitating achievement of these commitments (Garrett et al., 2006, p. 203; McLoyd, 2006, p. 131).

1992   APA's Public Interest Directorate sponsors the first APA miniconvention (at the Washington, DC, APA Centennial Convention) focused on ethnic minorities: "Ethnic Minorities: Issues and Concerns for Psychology, Now and in the Future." The miniconvention was organized by OEMA director, L. Philip Guzman, PhD (Holliday, 1992).

At the Centennial APA Convention in Washington, DC, the Council of National Psychological Associations for the Advancement of Ethnic Minority Interests (CNPAAEMI) is established on adoption of the CNPAAEMI governing rules. CNPAAEMI comprises the presidents of the nation's ethnic minority psychological associations and APA (Holliday, 2006).

Gail E. Wyatt, PhD, an African American, is first the person of color to receive a NIMH Research Scientist Career Award (Street, 1994).

1993   With the leadership of African American psychologist Jessica Henderson Daniel, PhD, and chair of the Massachusetts Board of

Registration of Psychologists, Massachusetts becomes the first state to require program and experience related to racial/ethnic basis of behavior for licensure (Daniel, 1994).

APA Council of Representatives passes a resolution declaring ethnic minority recruitment and retention as a high priority (APA, 1997).

Vonnie McLoyd becomes the first African American to be appointed associate editor of SRCD's *Child Development* journal (McLoyd, 2006, p. 139).

(*table continues*)

Table 1 (*continued*)

Year	Event

1994   African American psychologist Brian Smedley, PhD, becomes the first ethnic minority to direct APA's Public Interest Public Policy Office. During his tenure, ethnic minority issues are formally placed on APA's legislative advocacy agenda for the first time.

1995   Jennifer Friday, PhD, is the first African American to be elected president of the Southeast Psychological Association.

APA Council of Representatives approves revised *Guidelines and Principles for Accreditation of Programs in Professional Psychology*, including "Domain D: Cultural and Individual Differences and Diversity," which calls for programs to make "systematic, coherent and long-term efforts to attract and retain students and faculty [or interns and staff] . . ." from diverse backgrounds, "ensure a supportive and encouraging learning environment appropriate for the training of diverse individuals," and implement a "coherent plan to provide students [or interns] with relevant knowledge and experience about the role of cultural and individual diversity in psychological phenomena . . ." (APA Office of Program Consultation and Accreditation, 2007, p. 10).

ABPsi issues position paper "A Holistic View of American Violence: A Position Paper on the Federal Violence Initiative" (*Psych Discourse* [ABPsi NewsJournal], *26*). ABPsi is recipient of grant for the Centers for Disease Control and Prevention for a national HIV/STD Technical Assistance Project (Noel Brathwaite, PhD, MPH, project director in 1995). Project issued a newsletter, *Nia* (Williams, 2008).

1996   With funding provided by the Office of Special Populations of the Center for Mental Health Services, APA initiates the HBCU Training Capacity Grant program through which small grants are competitively awarded to psychology departments at HBCUs for activities that will strengthen a department's capacity to effectively recruit, retain, and train students of color for careers in psychology (APA OEMA, 1996).

Publication of *Handbook of Tests and Measurements for Black Populations* (two volumes) edited by Reginald L. Jones, PhD.

APA's OEMA is awarded a $750,000 grant from the National Institute of General Medical Sciences for the purpose of demonstrating the effectiveness of a "systemic approach" for increasing the number of persons of color in the educational pipeline for biomedical research careers in psychology. Later in the year 2000, the grant is renewed for $1.43 million. Grant is renewed again in 2004.

1997   APA's Office of Ethnic Minority Affairs organizes within the annual APA convention a miniconvention on "Psychology and Racism" focusing on the three themes of (a) the psychology of racism, (b) racism in psychology, and (c) the psychology of antiracism and involving 121 events and 449 presentations (APA, 1997).

1999   APA's Division 45 (Society for the Psychological Study of Ethnic Minority Issues) in collaboration with Divisions 17 (Counseling) and 35 (Psychology of Women) organize the first National Multicultural Conference and Summit in Newport Beach, California, chaired by Derald W. Sue, PhD.

APA's Division 45 initiates publication of its journal *Cultural Diversity and Ethnic Minority Psychology* with Lillian Comas-Diaz, PhD, as its first editor.

APA Council of Representatives passes a resolution on affirmative action and equal opportunity that encourages "psychological and public policy research that would illuminate sources of bias in institutional policies and practices . . ."

At the opening ceremony of the annual APA convention in Boston, then-APA President Richard M. Suinn presents a presidential citation to the presidents of the four national ethnic minority psychological associations that formally acknowledged their value and contributions. The ABPsi citation was accepted by its president, Samella Abdulla, PhD (personal correspondence: Suinn to Abdullah, March 11, 1999; Abdullah to Suinn, June 17, 1999).

2000	The APA Council of Representatives authorizes funding for a Commission on Ethnic Minority Recruitment, Retention, and Training in Psychology (CEMRRAT) Textbook Initiatives Work Group that is charged to develop guidelines on the inclusion of information and research on diverse populations for publishers and authors of introductory psychology textbooks (APA, 2001).

APA's OEMA establishes its Psychology in Ethnic Minority Services Institutions initiative aimed at strengthening relationships between APA and these institutions and promoting increased psychological education, training, and research at these institutions (APA OEMA, 2000).

ABPsi holds is annual convention in Accra, Ghana.

APA's Committee of State Leaders, with financial support from APA's Practice Directorate and CEMRRAT Grant Fund, initiates its diversity initiative through which state, territorial, and provincial psychological associations (SPTAs) are encouraged to send ethnic minority delegates to APA's annual state leadership conference and mentor them into SPTA leadership positions. By 2007, four African American and three other diversity delegates had been elected president or president-elect of their SPTAs.

2001	APA Council of Representatives passes a resolution "Racial/Ethnic Profiling and Other Racial/Ethnic Disparities in Law and Security Enforcement Activities" (APA OEMA, 2001c).

APA Council of Representatives passes a resolution "Racism and Racial Discrimination: A Policy Statement in Support of the Goals of the 2001 World Conference Against Racial Discrimination, Xenophobia, and Related Intolerance" (APA OEMA, 2001b).

APA's Office of International Affairs and OEMA provide financial support for an APA six-member delegation to the U.N. World

Conference Against Racism, Racial Discrimination, Xenophobia, and Related Intolerance in Durban, South Africa. Delegates are Corann Okorodudu, EdD, (delegation chair and the APA main representative to the U.N.); Thema Bryant, PhD (an APA representative to the U.N.); A. J. Franklin, PhD (president, Division 45); Bertha G. Holliday, PhD (director, OEMA); James S. Jackson, PhD (president-elect, APA's Committee on International Relations in Psychology); and William Parham, PhD (presidentelect, APA's Committee on Ethnic Minority Affairs; APA, 2002b;APA OEMA, 2001a).

SRCD initiates the Millennium Fellows Program, which provides travel funds, registration fees, and graduate and professional mentors and meetings with some of SRCD's leaders for undergraduate minority students to attend biennial SRCD meetings (Slaughter-Defoe et al., 2006, p. 190).

Establishment of ABPsi's Licensure, Certification, and Proficiency in Black Psychology program that seeks to prepare psychologists to work with Black children and families (ABPsi president's message posted August 12, 2007, at http://www.abpsi.org/president.htm).

2002	APA's Council of Representatives unanimously confirms African American psychologist Norman B. Anderson, PhD, as the APA chief executive officer, effective January 1, 2003.
2004	Psychologist Vonnie McLoyd (a 1997 recipient of the McArthur "genius" award) is elected president of the Society for Research in Adolescence (Harrison-Hale, 2006, p. 46).

(table continues)

Table 1 (*continued*)

Year	Event
2005	In response to the horrific absence and shortcomings of first-responders to the New Orleans victims of Hurricane Katrina, ABPsi issues *Guidelines for Providing Culturally Appropriate Services for People of African Ancestry Exposed to the Trauma of Hurricane Katrina* authored by Kevin Cokley, PhD, Benson G. Cooke, EdD, and Wade Nobles, PhD. Jessica Henderson Daniel becomes first African American female elected to the APA Board of Directors. James S. Jackson is appointed director of the University of Michigan's Institute for Social Research.
2006	The ABPsi Foundation is founded with the purpose of raising funds for scholarships, research, and other endeavors that promote the mission and vision of the ABPsi (Association of Black Psychologists, 2007; ABPsi president's message posted August 12, 2007, at http://www.abpsi.org/president.htm). Gwendolyn P. Keita becomes the first African American female APA executive director (Public Interest Directorate).

2007	The Society for the Psychological Study of Ethnic Minority Issues (APA Division 45) establishes the Psi Alpha Omega, "the national honor society in psychology for students of color and students interested in the study of ethnic and cultural issues" (retrieved October 15, 2007, from http://www.psialphaomega.com).
	The APA Council of Representatives authorizes a membership vote on an APA bylaws change that would establish a seat on the APA council for each of the national ethnic minority psychological associations. APBsi is unwilling to commit to assume such a seat, whereas the other minority psychological associations express a willingness to do so. The required two-thirds vote is not achieved.
	The APA council authorizes a second bylaws vote in 2008 on seats for the national ethnic minority psychological associations. Again, the vote falls short of the two-thirds majority needed for approval, this time by 126 votes of more than 10,300 votes cast on this amendment.
2008	Archie Turner is appointed as APA's first African American chief financial officer.
2009	In response to the nation's economic downturn, APA effects a significant disinvestment of its funding of ethnic minority programs and initiatives.

Later that year, consistent with its petition, ABPsi issued its 6-point statement related to a need for a moratorium on testing that placed Black children disproportionately at educational and developmental risk. In 1970, ABPsi sent to all graduate psychology departments its 10-point program for recruitment and retention of Black doctoral students. At least 35 departments reportedly adopted the entire program and numerous others adopted parts of the program. Also in 1970, ABPsi and APA launched a 3-year Black visiting scientist program to approximately 30 Black colleges (Williams, 1974).

In 1971, ABPsi, for the first time, conducted its convention at a site separate from that of the APA convention. Nevertheless, ABPsi President Reginald L. Jones addressed APA's council and again noted the gulf in the interests of the two associations—as epitomized by the finding that the word *racism* occurred only once in the 182-page 1971 APA convention program. Jones also made recommendations for needed changes in APA's administrative and governance structures that would serve to enhance ethnic minority recruitment and retention and multicultural training (APA, 2003). In that same year, an ideological-political chasm began to emerge between ABPsi and BSPA. Meetings focused on effecting a merger between the organizations met with little success. This was a harbinger of the periodic challenges and struggles that ABPsi would have with its student members.

According to Williams (1974), during the 1971–1974 period, in addition to its concerns with minority recruitment and testing, ABPsi efforts also focused on developing publication functions, strengthening its organizational infrastructure, and developing public policy advocacy processes including cultivating a relationship with the Congressional Black Caucus. As a result of the leadership of Reginald L. Jones and others, ABPsi launched its *Journal of Black Psychology* in 1974.

Currently, ABPsi is governed by a board of directors that includes four regional representatives. It also has a Council of Elders that advises the board, and a General Assembly that consists of volunteers from ABPsi chapters throughout the nation who carry out projects commissioned by the board. In addition, historically many ABPsi concerns have been taken on by one of its local chapters. For example, in 1972, the Bay Area chapter issued a position statement on use of IQ and ability tests, which demanded that the California State Department of Education declare a moratorium on these tests in assessing Black children (Richards, 1997); in 1980, the Bay Area chapter issued another position paper on the mental health needs of the Bay Area Black community (ABPsi, 1980, p. 11); in 1981, the Nashville chapter opposed the Tennessee Board of Education's implementation of a statewide proficiency examination of teachers, for which it solicited and received support from the Tennessee Psychological Association (B.

Holliday, personal files, 1981); and in 1985, the Nashville chapter developed on behalf of the national ABPsi a position paper on apartheid (B. Holliday, personal files, 1985).

In 1973, many of ABPsi's concerns were further legitimized through the conduct of landmark conferences. For example, African American counseling psychologists Thomas Gunnings and Gloria Smith held a national conference on counseling minority students that identified special concerns and

[margin notes: "moratorium on testing of educational & developmental risk — Black children"; "1970"; "cultivating a relationship w/ congressional black caucus"; "1974 ABPsi → Journal of Black Psychology"]

strategies in counseling these students. A national conference on testing was conducted in Hampton, Virginia, that focused on issues and concerns related to testing persons of color in education, government, and industry settings. And the attendance of 25 Blacks and other ethnic minority psychologists at the APA- and NIMH-sponsored 1973 Vail Conference, which examined the appropriateness of psychology's scientist-professional model of training, ensured that each of the conference's workshops included discussions of the relevance of such training for people of color.

Around 1975, ABPsi's annual convention program began to include African-centered presentations, thus marking the beginning of ABPsi's ideological transition to a more African-centered one. Th-is transition was neither easy nor without costs, and continues to be a source of signifi-cant tension within the organization.

Th-e distinct African American brand of "nationalism" (or post- colonial racialized perspectives) that currently underlies many of ABPsi's African-centered perspectives makes it diffi-cult for some of their adherents to enter into formal collaborative action with non-Black organizations and institutions, without fear of cooption, coercion, or loss of independence or clarity of vision. Th-is has served to limit ABPsi's ability (especially at the national level) to engage in long-term strategies in support of some of its original critical goals—such as enhancing the numbers and educational experiences of African American doctoral psychology students, and infl-uencing public policies and professional and technical standards related to testing. For example, in 1978, ABPsi refused to attend the Dulles Conference, which was cosponsored by APA and NIMH and focused on the roles of ethnic minority psychologists in organized psychology. Th-is refusal was due to "numerous attempts by ABPsi to work out strategies with APA which met with nonresponsiveness in addition to an apparent 'hidden agenda' to program the conference to deliver a recommendation for a Minority Division of American Psychological Association" (ABPsi, 1978, p. 7). In the letter of response to this invitation, ABPsi Chairwoman Ruth King noted, "We (ABPsi) will consider APA serious only when their Board of Directors is willing to sit with the Board of Directors of the Association of Black Psychologists on an equal basis and honestly deal with the serious psychological issues which face us all" (ABPsi, 1978, p. 7).

More recently, in response to a proposal to create a voting seat on the APA Council of Representatives for each of the ethnic minority psychological associations, ABPsi exhibited signifi-cant reticence and resistance. Th-e majority of members present at the 2006 business meeting of the ABPsi Annual Convention voted against accepting such a seat. Later, in 2007, the ABPsi president forwarded the following communication to APA:

> As long as it is clear that ABPsi has at present elected to not avail itself of the voting seat on Council, I see no inherent problem in OEMA or DIV [sic] 45 or whomever is responsible for moving this issue forward pursuing Council seats for all of the Ethnic Psychological Associations. I do not interpret such action as refl-ecting paternalism. I consulted with Dr. Holmes, our incoming president. She is of the opinion that it would be presumptuous and possibly inappropriate for ABPsi to tell APA how to mange their internal aff-airs. She sees the C/R seats as an issue subsumed under the large question of what type of relationship ABPsi wishes to have with APA, resolution of which she anticipates will require several years of dialogue within the ABPsi. (R. Atwell [personal communication] as cited in APA council, 2007, p. 68)

Th-e collaborative limitations of ABPsi's African-centered stance is counterbalanced by ABPsi's increasing focus on such priorities as nurturing the development of African-centered theory and practice in psychology, refi-ning internal and African-centered organizational procedures and rituals, and most recently, developing a program of certifi-cation and training of Afrocentric/African-centered clinicians, and establishing an ABPsi foundation that might eventually support training and community projects (Williams, 2008). However, such internal eff-orts from time to time have presented diffi-cult challenges, in part due to the inherent social conservatism of many "traditional" African tenets, which some members view as homophobic, sexist, and dogmatic. To ABPsi's credit, such concerns oft-en have been heard by ABPsi leadership, and related proposals and activities have been reconsidered or restructured (cf. Parham, White, & Ajamu, 1999, pp. 19–22). However, the energy required for the association to go through these periodic internal confl-icts has been draining and disillusioning to many ABPsi leaders and members. Nevertheless, most members view the annual ABPsi conventions as a respite and a homecoming: It is a place and intellectual space in psychology that African Americans craft-ed for themselves.

The APA and its Office of Ethnic Minority Affairs (OEMA), Committee on Ethnic Minority Affairs (CEMA), and Society for the Psychological Study of Ethnic Minority Issues (Division 45)

Th-e APA promotes itself as the nation's largest association of psychologists, with 148,000 members. It is also the leading publisher of psychological literature in the world and thus is the preeminent gatekeeper of psychological knowledge and research. Its current organization structure includes 54 divisions or special interest groups. It is governed by a Council of Representatives comprising representatives from each of its divisions and from each state, provincial, and territorial psychological association (SPTA).

APA's organizational growth has been characterized by a series of strategic decisions and eff orts that served to expand the scope of psychological research and practice. Such eff orts include those related to (a) the use of psychological tests as instruments for identifying diff erences among both social groups and individuals (Gossett, 1963/1965, pp. 368–376; Richards, 1997, chap. 4; Street, 1994, pp. 68, 74, 75, 83, 138); (b) the promotion of clinical and neurological assessments as necessary tools for diagnoses of mental diseases and disorders (Street, 1994, p. 205); (c) the use of psychotherapeutic and behavioral interventions as treatments for health, psychological, and behavioral problems (Street, 1994, p. 74); (d) the promotion of the salience of psychological research and interventions to critical national needs through an aggressive program of advocacy for both issues and programs of psychological import and federal funding for psychological research (Finison, 1986; Street, 1994, pp. 204–209); and (e) signifi cant control of the published psychological research literature (Street, 1994, chap. 3). In addition, psychological practice has been both protected and expanded through aggressive monitoring and advocacy of state licensing laws (APA approved its fi rst Model Legislation for State Licensure in 1955; Street, 1994).

APA's organizational policymaking oft en involves highly political decision-making processes— and prior to the late 1960s, on matters of race and civil rights, it was a North versus South divide. Indeed, Richards (1997) has argued that up until the 1970s, APA was "politically paralyzed by the sheer breadth of its members' interests and political attitudes. Any general statement about U.S. Psychology and the Civil Rights movement is thus impossible" (p. 238). Consequently, APA did not even acknowledge its near absence of participation of Black psychologists until 1963, when APA Division 9 (Society for the Psychological Study of Social Issues) insisted that APA establish the ad hoc Committee on Equality of Opportunity in Psychology (CEOP) to explore "the possible problems encountered in training and employment in psychology as a consequence of race" (Wispe et al., 1969,

p. 142, footnote 3). Th e committee's fi nal report (Wispe et al., 1969), based on 398 surveys completed by Black psychologists, documented the underrepresentation of Black psychologists and their alienation from mainstream U.S. psychology.

read again

In 1967, at the invitation of APA's Division 9, civil rights leader Rev. Dr. Martin Luther King, Jr., delivered an address at the APA convention on the role of the social scientist in the civil rights movement that called for more research on (a) Black leadership development, (b) political action and its effi cacy as a social change strategy, (c) psychological and ideological changes in Blacks , and (d) related implications for the relationship between Blacks and the greater society, including social institutions.

And then there was the drama of the wake-up call delivered at the 1968 APA convention in San Francisco when the ABPsi was established and its representatives walked in on the meeting of the APA Board of Directors and presented ABPsi's petition of concern. APA empowered a committee to respond to the petition (Baker, 2003). A report from this committee to the ABPsi Executive Committee indicated that (a) APA was willing to appoint a group to consider the psychological implications of the

look up

Kerner Report or commission a position paper on the report's psychological implications, but it was inappropriate for APA's board or council to make an endorsement on behalf of APA's members on any issue; (b) in February 1969, APA's board approved the expenditure of $4,000 for a working conference on recruitment of graduate students and faculty from disadvantaged groups; (c) the APA board had approved the convention committee's recommendation that the theme of the 1969 convention be "Psychology and Problems of Society," including several symposia organized by ABPsi; and (d) facilities would be made available at the APA convention for ABPsi's social hour and business meeting (Williams, 1974).

In 1969, in response to demands of the BSPA to increase ethnic minority student and faculty recruitment and retention, the APA council immediately adopted a motion that included (a) endorsement in principle of the statement presented by BSPA, (b) a commitment of APA funds to support the 4-point plan, and (c) the authorization of a committee and associated funding to work out details related to (a) and (b). Th e APA board also took action in support of BSPA's concerns and established a Commission for Accelerating Black Participation in Psychology, which comprised representatives of APA, APBsi, and BSPA. Later, APA provided 3 years of funding for a BSPA offi ce in the APA building. Th is marked the fi rst time that APA had embraced any organized group of psychology graduate students (FigueroaGarcia, 1994; Guzman et al., 1992; Pickren & Tomes, 2002; Street, 1994). It also marked the fi rst of several instances when Black psychology students would defy or question the preferred course of action of ABPsi. Undoubtedly, APA's failure to renew funding for a BSPA offi ce aft er the 3-year period was due to many factors, including the pending establishment of the APA Minority Fellowship Program (MFP). In addition, the continuing schism between BSPA and ABPsi certainly placed APA in a politically awkward position.

In 1970, African American psychologist Kenneth B. Clark, in his role as APA president, urged the APA Board of Directors to place high priority on issues of social responsibility. Consequently, in 1971, APA established the Department of Social and Ethical Responsibility and the ad hoc Committee on Social and Ethical Responsibility for Psychology. By vote of the APA membership, the ad hoc committee became a standing board in 1973 with responsibility for aspects of psychology involving solutions to problems of social justice, including issues related to ethnic minority participation in psychology (Pickren & Tomes, 2002).

In 1974, APA established its MFP, with funding provided by NIMH. Initially directed by Dalmas Taylor, PhD, later by James Jones, PhD, and currently by Andrew Austin-Daley, MDiv, MFP has to date provided fi nancial support for doctoral study and research in psychology and neuroscience to approximately 1,300 students of color.

Th e 1978 Dulles Conference titled "Expanding the Roles of Culturally Diverse Peoples in the Profession of Psychology" marked a major turning point for ethnic minority inclusion and participation in APA. Sponsored by the APA Board of Directors, the APA Board of Social and Ethical Responsibility, and NIMH, the conference's major recommendations focused on the need for an institutionalized ethnic minority presence in the governance and organizational structures of organized psychology. As a result, the APA Offi ce of Ethnic Minority Aff airs (OEMA) was established in 1979; the APA Board of Ethnic Minority Aff airs (BEMA) was established in 1980 aft er a successful related bylaws vote by the APA membership, with African American psychologist Henry Tomes, PhD, as its fi rst chair; and the Society for the Psychological Study of Ethnic Minority Issues (APA Division 45) was established in 1986 (Comas-Diaz, 1990; Guzman, Schiavo, & Puente, 1992; Street, 1994; S. Sue, 1994). BEMA and Division 45 each adopted a multicultural model wherein governance members were elected or appointed from ethnic-specifi c slates that ensured a balance in representation and concerns and interests of psychologists from each of the nation's major ethnic minority groups (African Americans, Asian American/ Pacifi c Islanders, American Indians/Alaska Natives, and Latinos[as]/Hispanics).

Over time, each of these entities has assumed a role that is distinct but mutually supportive. For example, Division 45, as a "speciality area" group, focuses its eff orts on providing a focal point for ethnic participation in APA, and promoting the stature and visibility of scientifi c and practice issues of concern to ethnic minority psychologists, primarily through establishment of both its journal and the biennial National Multicultural Conference and Summit, with its hallmark "honoring of elders" and "diffi cult dialogues." BEMA (and its successor, the APA Committee on Ethnic Minority Aff airs (CEMA), which was established as a result of APA's 1987 staff reorganization and subsequent 1990 realignment of its governance structure with the new staff directorate structure), in its role as an APA governance group, not only monitors and contributes to greater equity and less racial/ethnic bias in APA policymaking, but also identifi es and legitimizes major issues, strategies, and initiatives needed to increase within psychology both the participation of ethnic minorities and the stature of the needs and concerns of communities of color. In turn, many of the initiatives championed by these entities are actually carried out by staff of the OEMA. Examples of such initiatives include encouraging the establishment and development of more than 60 division and state psychological association committees (or sections) on ethnic minority aff airs and diversity as a strategy for increasing ethnic minority membership and participation and ensuring that ethnic minority psychological perspectives infl uence the policies and activities of divisions and SPTAs; maintaining a database and publishing a directory of ethnic minority psychologists to increase their visibility and ability to network; developing formats for communicating with ethnic minority psychologists; strengthening relationships and communication between minority-serving institutions and APA; developing a mini-convention on psychology and racism; operating and funding model minority student recruitment, retention, and training strategies; and encouraging increased ethnic minority leadership development (Comas-Diaz, 1990; Figueroa-Garcia, 1994; Holliday, 1992; Holliday and Holmes, 2003; Street, 1994).

In addition, in 1992, APA facilitated the establishment of the Council of National Psychological Associations for the Advancement of Ethnic Minority Interests (CNPAAEMI). Th is council consists of the presidents of APA, Division 45, and the four national ethnic minority psychological associations— the Asian American Psychological Association, ABPsi, National Latina/o Psychological Association, and the Society of Indian Psychologists. CNPAAEMI was established "for

the purpose of both discussing issues of mutual concern and developing joint strategies to address them" (*CNPAAEMI Governance Rules* as modifi ed February 1, 2002; CNPAAEMI, 2002). CNPAAEMI meets semiannually and is staff ed by OEMA. CNPAAEMI has developed a publication series focused on ethnic minority-centered perspectives on major psychological procedures. In 2006, CNPAAEMI established the Henry Tomes, PhD, Awards in honor of Tomes's continuous contributions to ethnic minority psychology.

Most recently, CNPAAEMI initiated eff orts to establish a voting seat on APA's Council of Representatives for each of the four national ethnic minority psychological associations. Eff orts related to this initiative refl ect the signifi cant political coordination that has developed among APA's ethnic minority entities. Division 45 assumed responsibility for introducing the proposal for the voting seats to APA's council, gaining council approval for presenting a necessary bylaws amendment for APA membership vote, and organizing a coalition of council members that developed a campaign to encourage members to vote in support of the bylaws amendment. OEMA actively provided consultation to other staff and committees assigned to draft the actual bylaws language and assure its conformity with both APA legal requirements and those of the national ethnic minority psychological associations. But, despite these eff orts, the bylaws amendment was rejected two times by very small margins (the second voted failed to gain the necessary two-thirds majority by 126 votes of 10,312 votes cast). In response, CEMA has assumed a liaison role with the APA council work group that was appointed to determine the next steps to be taken on the voting seats proposal.

APA's concerns with issues of ethnic minority students, faculty, and professional training were reinvigorated in 1994 when the APA Commission on Ethnic Minority Recruitment, Retention, and Training in Psychology (CEMRRAT) was established. It issued its fi nal report and plan in 1997 and a progress report on the implementation of that plan was issued in 2007 (APA CEMRRAT, 1997, 2007). In 1999, a CEMRRAT Implementation Fund was established by APA. Up until 2009, this was funded for $75,000 to $100,000 per year and used primarily for small grants to APA divisions, SPTAs, academic departments, APA offi ces, and other groups and individuals who proposed to engage in activities consistent with the APA/CEMRRAT plan. However, in 2009, because of fi nancial restraints associated with the nation's economic downturn, the APA Board of Directors and Council of Representatives voted to suspend funding for the CEMRRAT fund.

In 1999, in a gesture of reconciliation, honor, and gratitude, then-APA President Richard Suinn (APA's third president of color) presented a Presidential Citation to the ABPsi and to the other independent national ethnic minority psychological associations. Th e ABPsi citation, which was accepted by thenABPsi President Samella Abdullah, included citations of ABPsi's major contributions to psychology.

In 1991, Henry Tomes, PhD, became the fi rst African American hired by APA at the executive director level. In 2002, APA's Council of Representatives appointed psychologist Norman Anderson, PhD, as APA's fi rst African American chief executive offi cer. In 2005, Jessica Henderson Daniel, PhD, became the fi rst African American female elected to the APA Board of Directors. In 2006, Gwendolyn P. Keita, PhD, became the fi rst African American female APA executive director. In 2008, Archie Turner was hired as APA's fi rst African American chief fi nancial offi cer.

In 2001, the APA Offi ce and International Aff airs and OEMA funded a 6-member APA delegation to the UN World Conference Against Racism, Racial Discrimination, Xenophobia and Related Intolerances in Durban, South Africa. In 2002, the APA council approved *Th e Guidelines on Multicultural Education, Training, Research, Practice, and Organizational Change for Psychologists* (APA, 2002a), which was sponsored by APA Division 17 (Counseling Psychology). In 2007, at the urging of Joseph Horvat, Division 45 established Psi Alpa Omega as a national honor society. Horvat, an American Indian who had served as the president of the long-established Psi Chi Honor Society in psychology, believed Psi Chi was unwilling to aggressively reach out to ethnic minority students and address their special needs and experiences of marginalization (Autry, 2008; Psi Alpha Omega, n.d.). Psi Alpha Omega is the fi rst national honor society established to meet the needs of and honor ethnic minority and other students interested in multicultural and ethnic minority psychology issues.

The ACA and its Association of Multicultural Counseling and Development

Th-e roots of the counseling profession and discipline are found in educational settings (high schools and colleges), where vocational education and guidance became salient functions during the early 20th century. Later, counseling diversifi ed into other areas such as psychometrics, family and marriage, mental health, substance abuse, criminal justice, and human development. Th e American Counseling Association (ACA) defi nes itself as a "partnership" of associations representing professional counselors who enhance human development. As such, ACA is distinguished by its willingness to adapt and reinvent itself in the service of organizational growth. Prior to July 1, 1992, ACA was known as the American Association of Counseling and Development. And prior to 1983, it was known as the American Personnel and Guidance Association (APGA). APGA itself was created in 1952 through the merger of four independent associations (known as the "founding divisions"): the National Vocational Guidance Association, the National Association of Guidance and Counselor Trainers, the Student Personnel Association for Teacher Education, and the American College Personnel Association. Today, ACA consists of 19 divisions, each of which represents a specifi c area of interest and practice, as well as 56 branches (states, territories, and foreign countries), which were fi rst chartered in 1970 and organized into four regions.

Major accomplishments of ACA include (a) the continual cultivation of new divisions, (b) the leveling of a hierarchical governance structure, (c) the increased stature and regulation of the counseling professions as evidenced by the adoption of state licensure and certifi cation (state licensing was authorized by APGA in 1974, and the National Board for Certifi ed Counselors was established in 1983), (d) development of a structure and process for accreditation of counseling specialty training programs (Council for the Accreditation of Counseling and Related Educational Programs established in 1982), (e) an increased public policy presence, and (f) the establishment of a foundation (ACA, 2007a, 2007b, 2007c; History of Counseling, n.d.).

Because of African American psychologists' early tradition of working with children and youth in educational settings, large numbers of Black psychologists were trained in various areas of counseling. Consequently, signifi cant numbers of African American psychologists were affi liated with APGA during the Civil Rights era. During the 1969 APGA convention, a predominantly African American caucus presented a resolution to establish a salaried National Offi ce of Non-White Concerns to be located within APGA's Executive Offi ce. It has been reported that this action primarily refl ected Blacks' frustration with the absence of association support for a Black perspective on counseling that is characterized by such things as a color-conscious cultural-specifi c perspective, the recognition of a Black culture that contributes to identity and positive adaptations, transformative skills in response to the discriminatory or racist behavior of social systems and institutions, and community-based service delivery (cf. G. J. Jackson, 1977). Indeed, to a large extent, the history of African Americans within ACA refl ects the use of political strategies in pursuit of racial/ethnic-centered theories and practices of counseling. According to Daley (1972, as cited in G. J. Jackson, 1977, p. 495), caucus members were "tired of acquiescence; they were tired of an 'acceptable existence'; they were tired of all the rhetoric about warmth, acceptance, and development of each one's maximum potential."

In response to the 1969 caucus resolution, APGA established an Office of Non-White Concerns, which the caucus came to view as a powerless entity intended to pacify its efforts. Consequently, the caucus established itself as a somewhat parallel and alternative dues-paying nonvoting "interest group" of APGA. This interest group attracted more than 400 persons to its pre-APGA convention programs and banquets. Finally, in 1972, after several years of negotiation and struggle with its parent organization, the caucus reestablished itself as the Association of Non-White Concerns (ANWC) in Personnel and Guidance—a division of the APGA with voting rights in both APGA's Senate and on its Board of Directors (Anderson, 2007; Association for Multicultural Counseling and Development, n.d.). At its inception, ANWC defined its mission as follows:

> To recognize the human diversity and multicultural nature of our society; to enhance development, human rights and psychological health of all people; to identify and work to eliminate conditions that create barriers to individual development of non-Whites; to develop, implement and/or foster interest in charitable, scientific and educational programs that further the interests of non-Whites; to secure equality of treatment, advancement, qualifications, and status of people in personal and guidance work; to publish a journal and other materials with the purpose of raising the standards of all who work in guidance and counseling. (Anderson, 2007, p. 6)

Consistent with APGA's 1983 name change and its willingness to engage in organization transformation, in 1985, ANWC changed its name to its current one—the Association of Multicultural Counseling and Development (AMCD). A similar change was made in the titles of its newsletter and journal. Indeed, over the years, as the counseling discipline's membership became increasingly multiracial/ethnic, ANWC/AMCD progressively transformed itself into a multicultural organization, with equal standing with the other ACA partner associations and divisions. AMCD's current governance structure includes four vice presidents—each representing one of the nation's four major ethnic minority groups—as well as elected representatives of each of ACA's four regions. AMCD also charters state AMCD divisions (AMCD, 2007).

AMCD also seeks to actively engage multiple public and professional groups in its core mission. This is best exemplified in the origination, repeated revision, and promotion of multicultural competencies in counseling psychology, which were initially developed in 1992. The first statement of multicultural competencies was published in 1982 in the APA Division 17 journal, *The Counseling Psychologist* (D. W. Sue et al., 1982). In 1992, the AMCD president requested that the 1982 competencies be updated by a committee headed by the lead author of the 1982 document. The 1992 competencies were published in ACA's journal (D. W. Sue, Arredondo, & McDavis, 1992). A few years later, another revision was requested by the AMCD president. This revision was drafted by AMCD's Professional Standards Committee and featured a more "contextual" approach (Arredondo & Toporek, 2004). The 1996 competencies were published in AMCD's journal (Arredondo et al., 1996) and later served as the template for the drafting of APA's *Guidelines on Multicultural Education, Training, Research, Practice, and Organizational Change for Psychologists* (APA, 2002a), which initially was drafted by members of APA Divisions 17 (Counseling Psychology) and 45 (Ethnic Minority Issues).

Some of AMCD's most recent activities include the establishment of a leadership development institute, a Southern Africa initiative aimed at expanding multicultural competencies through cultural emergence in HIV/AIDS services settings, and a mentoring program for graduate students and early career professionals in counseling.

The SRCD and Its Black Caucus

Th e Society for Research in Child Development (SRCD) was established in 1933 as an outgrowth of a National Research Council subcommittee on child development, which was established in 1922–1923. Th e stated purposes of SRCD are "to promote multi-disciplinary research in the fi eld of human development, to foster the exchange of information among scientists and other professionals and various disciplines, and to encourage applications of research fi ndings" (SRCD, 2007). Its current major activities include promoting international interaction and communication related to human development, establishing and maintaining ethical standards for research with children, promoting research and training in diversity, bringing human development research to bear on social policy, and hosting biennial meetings on human development issues (SRCD, 2007). As a scientifi c society, SRCD members share a common focus of concern—human development research—and SRCD scientifi c meetings and governance activities are important professional networking opportunities for persons engaged in child and human development research. Indeed, the SRCD journal, *Child Development,* is viewed as the premier journal in this speciality area. Consequently, SRCD serves as the major national gatekeeper of research methods and issues as well as social policy and programs in the area of child and human development.

Inspired by the establishment of ABPsi, the Black Caucus of SRCD was founded in 1973. But in contrast to ABPsi's desire for organizational autonomy from APA and the rather strident positions taken by ANWC founders, the SRCD Black Caucus, a "special interest group," from its inception sought to be a means for advancing African Americans' professional careers *within* SRCD and for contributing to the improvement of the lives of Black children. Indeed, because of the stature and gatekeeping roles of SRCD, Black Caucus members believed the latter could not be accomplished in the absence of accomplishing the former. Consequently, in 1979–1981, when Black Caucus Chair Diana Slaughter-Defoe surveyed caucus members about their action preferences and needs, the three most highly ranked statements of preference were:

> (a) Identify key resource persons within such governmental and private foundation groups who might be of counsel, and so forth as regarding obtaining research funds; (b) Maintain close connections with the Committee on Minority Participation in SRCD in particular, so as to be a resource for nominations for various committees, appointments, and sharing grievances within the hierarchy of SRCD; (c) Maintain close contact with Black members of the various committees of SRCD so that we can promote the professional socialization of Black members of SRCD. (Slaughter-Defoe, 2006b, p. 21)

In 1977, at the urging of the Black Caucus, SRCD established the SRCD Committee on Minority Participation (COMP), thereby including ethnic minority concerns in the SRCD governance system. Since then, relations between the caucus and COMP have been close, with continual advocacy from the caucus to COMP, and with signifi cant permeability in membership and leadership between the two groups. Th us, COMP became one of the critical means through which the caucus gained legitimacy and SRCD Governing Council support for greater participation of Blacks in all SRCD activities. In its 1978 initial report to the SRCD Governing Council, COMP recommended strategies for increasing ethnic minority participation relative to governance, professional socialization (including increasing Black participation in the SRCD publication process), and professional integration (McLoyd, 2006).

But COMP and SRCD governance did not always see eye-to-eye. Prior to the 1980s, COMP focused strictly on issues and projects related to increasing Black participation in SRCD. But in 1982, the COMP chair, Raymond Yang, in his annual report to the council observed that it might be advisable for COMP to reassess its purpose and function. In particular, COMP requested funding for a special COMP meeting to conduct such reassessment; increased contact with SRCD's Social Policy Committee and with other SRCD committees, especially regarding advocacy of public policies affecting ethnic minority children and families; and a change of name to the Committee on Minority Issues. The SRCD council responded by saying "no" to the name change, requesting a detailed budget for the proposed meeting, and by sharply reminding COMP that its responsibilities were "carefully circumscribed by SRCD's scholarly and scientific functions" (Slaughter-Defoe, 2006a, pp. 55, 62). Shortly thereafter, Yang resigned as COMP chair. In 1985, a name change—from COMP to the Committee on Ethnic and Racial Issues—was approved (Garrett, Slaughter-Defoe, & Harrison-Hale, 2006, pp. 197, 200–201).

Another means used by the caucus for promoting its interests was the building of personal relationships with key SRCD scholars and governance leaders. This strategy is exemplified in the published letters exchanged between one of the caucus' founders, Algea Harrison-Hale, and renowned researcher Mary Ainsworth (Harrison-Hale, 2006). As a result of such efforts, African Americans gained access to major SRCD committees and boards. For example, Harriette Pipes McAdoo was appointed to the SRCD Council in 1979; in 1980, John McAdoo was appointed to the editorial board of *Child Development,* and by the end of that year, seven persons of color sat on that editorial board. In 1981, William Hall served as program chair of the biennial SRCD meeting; in that same year, SRCD established a study group on Black families and children that subsequently published an edited volume, *Beginnings: The Social and Affective Development of Black Children.* In 1990, a special issue of *Child Development* on ethnic minority children was edited by Margaret B. Spencer and Vonnie McLoyd, and in 1993, in recognition of the need for an associate editor with expertise on children of color and associate editors' manuscript overload, McLoyd became the first African American appointed as an associate editor of *Child Development* (McLoyd, 2006).

Such accomplishments within SRCD served not only to promote the scholarly careers of Black Caucus members, they also served to promote a revisionist perspective of Black families and children that emphasized their strengths, resiliencies, and the social contexts of their lives, with significant social policy implications. These accomplishments and their commonalities with the interests and concerns of other child development researchers of color resulted in the Black Caucus becoming a multicultural resource and a critical multicultural collegial support system. Consequently, SRCD's Black Caucus facilitated alliance among SRCD's ethnic minority child researchers in general. In 1991, the Black Caucus of SRCD explicitly voted to open its membership to persons of non-African American descent (Garrett et al., 2006).

In general, African Americans' organized efforts to increase their participation and influence within the psychological associations and societies significantly challenged the existing participatory and political processes and structures. Consequently, in each case examined, new governance structures were created resulting in dramatically expanding African American participation. This, in turn, enabled African Americans (often in collaborations with other ethnic minority psychologists) to establish other organizational venues (committees, work groups, study groups conferences, etc.) focused on further expanding ethnic minority participation in a variety of areas of society or association activity, including activities bearing on the discipline's theoretical and methodological racial biases and public policy issues of import to ethnic minority communities. Th ese were continuous and progressive eff orts over decades. Consequently, African American eff orts within the associations and societies (with the possible exception of ABPsi) served to increasingly galvanize political and intellectual alliances among all ethnic minority psychologists. Th is resulted in the ultimate creation of a multicultural perspective in psychology.

Intellectual Traditions and Contributions

African American psychologists' eff orts to gain full access to participation and infl uence within the scientifi c and professional associations and societies served to promote individual careers. But those eff orts also were motivated by a desire to eff ect and legitimize signifi cant changes in perspectives, methodology, scholarly and research literature, and public policy that would serve to revise and transform psychological knowledge and assumptions about African Americans and their families, institutions, and communities. Th is same "reformist/revisionist motive" provides the underpinning of meaning and signifi cance of the professional and scholarly career contributions of large numbers of contemporary African American psychologists. Th e following discussion seeks to identify some of these changes and contributions and to describe some of the major intellectual traditions that informed those eff orts. It should be noted that although the intellectual traditions are presented as distinct and independent, more oft en than not, these traditions to varying degrees interact with one another in infl uencing African American psychologists' individual and organizational perspectives and contributions.

The Social Contextual/Multidisciplinary Tradition

Th is tradition most oft en is associated with the social science faculty and students of the University of Chicago, especially as articulated and practiced during the 1930s through the 1950s. Because of its historical relationship with the Rosenwald Fund, which was a major fi nancial supporter of Black education prior to World War II, the University of Chicago provided training to relatively large numbers of Black scholars, especially in the social sciences (Holliday, 1989, 1999). For example, Greene's (1946) survey of Black recipients of doctoral degrees found that during the period of 1876 to 1943, a total of 381 Blacks were awarded doctorates, of which 234 (61.4%) were awarded by the University of Chicago, and Chicago was found to be the leading school in the number of doctorates awarded to Blacks in the social sciences. Its Black graduates included such luminaries as Charles Johnson, E. Franklin Frazier, Bertram Doyle, Allison Davis, Horace Mann Bond, and St. Clair Drake. Th ese and other Chicago graduates oft en went on to populate and lead academic departments at Historically Black Colleges and Universities (HBCUs), and later in their careers, oft en held academic posts at major White research institutions. From these posts and through their research and scholarship, the Chicago graduates infl uenced the education and training and intellectual and research perspectives of many contemporary Black psychologists (Holliday, 1999; Slaughter & McWhorter, 1985).

 During the pre-World War II years, Chicago signifi cantly infl uenced Black social science not only because it dominated the social sciences during that era, but also because the Chicago School of Social Science included a signifi cant focus on African American issues and communities and use of a "caste/ class" paradigm wherein the eff ects of both social class and racial status were examined. Other characteristics of the Chicago approach to social science research under the leadership of sociologist Robert E. Park include (a) use of multidisciplinary research methods and teams; (b) concern with social-ecological contexts—especially patterns of social relations and community characteristics and processes; (c) concern with social-historical contexts—that is, understanding the natural history of a phenomenon; (d) community-based research; and (e) the linking of research fi ndings to social policy concerns (Holliday, 1989, 1999; Slaughter & McWhorter, 1985).

Some view the American Council on Education studies on Negro youth personality development as one of the hallmarks of Black community social-psychological research conducted by the Chicago School. Th is was a national research project conducted during the late 1930s, resulting in the publication of seven books, and involving large samples, multiple geographical sites, and multidisciplinary interracial research teams. Th e project focused on social personality diff erences as observed and perceived at the levels of the individual, family, and community, with special attention given to the eff ects of segregation, isolation, and limited participation in civil, social, and occupational activities (Holliday, 1989, 1999).

Th e characteristics of Chicago's social/contextual multidisciplinary tradition continue to distinguish much of African American psychological research. Furthermore, this tradition has signifi cantly contributed to psychology's increased reliance on multicultural and population- and cultural-specifi c approaches to psychological knowledge, research, training, and practice.

The Empirical Social Science Tradition of the University of Michigan

Th is tradition is associated with social science faculty and students of the University of Michigan. Historically, the University of Michigan fostered an empirically based scientifi c approach to social issues. According to University of Michigan graduate Algea Harrison-Hale (2006),

> In the 19th century, when most educational institutions off ered a traditional classical curriculum of recitations and lectures, the University of Michigan off ered students a seminar on conducting research. By 1890, graduate students at the University of Michigan had to undertake research projects supervised by faculty who were also engaged in empirical studies. … In psychology, empirical work began when John Dewey came to the university in 1884 and encouraged the founding of its fi rst psychological laboratory in 1890. (p. 165)

Later, Michigan distinguished itself through the development and use of sophisticated sampling techniques and statistical analysis procedures appropriate for large-scale studies and surveys. Th us, in contrast to the Chicago School, the empirical tradition emphasized powerful sampling techniques, controlled collection and examination of data, and subsequent conduct of rigorous statistical data analyses.

Unfortunately, Black academics had little role in developing or refi ning Michigan's empirical approach. Indeed, APA's Committee on Equal Opportunity Psychology (CEOP) reported that between 1920 and 1966, the University of Michigan had awarded doctorates in psychology to only three African Americans (Wispe et al., 1969). Consequently, during the late 1960s and the 1970s, Michigan began an aggressive program of recruitment of Black students into its doctoral psychology programs.

Algea Harrison-Hale (2006), who was a doctoral psychology student at Michigan during the late 1960s, has described the extraordinary bonding that occurred among the newly recruited Black graduate students and faculty in Michigan's social science departments and how this bonding nurtured their social activism, sense of community, and academic careers.

Consequently, these new recruits oft en shared common research interests that were oft en grounded in Michigan's empirical approach. Outgrowths of this Black collegial network included several research programs (e.g., the Program for Research on Black Americans, the African American Mental Health Research Program, and the Center for Urban American Aging Research) of Michigan's renowned Institute of Social Research, which is now headed by African American psychologist and longtime Michigan faculty and researcher James S. Jackson. The university also hosts the Center for Research on Ethnicity, Culture, and Health as well as the Program on Poverty, the Underclass, and Public Policy. These programs have provided funding and empirical research opportunities for a generation of African American students and scholars, including large numbers of Black psychologists. In addition, Black psychology doctoral Michigan graduates of the 1970s era such as Vonnie McLoyd, A. Wade Boykin, and others have headed major research projects that are rooted in the empirical tradition (Harrison-Hale, 2006).

Another major legacy of Michigan's Black collegial network is the "Empirical Conferences on Black Psychology." These conferences were developed in response to the significant increase in the number of African American psychology scholars and researchers during the late 1960s and early 1970s and the unique challenges faced by these early career professionals (e.g., exceptional academic service loads, marginality within their academic departments, and devaluation of their research). Consequently, there was a need for some type of research support system that would serve to mentor and facilitate the research and publication efforts of young Black academic psychologists. In 1974, A. Wade Boykin and J. Frank Yates, who were then graduate students at the University of Michigan, convened the first Empirical Conference on Black Psychology at the University of Michigan with the financial support of the Russell Sage Foundation. This invited, closed forum was conceived as a means for convening "a limited number of persons to critique and present empirical studies, and, in general to promote a research orientation in the field of Black psychology" (Harrison, McAdoo, & McAdoo, 1995, p. 329). It also was a forum that helped persons prepare their papers for publication (Harrison-Hale, 2006, p. 169), and where it was required that all statements about African American children and families be substantiated by hard data (McAdoo & McAdoo, 1985).

The conference's planning committee was soon expanded to include William E. Cross, Anderson J. Franklin, Algea Harrison-Hale, and Harriette and John McAdoo. Between 1974 and 1992, a total of 13 conferences were convened at a variety of sites (e.g., Columbia, Cornell, Hampton, Howard, Lincoln [PA], Michigan State, and Oakland universities, as well as the Universities of California at Berkeley and San Diego, and Delaware), with funding provided by various sources including the National Institute of Education, NIMH, and the Ford Foundation (Harrison et al., 1995; Harrison-Hale, 2006). The conference planners issued several edited books that included papers emanating from the conferences. Examples include Boykin, Anderson, and Yates's (1979) *Research Directions of Black Psychologists* and McAdoo and McAdoo's (1985) *Black Children: Social, Educational, and Parental Environments.*

Collectively, the distinguishing contributions to African American psychology of the empirical social science tradition of the University of Michigan are its dual commitments to active intense career-long mentorship and to empirical research wherein theoretical and conclusionary statements are supported by empirical data.

The Black Scholar/Activist Tradition

This tradition is often associated with social science faculty of the historically Black Howard University in Washington, DC. Howard University is a private university that is governed by an independent board but funded by the federal government. Because of this unique set of characteristics and the consistent funding thus ensured, Howard has emerged as the "premier" historically Black university. Th us, over the years, Howard has been able to attract to its faculty some of the nation's most talented and well-known African American scholars. Th is was especially true prior to the Civil Rights era of the 1960s and 1970s, which ushered an increased recruitment of faculty of color to predominantly White universities.

Historically, as members of a small highly educated elite of the Black community and as ranking members of a major Black institution, Howard University scholars oft en were viewed as the nation's Black intellectual leaders. Consequently, Howard University scholars have forged what LaPoint and Th omas (2006) describe as a "historical legacy of articulating solutions to social problems and improving the human condition, especially for people of African descent" (p. 186). Th is legacy oft en has been characterized as the "Black scholar/activist" tradition. Th is tradition involves engagement in the multiple activities of research, scholarship, training, program or organization administration, and community leadership and advocacy. Th e tradition is epitomized by the lives of such persons as Charles S. Johnson (editor of the Urban League's magazine *Opportunity*, research director of the National Urban League, president of Fisk University), W. E. B. DuBois (academic scholar, world-class intellectual, a founder of the NAACP, and editor of its magazine *Crisis*), and Howard alumnae Mamie and Kenneth B. Clark. It is a tradition that is derived from life experience, Black community norms, and historical necessity.

According to LaPoint and Th omas (2006), during the 1970s, Howard University began its transition to a research institution. Th is transition included the creation of various centers, institutes, and other institutional supports to develop and sustain faculty research. Many of these research entities refl ect the scholar/activist tradition of using research in support of social change. For example, the Institute for Urban Aff airs and Research (IUAR), which existed during the 20-year period of 1972–1992, was committed to studying and solving social problems, especially those aff ecting underserved, poor, and urban communities. Th us, the institute not only conducted research but provided technical assistance to community groups, public and private agencies, and professional communities. According to LaPoint and Th omas, "IUAR directed various research projects that focused on understanding and advancing Black children's development in areas such as mental health, child abuse and neglect, the use of social workers in schools, unwed fathers, father involvement in preschool education, substance abuse prevention, and minority male socialization" (p. 184).

A second major Howard University center in which Black psychologists currently are prominently involved is the Center for Research on the Education of Students Placed at Risk (CRESPAR)/Touchstone Institute, which was established in 1994. CRESPAR is a collaborative federally funded project between Howard University and Th e Johns Hopkins University that seeks "to pursue a basic and applied research agenda, collaborative intervention projects, program evaluations, and scale-up and dissemination activities—all aimed at transforming schools, especially schools for children who have been placed at risk for educational failure" (LaPoint & Th omas, 2006, p. 185). Black psychologist A. Wade Boykin is the project's Howard University principal investigator.

Th e distinguishing contribution of the Black scholar/activist tradition to African American psychology is its emphasis on the use of research to support social change and empower Black communities, and its assumption that Black scholars have a responsibility to also take on the role of Black community activist.

The Afrocentric/African-Centered Tradition

Th is tradition is rooted in longstanding Black nationalist, Pan-African (emphasizing connections of various types among persons and communities of African descent), and culturally centered traditions within African communities throughout the African diaspora. Afrocentric/African-centered perspectives have been constructed in response both to the need to explain the integrity of the African American experience and to assumptions that enslavement resulted in African Americans having no cultural referent other than that of the United States (i.e., Eurocentric). It is a tradition that can be traced to several sources, including Marcus Garvey, who during the fi rst quarter of the 20th century founded the 6 million member United Negro Improvement Association and argued for Black economic independence and repatriation to West Africa; the 1920s Black literary movement known as Harlem Renaissance, which celebrated Black culture and a Black aesthetic (i.e., a Black perspective of the substance of beauty and truth); Elijah Muhammed's establishment of the Black Muslims in the 1930s and its cultural, political, and religious ethos in support of Black self-determinism and in opposition to Eurocentric perspectives; the French Negritude movement, which championed the integrity of African culture during the African independence movements of the 1950s and 1969s; the ideology of Black Power as articulated by Stokey Carmichael and others during the late 1960s; and Black cultural and nationalist movements of the late 1960s that continue to fi nd adherents such as Ron Karenga's African-centered cultural nationalism that purportedly serves to galvanize the minds of Black people through cultural unity, the Republic of New Africa's desire to create a African-inspired nation to be carved out of the U.S. South, and the socialpolitical nationalism of the Black Panthers (Betts, 1971, Introduction).

Within psychology, the Afrocentric/African-centered tradition represents a continuum of thought that is linked by its recognition of the relevance of both African culture and the history of Black oppression to the psychology of African Americans (cf. Parham et al., 1999; Whitten, 1993). Th e psychological Afrocentric perspective was initially articulated to a mass audience by Joseph L. White in 1970 in both *Ebony* and the *Black Scholar* publications. According to White (2004), "Rather than anchoring the search for identity and values in a Euro American perspective, the Afrocentric approach looks within and articulates a point of view that is congruent with the history and culture of African American people" (pp. 13–14).

Th e more conservative wing of this tradition, the Black psychology/Afrocentric perspective, has been described by Na'im Akbar (2004) as follows:

> Th e axiological [values] of Black Psychology is racialism. Th e value assumes race to be the critical human issue in the study of African American behavior … and views the critical relationship of Black-to-White as the paradigmatic relationship … the essential value of Black
> Psychology is mastery over oppression and the oppressor. (p. 24)

Th is Black psychology/Afrocentric perspective includes those African American psychological perspectives that acknowledge that Black culture and the psychology of Black people involve a fusion and use of African and Eurocentric elements (i.e., biculturalism) to eff ect necessary adaptations to both oppression and the dominant European culture. Th us, this perspective incorporates the consideration of both cultural and historical factors of African American life. Examples of such perspectives include Aldebert Jenkins' (1982) humanistic theory and Anderson J. Franklin's (1993, 2004) theory of invisibility.

Th e Black psychology/Afrocentric perspective also includes those psychological theories that emphasize the critical role of ethnic/racial identity development. Th ese theories, which oft en take the form of dynamic stage models, typically attempt to describe how people seek to develop a positive sense of self in the context of devalued ethnic minority and nondominant group status. Examples include William Cross's (1971, 1991) model of Negro-to-Black conversion; Th omas Parham's (1989)

African-centered theory of cycles of nigrescence, which postulates identity development processes throughout the life cycle; and Janet Helms's (1990) Black and White racial identity theory.

Th e Black psychology/Afrocentric perspective also is represented by Joseph White's (1984) own theory of African American psychology, which involves seven primary concepts: improvisation, resilience, transcendence of tragedy, connectedness to others, spirituality, valuing of direct experience, and emotional vitality. According to White, "Th ese concepts are expressed in all Black major social institutions and day-to-day living … "(p. 13). James M. Jones's (1991) theory presents a related set of concepts focused on fi ve dimensions of human experience: time, rhythm, improvisation, oral expression, and spirituality (TRIOS), which represent basic ways in which individuals and cultures make decisions, organize life, establish beliefs, and derive meaning.

In contrast, the more radical African-centered perspective of the Afrocentric/African-centered tradition is rooted primarily in an African worldview as defi ned by African philosophy, values, culture, and systems of spirituality. As Akbar (2004) has observed, "Th e essential value of the African Psychological system is the centrality of the human being … [with] a Divine Creator as the originator and sustainer of man, Nature is in harmony with herself and the desirable [human] state is a harmonious relationship with nature" (p. 25). Others, such as Cheryl Taweda Grills (2004), concur that philosophical and metaphysical concerns underpin African psychology, but locate African psychology as more centrally related to "the healing art and science of traditional African medicine" (p. 171), with communal self-knowledge being the key to mental health.

Some of the key concepts of the African-centered perspective that serve to eff ect a conceptual bridge between traditional African philosophy and more contemporary concerns include the following: (a) Ma'at, which is viewed as a cardinal principle guiding human behavior that includes the seven cardinal virtues of truth, justice, propriety/compassion, harmony, balance, reciprocity, and order; Maafa, which refers to the horrors of African enslavement and the African diaspora and the associated denial of the validity of African people's humanity; and Sankofa, which refers to the use of one's historical past and traditions as a guide to action in the future (Grills, 2004).

Although frequently implicitly advocating an idealized cultural nationalism, many African-centered psychological theories do not themselves refl ect cultural integrity, but instead oft en draw concepts from widely diff ering African cultures. Akbar (2004) in part explains this theoretical anomaly by noting that African psychology theoreticians view philosophical foundations of African psychology to "represent a pure model of the African person in particular and universal man in general" (p. 22). Examples of African-centered theories include Wade Nobles' (1972) theory, which builds on the African notion of the importance of the group to the individual's sense of identity; Akbar's (1977) theory, which highlights the African cultural emphasis on aff ective orientation including caring, empathy, and cooperative efforts as signifi cant sources of behavioral motivation; Joseph Baldwin's (aka Kobi K. K. Kambon) (1981) theory in which cultural traits of African people are viewed as at least partially biogenetic in origin, and maladjustment is viewed as the result of cognitive misorientation associated with loss of contact with one's cultural roots; and Linda James Myers' (1988) optimal psychology theory, which emphasizes the oneness of all, the individual's embeddedness in a larger spiritual force, and individual's construction of reality.

Th e Afrocentric/African-centered tradition has successfully served to infuse the notion of "culturally centered" and "culturally specifi c" theory and applications into psychology. Th ese theories and applications have revealed the limitations of a search for "universal" theory and "normative" development, behavior, and related intervention in psychology. Consequently, theory and practice in psychology have progressively shift ed to population-specifi c perspectives as well as increased recognition of the variability and social-cultural embedment of development and behavior.

Conclusion

I have briefl y described the social and historical contexts of African American psychology, which are marked both by the oppression and denigration that were generally experienced by African American communities and by the restricted professional opportunities in psychology up until the 1960s. Embedded in that history is the story of the contributions that the fi rst cohort of signifi cant size of African American psychologists sought to make, and the types of authority they have pursued, as they made a place and an intellectual space for themselves in psychology. Th e activities of this fi rst cohort suggest that African American history, skills, knowledge, and abilities it has honed among Black people over generations are not ones that strongly encourage individual achievement of the type involved in the development of an elegant abstract theory of learning. Instead, it is a history that speaks to the need to affi rm and contribute to the collectivity—that is, the group and the community.

I also have explored the relatively short history (less than half of a century) of African American's participation in psychology's associations and societies. Here, again, we see collective action that is brilliantly envisioned and strategically tailored to the values and structures of a particular organization: Strategies within smaller societies tend to involve appeals that are both personal and political, whereas strategies used in the larger professional associations tend to be more directly political and challenging. Within each of the associations and societies examined, the push for ethnic minority participation and concerns always started as a focus on African Americans, and always (with the exception of ABPsi) ended in multiracial/multicultural structures and solutions. Th us, African American psychologists forged coalitions that resulted in a new stream in the history of psychology—the history of multicultural psychology. Consequently, especially within the larger associations, one nearly loses the trail of a distinctly African American history in psychology. Th us, it would seem that it falls to ABPsi to maintain and strengthen an identifi able African American history in psychology.

I also have described the intellectual infl uences on African American psychology. Th ose infl uences are themselves best understood in the context of the social histories and experiences of African American scholars, the history of their patterns of participation (and nonparticipation) in U.S. academic institutions, and the legacy of ideas indigenous to the African American community. Th e intellectual infl uences identifi ed in this article have actively interacted with one another across space and time, resulting in the rich diversity of ideas and approaches that now serve to profoundly change psychology and promote its transformation from a Eurocentric discipline to a multicultural discipline appropriate for a global and diverse perspective of human behavior.

I have primarily addressed the contributions of that fi rst cohort of signifi cant size of African Americans psychologists who received their doctoral degrees in the 1970s and 1980s as a result of the gains of the
Civil Rights era. Regretfully, it was beyond the scope of this article to discuss the second major cohort who received their doctoral degrees during the 1990s. Th is cohort was benefi tted and privileged by the signifi cant mentorship provided them by the fi rst cohort and by the changes that their elders had effected in the organized entities of psychology—its associations and societies, its academic departments and institutes, its licensing boards. Th is second cohort was further benefi tted and

privileged by the rich intellectual legacy that their elders affi rmed, broadened, deepened, and fought to legitimize so that those who followed them might drink the wealth of this legacy without trepidation (cf. Slaughter-Defoe, Garrett, & Harrison-Hale, 2006). Th is second major cohort has tremendous occupational options, which it appears to be using both to extend the four major intellectual traditions identifi ed in this article and to establish new ones that are consistent with the increasing entry of African Americans into newer and growing areas of psychology such as health and industrial/organization psychology, neuropsychology, and neuro- science.

Th e history of African American psychology is entrusted to the second and subsequent cohorts of African American psychologists in the spirit of Sankofa: May you learn from the past and may the past guide your visions of the future.

References

Akbar, N. (1977). *Natural psychology and human transformation.* Chicago: Nation of Islam Offi ce of Human Development.

Akbar, N. (2004). Th e evolution of human psychology for African Americans. In R. Jones (Ed.), *Black psychology* (4th ed., pp. 17–40). Hampton, VA: Cobb & Henry.

American Counseling Association. (2007a.). *ACA divisions, regions and branches.* Retrieved October 16, 2007, from http://www.counseling.org/AboutUs/Divisions Branches And Regions/TP/Home/CT2.aspx

American Counseling Association. (2007b). *ACA milestones.* Retrieved October 16, 2007, from http://www.counseling.org/AboutUs/OurHistory/ TP/Milestones/CT2.aspx

American Counseling Association. (2007c). *Our history.* Retrieved October 16, 2007, from http://www.counseling. org/AboutUs/OurHistory/TP/ Home/CT2.aspx

American Psychological Association. (1963). Proceedings of the American Psychological Association. *American Psychologist, 18,* 769.

American Psychological Association. (1997, October). Psychology and racism. *Monitor, 28,* 38–46.

American Psychological Association. (2001, November). A primer of diversity. *Monitor, 32,* 76–77.

American Psychological Association. (2002a). *Guidelines on multicultural education, training, research, practice, and organizational change for psychologists.* Washington, DC: Author.

American Psychological Association. (2002b, January). Psychology bolsters the world's fi ght against racism. *Monitor, 33,* 52–53.

American Psychological Association. (2003). Reginald L. Jones: Award for distinguished career contributions to education and training. *American Psychologist, 58,* 926–929.

American Psychological Association Commission on Ethnic Minority Recruitment, Retention, and Training in Psychology. (1997). *Visions and transformations: Th e fi nal report.* Washington, DC: American Psychological Association Offi ce of Ethnic Minority Aff airs.

American Psychological Association Commission on Ethnic Minority Recruitment, Retention, and Training Task Force. (2007). *A portrait of success and challenge—Th e progress report: 1997–2005. Th e American Psychological Association/CEMRRAT plan.* Washington, DC: American Psychological Association Offi ce of Ethnic Minority
Aff airs.

American Psychological Association Council of Representatives (2007, August). R. Atwell, personal communication. In *Council of Representatives Agenda—San Francisco.* Washington, DC: American Psychological Association.

American Psychological Association Offi ce of Ethnic Minority Aff airs. (1996, February). American Psychological Association launches training capacity grants for the recruitment, retention and training of psychologists of color in historically Black colleges and universities. *Communique,* 13–14.

American Psychological Association Offi ce of Ethnic Minority Aff airs. (2000, May). Psychology and ethnic minority serving institutions. *Communique,* 43–53.

American Psychological Association Offi ce of Ethnic Minority Aff airs. (2001a, July). American Psychological Association board approves resolution on racism. *Communique,* 32–48.

American Psychological Association Offi ce of Ethnic Minority Aff airs. (2001b, July). American Psychological Association to participate in the World Conference Against Racism, Racial Discrimination, Xenophobia, and Related Intolerance. *Communique,* 3–5.

American Psychological Association Offi ce of Ethnic Minority Aff airs. (2001c, February). Taking a position on racial profi ling and other related racial/ethnic disparities in law and security enforcement. *Communique,* 38–50.

American Psychological Association Offi ce of Program Consultation and Accreditation. (2007). *Book 1: Guidelines and principles for accreditation of programs in professional psychology and Book 2: Accreditation operating procedures.* Washington, DC: Author.

Anderson, A. (2007). AMCD historical notes (1997–2007). *Th e Multicultural Counselor—Newsletter of AMCD, 1*(2), 6.

Arredondo, P., & Toporek, R. (2004). Multicultural counseling competencies = ethical practice. *Journal of Mental Health Counseling, 26,* 44–55.

Arredondo, P., Toporek, R. Pack-Brown, S. Jones, J., Locke, D. C., Sanchez, J., & Stadler, H. (1996). Operationalizing of the multicultural counseling competencies. *Journal of Multicultural Counseling and Development, 24,* 42–72.

Association for Multicultural Counseling and Development. (2007). *AMCD by-laws.* Retrieved November 1, 2007, from http://www.amcdaca .org/amcd/bylaws.pdf

Association for Multicultural Counseling and Development. (n.d.). *A historical sketch (1972–2007).* Retrieved November 15, 2007, from http://www.amcdaca.org/amcd/ history.cfm

Association of Black Psychologists. (1978, Summer). *ABPsi Newsletter, 7.*

Association of Black Psychologists. (1979, Fall). *ABPsi Newsletter.*

Association of Black Psychologists. (1980, Summer). *ABPsi Newsletter, 11.*

Association of Black Psychologists. (2006). LCPP Standards. Retrieved September 29, 2009, from http://www. abpsi.org/index.php/component/ content/article/cpp/81-lcpp-standards

Association of Black Psychologists. (2007, August). *ABPsi president's message.* Retrieved August 12, 2007, from http://www.abpsi.org/ president.htm

Autry, B. (2008, August). Th e founding and future of Psi Alpha Omega—Th e Division 45 national student honor society: An interview with its founder and director. *OEMA Communique Newsjournal* (pp. 17–19). Washington, DC: American Psychological Association. Retrievable from http://www.apa.org/pi/oema/july_2008_communique.pdf

Baker, D. B. (2003). Th e challenges of change: Formation of the Association of Black Psychologists. In I. B. Weiner (Series Ed.) & D. K. Freedheim (Vol. Ed.), *Handbook of psychology; Vol. 1. History of psychology* (pp. 492–495), Hoboken, NJ: Wiley.

Baldwin, J. A. (1981). Notes on an Afrocentric theory of Black personality. *Th e Western Journal of Black Psychology, 5,* 172–179.

Benimoff , M. (1995). Eastern Psychological Association: Report of the sixty-sixth annual meeting. *American Psychologist, 50,* 1086–1088.

Benjamin, L. T., Jr., & Crouse, E. M. (2002). Th e American Psychological Association's response to *Brown v. Board of Education:* Th e case of Kenneth B. Clark. *American Psychologist, 57,* 38–50.

Benjamin, L. T., Jr., Henry, K. D., & McMahon, L. R. (2005). Inez Beverly Prosser and the education of African Americans. *Journal of the History of the Behavioral Sciences, 41,* 43–62.

Betts, R. F. (1971). *Th e ideology of blackness.* Lexington, MA: Heath.

Blau, T. H. (1970). American Psychological Association Commission on Accelerating Black Participation in Psychology. *American Psychologist, 25,* 1103–1104.

Bowser, B. (1996). Towards a liberated education: Asa G. Hilliard, III. *Sage Race Relations Abstracts, 21,* 6–24.

Boykin, A. W., Anderson, J., & Yates, F. (1979). *Research directions of Black psychologists.* New York: Russell Sage Foundation.

Canady, H. G. (1939, June). Psychology in Negro institutions. *West Virginia State Bulletin,* 3.

Comas-Diaz, L. (1990). Ethnic minority mental health: Contributions and future directions of the American Psychological Association. In F. Serafi ca, A. Schwebel, R. Russell, P. Isaac, & L. Myers (Eds.), *Mental health of ethnic minorities* (pp. 275–301). New York: Praeger.

Council of National Psychological Associations for the Advancement of Ethnic Minority Interests. (2002). *Governing rules.* Washington, DC: American Psychological Association Offi ce of Ethnic Minority Aff airs.

Cross, W. E. (1971). Th e Negro to Black conversion experience: Towards a psychology of Black liberation. *Black World, 20*(9), 13–27.

Cross, W. E. (1991). *Shades of Black: Diversity in African American identity.* Philadelphia: Temple University Press.

Daley, T. T. (1972). Life ain't been no crystal stair. *Personnel and Guidance Journal, 50,* 491–496.

Daniel, J. H. (1994, November). Leadership and legacy in psychology. *Focus, 8,* 14–15.

Evans, R. B. (1999, December). Th e long road to diversity. *Monitor,* 24.

Figueroa-Garcia, A. (1994, August). *Th e making of an ethnic minority psychologist.* Paper presented at the Annual Convention of American Psychological Association, Los Angeles.

Finison, L. J. (1986). Th e psychological insurgency: 1936–1945. *Journal of Social Issues, 42,* 21–33.

Franklin, A. J. (1993). Th e invisibility syndrome in psychotherapy with African American males. In R. Jones (Ed.), *African American mental health: Th eory, research and intervention* (pp. 395–411). Hampton, VA: Cobb & Henry.

Franklin, A. J. (2004). *From brotherhood to manhood: How Black men rescue their relationships and dreams from the invisibility syndrome.* New York: Wiley.

Franklin, J. H., & Moss, A. A., Jr. (2000). *From Slavery to Freedom: A History of African Americans* (8th ed.). Boston: McGraw-Hill.

Garrett, A. M., Slaughter-Defoe, D. T., & Harrison-Hale, A. O. (2006). Appendix A: Th e chronological history of the Black caucus, 1973–1997. In D. Slaughter-Defoe, A. Garrett, & A. Harrison-Hale (Eds.), Our children too: A history of the Black caucus of the Society for Research in Child Development: 1973–1997. *Monographs of the Society for Research in Child Development,* 71(1, Serial No. 283), 193–207.

Gossett, T. F. (1965). *Race: Th e history of an idea in America.* New York: Schocken Books. (Original work published 1963)

Great Migration. (1999). In K. Appiah & H. Gates (Eds.), *Africana: Th e encyclopedia of the African and African American experience* (pp. 869–872). New York: Basic Books.

Greene, H. (1946). *Holders of doctorates among American Negroes: An education and social study of Negroes who have earned doctoral degrees in course, 1876–1943.* Boston: Meador.

Grills, C. T. (2004). African psychology. In R. Jones (Ed.), *Black psychology* (4th ed., pp. 171–208). Hampton, VA: Cobb & Henry.

Guthrie, R. V. (1976). *Even the rat was white: A historical view of psychology.* Boston: Allyn & Bacon.

Guthrie, R. (1994, November). African Americans in psychology. *Focus, 8,* 4–6.

Guthrie, R. V. (1998). *Even the rat was white: A historical view of psychology* (2nd ed.). Boston: Allyn & Bacon.

Guzman, L. P., Schiavo, S., & Puente, A. E. (1992). Ethnic minorities in the teaching of psychology. In A. Puente, J. Matthews, & C. Brewer (Eds.), *Teaching psychology in America: A history* (pp. 182–213). Washington, DC: American Psychological Association.

Harris, B. (1986). Reviewing 50 years of the psychology of social issues. *Journal of Social Issues, 42,* 1–20.

Harrison, A. O., McAdoo, J. L., & McAdoo, H. P. (1995). History of the Empirical Conferences on Black Psychology, *Journal of Black Psychology, 21,* 329–331.

Harrison-Hale, A. O. (2006). Contributions of African Americans from the University of Michigan to social science research on Black children and families. In D. Slaughter-Defoe, A. Garrett, & A. Harrison-Hale (Eds.), Our children too: A history of the Black caucus of the Society for Research in Child Development: 1973–1997. *Monographs of the Society for Research in Child Development,* 71(1, Serial No. 283), 164–172.

Helms, J. (1990). *Blacks and White racial identity: Th eory, research, and practice.* Westford, CT: Greenwood Press.

Hilliard, A. G. (1983). IQ and the courts' *Larry P. vs. Wilson Riles* and *PASE vs. Hannon. Journal of Black Psychology, 10,* 1–18.

History of Counseling. (n.d.). Retrieved October 16, 2007, from University of Missouri at St. Louis Web site: http:// www.umsl.edu/~pope/ history.html

Holliday, B. G. (1986). African-American families and social change: 1940 to 1980. *Family Perspective Journal, 20,* 289–305.

Holliday, B. G. (1989). Trailblazers in Black adolescent research. In R. Jones (Ed.), *Black adolescents* (pp. 39–54). Berkeley, CA: Cobb & Henry.

Holliday, B. G. (1992, August). *Roots of the mini-convention on ethnic minorities at the Centennial Convention of the American Psychological Association.* Paper presented at the Annual American Psychological Association Convention, Washington, DC.

Holliday, B. G. (1999). Th e American Council on Education's studies on Negro youth development: An historical note with lessons on research, context, and social policy. In R. Jones (Ed.), *African American children, youth and parenting* (pp. 3–30). Hampton, VA: Cobb & Henry.

Holliday, B. G. (2006). Council of National Psychological Association for Advancement of Ethnic Minority Interests. In Y. Jackson (Ed.), *Encyclopedia of Multicultural Psychology* (pp. 113–114). Th ousand Oaks, CA: Sage.

Holliday, B. G., & Holmes, A. L. (2003). A tale of challenge and change: A history and chronology of ethnic minorities in psychology in the United States. In G. Bernal, J. Trimble, A. Burlew, & F. Leong (Eds.), *Handbook of racial and ethnic minority psychology* (pp. 15–64). Th ousand Oaks, CA: Sage.

Hopkins, R., Ross, S., & Hicks, L. H. (1994). A history of the Department of Psychology at Howard University. *Journal of the Washington Academy of Sciences, 82,* 161–167.

Jackson, G. J. (1977). Emergence of a Black perspective in counseling. *Th e Journal of Negro Education, 46,* 230–253.

Jackson, J. P., Jr. (2006). Kenneth B. Clark: Th e complexities of activist psychology. In D. Dewsbury, L. Benjamin, Jr., & M. Wertheimer (Eds.), *Portraits of pioneers in psychology, Volume VI* (pp. 273–286). Washington, DC: American Psychological Association.

Jenkins, A. A. (1982). *Th e psychology of the Afro-American: A humanistic approach.* New York: Pergamon Press.

Jenkins, M. (1994). Section VI: Clinical psychology of ethnic minorities. *Th e Clinical Psychologist, 47,* 16.

Jones, J. (1991). Psychological models of race: What have they been and what should they be? In J. Goodchilds (Ed.), *Psychological perspectives on human diversity in America. Master lectures in psychology* (pp. 3–36). Washington, DC: American Psychological Association.

Katz, I. (1969). A critique of personality approaches to Negro performance, with research suggestions. *Journal of Social Issues,* 25(3), 13–27.

LaPoint, V., & Th omas, V. (2006). Contributions of Howard University to social science research on Black children. In D. Slaughter-Defoe, A. Garrett, & A. Harrison-Hale (Eds.), Our children too: A history of the Black caucus of the Society for Research in Child Development: 1973–1997. *Monographs of the Society for Research in Child Development, 71*(1, Serial No. 283), 173–187.

McAdoo, H. P., & McAdoo, J. L. (1985). Preface. In H. McAdoo & J. McAdoo (Eds.), *Black children: Social, educational, and parental environments* (pp. 9–13). Beverly Hills. CA: Sage.

McLoyd, V. C. (2006). Th e role of African American scholars in research on African American children: Historical perspectives and personal refl ections. In D. Slaughter-Defoe, A. Garrett, & A. Harrison-Hale (Eds.), Our children too: A history of the Black caucus of the Society for Research in Child Development: 1973–1997. *Monographs of the Society for Research in Child Development, 71*(1, Serial No. 283), 121–144.

Miller, D. K. (1986). Screening people in, not out: Comment on Morawski. *Journal of Social Issues, 42*(1), 127–131.

Morawski, J. G. (1986). Psychologist for society and societies for psychologists: SPSSI's place among professional organizations. *Journal of Social Issues, 42,* 111–126.

Myers, L. J. (1988). *Understanding an Afrocentric world view: Introduction to an optimal psychology.* Dubuque, IA: Kendall/Hunt.

Nobles, W. W. (1972). African philosophy: Foundations for Black psychology. In R. Jones (Ed.), *Black psychology* (pp. 99–105). New York: Harper & Row.

Parham, T. A. (1989). Cycles of psychological nigrescence. *Counseling Psychologist, 17,* 187–226.

Parham, T. A., White, J. L., & Ajamu, A. (1999). *Th e psychology of Blacks: An African-centered perspective* (3rd ed.). Upper Saddle River, NJ: Prentice Hall.

Parron, D. L. (1990). Federal initiatives in support of mental health research on ethnic minorities. In F. C. Serafi ca, A. E. Schwebel, R. K. Russell, P. D. Isaac, & L. B. Myers (Eds.), *Mental health of ethnic minorities* (pp. 302–309). New York: Praeger.

Pearl, A. (1970). Th e poverty of psychology—An indictment. In V. Allen (Ed.), *Psychological factors in poverty* (pp. 348–364). Chicago: Markham.

Pickren, W. E., & Tomes, H. (2002). Th e legacy of Kenneth B. Clark to the American Psychological Association: Th e Board of Social and Ethical Responsibility for Psychology. *American Psychologist, 57,* 51–59.

Psi Alpha Omega. (n.d.). *Welcome to Psi Alpha Omega.* Retrieved December 20, 2007, from http://www.psialphaomega.com/

Rainwater, L. (1970). Neutralizing the disinherited: Some psychological aspects of understanding the poor. In V. Allen (Ed.), *Psychological factors in poverty* (pp. 9–28). Chicago: Markham.

Richards, G. (1997). *"Race," racism and psychology: Towards a refl exive history.* New York: Routledge.

Sitkoff , H. (1978). *A new deal for Blacks: Th e emergence of civil rights as a national issue: Vol. 1. Th e depression decade.* New York: Oxford University Press.

Slaughter, D. T., & McWhorter, G. A. (1985). Social origins and early features of the scientifi c study of Black American families and children. In M. Spencer, G. Brookins, & W. Allen (Eds.), *Beginnings: Th e social and aff ective development of Black children* (pp. 5–18). Hillsdale, NJ: Erlbaum.

Slaughter-Defoe, D. T. (2006a). On becoming a governing council member and maximizing membership. In D. Slaughter-Defoe, A. Garrett, & A. Harrison-Hale (Eds.), Our children too: A history of the Black caucus of the Society for Research in Child Development: 1973–1997. *Monographs of the Society for Research in Child Development, 71*(1, Serial No. 283), 48–65.

Slaughter-Defoe, D. T. (2006b). Personal perspective on the beginnings of the Black caucus of SRCD. In D. Slaughter-Defoe, A. Garrett, & A. Harrison-Hale (Eds.), Our children too: A history of the Black caucus of the Society for Research in Child Development: 1973–1997. *Monographs of the Society for the Research in Child Development, 71* (1, Serial No. 283) 12–24.

Slaughter–Defoe, D. T., Garrett, A. M., & Harrison-Hale, A. O. (2006). Affi rming future generations of ethnic minority scientists. In D. Slaughter-Defoe, A. Garrett, & A. Harrison-Hale (Eds.), Our children too: A history of the Black caucus of the Society for Research in Child Development: 1973–1997. *Monographs of the Society for Research in Child Development,* 71(1, Serial No. 283), 188–192.

Society for Research on Child Development. (2007). *About the society.* Retrieved January 9, 2008, from http://www.srcd.org/about.html

Street, W. R. (1994). *A chronology of noteworthy events in American psychology.* Washington, DC: American Psychological Association.

Sue, D. W., Arredondo, P., & McDavis, R. J. (1992). Multicultural counseling competencies and standards: A call to the profession. *Journal of Counseling and Development, 70,* 477–486.

Sue, D. W., Bernier, Y., Durran, A., Feinberg, L., Pedersen, P. B., & Smith, E. J. (1982). Position paper: Crosscultural counseling competencies. *Th e Counseling Psychologist, 10,* 45–52.

Sue, S. (1994). Asian Americans in psychology. *Focus, 8*(2), 6–8.

Sullivan, P. (1999). Civil Rights movement. In K. Appiah & H. Gates (Eds.), *Africana: Th e encyclopedia of the African and African American experience* (pp. 441–455). New York: Basic Books.

Valentine, C. (1971). Defi cit, diff erence and bicultural models of Afro-American behavior. *Harvard Educational Review, 41,* 137–157.

White, J. L. (Ed.). (1984). *Th e psychology of Blacks.* Englewood Cliff s, NJ: Prentice Hall.

White, J. L. (2004). Toward a Black psychology. In R. Jones (Ed.,) *Black psychology* (4th ed., pp. 4–15). Hampton, VA: Cobb & Henry.

Whitten, L. A. (1993). Infusing Black psychology into the introductory psychology course. *Teaching of Psychology, 20,* 13–21.

Williams, R. (1974). A history of the Association of Black Psychologists: Early formation and development. *Journal of Black Psychology, 1,* 9–24.

Williams, R. (2008). A 40-year history of the Association of Black Psychologists. *Journal of Black Psychology, 34,* 249–260.

Wispe, L., Awkard, J., Hoff man, M., Ash, P., Hicks, L. H., & Porter, J. (1969). Th e Negro psychologist in America. *American Psychologist, 24,* 142–150.

Racial Microagressions Against Black Americans Implications for Counseling

Derald Wing et al.

Racial microaggression themes were identifi-ed using a focus-group analysis of self-identifi ed Black participants. Six categories of demeaning and invalidating messages refl-ected beliefs of White supremacy that were unintentionally conveyed by perpetrators. Implications for counselors and the counseling process are discussed.

The counseling and helping professions have acknowledged the importance of developing cultural competence in providing services to an increasingly diverse population (American Psychological Association, 2003; Sue, Arredondo, & McDavis, 1992). One of the steps to achieving that goal is for counselors to become aware of their worldviews: the standards used to judge normality and abnormality; the implicit values and assumptions about human behavior; and the biases, prejudices, and stereotypes inherited from their social conditioning in society (Ridley, 2005; Sue, 2003). It is clear that the counseling profession has taken important steps to point out that (a) racism detrimentally aff-ects the mental health of Black Americans (American Counseling Association, 1999), (b) counseling may represent cultural oppression for culturally diverse groups (Ridley, 2005), and (c) high rates of underuse of mental health services and premature termination may be due to individual and institutional bias toward clients of color (Burkard & Knox, 2004; Kearney, Draper, & Baron, 2005).

Although it can be acknowledged that the helping professions have done much to directly combat the overt forms of counselor and institutional bias through their production of competency standards and guidelines, the counseling profession has been less successful in addressing insidious forms of racism that invisibly infect the worldviews of well-intentioned helping professionals and the biased policies and practices within mental health delivery systems. Part of the problem is related to the profession's confusion regarding what the U.S. public views as racism and the profession's failure to understand racism's more insidious manifestations (Sue, 2003).

Th-e nature of racism in the United States has evolved over time from the old-fashioned overt expressions of White supremacy and racial hatred to the more subtle, ambiguous, and unintentional expressions called *aversive racism* (Dovidio & Gaertner, 2000). Because most White Americans associate

Derald Wing Sue, Kevin L. Nadal, Christina M. Capodilupo, Annie I. Lin, Gina C. Torino, & David P. Rivera, "Racial Microaggressions Against Black Americans: Implications for Counseling," *Journal of Counseling and Development*, vol. 86, no. 3, pp. 330–338. Copyright © 2008 by American Counseling Association. Reprinted with permission. Provided by ProQuest LLC. All rights reserved.

racism with hate crimes and White supremacist groups such as the Ku Klux Klan and skinheads, they are unaware how bias and discrimination have taken on an invisible nature that protects them from realizing their own complicity in the perpetuation of unintentional racism toward persons of color (Dovidio, Gaertner, Kawakami, & Hodson, 2002; Sue, 2004). As a result, most White Americans believe that discrimination is on the decline, that racism is no longer a signifi-cant factor in the lives of people of color, that they are personally free of bias, and that equality will be shortly achieved (Sue, 2003).

 Black Americans, however, perceive the situation quite diff-erently. Th-ey claim that racism is a constant and continuing reality in their lives and that many well-intentioned, White individuals continue to respond toward them with racial insensitivity, to act as if White people are superior, to possess a need to control everything, and to treat them poorly because of their race (Sue, Capodilupo, & Holder, in press). According to Black Americans, these attitudes and behaviors are frequently communicated by White persons through racial microaggressions directed toward them (Solórzano, Ceja, & Yosso, 2000). Because counselors and helping professionals seem no more immune than other individuals from inheriting the biases of their forebears, research now indicates that White counselors also deliver racial microaggressions in their counseling sessions with Black clients and Black supervisees (Constantine, 2007; Constantine & Sue, 2007).

The New Face of Racism: Racial Microaggressions

According to Sue, Bucceri, Lin, Nadal, and Torino (2007),

> raical microaggressions are brief and commonplace daily verbal, behavioral and environmental indignities, whether intentional or unintentional, that communicate hostile, derogatory, or other negative racial slights and insults to the target person or group, and are expressed in three forms: microassaults, microinsults and microinvalidations. (p. 72)

Microassaults are probably most similar to what has been called *old-fashioned racism* because their expression is deliberate, conscious, and explicit. Calling someone a "nigger," displaying the hood of the Ku Klux Klan, or refusing to serve a Black person are examples of microassaults. Th-ese expressions of racism are most oft-en deliberate on the part of the miccroaggressor, whose intent is to hurt, oppress, or discriminate against a person of color (Dovidio & Gaertner, 2000).

Microinsults and microinvalidations are signifi-cantly diff-erent from microassaults in that they are not usually expressed intentionally by perpetrators because the racial biases and prejudices that underlie these behaviors are outside the perpetrators' conscious awareness (Banaji, 2001; DeVos & Banaji, 2005). Th-e power that these microaggressions have to hurt and oppress people of color is due to their invisible nature. In fact, many Black individuals may fi-nd it easier to deal with microassaults because the intent of the microaggressor is clear and obvious, whereas microinsults and microinvalidations involve considerable guesswork because of their ambiguous and invisible nature (Sue et al., in press).

Microinsults can be defi-ned as actions (verbal, nonverbal, or environmental) that convey insensitivity, are rude, or directly demean a person's racial identity or heritage. Microinvalidations are actions that exclude, negate, or nullify the psychological thoughts, feelings, or experiences of people of color. Telling a Black American that "You are a credit to your race" or telling the person "You are so articulate" are examples of microinsults, whereas complimenting an Asian American for speaking good English or constantly asking the person "Where were you born?" are classifi-ed as microinvalidations. Both forms of microaggressions convey a hidden message and meaning to the recipient. In the former, the message is that "People of color as a group are unintelligent," and, in the latter, the message is "You are a foreigner or alien in your own land."

Aft-er proposing a hypothetical taxonomy of racial microaggressions, researchers were able to identity four microinsult themes in previous studies. Th-ese themes were as follows: (a) ascription of intelligence (assigning low or high intelligence on the basis of race), (b) assumption of criminal status (belief a group is more prone to crime), (c) pathologizing cultural values/communication styles, and (d) second-class citizenship (treating others as lesser beings). Th-is line of research also resulted in the uncovering of four microinvalidation themes: (a) being alien in one's own land, (b) color blindness, (c) denial of personal racism, and (d) the myth of meritocracy (Sue, Capodilupo, et al., 2007).

Other researchers note that racial microaggressions have a cumulative and harmful impact on people of color by assailing their sense of integrity, invalidating them as racial/cultural beings, sapping their spiritual and psychic energies, and imposing a false reality on them (Franklin, 2004; Solórzano et al., 2000; Sue et al., in press). Black Americans frequently report feelings of racial rage, frustration, low self-esteem, depression, and other strong emotional reactions when subjected to microaggressions. Investigators have also confi-rmed that racial microaggressions may be more harmful to people of color than overt acts of racial hatred and bigotry because the hidden, unintentional nature of microaggressions allows them to fl ourish outside the level of conscious awareness of the perpetrators, thereby infecting interracial interactions, institutional procedures and practices, and social policies (Franklin, 2004; Hintan, 2004; Sue, 2003).

Microaggressions refl ect an unconscious worldview of White supremacy that directly assails the racial reality of Black Americans. Th ese unique forms of aggression result in the perpetuation of various injustices that have major consequences not only on the mental health of the recipients, but also in creating and maintaining racial inequities in health care, employment, and education (U.S. Department of Health and Human Services, 2001). As such, eliminating racial microaggressions and minimizing their impact on achieving equal access and opportunity become issues of vital importance for counselors who embrace a multicultural/social justice helping perspective (Sue & Sue, 2008).

Getting White Americans to become aware of their unintentional racist communications is a major challenge to society and the helping professions. Although research on overt forms of racism is valuable, few scholars have explored the hidden and denigrating messages of racial microaggressions that are directed toward Black people. Th e fi rst step toward reversing the endless cycle of microaggressions that is perpetuated in the United States involves unmasking the hidden themes that refl ect a racially biased worldview that harms and oppresses others. Th e following qualitative study of Black Americans was designed to delineate some of the hidden messages that are inherent to microaggressions and indirectly tests the taxonomy developed by Sue, Capodilupo, et al. (2007) in previous research.

Method

Th e current investigation used a qualitative approach to explore the types of microaggressions experienced by Black Americans, the meanings they construed to them, and their emotional reactions to diff erent microaggressions. Qualitative approaches are highly appropriate when conducting research with marginalized populations, especially when contextualizing issues of power and privilege (Morrow & Smith, 2000). To fully explore a new area of investigation and capture the depth of participants' experiences, we used focus groups (Krueger, 1994,1998; Seal, Bogart, & Ehrhardt, 1998). Focus groups allow the social interaction of participants to generate meaning of the phenomenon under investigation (Krueger, 1998). Th is method has been successful in generating knowledge with racial/ethnic groups in other studies as well (Saint-Germain, Bassford, & Montano, 1993; Solórzano et al., 2000). Th rough describing, comparing, and categorizing microaggressive events produced from the focus groups, we were able to categorize them into themes and uncover their hidden messages.

Participants

Th e research participants were solicited through various means: fl yers posted at a local graduate school in the Northeast, classroom visits, and e-mail requests to Black student organizations. All participants had to identify as being either Black or African American, agree that subtle racism and discrimination existed in the United States, and indicate that they had personally experienced or witnessed racist incidents.

Two focus groups were formed, with membership of 8 individuals in one group and 5 in another. Of the 13 self-identifi ed Black Americans who participated in the study, 4 were men and 9 were women. Participants' ages ranged from 23 to 33 years. Nine participants were graduate students in either master's or doctoral programs in counseling psychology, and 4 worked in higher education settings.

Researchers

Th e research team was composed of four Black Americans, three Asian Americans (including the fi rst author and one of the coauthors), one Latino, and two White Americans (including two of the coauthors). Th e pivotal role of investigators, who are involved in the data collection and analysis processes generated from qualitative research methods, demands the identifi cation of the researchers' values, assumptions, and biases to check for potential bias (Fassinger, 2005). Th e members of the research team met to discuss these issues prior to collecting and analyzing the data generated in this study. Assumptions of the team members included a belief that racial microaggressions exist, that they are committed against Black Americans, that their eff ects have detrimental emotional consequences, and that they may be race/ ethnic group specifi c. Th e purpose of acknowledging such assumptions is to minimize bias in the datacollection and analysis process.

Measure

Data were collected through a demographic questionnaire seeking information about the research participants' ethnicity, age, gender, occupation, level of education, and information generated from the use of a semistructured interview protocol (available from the fi rst author upon request). Th e protocol consisted of eight questions that were aimed at producing diverse examples of microaggressions, investigating their eff ect on the recipients, exploring their meaning, and summarizing the responses of the participants.

Procedure

Th e research participants were assigned to one of two focus groups on the basis of their availability. Financial compensation was not off ered to the participants. Basic information about the study on racial microaggressions was shared with the participants. Both the group facilitators and observers were Black. Th ese persons conducted 90-minute focus groups with the participants who composed the two groups in this study. Th e racial similarity of the participants, facilitators, and observers was intentional to promote ease of disclosure and reduce negative feelings related to interacting with non-Black persons. Th e roles of the facilitators and observers were to lead the focus-group discussions and unobtrusively observe the group dynamics and the participants' nonverbal behaviors in these group meetings (Krueger, 1998).

Th e focus-group meetings were facilitated in a private room at the researchers' university. Prior to the onset of the group discussions, all participants signed consent and audiotape permission forms. At the end of the group meetings, a debriefi ng was immediately conducted between the facilitators and observers to check their observations about the group dynamics and issues of concern that arose during the group meetings. Th e focus-group sessions as well as the debriefi ng sessions were audiotaped and transcribed verbatim aft er removing the identity of the participants. Th e tapes were destroyed aft er transcription, and the transcripts were checked for accuracy before analysis.

A subteam of researchers that included three research team members identifi ed the domains used to categorize the narratives produced from the group meetings in accordance with the principles of focus-group analysis (Krueger, 1998; Miles & Huberman, 1994; Seal et al., 1998). Th e central task of the subteam was to make sense of the particular forms of microaggressions reportedly experienced by Black Americans; the messages conveyed through these microaggressions; and the behavioral, cognitive, and emotional reactions the research participants had to these microaggressions. Data analysis was conducted on the following: (a) identifi cation of the microaggressions, (b) description of critical incidents, (c) examination of emerging themes, (d) categorization of consequences, and (e) narration of common responses to the microaggressions.

Upon formulating domains, the subteam reconvened with the fi rst author, who served as the auditor, following an essential procedure that is used in consensual qualitative research (Hill et al., 2005; Hill, Th ompson, & Williams, 1997). Using a modifi ed consensual qualitative research approach is considered an acceptable methodology because qualitative studies are fundamentally interested in the richness of an experience as reported by the research participants (Polking-horne, 2005). Th us, the transcript analysis was accomplished through uniform agreement of the subteam members, who were required to independently extract core ideas from the aforementioned domains.

Core ideas are notions derived from the aforementioned domains that detail and holistically integrate the data given the context of the subject under examination (Hill et al., 2005; Hill et al., 1997). Upon extracting core ideas from the participants' responses, the subteam members then presented, discussed, and negotiated their own analytical results among themselves. Th e goal of reaching consensus among the subteam members was to enable an ultimate presentation to the auditor. Th e auditor then (a) compared the individual contributions of the subteam members, (b) curtailed groupthink tendencies, (c) encouraged diverse viewpoints, and (d) confi rmed or disconfi rmed the themes manifested in the focus groups. Th is process of data analysis was completed separately for each transcript before the results from the two groups were compiled.

Results

Six themes emerged from the data analysis and represent the meanings participants made of specifi c microaggressive incidents. Meaning making usually involves interpreting the events in question, unmasking their hidden messages, and surmising the intention of the microaggressor. To be considered a freestanding microaggression theme, only those incidents endorsed by multiple participants in both focus groups are recognized as such. One category of undeveloped incidents/responses was included because several incidents could not be classifi ed under any of the themes or did not reach group consensus.

Theme 1: Assumption of Intellectual Inferiority

Th is theme refers to microaggressions that assume Black Americans to be intellectually inferior, inarticulate, or lacking common sense. Both male and female participants spoke of negative reactions to being told, "You speak so well" or "You are so articulate." Such statements usually allow the microaggressor to maintain a belief in Black inferiority by considering the speaker to be an exception to his or her racial group. Th ese incidents occurred frequently in the workplace and in academic settings. One 25-year-old female participant stated, "In a class, if I say something that's insightful, quote unquote, you get a reaction. Like, 'Oh, that was really smart.' Like, 'Th at was really insightful' or some words like that." Although such statements were intended as compliments, they were generally interpreted as insults.

Participants also described multiple incidents of being treated diff erently when someone erroneously assumed that they were White because of their stellar résumés or through conversations over the phone. One 31-year-old female participant stated, "Every time I go on an interview, my résumé doesn't speak Black. … [When I show up for the interview] I get the same reaction from people. Sometimes it's more blatantly obvious than others, but it's always like, 'Oh, you're Silvia [pseudonym]?'" Th e hidden message communicated by the microaggressor was that educational and occupational accomplishments are "normal" for White individuals, but not for Black individuals. A number of Black persons entertained the notion that they would not have been called for an interview if the interviewer had known that they were Black.

One 22-year-old male participant described the following classroom situation: "You say something, [and] someone repeats back the exact same thing that you have said." He described incidents in which his comments were seemingly ignored or not acknowledged by the instructor or other students. However, when White students would make similar statements, the professor would positively acknowledge them. Many participants felt that their contributions were deemed "worthless" or "lacking in intellectual substance."

Theme 2: Second-Class Citizenship

Being perceived and treated as a lesser being was a frequent microaggressive theme. A typical incident includes the type of service that an individual receives at a store or restaurant. One 28-year-old male participant shared the following in describing his experience with this type of microaggression: "I go to the supermarket and there's an opportunity. [Th e salesperson says,] 'Who's in line next?' [and then chooses] someone who was not in line next, and I was standing there." Participants described many examples in which they were served last or ignored altogether.

Th e notion of second-class citizenship was further exemplifi ed by a 25-year-old female participant who reported the following experience: "I put money in someone's hand and they won't put the money back in my hand. Th ey'll make sure that they put the money on the counter as if I'm toxic." Th is Black participant believed that the microaggressor did not want to have any physical contact with her because she was a lesser being. Th is belief is reinforced by observations that the salesperson would hand change directly to others if they were White.

Theme 3: Assumption of Criminality

A belief that Black Americans are potential criminals and prone to antisocial or violent behaviors was another common theme that emerged in this study. A typical situation involving this theme was described by a 22-year-old female participant: "I've walked down the block from where I live and had a White woman cross the street and go to the other side and continue up." In this situation, the Black female participant recognized that a White woman would go out of her way to cross the street because she was either physically afraid of the research participant or assumed the participant had criminal intent.

Other situations occurred in which Black individuals were viewed as thieves or shoplift ers. One 30-year-old male participant stated, "Sometimes they follow you [in a store]. ... Somebody's walking behind me trying to monitor me or whatever." Th e meaning construed was that White individuals automatically assume that Black people are likely to steal, cannot be trusted, are immoral, and are likely to engage in criminal misconduct.

Most participants in both groups endorsed having experienced or knowing other Black individuals who were followed in stores, scrutinized closely by security guards in shopping malls, and pulled over by police while driving. All participants interpreted close surveillance behavior to be an assumption that they are "up to no good" or "dangerous." As one 40-year-old female participant stated, "It makes you feel like you are guilty of something ... like you're a criminal."

Theme 4: Assumption of Inferior Status

Believing that Black individuals are inferior in status and credentials was the fourth theme that emerged in this study. Some participants indicated how they were assumed to hold lower paying jobs and to occupy lower status career positions; in social situations, they were assumed to be poor or uncultured. One 26-year-old male participant described his entering a new building for business purposes as follows:

> I was in shoes, dress slacks, dress shirt, carrying a messenger bag, and so I walked in. ... [Th e] fi rst person I see is a guard, and the guard's like, "OK you go through that door right there." So I go through the door, and it turns out to be the messenger area, you know?

Th is participant immediately recognized the guard's assumption that he could not possibly be a manager or corporate executive, but instead was a lesser worker.

Another male participant described numerous incidents in which unhappy White individuals would come to his store and complain, "I need to see a manager!" in which case the Black participant replied "I am the manager!" Th is response was, in turn, met with incredulous and dubious looks from the microaggressor. In this situation, the microaggressor seemed to assume that the Black individual could not possibly occupy a position of authority or responsibility.

Th ere were also reported instances in which an assumption of inferior status involved believing that a Black individual is poor, primitive, or unsophisticated. One 31-year-old female participant recollected an incident that happened at a restaurant; she and a friend wanted to sit in the main dining room of a fancy restaurant but were instead seated in a casual dining area: "[Th e hostess says,] 'I wasn't aware that you wanted the main dining room.' My friend's like, 'Is it because we're Black and we're young?'"

In this situation, both the participant and her friend believed that the hostess assumed that they could not aff ord to dine in the main room (as opposed to the less expensive casual dining area in the back of the restaurant). It was further suggested that the hostess may also not want Black patrons to be seen in the main dining room and thus treated them as second-class citizens (an example of the additive nature and interaction of more than one microaggression theme).

Theme 5: Assumed Universality of the Black American Experience

Many participants reported numerous instances of being asked to speak for all members of their race. For example, a 27-year-old male participant stated, "I had a manager who would get résumés of people and whenever the name he thought looked Black, he would come, 'How do I pronounce this name?'" Th e manager assumed that the research participant knew how to pronounce all Black-sounding names by virtue of his being Black. Th e manager also seemed to believe that all Black people share identical experiences and were all the same.

Another male participant described the following incident:

> Th is White woman had called the offi ce, and she was asking for Tyrone. And I was the only brother working there and my name is Leroy. And I know she had just lost it, and she knew it was one of those Black-sounding names.

Th is participant stated that he felt a negation of his individual experience because he was viewed as being interchangeable with other Black people.

A female participant shared this sentiment when she discussed being the "only Black person on an all-White board" at a nonprofi t organization. She oft en believed that White members thought that her presence "brought a certain degree of authenticity" to the board, as if she alone could represent all Black people.

Many participants endorsed the feeling that in work and school settings, they were oft en looked to as the "Black representative" who could "speak for all Black people."

Several other participants reported incidents in which coworkers or managers "consulted" them when they had a question about a Black person the participant did not know. One male participant described the following experience in this regard: "[A coworker] asked me, 'Do I say African American or Black when referring to another coworker?'" Th e participant felt frustrated by this question, wondering, "[How] should I know what he/she prefers?" alluding to the notion that there is not just one way that people self-identify and that it is impractical to assume a universal experience for all Black people.

Theme 6: Assumed Superiority of White Cultural Values/Communication Styles

Nearly all of the research participants discussed incidents in which Black cultural values and communication styles were devalued and deemed inferior while the superiority of White values and ways of communicating were upheld. Speaking about the pressure to conform to White standards in her workplace, a 25-year-old female participant asserted the following:

> In a professional setting, you really have to sort of masquerade your responses. You can't say what's really on your mind, or you have to fi lter through so many diff erent lenses till it comes out sounding acceptable to whoever's listening.

This participant indicated feeling that she could not be her authentic self or use her true voice, because it may not be "acceptable" to White supervisors or coworkers. She further described messages (direct and indirect) at her workplace to "act White" in order to be "acceptable" and "professional."

A similar sentiment was echoed by a male participant: "Yeah and that sort of way of interacting is not, in terms of a cultural experience, is not always what I value nor even always want to do but it's something you have to learn how to do." This participant was discussing how he negotiates his workplace, specifically his feeling that he has to adopt White cultural values to "fit in" and "be successful."

Another male participant immediately followed up this statement by adding, "I don't like the small talk of 'How's your baby?' that I feel pressured to get involved in or I'm seen as rude, or disengaged." Both of these research participants concluded that White workplace norms could not be rejected without negative consequences. Not only could these norms not be followed, but many expressed feeling pressure to assimilate and acculturate to White standards if they were to have a chance to advance in the organization. Illustrating this further, a 30-year-old female participant explored how she learned to get involved in the office small talk that was common among White coworkers: "The way you interact, like I had to learn how to [engage in] the casual banter. … There is a certain rhythm that I had to learn… when you're asking questions and you have no real interest in the answers."

Several other participants discussed classroom experiences in which they were teased by classmates or corrected by their instructors for using words that were common and natural for them. As a 27-yearold male participant stated, "It was not uncommon for teachers to ask me to repeat myself, or make it clear that I needed to change my words to be understood." The message being communicated to these participants was that they needed to "learn the correct (read White) manner of speaking" to be successful in life.

A subtheme that emerged from the aforementioned major theme was titled *White standards of beauty are superior*. Endorsed only by female participants in both groups, this subtheme focused on one's physical appearance (hair texture and style). Commenting on this microaggression, women in both groups shared multiple incidents in which they felt that White women and men communicated to them that their way of wearing their hair (i.e., natural) is abnormal and strange. A 23-year-old female participant corroborated this subtheme by pointing out the following:

> I went on a job interview, so I think I twisted my hair so it looked a little calmer and so to not scare them. … We're wearing it our natural way, but my natural is different, you know, it's not natural.

This participant felt pressured to "twist her hair" because wearing it natural is "different" and "not natural" and may detrimentally affect her job interview.

Acknowledging a similar incident, a 31-year-old female participant stated,

> I used to work in a high school, a very White high school, and over the summer I got my hair braided. I went up there to do some business and oh, the reactions! "Oh my God! I mean, what's happening to you?" Like this whole militant and "What are you doing this summer?" They treated me like the angry Black woman, afraid of how I was going to come back. The comments were just all like cautionary "Are you OK?"

The immediate response by coworkers to the participant's braided hair is that she is "militant" and to be feared.

Both incidents, described previously, convey the idea that the more "Black" (i.e., natural) a woman wears her hair, the stronger the assumption that she fits the stereotype of the "angry Black woman." It seems inherent in these messages that conforming to White standards of beauty (i.e., relaxing or straightening hair) will result in more acceptance from White coworkers and/or friends.

With regard to their hair, women in both focus groups also discussed feeling that their hair was "on display" for White people to comment on. For example, a 40-year-old female participant, who had recently straightened her hair, was approached by a coworker who commented, "Oh, you look like Diana Ross and the Temptations!" This experience resonated with many of the other women in the group, who agreed with verbal yesses and head nods. Another female participant responded, "It's like they need to pass out a memo that I've changed my hairstyle. Want to take a picture and pass it around, so everyone can see how I've changed my hair?"

Other female participants likened the excitement over their changed hairstyle to a "news story" in the office, despite feeling that they were not doing anything different or worthy of such attention. They pondered aloud about whether a White coworker's haircut would generate as much attention and generally felt that their privacy was invaded with regard to their personal aesthetic.

Theme 7: Underdeveloped Incidents/Responses

Both focus groups mentioned a number of incidents that could not easily be classified into any of the aforementioned six major themes, because they were not fully endorsed by all group members. Additionally, because these incidents were not probed further, it was difficult for the entire research team to reach consensus. For example, one female participant shared a story in which she felt dehumanized: "This White woman approached a Black family and looked at a baby in the stroller and said, 'Oh, ain't that a cute little monkey!'" In this situation, the participant was appalled that the woman made a blatantly racist comment referring to a Black baby as a "monkey," particularly because the racial epithet is outdated and obviously offensive.

A male participant shared his reaction to an acquaintance's use of the term *nigger rigging*: "I was like, 'What did you just say?' [which the acquaintance follows with] 'No, I'm not being racist, calm down. ... Oh, you know, you know what I mean?'" The participant was frustrated that the microaggressor wholeheartedly denied that his comment was racist, thereby denying the racial reality of the individual who is insulted. Furthermore, the Black individual is now seen as angry and oversensitive, hence perpetuating the stereotype that Black Americans are "angry minorities."

Finally, one male participant disclosed that "two of my friends were talking about how rap music is always blasting in cars and how [they] hate that ... and I walked into the conversation [and they reacted,] 'Oh but not you ... you're not like that.'" The participant in this case felt tokenized in that because he may not engage in what is stereotyped as "typical Black behavior" (i.e., listening to rap music), he is viewed as exceptional and more acceptable to White people.

Limitations of the Study

It is important to note several limitations of this study. First, our findings were drawn from a nonrepresentative population of Black individuals: 13 total participants, twice as many women as men, and all with college experience. Although we believe that the findings have validity for most Black individuals in U.S. society, further qualitative and quantitative studies would prove fruitful to explore the generalizability of our findings.

Second, it must be cautioned that the terminology used in identifying microaggressive themes may have been infl uenced by the questions in the interview protocol. Th e researchers in the present study tried to guard against this possibility by making sure the participants could readily provide multiple examples under each microaggressive theme.

Th ird, although this study provided an in-depth exploration of racial microaggressions for Black individuals, future studies should probe the experiences of Latinos/Latinas and Native Americans, Black and Caribbean Americans, and the myriad ethnic groups that compose Asian Americans/Pacifi c Islanders.

Fourth, given the limited generalizability of qualitative research that involves focus-group discussions composed of a small number of participants, it would be helpful if instruments quantifying racial microaggressions could be created with subscales that measure specifi c themes identifi ed in this and other studies among larger numbers of research participants. Such a development would allow counselors to quantitatively measure the types of racial microaggressions people of color experience, identify similar and diff erent race-specifi c expressions, and determine the degree of psychological distress produced among larger samples.

Fift h, the present study focused exclusively on racial microaggressions. Recognizing the ways that persons in other devalued groups are likely to routinely experience similar microaggressions, future research that focuses on microaggressions associated with gender, sexual orientation, and other sociodemographic characteristics may prove equally valuable as those related to race.

Discussion

Th e results of this study support and extend the microaggression taxonomy proposed by Sue, Capodilupo, et al. (2007). Of the original proposed eight microaggression themes, four were similar or overlapping: ascription of intelligence, second-class citizenship, assumption of criminal status, and pathologizing cultural values/communication styles. One of the original proposed themes, denial of personal racism, was listed as an underdeveloped theme because only 1 participant mentioned such an incident in the groups. Two new themes emerged from the present study that are referred to as *assumption of inferior status* and *assumed universality of the Black American experience.*

Our ongoing investigations in this area indicate that racial microaggressions lead to psychological distress in Black Americans and that race-related stress occurs not only in response to overt racism but also in response to more indirect and subtle forms of racism. Microaggressions have a harmful and lasting psychological impact that may endure for days, weeks, months, and even years. Participants reported feelings of anger, frustration, doubt, guilt, or sadness when they experience microaggressions and noted further that the emotional turmoil stayed with them as they tried to make sense of each incident. Th e research team members' observations that many participants seemed to become distressed as a result of retelling their stories (e.g., crying/tearing, fl uctuations in voice volume, stammering over words) provided additional evidence substantiating the long-lasting eff ects of the stress and trauma experienced from being subjected to various microaggressions.

Microaggressions were commonly perpetrated by all types of people—strangers, causal acquaintances, and even personal friends. Th e type of denigrating themes directed at Black persons seemed to be infl uenced by two dimensions: (a) whether the person was a casual or close acquaintance and (b) the social situation or environment in which the microaggression occurred. Our ongoing research of this phenomenon suggests, for instance, that a microaggressor treating a Black American as intellectually inferior tended to be a coworker, classmate, or authority fi gure at either the Black person's workplace or educational institution. Microaggressions that are classifi ed in the assumed universality of the Black American experience and the assumed superiority of White cultural values/communication styles categories frequently occurred at work or school as well.

On the other hand, microaggressions that refl ected themes of second-class citizenship or assumption of criminality or inferior status more typically came from strangers in public settings. In other words, Black Americans are more than likely to be stereotyped and treated in more discriminatory ways in public, whereas they are more likely to be invalidated or insulted in school or work settings.

Th e idea that microaggressions refl ect commonly held prejudicial beliefs and stereotypes suggests that certain microaggressions will be diff erentially experienced by diverse racial/ethnic groups. For example, in a qualitative study on Asian Americans (Sue, Bucceri, et al, 2007), the theme *alien in one's own land* captured experiences in which participants were reportedly treated as perpetual foreigners despite being born and raised in the United States. Although the original hypothetical taxonomy (Sue, Capodilupo, et al, 2007) included this theme, it did not arise in the present study with Black American participants.

Similarly, the theme *assumption of criminality* was not present in the Sue, Bucceri, et al. (2007) study of Asian Americans but was prevalent in the current study. It is possible that this theme refl ects a historical stereotype of Black Americans as violent and dangerous, whereas Asian Americans are regarded as law abiding and quiet. In other words, although microaggressions refl ect a worldview of White supremacy relative to other racial groups, some of their manifestations are specifi c for racial/ethnic group (e.g., Asian Americans are more likely to encounter incidents with the theme of being a foreigner, whereas Black Americans are more likely to encounter incidents with the theme of criminality).

Another new theme emerging from this study that was not included in the original taxonomy was the assumption of inferior status theme. Although some of the experiences participants reported concerning this theme were similar to those related to the second-class citizenship theme, the research participants described their being assumed to be from a lower status was qualitatively diff erent from their being treated as a second-class citizen. For example, being overlooked in store lines, being passed by cabs, and having change put on the counter instead of in one's hand were all examples of being treated like a second-class citizen. On the other hand, other persons' assuming that one was uneducated, poor, or a menial labor worker composed the theme of assumption of inferior status. Furthermore, the examples supporting this theme could be broken down into "credentials" and "social class" to characterize the nature of the assumption. An example of the former is when a microaggressor acted surprised that a Black participant had a master's degree, whereas an example of the latter is when a hostess seated one of the research participants in the more casual, less expensive area of a restaurant. When a person is viewed as a second-class citizen, the message is conveyed that he or she is "less than," unimportant, and invisible. On the other hand, microaggressions conveying inferior status refl ect the historical stereotype that Black Americans are uneducated, poor, and occupy low-status positions.

Both themes have relevance for counseling situations. Although counselors and therapists are unlikely to communicate that a client of color is a second-class citizen, they may be prone to indirectly communicating the assumption of lower status. For example, when reading an application for counseling or hearing an individual's voice over the phone, a counselor may make assumptions about the race of the applicant (on the basis of the applicant's reported socioeconomic status, level of education, or "articulate" way of speaking). Similar to an interviewer being "shocked" to meet a Black job applicant with sterling credentials, a counselor can convey expectation surprise (facially) when fi rst meeting a Black client in session Participants in this study were very sensitive to such racial microaggressions that left them distrustful, angered, and resentful.

Also, although counselors may not directly communicate that clients of color are second-class persons, this theme seems to have prevalence in both Black American and Asian American participants' lives. Th e experience of being invalidated, unimportant, and invisible has been well documented for both Black Americans and Asian Americans (Franklin, 1999; Sue, 2004). Th erefore, counselors should be mindful that this dynamic may be a reality that many clients of color experience on a daily basis. Counselors are also encouraged to be cognizant of their own reactions in sessions that refl ect microaggressive stereotypes, biases, and assumptions.

Another common trend that emerged in the data analysis of the present study included participants describing attempts to prevent future microaggressions from occurring. In this regard, participants reported making an intentional eff ort to speak "clearly" and "articulately" when entering new situations (e.g., social gatherings, interviews, and workplace meetings) to establish credibility and evade microaggressions that communicate intellectual inferiority. As one research participant stated, "In the fi rst meeting, I have to crush all those stereotypes in one conversation. ... OK, I know big words. ... I'm articulate. ... I can talk to you about things that interest you." In doing so, the individual is attempting to dispel any negative stereotypes that others may have about Black people's competence and intelligence.

Suff ocating the authentic Black orAfrocentric self to conform to White, Eurocentric standards has long been perceived as a threat to the mental health of Black Americans (Franklin, 1999). Th us, it would behoove White counselors to be aware of how their own stereotypes and implicit biases operate in sessions with clients of color (Ridley, 1995) and recognize how these clients may feel pressured to obscure their true selves for the comfort or the sake of the helping professional (Franklin, 1999).

Conclusion

When taken together, the results from the present study of Black Americans and the previous investigation of Asian Americans do not include two of the originally proposed themes: color blindness and the myth of meritocracy. Several reasons are possible for the absence of these themes in the Sue, Bucceri, et al. (2007) and the present study on microaggressions. First, the limited time of the focus-group discussions restricted sampling of the universe of possible microaggressions. Second, both of these themes might involve microaggressions that are situational and reactional, in that a microaggressor might only reply with a color-blind or meritocracy statement when confronted or provoked in a discussion (e.g., a microaggressor saying that he or she "doesn't see color" aft er being accused of something racist or an employer saying, "Anyone could have gotten the job if he or she worked hard enough").

Although these themes were not mentioned by the participants in either study, there is potential for both themes to be endorsed by well-intentioned White counselors. Th is is possible because it is not uncommon for White counselors to directly convey that they are color blind and do not see race or to indirectly convey that they do not believe race to be salient to the lived experiences of clients of color (Neville, Worthington, & Spanierman, 2001).

Finally, we return to our earlier assertion that racial microaggressions (a) oft en refl ect an invisible worldview of White supremacy in otherwise well-intentioned individuals; (b) are manifested in individuals, institutions, and the U.S. culture at large; (c) induce enormous psychological distress in people of color; and (d) create disparities in education, employment, and health care for the target groups. We believe that dealing with racial microaggressions represents a social justice issue and that counselors need to become proactive in addressing their biases and those of society. Sue and Sue (2008) made such a point in their defi nition of social justice counseling:

> Social justice counseling/therapy is an active philosophy and approach aimed at producing conditions that allow for equal access and opportunity, reducing or eliminating disparities in education, health care, employment and other areas that lower the quality of life for aff ected populations, encouraging mental health professionals to consider micro, meso, and macro levels in the assessment, diagnosis and treatment of client and client systems, and broadening the role of helping professionals to include not only counselor/therapist but advocate, consultant, psychoeducator, change agent, community worker, etc. (p. 74).

References

American Counseling Association. (1999). *Racism: Healing its eff ects*. Alexandria, VA: Author.

American Psychological Association. (2003). Guidelines on multicultural education, training, research, practice, and organizational change for psychologists. *American Psychologist, 58,* 377–402.

Banaji, M. R. (2001). Implicit attitudes can be measured. In H. L. Roediger III, J. S. Nairne, I. Neath, & A. Surprenant (Eds.), *Th e nature of remembering: Essays inhonor of Robert G. Crowder* (pp. 117–150). Washington, DC: American Psychological Association.

Burkard, A. W., &Knox, S. (2004). Eff ect of therapist color-blindness on empathy and attributions in cross-cultural counseling. *Journal of Counseling Psychology, 51,* 387–397.

Constantine, M. G. (2007). Racial microaggressions against African American clients in a cross-racial counseling relationship. *Journal of Counseling Psychology, 54,* 1–16.

Constantine, M. G., & Sue, D. W. (2007). Perceptions of racial microaggressions among Black supervisees in crossracial dyads. *Journal of Counseling Psychology, 54,* 143–154.

DeVos, T., & Banaji, M. R. (2005). American = White? *Journal of Personality and Social Psychology, 88,* 447–466.

Dovidio, J. F., & Gaertner, S. L. (2000). Aversive racism and selection decisions: 1989 and 1999. *Psychological Science, 11,* 315–319.

Dovidio, J. F., Gaertner, S. L., Kawakami, K., & Hodson, G. (2002). Why can't we all just get along? Interpersonal biases and interracial distrust. *Cultural Diversity and Ethnic Minority Psychology, 8,* 88–102.

Fassinger, R. E. (2005). Paradigms, praxis, problems, and promise: Grounded theory in counseling psychology research. *Journal of Counseling Psychology, 52,* 156–166.

Franklin, A. J. (1999). Invisibility syndrome and racial identity development in psychotherapy and counseling African American men. *Th e Counseling Psychologist, 27,* 761–793.

Franklin, A. J. (2004). *From brotherhood to manhood: How Black men rescue their relationships and dreams from the invisibility syndrome.* Hoboken, NJ: Wiley.

Hill, C. E., Th ompson, B. J., Hess, S. A., Knox, S., Williams, E. N., & Ladany, N. (2005). Consensual qualitative research: An update. *Journal of Counseling Psychology, 52,* 196–205.

Hill, C. E., Th ompson, B. J., & Williams, E. N. (1997). A guide to conducting consensual qualitative research. *Th e Counseling Psychologist, 25,* 517–572.

Hinton, E. L. (2004, March/April). Microinequities: When small slights lead to huge problems in the workplace. *Diversitylnc.* Retrieved March 17, 2008, from http://www.magazine.org/content/fi les/Microinequities.pdf

Kearney, L. K., Draper, M., & Baron, A. (2005). Counseling utilization by ethnic minority college students. *Cultural Diversity and Ethnic Minority Psychology, 11,* 272–285.

Krueger, R. A. (1994). *Focus groups: A practical guide for applied research* (2nd ed.). Th ousand Oaks, CA: Sage.

Krueger, R. A. (1998). *Analyzing & reporting focus group results.* Th ousand Oaks, CA: Sage.

Miles, M. B., & Huberman, A. M. (1994). *Qualitative data analysis: An expanded sourcebook* (2nd ed.). Th ousand Oaks, CA: Sage.

Morrow, S. L., & Smith, M. L. (2000). Qualitative research for counseling psychology. In S. D. Brown & R. W. Lent (Eds.), *Handbook of counseling psychology* (3rd ed, pp. 199–230). New York: Wiley.

Neville, H. A., Worthington, R. L., & Spanierman, L. B. (2001). Race, power, and multicultural counseling psychology: Understanding White privilege and color–blind racial attitudes. In J. G. Ponterotto, J. M. Casas, L. A. Suzuki, & C. M. Alexander (Eds.), *Handbook of multicultural counseling* (2nd ed, pp. 257–288). Th ousand Oaks, CA: Sage.

Polkinghorne, D. E. (2005). Language and meaning: Data collection in qualitative research. *Journal of Counseling Psychology, 52,* 137–145.

Ridley, C. (1995). *Overcoming unintentional racism in counseling and therapy: A practitioner's guide to intentional intervention.* Th ousand Oaks, CA: Sage.

Ridley, C. R. (2005). *Overcoming unintentional racism in counseling and therapy* (2nd ed.). Th ousand Oaks, CA: Sage.

Saint-Germain, M. A., Bassford, T. L., & Montano, G. (1993). Surveys and focus groups in health research with older Hispanic women. *Qualitative Health Research, 3,* 341–367.

Seal, D. W., Bogart, L. M., & Ehrhardt, A. A. (1998). Small group dynamics: Th e utility of focus group discussions as a research method *Group Dynamics: Th eory, Research, and Practice, 2,* 253–266.

Solórzano, D., Ceja, M., & Yosso, T. (2000). Critical race theory, racial microaggressions, and campus racial climate:

Th e experiences of African American college students. *Th e Journal of Negro Education, 69,* 60–73.

Sue, D. W. (2003). *Overcoming our racism: Th e journey to liberation.* San Francisco: Jossey-Bass.

Sue, D. W. (2004). Whiteness and ethnocentric monoculturalism: Making the "invisible" visible. *American Psychologist, 59,* 759–769.

Sue, D. W. Arredondo, P., & McDavis, R. J. (1992). Multicultural competencies/standards: A call to the profession. *Journal of Counseling & Development, 70,* 477–486.

Sue, D. W., Bucceri, J., Lin, A. I., Nadal, K. L., & Torino, G. C. (2007). Racial microaggressions and the Asian American experience. *Cultural Diversity and Ethnic Minority Psychology, 13,* 72–81.

Sue, D. W., Capodilupo, C. M., & Holder, A. M. (in press). Racial microaggressions in the life experience of African Americans. *Professional Psychology: Research and Practice.*

Sue, D. W., Capodilupo, C. M., Torino, G. C., Bucceri, J. M., Holder, A. M. B., Nadal, K. L., & Esquilin, M. (2007). Racial microaggressions in everyday life: Implications for clinical practice. *Th e American Psychologist, 62,* 271–286.

Sue, D. W., & Sue, D. (2008). *Counseling the culturally diverse: Th eory and practice.* Hoboken, NJ: Wiley.

U.S. Department of Health and Human Services. (2001). *Mental health: Culture, race, and ethnicity. A supplement to mental health: A report of the Surgeon General.* Rockville, MD: U.S. Department of Health and Human Services, Substance Abuse and Mental Health Service Administration, Center for Mental Health Services.

A Contemporary History of the Church, Hip Hop and Technology

Their Influence on African American Youth Development Marybeth Gasman and
Edward M. Epstein

Over the past 40 years, the societal infl uences on African American young people have changed signifi cantly. Hip-hop culture and electronic communications technology (e.g., computers, video, and television) have had a substantial impact on youth, providing venues for self-expression and empowerment, while simultaneously distracting some adolescents from the traditional learning process. At the same time, one long-standing infl uence in the lives of Black youth, the Church, has seen its sway erode in recent years (Lincoln & Mamiya, 1990). Th is chapter focuses on the relationship between these three societal forces, showing how throughout history the Church has earned a venerable status in African American society as a provider and a mentor for youth—and how modernity has thrown this institution a curve ball. Comparisons with youth of other racial and ethnic backgrounds are off ered throughout the chapter.

THE BLACK CHURCH

Since its creation, the Black church has served as a means by which African Americans have weathered the oft en-turbulent storms they have faced in American society. Historians and sociologists emphasize that it was the mixture of social needs, response to White racism, and Black initiative that spurred the foundation of the Black church (Frazier, 1974; Lincoln, 1974; Lincoln & Mamiya, 1990; Woodson, 1921). Th e fi rst Black churches took root in the Northern states. Among them was the African Methodist Episcopal (AME) Church, which was established in Philadelphia in 1816 by a group of Black Methodists who were unhappy with the treatment they received in the White churches of that denomination. By 1846 the AME Church had 17,375 congregants who met in 206 member institutions, led by 176 clergymen. Also founded in the Northeast was the African Methodist Episcopal Zion Church, which grew from six congregations in 1821 to 132 congregations in 1864 with 113 clergy and 13,702 members (Frazier; Lincoln; Lincoln & Mamiya; Woodson).

According to Jones (1982), "Th e largest ingathering of blacks into the Christian church occurred in the fi rst half of the nineteenth century when many [Blacks] were converted during the extended "great awakening" (pp. 1801–1858). Th e majority of the congregants were located in the South and belonged to either the Methodist or Baptist denomination. Jones further notes, "As the nineteenth century drew to a close, black Christianity had achieved a fair degree of institutionalization and stability" (Jones, p. 9). Consequently, the AME Church had expanded its membership to include 494,777 persons, while the AME Zion Church reported a membership of 184,542. In addition, Th e Colored Methodist Church had increased its membership to 172,996.

Much has been written about the socially repressive culture at some Black churches up to the period before the Civil Rights Movement (Frazier, 1957, 1974). According to critics, the institutions tended to reinforce class distinctions and promote a kind of internalized racism in which lighter skin color imparted status (Green, 1982). Nevertheless, the Black church came to be one of the most eff ective mechanisms for advocating and promoting the social needs of Blacks in America (Adams, 1985). Jones (1982) indicates, "In point of fact, no institution or organization seeking to make an impact in black communities could do so without the support and cooperation of the churches" (p. 9). How then, did the Black church come to acquire the level of respect and prestige that it now has among the larger Black community? Has this level of respect changed among youth cultures?

A key test of the church's true character was its response to the Civil Rights Movement. Th e Black church's fi ght against racial injustice entered the national consciousness in 1955 in Montgomery, Alabama. On December 1 of that year, a Black seamstress named Rosa Parks refused to relinquish her seat on a segregated bus and was subsequently jailed. Th is event in turn started a social movement that would rock the foundation of America, and the Black church served as the movement's catalyst. Th e resulting bus boycott was organized largely out of the Dexter Avenue Baptist Church. Harris (1994) states, "An important lesson the black church should remember from the Civil Rights Movement is that while the movement served as a prophetic criticism of American society, it demanded prophetic self-criticism and internal transformation of the black church as well" (p. 2). Of note, African American youth were instrumental in the movement, but they were not always appreciated. Church leaders involved in the Southern Christian Leadership Conference (SCLC) enlisted the support of mainly adults and controlled the focus of the movement's eff orts. Eventually young people, mainly from historically Black colleges and universities, grew frustrated and formed the Student Nonviolent Coordinating Committee (SNCC). SNCC had a profound infl uence on the movement and brought considerable attention to inequities at the local level throughout the South (Garrow, 1987).

In a call to promote the racial equality of Black Americans, the Black church rose to the occasion. Consequently, during the mid-twentieth century the Black church became an institution that was both prepared and willing to serve as an active agent in the liberation of its congregants from social injustice and oppression. Whereas the Black Church served, in some capacity, as a liberator of Black Americans from social plights prior to 1955, the Civil Rights Movement allowed the Black Church to escalate that liberation to a level that was witnessed throughout the world (Lincoln, 1974; Lincoln & Mamiya, 1990). In the wake of the Civil Rights Movement, Black church membership—still largely composed of Baptist and Methodist denominations—continues to expand with nearly three million members making up the Black Baptist and Methodist churches (Lincoln & Mamiya).

Within a segregated society, the Black church was one of a few cohesive institutions, providing ample services and solace to the Black community at large. According to Lincoln and Mamiya (1990),

At the beginning of the last decade of the twentieth century the black churches are, on the whole, still healthy and vibrant institutions. While there has been some chipping away at the edges, particularly among unchurched underclass black youth and some college educated,

middle-class young adults, black churches still remain the central institutional sector in most
black communities (p. 382).

Scholars contend that the infl uence and popularity of the Black church has been diminished in recent years due to a bounty of opportunities such as sports and entertainment and infl uences such as hip hop and technology-based social networking stimulating youth culture (Billingsley, 1999; Lincoln & Mamiya, 1990). In addition, desegregation and secularization in the post-Civil Rights era have led to a weaker role for the church. Scholars also attribute the lack of participation among African American youth in the church to the dominance of church elders who want to maintain the status quo rather than change with the times (Lincoln & Mamiya).

Th roughout American history, Black churches have provided ample opportunity to young African Americans, helping them to develop their talent and leadership skills. In fact, many young people have used the church to launch professional careers in education, politics, music, and entertainment (Lincoln & Mamiya, 1990). Th e success that the Black church has with young people is linked to the church's "holistic ministry" and emphasis on humans as "not only spiritual, but also physical and social creatures" (Lincoln & Mamiya, p. 400). In recent years, Black churches have turned their attention to bolstering the self-esteem and racial and cultural identity of African American youth. Research shows that church role models, both clerical and lay, play a signifi cant part in the lives of those youth active in the Black church (Johnson, Jang, Spencer, & Larson, 2000). Of note, the church is also of great signifi cance in the lives of Latino youth, with research showing that involvement leads to higher grades, less trouble with delinquency in school, and higher self-esteem. Moreover, Latino churchgoers "engage more in activities with their children"—activities that enhance the family learning environment (Sikkink & Hernandez, 2003, p. 13).

According to Johnson et al. (2000), church-going inner city youth are more resilient and able to "escape from the world of poverty, drug use, and crime" at greater rates than their non-churchgoing counterparts (p. 481). Th is resiliency is oft en fostered by church-affi liated mentors "who are involved in young people's lives and who help them make important decisions." (Cook, 2000, p. 719). Moreover, research by Freeman (1986) shows that Black and Latino males living in high poverty areas of Philadelphia, Boston, and Chicago who attend church are signifi cantly less likely to participate in criminal activities. Churches instill faith in individuals and provide much needed structural supports in many communities. Th ese individuals were more likely to stay in school, have an aft er-school job, and less likely to behave in ways termed "socially deviant" (Cook; Freeman; Sikkink & Hernandez, 2003). In particular, Latino youth who attended church were more likely to feel close to their peers at school and more likely to get along with their teachers (Edwards, Fehring, Jarrett, & Haglund, 2008; Sikkink & Hernandez). Interestingly, Johnson et al. found that African American youth living in high-crime neighborhoods that were active in the church were less likely to become involved in criminal activity than those non-church-going young people living in low-crime areas. Th is relationship, in the words of Johnson et al., could be attributed to what Stark (1996) calls a moral community or, in other words, a community in which the vast majority of individuals are connected to a religious institution and active in their connectedness. According to Sikkink and Hernandez, the church and religion in general are "sometimes the only form of social support in inner city areas" for Black and Latino youth (p. 20).

In addition to helping young people avoid a life of crime, there is some evidence that youth involvement in the church is highly correlated with these individuals having "a better chance of moving out of poverty conditions than those [youth] condemned to the anonymity of poverty" (Edwards et al., 2008; Lincoln & Mamiya, 1990, p. 403; Sikkink & Hernandez, 2003). Some churches have been quite purposeful in their attempts to change the life of young African Americans, feeling that the church is "the only institution capable of turning their lives around" (Billingsley, 1999, p. 102). For example, many churches provide support services for young, pregnant Black and Latino women, including child rearing, fi nancial management, and counseling classes. Other churches have directed their attention to crises in the Black and Latino male youth community, creating programs that empower young Black and Latino men. Th ese programs provide Black and Latino male role models for young people who do not have a stable father fi gure in their lives. According to the minister at Atlanta's Antioch Baptist Church, for example, "Th e presence of men attracts other men. It signifi es that the men of Antioch are respected and empowered" and this message has a signifi cant impact on Black, male youth *(Christian Century,* 1994, p. 1). And research shows that church-going African American youth are more likely to have mentors than their non-church-going counterparts (Cook, 2000). Many times these mentors help their mentees make important decisions about family and career.

In recent years, Black mega churches (large nondenominational churches that off er religion as well as a variety of social services) have been established throughout the country. Supporters of the Black mega church movement claim that during this time of disengagement among youth, these churches are playing a disproportionate role in educating and mentoring young African Americans, especially the urban poor *(Christian Century,* 1994). Unfortunately, in the minds of Black church leaders, Black youth are not engaging with the Black church at the same levels as in the past. When Frazier wrote his classic *Th e Negro Church in America* a generation ago, over 80% of African American youth participated in the Church or Sunday school *(Christian Century;* Frazier, 1974). However, today, some researchers estimate that almost 60% of Black youth have no contact at all with the church *(Christian Century).* According to a recent article in *Christian Century,* the reasons for the lack of engagement are many:

> *Some are children of those drawn to Islam by the preaching of Malcolm X. Others fi nd the turn-the-other-cheek Christian pacifi sm that was a hallmark of the civil rights era irrelevant. Some, turned off by images of a white Jesus, reject Christianity as a faith imposed on slaves that replaced their original beliefs in animism or Islam. Others simply fall victim to the temptations of a consumerist popular culture or the violent ethos of the street (*Christian Century, *1994, p. 2).*

Other scholars, including Bachman, Johnston, and O'Malley (2005) found the situation to be less dire for the Black church, with 56% of African American high-school seniors believing in the importance of religion and 45% regularly attending religious services.

In the words of one scholar, "Being a faithful, moral person is against the odds and weight of the entire [inner city] culture" and it is here in the inner city where most of the drop-in African American (as well as Latino) youth engagement has taken place (Franklin in *Christian Century,* 1994, p. 2). Th e inner city culture to which the author refers includes a strong dose of hip hop—rap music, dancing, and visual art.

According to Cone (1990), Herndon, (2003), McAdoo (1993), and Sikkink and Hernandez (2003), whereas Blacks and Latinos traditionally and typically "embrace the value of religion, its liberating power, the reliance on a higher power, and the practical application of spiritual principles in life," Whites tend to view religion as something more abstract or intellectual (Herndon, p. 76). Th ese researchers attribute this diff erence to issues of race, social conditions, class, and stress, noting that African Americans, Latinos, and some Asian American groups may use religion as a coping mechanism for the stress in their lives (Chau, 2006; Cone; Edwards et al., 2008; Herndon; McAdoo; Sikkink & Hernandez). Of course, Whites may also use religion to address issues of stress but less oft en. Some researchers have focused on the impact of faith on the lives of young African Americans and Latinos, noting that faith serves as the "ultimate support when the other things they depend on in their lives collapse around them" (Sikkink & Hernandez; Stewart, 2002, p. 581). Many young African Americans and Latinos who have participated in studies pertaining to the Black church and resilience have noted that their ability to pray, attend church, and read scripture has helped them during times of personal turmoil (Sikkink & Hernandez). According to research by Herndon, African American church-going youth "believed that these acts [church attendance and praying] assisted in shouldering the stresses and strains of life and caused them to excel in the face of academic and social adversities" (p. 78).

Still, some researchers have found that an affi liation with the church provides mentoring, fosters comfort with public discussion and disagreement, and enables young African American men and women to view each other as equals or peers, which in turn helps to build a strong nuclear African American family unit (Franklin in *Christian Century,* 1994). Other researchers have found that churches off er several other mechanisms for supporting resilience among African American youth. Th ese include assisting Black teenagers to "develop self-regulatory abilities, fostering identity development … and off ering a relationship with a powerful and loving Other" (Cook, 2000, p. 3). Self-regulatory abilities are particularly important, as these skills help young people to modify their behavior when necessary. Th e Black church's assistance with identity formation is also vitally important in that "if young people are willing to negotiate life within the context of the church rather than a gang, they have a better chance of avoiding prison, early pregnancy, and the numerous other negative outcomes that limit their ability to achieve health and happiness" (Cook).

According to researchers, the Black church, like all religion, has the ability to provide a sense of structure that is sought by youth in general and inner city African American youth in particular (Ianni, 1989). African American youth involved in the church are off ered "a standard for behavior" and taught right and wrong (Cook, 2000, p. 8). Many of these young people, when confronted with a potentially negative or dangerous situation, report hearing the voice of their pastor or youth minister telling them not to make the wrong decision (Cook). Moreover, these young people credit the Black church with providing a sense of purpose and direction in their lives, labeling their spirituality their "inner core" or "peace of mind" (Herdnon, 2003, p. 79). Th is crediting of the Black church is particularly poignant when students are in college; the church serves as a home away from home, an extended family, and a venue for exploring their spirituality.

In addition, congregants of the Black church have the potential to act as a close-knit web of support for young African Americans. Th ough it sounds simplistic, when youth are kept busy, they tend to stay out of trouble. Of greater importance, they participate in activities that have a positive impact on their lives. According to Cook (2000), "the church provides youths with a place to go and things to do, instead of watching television all aft ernoon or hanging out with friends, a situation in which trouble easily develops" (p. 9). Although church is oft en thought of as a Sunday-only event, most Black churches and especially megachurches off er young people "youth groups, Bible classes, sports events, or aft er-school tutoring programs" throughout the week (Cook, p. 9). However, researchers also note that young people may not be spiritually mature enough to actually reap the benefi ts that the Black church has to off er until later in life (Stewart, 2002).

HIP HOP

Th e Black church, for the most part, has been seen throughout American history as a positive infl uence on African American youth development. On the other hand, hip hop is oft en viewed as a negative factor in the lives of young Blacks as well as Latinos and some Asian American groups, labeled as nihilistic and destructive by a host of scholars, journalists and leaders, Black and White, from across the political spectrum (McWhorter, 2003). Hip hop, with roots in the U.S. Black, Caribbean, and African traditions, came into being on the streets of the Bronx, New York, during the 1970s; beginning as a local movement, it quickly spread nationally and internationally (Chang, 2005; Hill, in press; Petchauer, 2009; Rose, 1994). Kitwana claims that those Blacks born between 1965 and 1984 represent the "hip hop generation" and are infl uenced by a particular set of values and attitudes that play a role in their learning process (2003). In eff ect, the hip hop movement introduced a culture, lifestyle and musical genre into society. According to Hill (in press),

> *From the i-Pods of suburban American teens to revolutionary movements of the Global South, the sites, sounds, and spectacles of hip-hop have become a central feature of an increasingly globalized cultural landscape (p. 1).*

For contemporary youth, hip hop *is* culture. Th ey have grown up in a world where styles of music and dance pioneered by the hip-hop generation are all-pervasive. Th ese styles are as well known to White suburbanites as Black inner city dwellers.

Of signifi cance is the fact that hip-hop culture fi rst appeared as the Civil Rights Movement waned. Aft er nonviolent civil disobedience had given way to rioting in the inner cities; aft er "urban renewal" had eviscerated cities' physical and social infrastructure; and as the mostly white suburb was entrenched as a convenient replacement for legalized segregation—at this moment, a group of creative individuals fashioned what we now know as hip hop. Although they did not experience the Civil Rights struggle directly, hip-hop pioneers like Kool Herc and Afrika Bambaataa would have seen the confrontations unfolding on television. Th is partially explains the distinct political consciousness present in much rap music. However, most hip-hop pioneers grew up with a very diff erent world view than the civil rights protesters. Hip hop's epicenter was the Bronx, one of the areas hardest hit by urban decline—and also a melting pot of West Indian and Latino immigrants. Consequently, the ideological leanings of hip-hop innovators were a mixed bag as well. DJ Kool Herc, for example, came from Jamaica and would have been aware of freedom struggles there as well as in the United States. Afrika Bambaataa's Zulu Nation too was inspired by worldwide anticolonial movements (Chang, 2005; Rose, 1994). It would not be accurate, then, to say that hip hop's social consciousness was a product of the Black Church's protest tradition.

For many Americans, hip hop is synonymous with rap music; the words "hip hop" and "rap" are oft en used interchangeably. Th ose more knowledgeable about the movement identify four pillars—rapping, DJing, graffi ti, and break dancing—as the primary forms of expression the movement spawned (Chang, 2005). But hip hop also encompasses fashion, advertising, linguistic characteristics, postures, and more recently, various forms of activism (Petchauer, 2009). Chang (2005) claims that "Hip-hop off ers a generational worldview that encompasses the shoes you choose to whether you're inclined to vote or not to how you understand the issues of race" (p. 1). Because hip-hop culture includes elements of material culture, Kitwana (2003) asserts that the hip-hop generation is more career-oriented and material-based than previous generations of African Americans, who were more focused on gaining their legal rights. Specifi cally, he notes:

For many, the American Dream means not just living comfortably but becoming an overnight millionaire while still young. Many of us can't imagine waiting until we are forty, or even thirtyfi ve, for that matter. Th is desire for wealth is accompanied by a sense of entitlement. Th at a handful of widely celebrated hip-hop generationers have achieved the dream makes the possibility real, despite the odds. And this desire to achieve not simply fi nancial security but millionaire status is the driving force of our generation's work ethic (Kitwana, 2003, p. 46).

In this sense, hip hop picks up where the Civil Rights Movement left off : pursuing the yet unfulfi lled promise of economic equality that should rightly follow legal equality.

According to Morrel and Duncan-Andrade (2002), hip hop also "represents a resistant voice of urban youth through its articulation of problems that this generation and all Americans face on a daily basis" (p. 88). And, hip hop is the "representative voice of urban youth, since the genre was created by and for them" (p. 88). It refl ects the hopes, dreams, aspirations, and concerns of urban youth of all racial and ethnic backgrounds; every issue and aspect of life in the inner city is the subject of interpretation (Powell, 1991 and Rose, 1991). Hip-hop culture is a "multiracial, multiethnic phenomenon" (McFarland, 2008, p. 173). Hip hop emerged as an alternative source of identity development and social status for youth at a moment when "economic and social disparity left the traditional support pillars of the church, school, and neighborhood—literally and fi guratively—crumbling" (Petchauer, 2009, p. 28). Th e identity formed by the hip-hop generation and its descendents is highly diff erent from those reared during the

Civil Rights Movement. As Petchauer (2007) explains,

Th e old racial politics and defi nitions ... are rigid constructions of race, ethnicity, and cultural ownership—the kind from which many accusations of cultural thievery are posited (e.g., Elvis and rock and roll). Hip-Hop is frequently perceived as a participatory culture, one that operates upon notions of civic (rather than primordial) membership and challenges the older notion that Black culture is only available to individuals who are phenotypically Black (p. 31).

An explanation for the more fl uid identity of the hip-hop generation's members rests in the art forms themselves, which, moreso than previous African American art forms, rely on recycling. Hip hop's earliest originators were DJs, individuals like Kool Herc and Grandmaster Flash, whose main contribution was to refashion prerecorded sounds to create new beats. Th e break beat—the kernel of rhythm these DJs sampled and repeated to generate a hip-hop groove—oft en came from a funk track such as James Brown's "Funky Drummer" or the Winstons' "Amen, Brother." But they would add to that a rich palette of sounds that included pop, rock and roll, disco, voice overlays, and raw noise. Consider this description by hip-hop critic Nelson George (1999) of a Grand Master Flash performance:

It begins with "you say one for the trouble," the opening phrase of Spoonie Gee's "Monster Jam," broken down to "you say" repeated seven times, setting the tone for a record that uses the music and vocals of Queen's "Another One Bites the Dust," the Sugar Hill Gang's "8th Wonder," and Chic's "Good Times" as musical pawns that Flash manipulates at whim. He repeats "Flash is bad" from Blondie's "Rapture" three times, turning singer Deborah Harry's dispassion into total adoration. While playing "Another One Bites the Dust," Flash places a second record on the turntable, then shoves the needle and the record against each other. Th e result is a rumbling, gruff imitation of the song's bass line. As guitar feedback on "Dust" builds, so does Flash's rumble, until we're grooving on "Good Times."

As hip hop was multilayered, so were the people who made it. Many break dance innovators were Latino (e.g., Richie "Crazy Legs" Colon), as were graffi ti writers (Lee "LEE" Quinones). Kool Herc himself was Jamaican-born, and many of his stylistic innovations paralleled Jamaican forms such as dub (Chang, 2005). According to McFarland (2008),

> *Rap music and hip-hop have most commonly been understood as black American phenomena. While it is undoubtedly true that black American youth have been the driving force in the creation of hip-hop, numerous other cultures and peoples have contributed to it. Jamaican music, dance, and oral tradition, Asian martial arts and philosophy, Italian gangster fantasy, Japanese technology, Chicano dress and style, Islam, Euro-American capitalist ideology, and Puerto Rican dance and music all played a role in the early development of hip-hop culture and music (pp. 173–174).*

Given the mixed provenience of this genre, it is not surprising that hip hop-infl uenced African American youth construct race and ethnicity diff erently from previous generations of Black Americans.

According to some researchers, hip-hop artists consider themselves to be educators, seeking to promote "consciousness within their communities" (Morrell & Duncan-Andrade, 2002, p. 89). Th ese researchers consider hip hop to be "prophetic and empowering" (Petchauer, 2009, p. 3). Although the primary discussion in this chapter focuses on African Americans, it should be noted that the infl uence of hip hop transcends race and as mentioned above, young people from various ethnic and racial backgrounds have been strongly infl uenced by hip-hop culture (Morrel & Duncan-Andrade). While hip hop began in the African American community, 70% of compact discs have been purchased by White youth; more recently, song downloads have also been mainly consumed by White youth although there is less of a gap. And, it should be noted that African American and hip-hop cultures are "neither identical nor completely separate entities" (Petchauer, p. 21). According to Petchauer,

> *Although hip-hop in many ways is a subset of Black culture–exhibiting many characteristics of African American culture, maintaining some of the ideological underpinnings of the civil rights and Black power movements, and having been assembled by marginalized African American and Latino youth—participation and cultural membership in hip-hop in the Twenty First century is not limited to individuals who are phenotypically Black (p. 21).*

Petchauer (2007) claims that hip hop lacks the clear components of a social movement, including "grievance, common goals, [and a] communication network," which is fundamentally diff erent from the Civil Rights Movement (Petchaur, p. 30). Lang (2000) describes hip hop as even more apolitical, noting that young African Americans engaged in hip-hop culture tend to:

> *View cultural expression as resistance in and of itself, ignoring the importance of organized, state-directed activity around material conditions. Th us, one hears oft en references to hip-hop being a social movement in the same vein as civil rights and Black Power. Yet hip-hop, like all forms of art and culture, has no fi xed political character (p. 127).*

Hill (in press) as well at Petchauer (2009) contend that hip-hop music and culture shape youth identity, including the identity of African Americans, Latinos, Asian Americans, and Whites. In Petchauer's opinion, "Th e magnitude of hip-hop's cultural infl uence upon youth and young adults is much greater than the literal meanings of commercial, mainstream rap music" (p. 28). And in fact, both scholars advocate for a curriculum in schools that uses hip hop to engage students in meaningful ways. Hip hop, according to some, can be used to bridge the world of the street with academics (Morrel & DuncanAndrade, 2002). For example, some scholars suggest that juxtaposing hip-hop lyrics with "traditional" poets can help African American and Latino youth to understand how people of diff erent generations view and comment on their "rapidly deteriorating societies." (Morrell & Duncan-Andrade, p. 91; Pulido, 2009). Of course, according to critics, this kind of curriculum is controversial given the sexual and misogynistic lyrics of many hip-hop songs and the culture in general (Giroux, 1996; McWhorter, 2003). Moreover, scholars argue that some young people have constructed a "generational identity of being more morally corrupt compared to previous generations" (Petchauer, p. 18) and this could hold back these individuals' potential. But, those who support the incorporation of hip hop into curricula, according to Morrel and Duncan-Andrade, think that "the knowledge refl ected in these lyrics could engender discussions of esteem, power, place, and purpose or encourage students to further their own knowledge of urban sociology and politics" (p. 89). According to some scholars, historic images from the Civil Rights Movement or of Martin Luther King Jr. are too far removed from the lives of young people to be a strong infl uence (Petchauer, 2007). Instead, other scholars claim that "constructing a myth that Tupac survived his fatal 1996 shooting helped students transcend feelings of vulnerability in their local spaces" (Petchauer, 2009, pp. 17 and 18). Perhaps the best way to describe the infl uence of hip hop on African American youth culture is to quote Petchauer (2007) when he says "Hip-hop, now integrated into the fabric of American culture, is both a cause and eff ect of these shift ing and more open constructions of ethnicity among young adults" (p. 31).

TECHNOLOGY

A rat done bit my sister Nell
And Whitey's on the moon
Her face and arms began to swell
With Whitey on the moon
Th e revolution will not be brought to you by the
Schaefer Award Th eatre and will not star Natalie
Woods and Steve McQueen or Bullwinkle and Julia.
Th e revolution will not give your mouth sex appeal.
Th e revolution will not get rid of the nubs. Th e
revolution will not make you look fi ve pounds thinner,
because the revolution will not be televised, Brother. —
Gil Scott Heron (1971)

Previous generations of African Americans viewed technology with a certain mistrust. Scientifi c innovations—whether in space, medicine, or communications—were seen by some African Americans as at best a distraction from the real problems of life, and at worst a conspiracy, part of a racist apparatus that kept them down. Th ese suspicions were borne out in certain baneful incidents in U.S. history, such as the Tuskegee experiment in which African Americans were used as lab rats to test the eff ects of syphilis contagion (Gray, 1998; Jones, 1981). Yet the hip-hop generation was diff erent. Th is is a generation whose point of reference is television and video games. An irony of the above quoted "Revolution will not be Televised" from Gil Scott Heron is that while it certainly takes aim at the deadening eff ects of television, it inadvertently tells us that he's been watching quite a bit of it. Heron's music, which predates hip hop by a few years, points the way toward rap—a music that oft en makes sly, ironic jabs at electronic culture, but also presumes a knowledge of it.

Perhaps one reason for hip hop's embrace of technology is that it is woven into the fabric of the music. It was a profound achievement of the early hip-hop innovators that, using analog sound equipment, they were able to build tapestries of sound rich enough to put today's digital technicians to shame. Kool Herc's claim to fame was his speaker system ("the Herculords"), which he carried proudly from one party to the next. Grand Master Flash was particularly adept with the use of electricity and electronics. When power was lacking, his crew famously wired the system to a streetlight pole. Flash also added a toggle to his headphone jack in order to monitor two turntables and seamlessly switch from one to the other. Th is innovation, along with techniques like the "backspin" and the "cut," made it possible to loop sound on the fl y, using only vinyl records (Hager, 1984). From the beginning, hip hop DJing displayed virtuosity in the use of technology, rather than in singing or playing an instrument.

Today's youth, and African American youth in particular, spend more time with various forms of electronic media than any other activity with the exception of sleeping (Roberts & Foehr, 2008). Th e average 8- to 18-year old, for example, uses technology (television, computers, video games, Ipods, etc.) more than 6 h a day (Fazzaro, 1999; Roberts & Foehr). And, according to a recent study by Roberts and Foehr, youth have become astute at media multitasking—or using several media concurrently— which increases their use to approximately 8.5 h a day. Televisions are in 99% of American households, and 95% of these same households have at least fi ve other forms of technology available to family members. Of note, according to the Kaiser Foundation, "68 percent of U.S. eight- to eighteen-year-olds and 33 percent of children from birth to age six had a TV in their bedroom (19 percent of children under age one roomed with a TV set)" (Roberts & Foehr, p. 15). Also of note, as of 2005, 45% of teens owned their own cell phones, and the number is on the increase with access to phone service lowering in cost (Roberts & Foehr). Although young people are benefi ting from their technological skills, they are being hindered by fewer hours of adult interaction and face-to-face social interaction in general.

Interestingly, Carver predicted in 1999 that African Americans and Latinos would fall on the wrong side of the digital divide. He is correct on some fronts; most African American and Latino communities do not have access to technology in the same ways as their White counterparts. Public schools and libraries have antiquated equipment and many African American and Latino homes do not have access to the internet. However, in certain respects, African American and Latino youth are well connected to technology. Most have access to cell phones, iPods, video games, and televisions (Mason & Dodds, 2005; Roberts & Foehr, 2008). In a report for the Kaiser Foundation, Rideout and Hamel (2006) found that African American adolescents had more media exposure than Hispanics and Whites, with 10, 9, and 8 h, respectively. In fact, African Americans spend double the amount of time in front of a television than their White counterparts. Th ey also use video games more oft en, averaging 65 min per day (Rideout & Hamel).

Unfortunately, their use of computers is signifi cantly lower than Whites. When Carver began his study in 1999, African American and Latino youth had 20% less access to computers than their White counterparts, and when they had access in schools or in their homes, it was typically access to 3- to 4-year-old equipment (Carver, 1999; Mason & Dodds, 2005). And, African American and Latino youth received and continue to receive inadequate training on computers—typically the focus is on remedial skill development rather than advanced technologies (Carver; Mason & Dodds; Roberts & Foehr, 2008). However, this access to technology has increased slowly over the past 10 years (U.S. Department of Commerce, 2002). Closing the digital divide has become the focus of a great deal of investment by foundations and universities, leading to such projects as the Microsoft School of the Future in Philadelphia, where students from an impoverished neighborhood learn on laptop computers. As a result, computer usage by African Americans and Latinos is up to about with about 33% of Latino's and 40% of African American's having Internet access at home (Fairlie, 2003).

CONCLUSION

When we look at young African Americans' interests (as well as Latinos and Asian Americans in some cases)—their embrace of the electronic media, their love of the sound wizardry found in hip-hop music—we begin to see why many are alienated from Church culture. As noted earlier in this chapter, Black churches are still led by an older generation that is suspicious of technology. Moreover, the church remains an essentially segregated institution. In fact, Martin Luther King Jr. once said that "Sunday is the most segregated day in America." Th is is true because White churches have traditionally been unfriendly toward Blacks, but also because Black churches have long fulfi lled a spiritual need that the White ones do not address. Black churches have diff erent music, preach diff erent sermons, and voice a diff erent perspective than the rest of America. Th ey assume the same rigid constructions of race, ethnicity, and cultural ownership that Petchauer (2009) notes have been rejected by the hip-hop generation. Hip-hop youth do acknowledge the depth of racial inequality in America—rap music, for example, oft en exposes police brutality—yet their take on race is fundamentally diff erent from that of the previous generation. Will the Black church (and other churches for that matter) adapt to the changing attitudes of these young people? It would seem that to do so would require more than just installing a pair of turntables in place of the church organ. With its embrace of the worldly—material success and the mastery of life's challenges through man-made technology—hip hop represents a marked departure from the church's emphasis on the other-worldly.

REFERENCES

Adams, J. H. (1985). Stewardship and the black church. *Urban League Review,* 9(1), 17–27.

Bachman, J. G., Johnston, L. D., & O'Malley, P. M. (2005). *Monitoring the future: A continuing study of American youth (8th, 10th, and 12th-grade surveys), 1976–2003 [Computer fi les].* Conducted by University of Michigan, Survey Research Center, Ann Arbor.

Billingsley, A. (1999). *Mighty like a river. Th e black church and social reform.* New York, NY: Oxford University Press.

Carver, B. A. (1999). Th e information rage: Computers and young African American males. In V. C. Polite & J. E. Davis (Eds.), *African American males in school and society: Practices and policies for eff ective education. New York, NY: Teachers College Press.*

Chang, J. (2005). *Can't stop won't stop: A history of the hip hop generation.* New York, NY: St. Martin's Press.

Chau, W. W. (2006). Th e relationship between acculturative stress and spirituality among Chinese immigrant college students in the United States. Unpublished Th esis. ERIC Online submission: ED491387.

Christian Century. (1994). Young black men and church. *Christian Century, 111*(14), 439–441.

Cone, J. H. (1990). God is black. In S. B. Th istlethwaite & M. P. Engel (Eds.), *Life every voice: Constructing Christian theologies from the underside.* San Francisco: Harper Collins Publishers.

Cook, K. V. (2000). 'You have to have somebody watching your back, and if that's God, then that's mighty big': Th e church's role in the resilience of inner city youth. *Adolescence, 35*(140), 717–730.

Edwards, L. M., Fehring, R. J., Jarrett, K. M., & Haglund, K. A. (2008). Th e infl uence of religiosity, gender, and language preference acculturation on sexual activity among Latino/a adolescents. *Hispanic Journal of Behavioral Sciences, 30*(4), 447–462.

Fairlie, R. W. (2003). *Is there a digital divide? Ethnic and racial diff erences in access to technology and possible explanations.* Final Report to the University of California, Latino Policy Institute and California Policy Research Center U.C. Santa Cruz.

Fazarro, D. E. (1999). Motivating African-American youth in technology education. *Tech Directions, 59*(1), 25–29.

Frazier, E. F. (1957). *Black bourgeoisie.* New York, NY: Free Press.

Frazier, E. F. (1974). *Th e Negro church in America.* New York, NY: Schoken Books.

Freeman, R. B. (1986). Who escapes? Th e relation of churchgoing and other background factors to the socioeconomic performance of black male youth from inner-city tracts. In R. B. Freeman & H. J. Holzer (Eds.), *Th e black youth employment crisis.* Chicago, IL: University of Chicago Press.

Garrow, D. (1987). *Martin Luther King Jr. and the Southern Christian leadership conference.* New York, NY: HarperCollins.

George, N. (1999). *Hip hop America.* New York, NY: Penguin Books.

Giroux, H. (1996). *Fugitive cultures: Race, violence, and youth.* New York, NY: Routledge.

Gray, F. D. (1998). *Th e Tuskegee syphilis study: Th e real story and beyond.* New York, NY: River City Publications.

Green, R. L. (1982). Growing up black, urban, and in the church. *Th e Crisis, 89*(9), 13–19.

Hager, S. (1984). *Hip hop: Th e illustrated history of break dancing, rap music, and Graffi ti.* New York, NY: St. Martins Press.

Harris, F. C. (1994). Something within: Religion as a mobilizer of African American political activism. *Th e Journal of Politics, 56*(1), 42–68.

Herndon, M. K. (2003). Expressions of spirituality among African American college males. *Journal of Men's Studies, 12*(1), 75–83.

Heron, G. S. (1971). *Pieces of man.* Record Album.

Hill, M. L. (in press). 'Stakes is high': Towards an anthropology of hip-hop based education. In M. L. Hill (Ed.), *Beats, rhymes, and classroom Life: Hip-Hop, pedagogy, and the politics of identity.* New York, NY: Teachers College Press.

Ianni, F. A. J. (1989). *Th e search for structure: A report on American youth today.* New York, NY: Free Press.

Johnson, B. R., Jang, S. J., Spencer, D. L., & Larson, D. (2000). Th e 'invisible institution' and black youth crime: Th e church as an agency of local social control. *Journal of Youth and Adolescence, 29*(4), 47–64.

Jones, J. H. (1981). *Bad blood: Th e Tuskegee syphilis experiment.* New York, NY: Free Press.

Jones, L. H. (1982). Th e black churches in historical perspectives. *Th e Crisis, 89*(9), 16–21.

Kitwana, B. (2003). *Th e hip-hop generation: Young Blacks and the crisis of African American culture.* New York, NY: Basic Civitas Books.

Lang, C. (2000). Th e new global and urban order: Legacies for the 'hip-hop generation. *Race and Society, 3,* 111–142.

Lincoln, C. E. (1974). *Th e black church since Frazier.* New York: Schoken Books.

Lincoln, C. E., & Mamiya, L. H. (1990). *Th e black church in the African American experience.* Durham, North Carolina: Duke University Press.

Mason, C. Y., & Dodds, R. (2005). Bridge the digital divide for educational equity. *Th e Education Digest,* 25–27.

McAdoo, H. P. (Ed.). (1993). *Family ethnicity: Strength in diversity.* Newbury Park: Sage Publications.

McFarland, P. (2008). Chicano hip-hop as interethnic contact zone. *Aztlán: A Journal of Chicano Studies, 33*(1), 173–183.

McWhorter, J. H. (2003). How hip-hop holds Blacks back. *City Journal, 13,* 3 Retrieved September 10, 2008, from http://www.city-journal.org/html/13_3_how_hip_hop.html

Morrell, E., & Duncan-Andrade, J. M. R. (2002). Promoting academic literacy with urban youth through engaging hip-hop culture. *English Journal,* 88–92.

Petchauer, E. M. (2007). African American and hip-hop cultural infl uences. In A. P. Robai, L. B. Gallien, Jr., & H. R. Stiff -Williams (Eds.), *Closing the African American achievement gap in higher education.* New York, NY: Teachers College Press.

Petchauer, E. M. (2009). Framing and reviewing hip-hop education research. *Review of Educational Research, 79*(2), 946–978.

Powell, C. T. (1991). Rap music: An education with a beat from the street. *Journal of Negro Education, 60*(3), 245–259.

Pulido, I. (2009). "Music fi t for us minorities": Latinas/os' use of hip hop as pedagogy and interpretive framework to negotiate and challenge racism. *Equity and Excellence in Education, 42*(1), 67–85.

Rideout, V. J., & Hamel, E. (2006). *Th e media family: Electronic media in the lives of infants, toddlers, preschoolers, and their parents.* Menlo Park, CA: Kaiser Family Foundation.

Roberts, D. F., & Foehr, U. G. (2008). Trends in media use. *Th e Future of Children, 18*(1), 11–37.

Rose, T. (1991). "Fear of a black planet": Rap music and black cultural politics in the 1990s. *Jounral of Negro Education, 60*(3), 276–290.

Rose, T. (1994). *Black Noise: Rap and Black Culture in Contemporary America.* Hanover, NH: Wesleyan University Press.

Sikkink, D., & Hernandez, E. I. (2003). *Religion matters: Predicting schooling success among Latino youth.* Notre Dame: University of Notre Dame, Institute for Latino Studies.

Stark, R. (1996). Religion as context. Hellfi re and delinquency one more time. *Social Relations, 57,* 163–173.

Stewart, D. (2002). Th e role of faith in the development of an integrated identity: A qualitative study of black students at a white college. *Journal of College Student Development, 43*(4), 579–596.

U.S. Department of Commerce. (2002). *A nation online: How Americans are expanding their use of the internet.* Washington, DC: U.S.G.P.O.

Woodson, C. G. (1921). *Th e history of the Negro church.* Washington, DC: Th e Associated Publishers.

Examining Race/Ethnicity and Fears of Children and Adolescents in the United States

Differences Between White, African American, and Hispanic Populations

Joy J. Burnham and Richard G. Lomax

Th e American Fear Survey Schedule for Children (FSSC-AM; J. J. Burnham, 1995, 2005) has been used to measure fears of children and adolescents. Th e FSSC-AM is based on the 2nd revision of a psychometrically sound and well-known fear scale (i.e., FSSC-II; E. Gullone & N. J. King, 1992). In this study, age and gender diff erences, fear intensity scores, and fear prevalence scores were analyzed across race/ethnicity (i.e., White, African American, and Hispanic populations). Multivariate analyses of variance yielded signifi cant eff ects for race/ethnicity.

Close connections between developmental theory and fear research are found throughout the body of literature related to fear (Angelino, Dollins, & Mech, 1956; Bauer, 1976; Davidson, White, Smith, & Poppen, 1989; Derevensky, 1979; Gullone & King, 1993; Hall, 1897; Jersild & Holmes, 1935a, 1935b; King & Ollendick, 1989; Morris & Kratochwill, 1985; Ollendick, 1979). Although many of these studies are dated at this time, they are a reminder of the predictable patterns of fears that have been documented through the centuries. Fears are considered to be a normal part of development (Morris & Kratochwill, 1985). Gullone (1996) described fear in children as "an adaptive reaction to a real or imagined threat" (p. 144). With cognitive and social development, the fears of children and adolescents change quantitatively (Campbell, 1986). For example, young children fear imaginary things (Ollendick, Matson, & Helsel, 1985), whereas by the ages of 5 to 6 years, school fears manifest (Ollendick, 1979). In contrast, "fears remain relatively constant and consist primarily of fears related to injury, natural events, and social anxiety" by age 6 years to adolescence (Ollendick, Matson, & Helsel, 1985, p. 465).

Diff erences related to age and gender are oft en reported in studies on fear. Fears usually decrease as children get older (Burnham, 1995; Burnham & Gullone, 1997; Davidson et al., 1989; Gullone & King, 1992, 1993), although exceptions to the characteristic pattern can be found. For example, Angelino et al. (1956) reported that fears related to economic and political issues increase with age, whereas

Gullone and King (1993) noted that the fear of criticism increased during the middle years of school. In addition, Burnham, Schaefer, and Giesen (2006) found in their study that boys and adolescents were more likely to have school-related and peer-related fears (e.g., from bad grades to losing friends) than were the younger participants and the girls. Overall in fear-related studies, girls, by a large majority, have reported more fears than have boys (Angelino et al., 1956; Burnham, 1995; Burnham & Gullone, 1997; Gullone & King, 1993; Ollendick, 1983).

Th roughout a century of research on fear (Gullone, 1999, 2000), studies have examined crosscultural diff erences, for example, between Australian and American children (Burnham & Gullone, 1997; Ollendick, King, & Frary, 1989), British children (Ollendick & Yule, 1990), and youth from the Netherlands (Muris & Ollendick, 2002). Other studies have focused on fears of children in Israel (Elebedour, Shulman, & Kedem, 1997) and South Africa (Burkhardt, Loxton, & Muris, 2003). Regarding cross-cultural fears, Burkhardt et al. concluded that "childhood fears are at least to some extent culturally determined" (p. 95). Th ese authors found that among three cultural groups of children in South Africa, fears were diff erent across the cultures, with White youth being the least fearful. In addition, Shore and Rapport (1998) reported that "recent cross-national and cross-cultural studies suggest that ethnocultural factors may infl uence the dimensional nature of the construct as well as the developmental pattern of children's fears" (p. 456).

Despite relevance in cross-cultural research (Burkhardt et al., 2003; Shore & Rapport, 1998), we have found no fear studies that compare the diff erences in fears across the three largest racial/ethnic groups in the United States (i.e., African American, Hispanic, and White youth). One study compared the worries of African American, Hispanic, and White youth (Silverman, La Greca, & Wasserstein, 1995), albeit with a small Hispanic sample size.

Overall, "research on anxiety disorders in non-White youth is disturbingly sparse" (Ginsburg & Silverman, 1996, p. 517). With over 37 million African American citizens in the United States, accounting for 12% of the total population (U.S. Census Bureau, 2008); over 46 million of Hispanic origin in the United States, representing 15% of the total population (U.S. Census Bureau, 2008); and White citizens making up approximately 65% of the population (i.e., 199 million; U.S. Census Bureau, 2008), fear-related studies that consider race in the United States are needed to understand the fears of a diverse population of youth. In addition, the Fear Survey Schedule (FSS), the "exclusive assessment tool for fear assessment" (Gullone, 2000, p. 435), has been underutilized with African American and Hispanic populations because a majority of the studies have been done with White children and adolescents from the United States or abroad.

Very little data exist on the fears specifi cally of African American youth (Neal, Lilly, & Zakis, 1993), and of the studies that had been completed, most are outdated at this time. Researchers have found diff erences between the fears of African American youth and their White counterparts (Lapouse & Monk, 1959; Last & Perrin, 1993; Nalven, 1970; Neal et al., 1993). Two studies used the FSS to examine fears of African American children and to compare African American children with White children in this regard (Last & Perrin, 1993; Neal et al., 1993). Results from the African American studies included a correlation between anxiety and race/ethnicity (Neal & Turner, 1991), a higher incidence of fear of animals for African American children than for the White children (Nalven, 1970), and more fears in general reported by African American children than by White children (Lapouse & Monk, 1959). Last and Perrin reported that African American children had higher total scores on the FSS than did White children and that "African Americans are more likely to report phobic responses in general than

Whites" (p. 162). Neal et al. explained that the "diff erences in fears may be rooted in semantics. African American children are more likely to report specifi c fears, whereas White children are more likely to use generic terms" (p. 13 0). To explain this, although African American children might endorse a "fear of rats," White children, in contrast, would choose "fear of small animals (Neal et al., p. 130; Neal & Turner, 1991). In a similar vein, Silverman et al. (1995) studied worries and found that African American children endorsed more worries than did White or Hispanic children.

Very little data exist on fears of Hispanic youth. Owen (1998) noted that "an abundant [amount of] literature exists concerning the fears of middle-class Anglo children, but few studies examine other ethnic groups" (Introduction section, para. 1). Alva and de Los Reyes (1999) reiterated the same concern in stating that "few studies concerning childhood psychosocial stress have included Hispanics and other minority children and adolescents" (p. 344). Two studies with a Hispanic sample have used the FSS (i.e., Ginsberg & Silverman, 1996; Owen, 1998), with both studies comparing Hispanic populations with White populations. Owen reported the "fi rst-ever data on self-reported fears of a large group of Hispanic/Mexican American children" (Discussion section, para. 15), and Ginsberg and Silverman studied Cuban Americans. Owen found that for the Hispanic/Mexican group, girls were more fearful than boys. In their studies, both Ginsberg and Silverman and Owen found that Hispanic children's fears were very similar to White children's fears.

Cultural diff erences across countries have oft en emerged regarding fears (Burkhardt et al., 2003). Yet in the United States, no studies have examined fears across the three largest racial/ethnic groups, with the exception of one study on worries. Using Burkhardt et al.'s terminology, we hypothesized in the present study that fears among White, African American, and Hispanic children and adolescents in the United States would be "highly specifi c and idiosyncratic" (p. 95). Th e purpose of our study was twofold: (a) to examine diff erences in fear levels for children and adolescents (elementary, middle/secondary school levels, from Grades 2 through 12) across race/ethnicity (i.e., White, African American, and Hispanic populations) and (b) to report fear intensity and fear prevalence scores for the factors of race/ethnicity, gender, and school level (i.e., elementary, middle/secondary). We analyzed the following hypotheses: (a) there would be no racial/ethnic group diff erences based on the fi ve factor scores for the elementary school-level students; (b) there would be no racial/ethnic group diff erences based on the fi ve factor scores for the middle/secondary school-level students; (c) there would be no racial/ethnic, gender, or school-level diff erences based on the fear intensity variable; and (d) there would be no racial/ ethnic, gender, or school-level diff erences based on the fear prevalence variable.

Method

Participants

Th e data source was fear data collected from students ($N = 1,030$) in 28 schools (Grades 2 through 12) in two southeastern states. Th e sample consisted of elementary school-level students in Grades 2 through 6 ($n = 466$) and middle/secondary school-level students in Grades 7 through 12 ($n = 564$). Th ere were 481 White students (48.4%), 241 African American students (24.2%), 239 Hispanic students (24.0%), 23 Asian American students (2.3%), 6 Native American students (0.6%), 4 with an unspecifi ed racial/ ethnic background (0.4%), and 36 (3.5%) who did not specify their racial background. Th ere were 544 girls, 457 boys, and 29 students who did not identify gender.

Procedure

A version of the FSS, the American Fear Survey Schedule for Children (FSSC-AM; Burnham, 1995, 2005), was used in this study, with institutional review board approval. Written parental consent was obtained prior to administration of the FSSC-AM, and the directions on the survey were read aloud to all students. (Th e entire survey was read aloud to students in Grades 2 and 3.) Th e participants responded by marking an "x" in front of *not scared, scared, or very scared* for each fear item. Administration of the FSSC-AM was done in groups and typically took place in the classroom. During the administration of the survey, the researcher (the fi rst author) answered any questions from the students.

Analysis

Data collection and examination of variables followed the protocol described in previous research on fear using the FSS (Gullone & King, 1992, 1993). Fear intensity (i.e., the summation of the total fear scores, that is, *not scared, scared*, and *very scared* responses) and fear prevalence (i.e., the summation of the *very scared* responses) were examined across race/ethnicity, school level, and gender. Factor scores from previous factor analyses (Burnham, 2005; i.e., subscales for elementary school-level were Death and Danger Fears, School/Family-Related Fears, Fear of Scary Th ings, Animal Fears, and Fear of the Unknown, and subscales for middle/secondary school-level were Death and Danger Fears, Animal Fears, School-Related Fears, Fear of the Unknown, and Medical Fears) were computed and analyzed across race/ethnicity.

Instrument

Scherer and Nakamura (1968) introduced the FSS and examined the factor structure of the survey by using factor analysis. Since the 1960s, several versions and updates of the FSS have been introduced. Ollendick (1983) revised the FSS and named the revised scale the Fear Survey Schedule for Children— Revised (FSSC-R). In 1992, Australian researchers Gullone and King (1992, 1993) off ered the second revision of the FSS, the Fear Survey Schedule for Children-II (FSSC-II), which updated the fear content for the fi rst time (e.g., dropped the "Fear of Russia" and added "AIDS"). Gullone and King found evidence that the FSSC-II had high internal consistency, as measured by the Cronbach's alpha (.96) and 1 -week test-retest reliability (.90). Strong evidence of divergent, construct, and convergent validity for the FSSC-II were reported by Gullone and King.

Because the FSSC-II (Gullone & King, 1992) was an Australian version of the measure (e.g., referencing fears of dingoes, bushfi res), Burnham (1995) adapted and validated the FSSC-II for use in the United States. Burnham (1995, 2005) renamed the adapted version the FSSC-AM and added 20 contemporary fear items for use in the United States (e.g., "drive-by shootings," "having to fi ght in a war," "terrorist attacks"). Th e FSSC-AM is a self-report fear survey with 98 items for participants in Grades 7 through 12 and 95 items for students in Grades 2 through 6. Burnham (2005) found that the Cronbach's alpha estimate for the FSSC-AM was .97, which compared favorably with .96 reported by Gullone and King (1992). Elementary and middle/secondary school-level grades were analyzed separately with the FSSCAM because three fear items were removed from this measure for the younger participants (i.e, "being raped," "my getting pregnant or getting my girlfriend pregnant," and "cults/satanic worship/ voodoo"). Burnham (2005) examined factor analysis results for elementary school-level children in Grades 2 through 6 and middle/secondary school-level youth in Grades 7 through 12. For elementary schoollevel students, fi ve factors were extracted: Death and Danger Fears (e.g., "having to fi ght in a war," "drive-by shootings," "terrorist attacks"), School/Family-Related Fears (e.g., "failing a test," "getting bad grades," "my parents arguing"), Fear of Scary Th ings (e.g., "darkness," "thunderstorms"), Animal Fears ("snakes," "spiders," "mice"), and Fear of the Unknown (e.g., "being alone at home"). Cronbach's alpha reliability estimates for the fi ve factors (i.e, subscales) ranged from .60 to .97. For middle/secondary school-level students, fi ve factors were extracted. Th e fi rst factor was Death and Danger Fears, followed by Animal Fears, School/Family-Related Fears, Fear of the Unknown, and Medical Fears. Cronbach's alpha reliability estimates for the fi ve factors (i.e., subscales) ranged from .70 to .96.

Results

Th e fi ve subscale score variables were analyzed to determine whether racial/ethnic group diff erences existed. Because the instruments and subsequent factor analysis results were diff erent for the elementary and the middle/secondary school levels, separate one-factor analyses of variance (ANOVAs) were conducted for each school-level sample. For the elementary school-level sample, the multivariate analysis of variance (MANOVA) yielded a signifi cant eff ect for race/ethnicity, $F(10,530) = 7.80$, $p < .001$, $\eta2 = .13$. Th e univariate ANOVAs were only signifi cant for the following subscale score variables: (a) School/
Family-Related Fears, $F(2,269) = 3.75$, $p < .05$, $\eta2 = .03$; (b) Animal Fears, $F(2, 269) = 9.40$, $p < .001$, $\eta2 = .07$; and (c) Fear of Scary Th ings, $F(2,269) = 5.94$, $p < .005$, $\eta2 = .04$. Th ere was not a signifi cant race/ ethnicity eff ect for the Death and Danger Fears or for Fear of the Unknown. Th e following post hoc Bonferroni pairwise contrasts were signifi cant ($p < .05$) for the elementary school-level students: (a) White students had higher school/family-related fears than did African American students, (b) African American students had higher fear of animals than did White students, and (c) African American and Hispanic students both had higher fear of scary things than did White students.

For the middle/secondary school-level sample, the MANOVA yielded a signifi cant eff ect for race/ethnicity, $F(10,826) = 11.23$, $p < .001$, $\eta2 = .12$. Th e ANOVAs were signifi cant only for the following subscale score variables: (a) Death and Danger Fears, $F(2,417) = 3.26$, $p < .05$, $\eta2 = .02$, and (b) Animal Fears, $F(2,417) = 19.87$, $p < .001$, $\eta2 = .09$. Th ere was not a signifi cant race/ethnicity eff ect for School/Family-Related Fears, Fear of the Unknown, or Medical Fears. Th e following post hoc Bonferroni pairwise contrasts were signifi cant ($p < .05$) for the middle/secondary school-level students: (a) African American students had higher fear of animals than did both White and Hispanic students and (b) African American students had higher fear of death and danger than did White students.

For the fear intensity (i.e., summation of the fear responses) and fear prevalence (i.e., summation of very scared responses) composite variables, three-factor ANOVAs were conducted, with the factors being race/ethnicity, gender, and school level (elementary or middle/secondary). Th e results for fear intensity were as follows: (a) Th ere was a signifi cant eff ect for gender, $F(1,928) = 189.31$, $p < .001$, $\eta2 = .17$, with girls scoring higher than boys; (b) a signifi cant eff ect for school level, $F(1,928) = 27.79$, $p < .001$, $\eta2 = .03$, with elementary school-level students scoring higher than middle/secondary school-level students; and (c) no other eff ects were signifi cant. Th e results for fear prevalence were as follows: (a) Th ere was a signifi cant eff ect for gender, $F(1,928) = 130.75$, $p < .001$, $\eta2 = .12$, with girls scoring higher than boys; (b) a signifi cant eff ect for school level, $F(1,928) = 70.04$, $p < .001$, $\eta2 = .07$, with elementary school-level students scoring higher than middle/secondary school-level students; (c) a signifi cant eff ect for race/ethnicity, $F(1,928) = 6.96$, $p < .001$, $\eta2 = .02$, with African American students scoring higher than both White and Hispanic students (from post hoc Bonferroni pairwise contrasts); and (d) no other eff ects were signifi cant.

Discussion

Th e fear intensity and fear prevalence scores from this study were comparable with those of previous studies (i.e., Gullone & King, 1992, 1993). Girls have reported more fears than boys for years (Angelino et al., 1956; Burnham, 1995, 2005; Burnham & Gullone, 1997; Ollendick, 1983). In addition, girls in the elementary and middle/secondary school-level groups reported higher fear scores than did boys. Elementary school-level students also reported higher fear scores than did middle/secondary schoollevel students, which followed the typical marked decline in fears as children age (Burnham, 1995, 2005; Burnham & Gullone, 1997; Davidson et al., 1989; Gullone & King, 1992, 1993). Th e results for fear prevalence in the current study were also similar to results that have been found in the literature on fears. Girls have typically endorsed more fears than have boys (Angelino et al., 1956; Burnham, 1995, 2005; Burnham & Gullone, 1997; Ollendick, 1983). In this study, elementary school-level students had higher levels of fear than did middle/secondary school-level students, paralleling previous fear studies in the fi eld (Burnham, 1995; Burnham & Gullone, 1997; Davidson et al., 1989; Gullone & King, 1992,1993).

Conclusions have been fairly consistent when fears have been compared across two racial groups (i.e., White and African American, White and Hispanic). For example, Ginsberg and Silverman (1996) and Owen (1998) found Hispanic and White youth to be very similar regarding their reported fears using the FSSC-R, whereas Last and Perrin (1993) found similarities between White and African American children regarding their fears.

In this study, similarities between the three racial groups were detected. For example, in the elementary school-level study, two of the fi ve subscales on the FSSC-AM were not signifi cantly diff erent for the racial groups (i.e., Death and Danger and Fear of the Unknown), and for the middle/secondary school-level students, three of the fi ve fear subscale scores were not signifi cantly diff erent across the racial groups (i.e., School/Family-Related Fears, Fear of the Unknown, and Medical Fears). It can be postulated that homogeneity existed to some degree across the given fear subscale scores for the three racial groups.

Diff erences between the three racial groups were notable in the current study. Th e elementary schoollevel students had signifi cant subscale score diff erences for fears related to school and family, animals, and scary things. For the school and family fears, White elementary school-level children had a higher level of School/Family-Related fears than did the African American elementary school-level children. No previous fear study has reported higher scores for School/Family- Related fears for White children. However, Neal et al. (1993) found that African American children did not have a subscale related to related to school fear aft er factor analysis, suggesting possible consistency across Neal et al.'s study of African American children and the African American children in the current study. For the animal fears, African American students had signifi cantly higher scores for Animal Fears than did White students, which paralleled Nalven's (1970) work. Last, African American and Hispanic students had higher scores on the Fear of Scary Th ings subscale than did White students. Th is fi nding was unique. Studies have illustrated that "Hispanic and African American youth have been found to be exposed to more violent events as compared to White children" (Storch, Nock, Masia-Warner, Barlas, 2003, p. 441). Determining whether this fact played a role in the signifi cant diff erence between the three racial groups regarding scores on the Fear of Scary Th ings subscale in the current study would be of interest. Silverman et al.'s (1995) studies on worries of elementary school-level children off ered some comparable fi ndings. For example, they concluded that African American children worried more oft en about war, health, personal harm, and about their family than did White or Hispanic children. In addition, Silverman et al. found that African American and Hispanic children worried more about health issues than did White youth. In contrast to Silverman et al.'s conclusions about family worries for African American children, the current study found that White children had more family-related fears than did their counterparts. In comparison, this study indicated that African American and Hispanic elementary school-level children were more fearful of scary things than were White children, whereas Silverman et al. found that African American and Hispanic elementary school-level children had more health worries than did their White counterparts.

For the middle/secondary school-level students, signifi cant diff erences were found regarding the Death and Danger and Animal Fears subscales. Th e fi ndings in this study indicated that, similar to fi ndings for elementary school-level students, middle/secondary school-level African American students had higher fear of animals than did both White and Hispanic students at this level, again supporting the fi ndings of Nalven's (1970) study. Th e middle/secondary school-level African American students also endorsed higher fear of death and danger than did White students at this school level. Owen's work with
Hispanic children found death and danger fears to be "preeminent … regardless of ethnic background" (Discussion section, para. 15). Yet, no previous study with African American youth has reported higher death and danger fears for this group than for White youth of the same age.

Implications for Counseling and Counseling Research

Many studies have erred on representation of minority and underserved youth; fear research is no exception. By addressing race/ethnicity, this study found signifi cant fear diff erences between White, African American, and Hispanic elementary and middle/secondary school-level youth on several factors. Th e most unique contributions were fi ndings of (a) higher school/family-related fears for White elementary school-level students than for African American elementary school-level students, (b) higher fears of scary things for elementary school-level African American and Hispanic students than for White elementary school-level students, and (c) higher fear of death and danger endorsements for African American adolescents (middle/secondary school-level students) than for White adolescents (middle/secondary school-level students). Because these three trends have not been previously reported in race/ethnicity fear studies, there are implications for counselors who work closely with youth, as well as for the counselor educator who trains future counselors. Knowledge that racial/ethnic groups respond diff erently to certain fears related to school, family, death, and danger can assist the professional counselor with routine planning for counseling, consultation, and referral. Moreover, this information can be helpful during uncertain times, such as during present day concerns that aff ect children and adolescents, as well as parents, teachers, and communities (e.g., the aft ermath of disasters like 9–11 and Hurricane Katrina, the war in Iraq, shootings at schools and on college campuses, swine fl u). Th e information can also aid preparation for future crises as they develop over time.

Th is study not only off ered new fi ndings and fear factors that were "highly specifi c and idiosyncratic" (Burkhardt et al., 2003, p. 95), but it also underlined that fear commonalities exist among diff erent ethnic groups. Th ere were similarities between the fi ndings of this study and those of previous fear studies that compared two ethnic groups. Th is study supported certain fi ndings about relationships regarding fears between African American children and White children (Lapouse & Monk, 1959; Last & Perrin, 1993; Nalven, 1970; Neal et al., 1993), Hispanic children and White children (Ginsberg & Silverman, 1996; Owen, 1998), and the ethnic study that examined children's worries (Silverman et al., 1995).

Th e current study has research implications for the future. First, this study off ers updates to gaps found in fear-related research. For example, to compare the fears of African American and White children, it was necessary to use older studies (Lapouse & Monk, 1959; Nalven, 1970) because newer work did not exist. Second, the current study suggests that replication in other geographic regions of the United States is indicated. Th ird, this study restates the need for more investigations of minority youth, in general, and for fear-related research specifi cally. Sue, Arredondo, and McDavis (1992) established more than a decade ago that there was a "need for a multicultural approach to assessment, practice, training, and research" (p. 477). Because there are very few fear-related studies with minority youth, Sue et al.'s thoughts have not been integrated fully in relation to research on fear at this time. Ginsberg and Silverman (1996) reiterated this point when they explained that "there is little in the theoretical or empirical literature regarding anxiety/fear in Hispanic populations" (p. 518). Certainly, there are also limited studies on the fears of African American youth.

Not too long ago, Sue et al. (1992) posited that the United States was a "monocultural and monolingual" (p. 478) country. Nonetheless, with the current growing diversity, the United States is "fast becoming a multiracial, multicultural, and multilingual society" (Sue et al., 1992, p. 478). Data from the U.S. Census Bureau (2008) confi rm this claim. Unfortunately, the current study revealed the present monocultural nature of most fear studies completed in the United States. Because many counselors work closely with anxious, fearful, and phobic youth from a variety of cultural backgrounds, this fi nding is alarming. Without solid research that considers diversity, counselors will not have adequate information pertaining to assessment, treatment, and quality services when working with minority youth. Undoubtedly, for multiculturalism to truly be the fourth force in counseling (Pedersen, 1990), more diverse research is needed.

References

Alva, S. A., & de Los Reyes, R. (1999). Psychosocial stress, internalized symptoms, and the academic achievement of Hispanic adolescents. *Journal of Adolescent Research, 14,* 343–358.

Angelino, H., Dollins, J., & Mech, E. V (1956). Trends in the "fear and worries" of school children as related to socio-economic status and age. *Th e Journal of Genetic Psychology, 89,* 263–276.

Bauer, D. H. (1976). An exploratory study of developmental changes in children's fears. *Journal of Child Psychology and Psychiatry, 17,* 69–74.

Burkhardt, K., Loxton, H., & Muris, P. (2003). Fears and fearfulness in South-African children. *Behaviour Change, 20,* 94–102.

Burnham, J. J. (1995). *Validation of the Fear Survey Schedule for Children and Adolescents (FSSC-II) in the United States.* Unpublished doctoral dissertation, Auburn University, AL.

Burnham, J. J. (2005). Fears of children in the United States: An examination of the American Fear Survey Schedule with 20 new contemporary fear items. *Measurement and Evaluation in Counseling and Development, 38,* 78–91.

Burnham, J. J., & Gullone, E. (1997). Th e Fear Survey Schedule for Children-II: A psychometric investigation with American data. *Behaviour Research and Th erapy, 35,* 165–173.

Burnham, J. J., Schaefer, B., & Giesen, J. (2006). An empirical taxonomy of youths' fears: Cluster analysis of the American Fear Survey Schedule (FSSC-AM). *Psychology in the Schools, 43,* 673–683.

Campbell, S. B. (1986). Developmental issues in childhood anxiety. In R. Gittleman (Ed.), *Anxiety disorders of children* (pp. 24–57) New York: Guilford Press.

Davidson, P., White, P., Smith, D., & Poppen, W. (1989). Content and intensity of fears in middle children among rural and urban boys and girls. *Th e Journal of Genetic Psychology, 150*, 51–58.

Derevensky, J. L. (1979). Children's fears: A developmental comparison of normal and exceptional children. *Th e Journal of Genetic Psychology, 135*, 11–21.

Elebedour, S., Shulman, S., & Kedem, P. (1997). Children's fears: Cultural and developmental perspectives. *Behaviour Research and Th erapy, 35*, 491–496.

Ginsberg, G. S., & Silveman, W. K. (1996). Phobic and anxiety disorders in Hispanic and White youth. *Journal of Anxiety Disorders, 10*, 517–528.

Gullone, E. (1996). Developmental psychopathology and normal fear. *Behaviour Change, 13*, 143–155.

Gullone, E. (1999). Th e assessment of normal fear in children and adolescents. *Clinical Child and Family Psychology Review, 2*, 91–106.

Gullone, E. (2000). Th e development of normal fear: A century of research. *Clinical Psychology Review, 20*, 429–451.

Gullone, E., & King, N. J. (1992). Psychometric evaluation of a revised fear survey schedule for children and adolescents. *Journal of Child Psychology and Psychiatry and Allied Disciplines, 33*, 987–998.

Gullone, E., & King, N. J. (1993). Th e fears of youth in the 1990s: Contemporary normative data. *Th e Journal of Genetic Psychology, 154*, 137–153.

Hall, G. S. (1897). A study of fears. *Th e American Journal of Psychology, 8*, 147–249.

Jersild, A. T., & Holmes, F. B. (1935a). Children's fears. *Child Development Monographs, 20* (ix, No. 358). New York: Teachers College, Columbia University.

Jersild, A. T., & Holmes, F. B. (1935b). Some factors in the development of children's fears. *Journal of Experimental Education, 4*, 131–141.

King, N. J., & Ollendick, T. (1989). Children's anxiety and phobic disorders in school settings. Classifi cation, assessment, and intervention issues. *Review of Educational Research, 59*, 431–470.

Lapouse, R., & Monk, M. A. (1959). Fears and worries in a representative sample of children. *American Journal of Orthopsychiatry, 29*, 803–818.

Last, C. J., & Perrin, S. (1993). Anxiety disorders in African American and White children. *Journal of Abnormal Child Psychology, 21*, 153–164.

Morris, R. J., & Kratochwill, T. R. (1985). Behavioral treatment of children's fears and phobias: A review. *School Psychology Review, 14*, 84–93.

Muris, P., & Ollendick, T. H. (2002). Th e assessment of contemporary fears in adolescents using a modifi ed version of the Fear Survey Schedule for Children—Revised. *Journal of Anxiety Disorders, 16*, 567–584.

Nalven, F. B. (1970). Manifest fears and worries of ghetto versus middle-class suburban children. *Psychological Reports, 27*, 285–286.

Neal, A. M., Lilly, R. S., & Zakis, S. (1993). What are African American children afraid of? *Journal of Anxiety Disorders, 7*, 129–139.

Neal, A. M., & Turner, S. M. (1991). Anxiety disorder research with African Americans: Current status. *Psychological Bulletin, 109*, 400–410.

Ollendick, T. H. (1979). Fear reduction techniques with children. In M. Hersen, R. M. Eisler, & P. M. Miller (Eds.), *Progress in behavior modifi cation* (Vol. 8, pp. 127–168). New York: Academic Press.

Ollendick, T. H. (1983). Reliability and validity of the revised Fear Survey Schedule for Children (FSSC-R). *Behaviour Research and Th erapy, 21*, 685–692.

Ollendick, T. H., King, N. J., & Frary, R. B. (1989). Fears in children and adolescents: Reliability and generalizability across gender, age and nationality. *Behaviour Research and Th erapy, 27*, 19–26.

Ollendick, T. H., Matson, J. L, & Helsel, W. J. (1985). Case histories and shorter communications: Fears in children and adolescents: Normative data. *Behavior Research and Th erapy, 23*, 465–467.

Ollendick, T. H., & Yule, W. (1990). Depression in British and American children and its relation to anxiety and fear. *Journal of Consulting and Clinical Psychology, 58*, 126–129.

Owen, P. R. (1998). Fears of Hispanic and Anglo children: Real world fears in the 1990s [Electronic version]. *Hispanic Journal of Behavioral Sciences, 20*, 483.

Pedersen, P. B. (1990). Th e constructs of complexity and balance in multicultural counseling theory and practice. *Journal of Counseling & Development, 68*, 550–554.

Scherer, M. W., & Nakamura, C. Y. (1968). A Fear Survey Schedule for Children (FSS-FC): A factor analytic comparison with manifest anxiety (CMAS). *Behaviour Research and Th erapy, 6*, 173–182.

Shore, G. N., & Rapport, M. D. (1998). Th e Fear Survey Schedule for Children—Revised (FSSC-HI) [Hawaii revision]: Ethnocultural variations in children's fearfulness. *Journal of Anxiety Disorders, 12*, 437–461.

Silverman, W., La Greca, A. M., & Wasserstein, S. (1995).What do children worry about? Worries and relationship to anxiety. *Child Development, 66*, 671–686.

Storch, E. A., Nock M. K., Masia-Warner, C., & Barlas M. E. (2003). Peer victimization and social-psychological adjustment in Hispanic and African American Children. *Journal of Child and Family Studies, 12*, 439–452.

Sue, D. W., Arredondo P., & McDavis R. J. (1992). Multicultural counseling competencies and standards: A call to the profession. *Journal of Counseling & Development, 70*, 477–486.

U.S. Census Bureau (2008, March). *2008 population estimates* [Table T4-2008, Hispanic or Latino by race]. Retrieved May 27, 2009, from http://factfi nder.census.gov/servlet/DTTable?_bm=y&-geo_id=01000US&ds_name=PEP_2008_EST&-_lang=en&-redoLog=true&-mt_name=PEP_2008_EST_G2008_T004_2008&format+&-CONTEXT=dt

Advancing the Africentric Paradigm Shift Discourse

Building toward Evidence-Based Africentric Interventions in Social Work Practice with African Americans

Dorie J. Gilbert et al.

For over a decade, a number of social work scholars have advocated for an Africentric paradigm shift in social work practice with African Americans; yet the paradigm shift has been slow in coming with respect to infusing Africentric theory and interventions into social work practice, education, and research. Interventions that infuse Africentric values (such as interdependence, collectivism, transformation, and spirituality) have been shown to create signifi cant change across a number of areas important to social work practice with African Americans. However, a barrier to the full integration of Africentric models into social work practice is that Africentric programs lack cohesive documentation and replication and, thus, have limited potential to be established as evidence-based practices. Th e authors present an overview of various Africentric interventions, including their program components and methods of evaluation, with the aim of establishing guideposts or next steps in developing a discourse on Africentric interventions that are promising best practices or are emerging as evidence-based practices. Th e authors conclude with implications for social work practice, education, and research and a call for Africentric scholars to engage in increased discussion, dissemination of manualized treatments, and collaborative research to build the evidencebased Africentric knowledge base and foster replication of studies.

Social work practice with African Americans has evolved from a generalist perspective that tended to overlook cultural values to one that recognizes the need to incorporate cultural sensitivity and cultural competence. In particular, the strengths perspective (Hill, 1971, 1999; Saleebey, 1992), empowerment theory (DuBois & Miley, 1996; Solomon, 1976), and the person-in-environment framework (Germain, 1991) have supported the profession's move toward ethnic-centered interventions, which at minimum should emphasize the cultural competencies of the practitioners and attention to salient ethnocultural factors, such as beliefs, language, and traditions. Beyond recognizing strengths and cultural sensitivity, the Africentric paradigm is a complementary, holistic perspective that emerged as a response to traditional theoretical approaches that failed to consider the worldviews of historically

Dorie J. Gilbert, Aminifu R. Harvey, & Faye Z. Belgrave, "Advancing the Africentric Paradigm Shift Discourse: Building toward Evidence-Based Africentric Interventions in Social Work Practice with African Americans," *Social Work*, vol. 54, no. 3, pp. 243–252. Copyright © 2009 by National Association of Social Workers, Inc. Reprinted with permission.

oppressed populations. Africentric approaches address the totality of African Americans' worldview and existence, including their experiences of collective disenfranchisement and historical trauma as a result of slavery and persistent racial disparities. Interchangeably referred to as "Afrocentric," "Africentric," or "African-centered," interventions are based on the principle of reinstilling traditional African and African American cultural values in people of African descent. This approach stems from the premise that African Americans, for the most part, survived historically because of values such as interdependence, collectivism, transformation, and spirituality that can be traced to African principles for living (Akbar, 1984; Asante, 1988; Karenga, 1996; Nobles & Goddard, 1993). Over a decade ago, Schiele (1996, 1997), Harvey (1985, 1997),and Harvey and Rauch (1997) began to develop and advocate for Africentrism as an emerging paradigm for social work practice. Indeed, a number of social work scholars have weighed in on the discourse, calling for a much-needed Africentric paradigm shift in social work practice with African Americans (Carlton-LaNey, 1999; Daly, Jennings, Beckett, & Leashore, 1995; Daniels, 2001; Freeman & Logan, 2004; Gibson & McRoy, 2004; Manning, Cornelius, & Okundaye, 2004; A. Roberts, Jackson, & Carlton-LaNey, 2000; Sherr, 2006; Swigonski, 1996; White, 2004). Harvey (2003) provided a general guide for a social work shift away from Western approaches to social work conceptualizations and practices with African Americans via an Africentric paradigm. Yet the paradigm shift has been slow in coming with respect to infusing Africentric theory and constructs into social work practice, education, and research.

Furthermore, although *evidence-based practices* (EBPs), those counseling and prevention programs that have the best-researched evidence, have become the "gold standard" for practice and research, there is a growing recognition that EBPs do not automatically translate intact across cultural lines (Bernal & Scharron-del-Rio, 2001; Davis, 1997). In fact, few EBPs are culturally congruent for African Americans. Conversely, Africentric interventions are culturally congruent practices specifically for African American populations and have demonstrated significant positive outcomes across several areas important to social work practice with African Americans, including increases in positive child, adolescent, and family development (Belgrave, 2002; Belgrave, Townsend, Cherry, & Cunningham, 1997; Constantine, Alleyne, & Wallace, 2006; Dixon, Schoonmaker, & Philliber, 2000; Harvey & Hill, 2004; Thomas, Townsend, & Belgrave, 2003; Washington, Johnson, Jones, & Langs, 2007). Other Africentric interventions have shown improved outcomes for incarcerated individuals and decreases in substance abuse and HIV risk behavior (Gant, 2003, 2007; Gilbert & Goddard, 2007; Harvey, 1997; Longshore & Grills, 2000; Nobles & Goddard, 1993). Although many Africentric programs show great promise, they lack the replications needed to become recognized as EBPs, and so most are considered *emerging best practices*—interventions that are promising but less documented and replicated than EBPs. This article begins to address the gap between evidence-based and culturally congruent Africentric interventions for African Americans.

Following a discussion of contemporary psychosocial concerns of African Americans and the relevance of Africentric interventions, we present a case for greater documentation and dissemination of the current emerging Africentric best practices to accelerate the infusion of Africentric-based interventions into social work practice. Based on our larger, ongoing project to establish a collective volume on Africentric best practices, this article presents a selected sample of emerging Africentric best practices in two categories—child, adolescent, and family development and substance abuse and HIV prevention—and discusses implications for social work practice, education, and research.

BACKGROUND ON AFRICAN AMERICANS' PSYCHOSOCIAL CONCERNS

African Americans make up approximately 13 percent of the U.S. population (U.S. Census Bureau, 2004), and although the term "African American" may accurately reflect those individuals who are descended from slaves in this country, the more than 33 million individuals comprising various black ethnic subgroups (for example, Caribbean, Central and South American, and African immigrants) underscore the diversity of this population. Th e present discussion primarily addresses U.S.-born African Americans who have experienced deculturalization through historical trauma, starting with capture from Africa to the ongoing inequities in the United States.

Historical strengths of the African American family include a strong achievement orientation and work ethic, fl exible family roles, strong kinship bonds, and a strong religious orientation (Hill, 1971). Today, African Americans continue to build on traditional strengths of kinship and spirituality (Hill, 1999), yet subgroups of African Americans experience serious negative outcomes and disparities. Although somewhere between a quarter and a half of today's African American families are considered middle class, African Americans continue to experience serious disparities in education, earnings, and employment compared with white Americans (Attewell, Lavin, Th urston, & Levey, 2004).

Many current health and mental health problems of black Americans can be traced to historical trauma resulting from slavery and persistent societal oppression (DeGruy-Leary, 2005). Historical and current racism underlie current barriers to healthy living for African Americans (Myers, 1988; Nobles & Goddard, 1993). Twenty-one percent of African Americans have reported no usual source of medical care and generally use clinic or emergency room care. Even with diff erences in income, insurance status, and medical need accounted for, race and ethnicity signifi cantly aff ect access to and quality of health care for African Americans (Smedley, Adrienne, & Alan, 2002). Th e Offi ce of Minority Health and Health Disparities (OMHHD) (2002) reported the death rate for African Americans as higher than that for non-Hispanic white Americans for heart diseases, stroke, cancer, chronic lower respiratory diseases, infl uenza and pneumonia, diabetes, HIV/AIDS, and homicide.

From an Africentric perspective, the etiology of negative outcomes for African Americans lies in individual and structural barriers (for example, discrimination, institutionalized racism). When individuals lack cultural knowledge, self-appreciation, and positive racial identifi cation but internalize negative views, myths, and stereotypes, they become engaged in a constellation of coping responses that are not self-enhancing. Th ese include fatalism, overemphasis on materialism, and self-destructive behaviors—such as substance abuse, violence, and other risk behaviors—in addition to stress and depression (Myers, 1988; Nobles & Goddard, 1993).

Depression among African American women is almost 50 percent higher than it is among white American women; and suicide among African American youths between the ages of 10 and 14 rose 233 percent from 1980 to 1995, compared with a 120 percent rise for their white counterparts (OMHHD, 2002). Overall, African Americans account for approximately 25 percent of the mental health needs in this country, but only about 2 percent of the nation's trained mental health counselors are black (OMHHD, 2002), highlighting the urgent need to document and increase culturally relevant interventions and to establish collective work on emerging Africentric best practices, particularly interventions for resource-poor and marginalized African Americans.

AFRICENTRIC INTERVENTIONS: RATIONALE AND LITERATURE REVIEW

Africentric programs emerged as a response to traditional Eurocentric theories and psychological approaches that fail to consider the worldviews of historically oppressed populations (Akbar, 1984; Asante, 1988). From an Africentric perspective, psychosocial issues confronting African Americans are caused by historical oppression and distress and coping patterns in reaction to the oppression. Th e group's resilience rests on the development of an identifi cation and acceptance of a culture based on knowledge of its African heritage and the promotion of behaviors, thoughts, and emotions that foster the liberation of African people from oppression and repression. In short, the reclamation of African culture is key to the survival and positive existence of people of African descent and is a healing phenomenon (Hilliard, 1997; Nobles & Goddard, 1993). One value system (set of guiding principles) for African Americans that can assist them in addressing the root cause of social problems in the African American community is the *Nguzo Saba:* the seven principles representing "the minimum set of values African Americans need to rescue and reconstruct their lives in their own image and interest and build and sustain an Afrocentric family, community and culture" (Karenga, 1996, p. 543). These seven principles are *unity* (striving for unity in family, community, and race); *self-determination* (defining, naming, and creating for oneself); *collective work and responsibility* (building and maintaining community and solving problems together); *cooperative economics* (building and maintaining the economic base of the community); *purpose* (restoring people to their original traditional greatness); *creativity* (enhancing the beauty and benefits of self and community); and *faith* (belief in the righteousness of the black struggle).

Another value system for guiding the life and behavior of African Americans is rooted in the principles of *Maat*, a philosophical, spiritual, and cultural system that reflects principles for living "to support and facilitate the full expression of one's spiritual essence (sense of self)" (Parham, 2002, p. 41). The basic principles of Maat are translated through the Nguzo Saba, and together these principles assist individuals, families, and communities in obtaining wisdom about self in connection to the spiritual and material realms of being (Graham, 2005). Although African Americans are diverse and vary in the extent to which they endorse these principles, when these values are infused into Africentric interventions, they form the cornerstone of behavior change and empower communities in reaffirming purpose and meaning in life (Graham, 2005).

Chipungu et al. (2000) reviewed Africentric drug prevention interventions and identified three critical components of Africentric programs: (1) components implemented to instill Africentric values such as communalism and spirituality, which increase resiliency and other protective factors while decreasing or mediating risk factors; (2) components that emphasize the current conditions of African Americans to help reduce societal pressures and build positive African American ideals; and (3) components that include Africentric activities and projects to increase positive sense of self through African and African American historical examples. A number of different programs across the country include these components, yet there is no cohesive documentation of the various programs to determine whether and how they have been evaluated; and overall, we lack knowledge about the additional research and duplication required to advance the discourse on the needed Africentric paradigm shift. Schiele (2000) emphasized the need to evaluate Africentric programs and to replicate Africentric studies. By doing so, Africentric scholars will move closer to establishing criteria for EBP. The best available and most appropriate research evidence is usually ranked hierarchically according to its scientific strength and tends to fall into four levels of evidence (A. R. Roberts, Yeager, & Regehr, 2006; Thyer, 2006):

- *Level 1: Meta-Analyses and systemic reviews*: Meta-analyses present aggregate results across separate outcome studies using different outcome measures, and they typically include only randomized controlled trials (RCTs); alternatively, systemic reviews include quasi- and pre-experimental outcome studies and correlational, single-subject, and case studies.
- *Level 2: Individual and multisite RCTs*: Individual RCTs involve large numbers of clients randomly assigned to treatment and control groups. Multisite RCTs use several independent research teams in varying locations among diverse populations.

- *Level 3: Uncontrolled clinical trials or quasi-experimental clinical trials*: Uncontrolled clinical trials involve assessing many clients one or more times before an intervention, using identical pretest and posttest methods. Quasi-experimental clinical trials add comparison of diff ering treatment conditions to pretest and posttest procedures.
- *Level 4: Anecdotal case reports, correlations studies, descriptive reports, case studies, and singlesubject designs*: Th ese provide the lowest levels of research evidence yet are relevant for specifi c studies.

Th e eight Africentric programs chosen for discussion in this article adhere to this spectrum of EBP, and levels of evidence are indicated for each. With the goal of building increased evidence for Africentric interventions along this spectrum, we consider this a fi rst step in identifying and documenting various Africentric interventions to advance, in Proctor and Rosen's (2006) words, the "packaging and communicating [of] this information for better retrieval and application by practitioners" (p. 101).

AFRICENTRIC INTERVENTIONS: DEFINITION AND DISCUSSION

As part of a larger project to document an extensive collection of Africentric programs and evaluation studies, we performed a systematic review of interventions that are grounded in Africentric principles across social work, psychology, and affi liated professional disciplines over the past decade. Intervention programs for review were identifi ed through fi ve methods: (1) computer searches of over 15 diff erent electronic databases (for example, Social Sciences Citation Index, Science Citation Index Expanded, Social Work Abstracts, Sociological Abstracts, Info Trac Web, PsycINFO, Medline); (2) manual searches for studies reported from 1997 through 2007 in major journals and journals focusing on African American issues; (3) examination of the bibliographies of selected articles; (4) Web site searches across a number of the National Institutes of Health, including the National Institute of Mental Health, the National Institute on Drug Abuse, and the National Institute of Child Health and Human Development; and (5) contact with individual Africentric scholars and institutions.

In defi ning "Africentric," we included programs with reported fi ndings that specifi cally included the following: Africentric methods in the description of the program; discussion of Africentric principles such as spirituality, collectivism, and transformation in the description of the background or conceptual framework of the study; infusion of Africentric practices (for example, unity circles, rituals, Nguzo Saba, Maat, African proverbs) in delivery of the intervention; and (4) intervention components addressing African Americans, Africans, or both within the context of their historical and current oppression. Th e results revealed a myriad of Africentric programs, ranging from small, community-based programs with and without major funding to large-scale, multisite RCTs.

For the purposes of this discussion, we chose eight programs as a representative sample of interventions to highlight in terms of their objectives, outcomes, and methods of evaluation.Th e programs fall into two basic categories: (1) child, adolescent, and family development and (2) substance abuse and HIV prevention. Th e following overview is in no way exhaustive, but it provides a snapshot of the current state of Africentric interventions to identify next steps in developing guideposts for best practices that would signifi cantly advance the fi eld toward evidence-based Africentric interventions. Th e intent of this discussion is not to endorse the broad-scale adoption of EBP, which has both merit and limitations; instead, we are primarily interested in disseminating knowledge and building opportunities for replication of studies and programs—which, naturally, will lead to best practices and EBPs.

Child, Adolescent and Family Development

Structural racism, poverty, high rates of violence in the community, and poor racial and ethnic identity are some risk factors that work against positive well-being among African American youths. However, strong racial and ethnic identity and Africentric values among children and adolescents have been shown to be positively correlated with healthy development in several studies. We highlight fi ve programs that support these identities and values.

Th e NTU Project (Quasi-experimental, Level 3). Cherry et al. (1998) enlisted African American fi ft h- and sixth-graders in an Africentric-based program designed to decrease risk factors and increase protective factors for substance use. *Ntu* is a Bantu word that means "essence of life." Intervention components for fi ft h-graders included an Africentric education program, a substance use education program, a rites of passage program, a family therapy program, and a parenting program; sixth-graders completed a booster program designed to reinforce skills. Findings supported signifi cant eff ects for protective factors, particularly knowledge of African culture, increased racial identity, improved selfesteem, and improved school behaviors for intervention but not comparison participants.

A Journey Toward Womanhood (Quasi-experimental, Level 3). Th is is an intensive and comprehensive program designed for girls of African descent ages 12 to 17 (Dixon et al., 2000). Rooted in the African "rites of passage" tradition, the program aims to instill knowledge of cultural roots and community awareness. Th e goals are to build and maintain healthy self-esteem; instill cultural pride and self-appreciation; teach life and social skills for self-suffi ciency; and discourage teenage pregnancy, juvenile delinquency, school dropout, and drug abuse. Th e program has been evaluated over a 10-year period, and fi ndings include the following: Rates of sexual activity were signifi cantly higher among program nonparticipants (70 percent) than participants (27 percent); program participants were less likely to get pregnant as teenagers than non-participants; program participants were signifi cantly more likely than nonparticipants to demonstrate positive behaviors and endorse the importance of heritage and ethnic pride; and (4) program participants missed fewer school days.

Sisters of Nia. (Quasi-experimental, Level 3). Sisters of Nia is a cultural intervention for African American girls in early adolescence, aiming to increase cultural values and beliefs, such as ethnic identity, and positive gender roles and relationships (Belgrave et al., 2004). Th e curriculum includes 14 sessions led by a female African American facilitator. Some of the session topics are African culture, relationships, appearance, media messages, African American women in leadership, and faith. Th e Principles of Nguzo Saba and African proverbs are used along with relational and Africentric methods. Intervention group participants demonstrated signifi cant increases in ethnic identity, marginally signifi cant gains in androgynous gender roles, and decreases in relational aggression in comparison with participants who were not in the intervention group. Findings suggest that pre-early adolescence may be an opportune period for implementing prosocial, cultural interventions for girls, particularly to promote resiliency factors. Th is study replicated previous results showing increased resilience among girls in an intervention group (Belgrave, Chase-Vaughn, Gray, Dixon-Addison, & Cherry, 2000).

MAAT Africentric Adolescent and Family Rites of Passage Program (Quasi-experimental, Level 3). Harvey and Hill (2004) implemented the Africentric Adolescent and Family Rites of Passage Program at the MAAT Center for Human and Organizational Enhancement in Washington, DC. Th e project targeted African American adolescents between the ages of 11.5 and 13.5 years and their families. Th e program aims to reduce substance abuse and antisocial behaviors and attitudes. Th e program's Africentric, strengths-based, family-centered approach is based on the ancient Egyptian principle of Maat. Components included an aft er-school program, activities to promote family enhancement and empowerment, and individual family counseling, all emphasizing African and African American culture. Findings from a three-year evaluation of the program demonstrated signifi cant gains in participating adolescents' self-esteem and knowledge about substance abuse. Among parents, sizeable but nonsignifi cant gains were made in parenting skills, racial identity, and community involvement. Additional evidence from focus groups suggests that the program's family-oriented, Africentric approach was advantageous for at-risk youths and that indigenous staff may have contributed to positive outcomes.

Kuumba Group (Uncontrolled, Pre-Post, Level 3). Th e Kuumba Group was piloted as a therapeutic, recreational group intervention with an emphasis on Afrocentric values, providing mentoring for male African Americans between the age of 9 and 17 (Washington et al., 2007). Th e purpose of the project was to prevent youths from being placed in foster care.Th e central strategy was to infuse Nguzo Saba themes into discussions and interactions as an inoculation to counteract the values associated with self-destructive behaviors and stereotypical media images. Implemented with individually and family-focused traditional child welfare and clinical services, curriculum components used previously tested comprehensive rites of passage program activities to aff ect cultural identity, self-exploration, value clarifi cations, and nonviolent confl ict resolution. Postintervention interviews with relative caregivers indicated slight increases in participants' spiritual orientation and improved school and home behavior among youths.

Substance Abuse and HIV Prevention

Substance abuse among African Americans has been linked to hopelessness, deterioration of communities, and self-destructive behavior associated with responses to oppressive conditions. Th e epidemic of substance abuse has existed in tandem with that of HIV infection, and although African Americans make up only 13 percent of the U.S. population, they accounted for over 50 percent of HIV and AIDS cases in 2003 (OMHHD, 2002). Africentric interventions to prevent and reduce substance abuse and HIV incidence include elements to help individuals counter oppressive conditions, maintain values congruent with healthy cultural identity, and participate in culturally congruent rituals.

Th e Culturally Congruent African-Centered Treatment Engagement Project (Quasi-Experimental, Level 3). Th is culturally congruent intervention applies Africentric concepts in single-session counseling with African American drug users (Grills, 2003; Longshore & Grills, 2000).Th e intervention method involves the client, the counselor, and a former drug user (peer) viewing a video about drug use together and discussing the topics together as a means of recovery; a dyadic counseling session follows, led by the counselor and joined by the peer,—to bolster recovery-related motivation. Integral to the content and format of the intervention are African and African American values— including spiritualism, interdependence, and transformative behavior based on the principles of Maat— and sociopolitical consciousness raising, in which drug abuse treatment and recovery is reframed as healing the African American community. Th e project evaluation determined that participants in the motivational Africentric intervention experience were signifi cantly less likely to be using drugs one year later. Findings suggest that culturally congruent values partnered with motivational interviewing techniques may help to advance participants through the transtheoretical stage-of-change process and promote overall recovery.

Healer Women Fighting Disease (Quasi-experimental, Level 3). Th is is an integrated HIV and substance abuse prevention program targeting African American women (Gilbert & Goddard, 2007; Nobles, Goddard & Gilbert, in press). Rooted in the African-centered behavioral change model, program components emphasize infusion of traditional African and African American cultural values based on the Nguzo Saba and Maat to address women's self-worth and sense of control of life; reinstill traditional cultural values to transform thoughts, feelings, and behavior; and help women develop protective factors that make them less likely to engage in risk-taking behaviors. Sixteen weekly two-hour sessions are delivered by African American facilitators in a community setting; components include behavioral skills practice, group discussions, role playing, and viewing of a prevention video. Findings show signifi cant changes from pretest to posttest in increasing motivation and decreasing depression (cultural realignment), increasing HIV/AIDS knowledge and self-worth (cognitive restructuring), and adopting less risky sexual practices (character development) for intervention participants relative to the comparison group. Outcomes suggest that integration of an African-centered approach demonstrates promise as a critical component in health promotion interventions for African Americans.

Th e JEMADARI Program (RCT, Level 2). Th is program is based on a Swahili word meaning "wise companion," which serves as a symbol of positive masculinity. Th e program is a culturally congruent, RCT intervention for African American men ages 18 to 63 residing in residential treatment programs. Th e program targets participants' drug and sexual risk-related behaviors (Gant, 2003).Th e intervention content is based on elements of the Nguzo Saba and includes vignettes and case studies taken from the works of contemporary and classic African American male writers and artists, literature on African American male sexuality, discussions of conditions of African American life (for example, slavery, economic hardship, social discrimination, social inequality, political disenfranchisement, racism), and themes of African American life (for example, political activity; achievement for self and family, race, and society; self-integrity; creativity; struggle). In a six-month follow-up evaluation, investigators assessed adaptive copings skills, perceptions of personal control, satisfaction with life direction, ethnic identity, and adaptive peer group support. In the preliminary fi ndings, JEMADARI program participants demonstrated drug abstinence, condom use, and reduction of sexual partners beyond levels achieved in the standard residential treatment program; the fi nal analysis indicated a statistically signifi cant decrease in number of sexual partners in the past three months from pretest to posttest for the JEMADARI group as compared with the control group (Gant, 2007).

SOCIAL WORK IMPLICATIONS

Th e general fi ndings for the sample programs presented here support the effi cacy of infusing Africentric values and an African-centered approach in programs that target the healthy development of African American children and adults. Th e hierarchical range of these studies indicates that Africentric research is moving beyond anecdotal and descriptive cases and replication of existing interventions showing effi cacy would build a strong case for evidence-based Africentric practice. Although nonrandomized studies can provide relevant empirical support, whenever possible, Africentric interventions should involve randomized selection of treatment and control groups, building toward at least two RCTs conducted by diff erent research teams. To advance the replication of studies across diff erent research teams, researchers must produce and disseminate treatment manuals with clear and detailed descriptions of the intervention components. For example, of the programs discussed here, the recently manualized Sisters of Nia and Healer Women Fighting Disease interventions can now be replicated by other teams of researchers. Finally, researchers should work toward increasing peer-reviewed publication of results across multiple teams of researchers, which will build the knowledge base for Africentric EBP.

A number of implications can be drawn from the discussion, centering on the intersection of education, practice, and research—specifically implications related to the profession's slowness in incorporating Africentric teaching and research. Over the past decade, there have been a number of appeals to social work to take a lead in addressing the inequities and social conditions that afflict many African Americans. Allen-Meares and Burman (1995) described the lack of social work leadership in this area as a "discomforting silence from the social work community" (p. 271). Social workers are on the frontlines of working with clients who experience social, mental health, and health disparities, and they are in the best position to create better awareness and advocacy at local, state, and national levels.

Further discussion of Africentric approaches to working with African American children, adults, families, and community groups is warranted given the significant disparities in areas where social work is highly engaged. Schools of social work are held accountable for developing comprehensive curriculums that prepare students to deliver social services effectively within a complex society. Greater infusion of Africentric theory and research fits with the NASW (2000) *Code of Ethics* on acquisition of cultural competence as an ethical standard and with the Council on Social Work Education's mandate to teaching cultural competency. Awareness of and knowledge about Africentric interventions should be well integrated into professional schools of social work, as are other models of practice. Schiele (1997) noted that "Afrocentric knowledge should not be marginalized or relegated to discrete, elective, or required courses but rather infused throughout all areas of social work curricula" (p. 816). Advancing these ideas within the social work academic and research setting will require continued focus on engaging social work education and practice professionals.

One major barrier to full integration of an Africentric paradigm into social work curriculums and practice is that Africentric programs lack cohesive documentation, which limits their chances of being established as best practices or EBPs through replication and multiple trials. At the same time, we know that culturally relevant interventions are more likely to lead to enduring behavior change than are interventions that do not consider a client's culture and social context (Davis, 1997; Nobles & Goddard, 1993). Advocacy for increased Africentric discourse on EBP will begin to close this gap. Africentric scholars who want to advance Africentric interventions are encouraged to work in interdisciplinary teams, especially when they are disseminating information or seeking state and federal funding sources. Building professional and research alliances within the field of psychology, specifically among Africentric psychologists and other affiliated professionals, is also important to advancing the scientific discourse on the effectiveness of Africentric interventions.

CONCLUSION

Although African Americans are widely resilient, many of the problems they face are rooted in impoverished living conditions and stressful life events resulting from historical oppression and loss of culture and identity. Africentric interventions address structural (macro) and individual (micro) challenges to promote well-being and, as such, are consistent with social work's commitment to social justice for vulnerable populations. More efforts should be made to disseminate information about existing Africentric interventions, with emphasis on documenting those that have been evaluated and those that are in need of additional studies, with the aim of developing guidelines for evidence-based

Africentric practice. Our work here is a start in that direction. On the evidence of the literature review, a number of programs are achieving success with various African American subpopulations; programs are being implemented by both psychologists and social workers who are committed to working with African American populations. Funding to increase the number of RCTs will help in developing the necessary evidence of eff ectiveness. Smaller projects and community-based grassroots programs continue to struggle with funding, but incorporating manualized interventions and control groups at this level would add substantially to the research base. Th rough documentation of the existing programs, dissemination can lead to replication, and the discourse will be advanced to develop guidelines and further studies of Africentric best practices. Our larger work of capturing the comprehensive scope of Africentric interventions in a single volume will help to facilitate greater dissemination and replication of promising interventions. We hope this article starts a trend of Africentric scholars talking to each other across disciplines, sharing manualized treatments, and working collaboratively to build evidence-based Africentric research.

REFERENCES

Akbar, N. (1984). Africentric social sciences for human liberation. *Journal of Black Studies, 14, 395–414.*

Allen-Meares, P., & Burman, S. (1995).Th e endangerment of African American men: An appeal for social work action [Comments on Currents]. *Social Work, 40,* 268–274.

Asante, M. (1988). *Afrocentricity: Th e theory of social change.* Trenton, NJ: Africa World Press.

Attewell, P., Lavin, D., Th urston, D., & Levey, T. (2004).Th e black middle class: Progress, prospects and puzzles. *Journal of African American Studies, 8*(1/2), 6–19.

Belgrave, F. Z. (2002). Relational theory and cultural enhancement interventions for African American adolescent girls. *Public Health Reports, 117,* 76–81.

Belgrave, F. Z., Chase-Vaughn, G., Gray, F., Dixon-Addison, J., & Cherry,V. R. (2000).Th e eff ectiveness of a culture and gender-specifi c intervention for increasing resiliency among African American preadolescent females. *Journal of Black Psychology, 26,* 133–147.

Belgrave, F. Z., Reed, M. C., Plybon, L. E., Butler, D. S., Allison, K. W, & Davis, T. (2004).An evaluation of Sisters of Nia: A cultural program for African American girls. *Journal of Black Psychology, 30,* 329–343.

Belgrave, F. Z.,Townsend, T., Cherry, V., & Cunningham, D. (1997). Th e infl uence of an Africentric worldview and demographic variables on drug knowledge, attitudes, and use among African American youth. *Journal of Community Psychology, 25,* 421–433.

Bernal, G., & Scharron-del-Rio, M. R. (2001). Are empirically supported treatments valid for ethnic minorities? Toward an alternative approach for treatment research. *Cultural Diversity and Ethnic Minority Psychology, 7,* 328–342.

Carlton-LaNey, I. (1999). African American social work pioneers' response to need. *Social Work, 44,* 311–321.

Cherry, V. R., Belgrave, F. Z., Jones,W., Kofi Kennon, D., Gray, F. S., & Phillips, F. (1998). NTU: An Africentric approach to substance abuse prevention among African American youth. *Journal of Primary Prevention, 18,* 319–339.

Chipungu, S. S., Hermann, J., Sambrano, S., Nistler, M., Sale, E., & Springer, J. F. (2000). Prevention programming for African American youth: A review of strategies in CSAP's national cross-site evaluation of high-risk youth programs. *Journal of Black Psychology, 26,* 360–385.

Constantine, M. G., Alleyne,V. L., & Wallace, B. C. (2006). Africentric cultural values: Th eir relation to positive mental health in African American adolescent girls. *Journal of Black Psychology, 32,* 141–154.

Daly, A., Jennings, J., Beckett, J. O., & Leashore, B. R. (1995). Eff ective coping strategies of African Americans. *Social Work, 40,* 240–248.

Daniels, J. (2001). Africentric social work practice. *International Social Work, 44,* 301–310.

Davis, K. (1997). *Consumer driven standards and guidelines in managed mental health for populations of African descent: Final report on cultural competence.* Rockville, MD: Center for Mental Health Services.

DeGruy-Leary, J. (2005).Th e African American Adolescent Respect Scale: A measure of a prosocial attitude. *Research on Social Work Practice, 15*, 462–469.

Dixon, A., Schoonmaker, C., & Philliber.W. (2000). A journey towards womanhood: Eff ects of an Acrocentric approach to pregnancy prevention among African-American female adolescents. *Adolescence, 35*, 425–429.

DuBois, B., & Miley, K. (1996). *Social work: An empowering profession* (2nd ed.). Boston: Allyn & Bacon.

Freeman, E. M., & Logan, S. L. (2004). Common heritage and diversity among black families and communities: An Afrocentric research paradigm. In E. M. Freeman & S. L. Logan (Eds.), *Reconceptualizing the strengths and common heritage of black families: Practice, research and policy issues* (pp. 5–24). Springfi eld, IL: Charles C. Th omas.

Gant, L. M. (2003, July). *Evaluation of the JEMADARI Program.* Paper presented at the National HIV Prevention Conference, Atlanta.

Gant, L. M. (2007,April). *HIV/AIDS risk reduction programs for drug dependent persons: Th e JEMADARI Research Project.* Paper presented at the University of Pittsburgh School of Social Work.

Germain, C. B. (1991). *Human behavior in the social environment.* New York: Columbia University Press.

Gibson, P. A., & McRoy, R. G. (2004). Cultural maintenance: Building on the common heritage of black families. In E. M. Freeman & S. L. Logan (Eds.), *Reconceptualizing the strengths and common heritage of black families: Practice, research, and policy issues* (pp. 237–265). Springfi eld, IL: Charles C Th omas.

Gilbert, D., & Goddard, L. (2007). HIV prevention targeting African American women: Th eory, objectives, and outcomes from an African-centered behavior change perspective. *Family & Community Health, 30*(Suppl. 1), S109–S111.

Graham, M. (2005). *Maat*: An African-centered paradigm for psychological and spiritual healing. In R. Moodley & W. West (Eds.), *Integrating traditional healing practices into counseling and psychotherapy* (pp. 210–220). Th ousand Oaks, CA: Sage Publications.

Grills, C. T. (2003). Substance abuse and African Americans: Th e need for Africentric-based substance abuse treatment models. In D. J. Gilbert & E. M.Wright (Eds.), *African-American women and HIV/AIDS: Critical responses* (pp. 51–72). Westport, CT: Praeger.

Harvey, A. R. (1985). *Th e black family: An Afro-centric perspective.* New York: United Church of Christ Commission for Racial Justice.

Harvey, A. R. (1997). Group work with African-American youth in the criminal justice system. In G. L. Grief & Ph. H. Ephross (Eds.), *Group work with populations at risk* (pp. 160–174). New York: Oxford University Press.

Harvey, A. R. (2003). A general paradigm of African-centered social work: A social work paradigm shift in the liberation for the liberation of African people. In D. A.Azibo (Ed.), *African-centered psychology: Culture-focusing for multicultural competence* (pp. 109–128). Durham, NC: Carolina Academic Press.

Harvey, A. R., & Hill, R. B. (2004). Africentric youth and family rites of passage program: Promoting resilience among at-risk African American youths. *Social Work, 49*, 65–74.

Harvey, A. R., & Rauch, J. B. (1997). A comprehensive Afrocentric rites of passage program for black male adolescents. *Health & Social Work, 22*, 30–37.

Hill, R. B. (1971). *Strengths of black families.* New York: Emerson-Hall.

Hill, R. B. (1999). *Strengths of African American families: Twenty-fi ve years later.* Lanham, MD: University Press of America.

Hilliard, A. S. (1997). *Th e reawakening of the African mind.* Gainsville, FL: Makare.

Karenga, M. (1996).Th e Nguzo Saba (the seven principles): Th eir meaning and message. In M. K. Asante & A. S. Abarry (Eds.), *African intellectual heritage: A book of sources* (pp. 543–554). Philadelphia: Temple University Press.

Longshore, D., & Grills, C. (2000). Motivating illegal drug use recovery: Evidence for a culturally congruent intervention. *Journal of Black Psychology, 26*, 288–301.

Manning, M., Cornelius, L., & Okundaye, J. (2004). Empowering African Americans through social work practice: Integrating an Afrocentric perspective, ego psychology, and spirituality. *Families in Society, 85*, 229–235.

Myers, L. J. (1988). *Understanding an Afrocentric world view: Introduction to an optimal psychology*. Dubuque, IA: Kendall/Hunt.

National Association of Social Workers. (2000). *Code of ethics of the National Association of Social Worker*. Washington, DC: Author.

Nobles, W. W., & Goddard, L. L.(1993). Toward an African-centered model of prevention for African American youth at high risk. In L. L. Goddard (Ed.), *An African-centered model of prevention for African American youth at high risk* (pp. 115–129). Rockville, MD: U.S. Department of Health and Human Services/Public Health Service/Substance Abuse and Mental Health Services Administration.

Nobles,W. W., & Goddard, L. L., Gilbert, D. J. (in press). Culturecology, women and African-centered HIV prevention .*Journal of Black Psychology.*

Offi ce of Minority Health & Health Disparities. (2002). *Eliminate disparities in mental health [Fact sheet]*. Retrieved
January 19, 2009, from http://www.cdc. gov/omhd/AMH/factsheets/mental.htm

Parham. T. A. (2002). *Counseling persons of African descent*. Th ousand Oaks, CA: Sage Publications.

Proctor, E. K., & Rosen, A. (2006). Concise standards for developing evidence-based practice guidelines. In A. R. Roberts & K. Yeager (Eds.), *Foundations of evidence- based social work practice* (pp. 93–102). New York: Oxford University Press.

Roberts, A., Jackson, M., & Carlton-LaNey, I. (2000). Revisiting the need for feminism and Afrocentric theory when treating African-American female substance abusers. *Journal of Drug Issues, 30*, 901–917.

Roberts, A. R.,Yeager, K., & Regehr, C. (2006). Bridging evidence-based health care and social work: How to search for, develop, and use evidence-based studies. In A. R. Roberts & K. Yeager (Eds.), *Foundations of evidencebased social work practice* (pp. 3–20). New York: Oxford University Press.

Saleebey, D. (1992). *Th e strengths perspective in social work practice*. New York: Longman.

Schiele, J. H. (1996). Afrocentricity: An emerging paradigm in social work practice. *Social Work, 41*, 284–294.

Schiele, J. H. (1997).Th e contour and meaning of Afrocentric social work. *Journal of Black Studies, 21*, 800–819.

Schiele, J. H. (2000). *Human services and the Afro-centric paradigm*. Binghamton, NY: Haworth Press.

Sherr, M. (2006).Th e Afrocentric paradigm: A pragmatic discourse about social work practice with African Americans. *Journal of Human Behavior in the Social Environment, 13*(3), 1–17.

Smedley, B. D, Adrienne Y. S., & Alan R. N. (Eds.). (2002). *Unequal treatment: Confronting racial and ethnic disparities in healthcare*. Washington, DC: National Academies Press.

Solomon, B. B. (1976). *Black empowerment: Social work in oppressed communities*. New York: Columbia University Press.

Swigonski, M. (1996). Challenging privilege through Africentric social work practice. *Social Work, 41*, 153–161.

Th omas, D., Townsend,T., & Belgrave, E. (2003).Th e infl uence of cultural and racial identifi cation on the psychosocial adjustment of inner-city African American children in school. *American Journal of Community Psychology, 32*, 217–228.

Th yer, B. A. (2006).What is evidence-based practice? In A. R. Roberts & K.Yeager (Eds.), *Foundations of evidencebased social work practice* (pp. 35–46). New York: Oxford University Press.

U.S. Census Bureau. (2004). *U.S. interim projections by age, sex, race, and Hispanic origin*. Retrieved January 19, 2009, from http://www.census.gov/ipc/www/ usinterimproj

Washington, G., Johnson,T., Jones, J., & Langs, S. (2007). African-American boys in relative care and a culturally centered group mentoring approach. *Social Work with Groups, 30*(1), 45–68.

White, R. (2004). Social work and African-centered world views. *Journal of Ethnic & Cultural Diversity in Social Work, 13*, 122–125.

Building on Strengths

Intergenerational Practice with African American Families
Cheryl Waites

Intergenerational kinship and multigenerational families (three or more generations) have been a source of strength for African Americans. Th is article presents a culturally responsive intergenerational practice model for working with African American families that draws on this legacy. Th e model looks at intergenerational kinship and multigenerational families through an Afrocentric, intergenerational solidarity framework. It provides a means to understand and support the strengths and resource richness of intergenerational relationships; the Afrocentric paradigm's affi rmation of family and cultural strengths; and the power of intergenerational kinship, family solidarity, and support across generations. Building on the six solidarity elements of the intergenerational solidarity framework, this model provides an empowerment-oriented approach for social work practice with African American families that takes into consideration cultural values and practices.

Family networks, composed of several generations (three of more), have been a source of strength for African American families. Multigenerations providing support and care for family members and fi ctive kin (non-blood relatives) across the life course have been well documented (Billingsley, 1992; Billingsley & Morrison-Rodriguez, 1998; Hill, 1971, 1993, 1998, 1999; Martin & Martin, 1985; McAdoo, 1998; Schiele, 1996, 2000). Born out of African traditions and adaptation to a harsh environment, multigenerational families have persevered in the face of disparity and oppression spanning 400 years of slavery, years of "Jim Crow," and decades of segregation, marginalization, and intentional and unintentional racism (Christian, 1995). Despite these obstacles, people of African descent have a legacy of intergenerational kinship, resilience, spirituality, and hope (Bagley & Carroll, 1998; Denby, 1996). Multigenerational families and intergenerational kinships have played a signifi cant role in preserving and strengthening African American families.

As our society ages, multigenerational families will be more common, resulting in longer years of "shared lives" across generations (Bengtson, 2001; Bengtson & Roberts, 1991). It has been predicted that there will be almost equal bands of older adults, middle generation adults, young adults, adolescents, and children as we move deeper into the 21st century (U.S. Census Bureau, 2004). Th is statistic holds true for African Americans. Th e numbers of African American elders, age 65 and older, are increasing. Between 1980 and 1995, the number of African Americans increased from 2.1 million to 2.7 million (a 29 percent increase). Th is group is expected to expand to 6.9 million by 2030 and 8.6 million by 2050 (Miles, 1999). Individuals are now more likely to grow older in four-, or even more, generation families;

spend an unprecedented number of years in family roles such as grandparent and great-grandparent; and remain part of a network of intergenerational family ties (Bengtson, 2001; Bengtson, Rosenthal, & Burton, 1990; Hagestad, 1996; Riley, 1987). Kin, and non-kin, will be available to provide care and assistance to younger families (King, 1994; Silverstein, Parrott, & Bengtson, 1995) and caregiving for dependent elders (Bengtson et al., 1990). In view of the changing demographics, it is important to revisit cultural values regarding how families interact across generations.

Historically, cultural values, family practices, and strengths, such as special care for children and elders, kinship ties, and collectivism have been part of African American life (Barnes, 2001). Hill (1971, 1999) wrote eloquently about five strengths of African American families: strong achievement orientation, strong work orientation, flexible family roles, strong kinship bonds, and strong religious orientation. Hill and others have pointed to strengths that are linked to history, culture, values, and cultural adaptations and suggested that building on these strengths is a good strategy for working with African American families (Freeman & Logan, 2004; Logan, 2001; McAdoo, 1998; McCullough-Chavis & Waites, 2004; Staples, 1999). Strong kinship ties, intergenerational support, faith, and coming together during times of need have been effective resources for African American families.

Today's social environment, and the challenges individuals and families face, warrant use and revitalization of cultural strengths. Problems such as drug and alcohol addiction, overrepresentation of African American children in foster care, HIV and AIDS, health disparities, high rates of incarceration, unemployment, and poverty are severe and complex. Many individuals and families have demonstrated remarkable resilience; others have suffered. Effective strategies to help families as they contend with pressing issues are rooted in African American cultural strengths. Cultural values and practices that sustained families in the past can be used to empower families today. Use of the power of intergenerational kinships and multigenerational family support can serve to preserve and strengthen vulnerable African American families.

Over the past 20 years, a number of practice approaches have been proposed for culturally competent practice with African Americans and other ethnic and racial groups. Strengths-based, empowermentoriented, ethnically sensitive, constructionist, Afrocentric, and social justice frameworks have been used to guide practice with African American families. Such frameworks provide models by which social problems are assessed and intervention strategies are outlined. Many recognize multigenerational and extended family strengths. However, there is a need for an approach that builds on and restores the strengths of multigenerational families and intergenerational kinship. This approach may include restoring the influence of the extended family's multigenerational network so that relatives and fictive kin are encouraged to remain involved with family members and step forward to provide support and care. An Afrocentric, intergenerational solidarity approach that acknowledges the family life cycle, as well as the values and traditions that have sustained people of African descent, is a mechanism for promoting family closeness and responsibility. Embracing the legacies and wisdom of past generations and the hope and promise of the future is a framework for best practice. This article describes an intergenerational model that can be used to understand and provide support and assistance to African American families. The model defines families of African descent from an Afrocentric intergenerational perspective. It highlights the history and interconnectedness of African American families and communities and takes into account the temporal nature of the family life cycle.

AN INTERGENERATIONAL PERSPECTIVE: THEORETICAL FOUNDATIONS FOR PRACTICE

An intergenerational perspective is relevant to social work practice with African American families. It brings an awareness of and attention to kinship, intergenerational relationships, and multigenerational families. Strengths, values, and practices that are transmitted across generations, family life cycle stages, intergenerational support, and current cultural context are central to this perspective (Waites, 2008). It provides a framework for understanding the past, exploring the current environment, and using culturally relevant strategies and practices to empower families.

Intergenerational Solidarity

Family relationships across generations are becoming increasingly important. Changes in family age structures are creating longer years of shared lives (Bengtson, 2001). Bengtson stated that "intergenerational bonds are more important than nuclear family ties for well-being and support over the life course" (Bengtson, 2001, p. 7). With increased longevity, parents, grandparents, and other relatives can be available to serve as resources for younger generations. Kin, across several generations, will increasingly be called on to provide essential family functions; intergenerational support and care will increase over time.

Bengtson and his colleagues (Bengtson & Roberts, 1991; Bengtson & Schrader, 1982) provided a multidimensional construct for understanding intergenerational relationships. Derived from classical social theory, social psychology, and family sociology, their intergenerational solidarity model examines social cohesion between generations. Th e construct evolved from a longitudinal study consisting of a cross-sectional survey with more than 2,044 participants from three generational families. Data were collected at three intervals, including the great-grandchild generation. From this research, Bengtson and others (Bengston & Mangen, 1988; Bengston & Schrader, 1982; Roberts, Richards, & Bengtson, 1991) constructed an intergenerational solidarity taxonomy for understanding intergenerational relationships. Th ese six elements provide a mechanism for understanding intergenerational relationships and are discussed later in greater detail.

Afrocentric Worldview

An Afrocentric paradigm fi ts nicely with the intergenerational solidarity framework because it affi rms human capacities and family and cultural strengths and promotes intergenerational connections. It presents a worldview that highlights traditional African philosophical assumptions, which emphasize a holistic, interdependent, and spiritual conception of people and their environment (Schiele, 2000).

Th e Afrocentric paradigm affi rms that there are universal cultural strengths and an African worldview that survived the generational devastations caused by the transatlantic slave trade and the oppression that followed. As a result, it is important to understand and respect the customs, practices, and values that are central to African American families and communities.Th ese cultural strengths, as previously described, can be used in micro, meso, and macro interventions to enhance the lives of all people, particular people of color (Schiele, 2000). Families are at the heart of the intergenerational perspective. Families have shared history and futures (Carter & McGoldrick, 1999); they move through time together. Th e sharing of history and futures and the moving through time together are oft en referred to as family life cycle stages. Th eses stages have been identifi ed as leaving home, single young adults joining of families through marriage, the new couple, families with young children, families with adolescents, launching children and moving on, and families in later life (Carter & McGoldrick, 1999). Relationships with parents, siblings, grandparents, and other family members experience transitions as each group moves along the family life cycle. Multiple family units are formed (for example, families with young children and families in later life), and all are a part of the larger multigenerational family. In this respect, there is a temporal reality associated with multigenerational families, and the family life cycle provides some descriptive information regarding how families move across time.

Th e stages described by Carter and McGoldrick (1999) laid a foundation for understanding African American families and family life cycle stages. African cultural traditions, environmental realities, and the diversity of family forms—which evolved from cultural traditions and adaptations to hardships—are also relevant. Th ey provide insights regarding intergenerational relationships and temporal stages. A legacy of strong intergenerational kinship, multi-generational families, and extended family networks is refl ected in Hill's (1999) fl exible family roles. For example, caregiving is an important value for African American families. Grandparents may step in to assist or raise a grandchild. A single parent may depend on support from parents, or grandparents, aft er a child is born. African American children raised by grandparents oft en feel fi lial obligations to care for parents and grandparents (Ruiz & Carlton-LaNey, 1999). Extended family may play important roles and provide support and care to young and older adult relatives. Multigenerations may live in the same residence and pool their resources. For African American families, the family life cycle stages have signifi cant intergenerational patterns of assistance and care that are reciprocal over time. Th ese intergenerational supports, in some cases, may be in need of validation, nurturing, and revitalization to strengthen and support troubled families (Waites, 2008).

AFROCENTRIC INTERGENERATIONAL PRACTICE

Th e Afrocentric intergenerational practice model presented here builds on the solidarity construct and the Afrocentric paradigm. It acknowledges the diversity and fl exibility of the family life cycle and brings attention to traditions and cultural infl uences, specifi cally, caregiving, kinship bonds, the intercon- nectedness of families, and extended families. It refl ects an approach that respects and supports the strengths and resilience of intergenerational kinship. Th is practice model's basic principles promote a society that values all generations and

- recognizes that each generation has unique strengths—each person, young and older, is a resource
- recognizes the roles of youths, middle generations, and elders in families and communities
- acknowledges confl icts that may occur in intergenerational relationships
- encourages collaboration and support across generations
- fosters intergenerational kinship and interdependence
- fosters public policy that recognizes and addresses the needs of all generations
- supports and nurtures family and cultural strengths

Th is model is culturally responsive in that it uses strategies that are compatible with culturally competent practice and transforms knowledge and cultural awareness into interventions that support and sustain healthy family functioning (McPhatter, 1997; Waites, Macgowan, Pennell, Carlton-LaNey, & Weil, 2004).

Afrocentric Intergenerational Solidarity Model

Th e Afrocentric intergenerational solidarity model consists of six solidarity elements and provides indicators of intergenerational cohesion. Th e infusion of an Afrocentric worldview provides culturally relevant issues, questions, and empowerment-oriented strategies. Th e fi rst element, *associational solidarity*, focuses on the type and frequency of contact between generations (see Table 1). Examining the amount and nature of intergenerational contact is at the forefront. Within an Afrocentric worldview, assessing family traditions and history regarding communication is important. Once information is obtained, a process of nurturing, reinforcing, and revitalizing contact and communication among family members can be undertaken. Intergenerational communication may go beyond phone calls; traditions such as Sunday dinners, regular family visits, family reunions, special events, and other celebrations are mechanism for connections. Intergenerational communication can lead to strong supportive networks and enhance the amount and quality of intergenerational contact.

Th e second element, *aff ectional solidarity*, addresses the expressed closeness, warmth, and trust found in intergenerational kinships. Th e indicators call for the practitioner to look at emotional ties to family and community, signs of intergenerational confl ict, and the overall reciprocity of positive sentiment among family members and across generations. With an Afrocentric view, affi liations with and sentiments toward the extended family, and the African American community as a whole, must also be explored.Th e goal is to assess and address the issues of aff ection, trust, and closeness and to support and nurture relational understanding and reciprocity across generations.

Th e third element, *consensual solidarity*, looks at agreements of values and beliefs. Th e indicators call for an assessment of intrafamilial concordance. Assessing the transmission and agreement of Afrocentric values, beliefs, and traditions, as well as the cultural strengths, enhances the cultural relevance of practice. Understanding family members' generational diff erences and their willingness to build intergenerational respect, dialogue, and collaboration is also important. Th e model suggests that practitioners encourage the understanding and recognition of cultural strengths. In addition, attempts should be made to support family and extended family as they engage in history reminding, consciousness raising, and intergenerational understanding and respect.

Th e fourth element, *functional solidarity*, addresses the frequency of intergenerational exchanges of assistance and resources. Th e indicators direct the assessment of help giving and receiving and how families assist and support each other. Th e role of collectivism, extended family support, and community support from churches, lodges, fraternal orders, and so forth are also assessed. Mechanisms to support equable intergenerational care and the use of formal and informal resources are suggested. Th is may include extended family, fi ctive kin, church family, intergenerational programs, or other community resources.

Normative solidarity, the fi ft h element, looks at fi lial responsibility and obligations. Th e indicators are family roles and the strength of obligation to those roles. Th e Afrocentric worldview expands this sense of obligation not only to parents, grandparents, children, and grandchildren, but also to the extended family, fi ctive kin, and the community as a whole. Intergenerational family and extended family support, and the use of community programs and formal resources, are encouraged.

Th e sixth and last element, *structural solidarity*, highlights the opportunity for intergenerational interaction as it relates to residential propinquity. For example, some older adults reside with their children or grandchildren in coresidential situations or in the same community. Th is arrangement aff ords them great intergenerational access. Some families, however, may move far away and relocate due to employment opportunities elsewhere. Older adults may be unable to travel to family or community events due to distant locations, health issues, or limited access to convenient and aff ordable transportation. Both latter situations aff ect opportunities to maintain close contact. Th e empirical indicators focus on the residential proximity of family members, the number of family members, and health and disability issues.

Table 1: Intergenerational Solidarity with an Afrocentric Worldview

Construct - Element	Definition	Indicators	Culturally Relevant Issues
Associational solidarity	Frequency and patterns of interaction in various types of activities in which family members engage	• Frequency of intergenerational interaction (that is, face-to-face, telephone, mail) • Types of common activities shared (that is, recreation, special occasion, and so forth)	• Family history, traditions, and practices regarding family communication patterns, and family gatherings and activities • Intergenerational family members' access to one another (that is, transportation, telephone, computer literacy)
Affectional solidarity	Type and degree of positive sentiments about family members, and the degree of reciprocity of these sentiments	• Ratings of affection, warmth, closeness, understanding, trust, and respect for family members • Ratings of perceived reciprocity in positive sentiments among family members	• Preeminence of close parent–child relationship, grandparent relationships, extended family relationships, and so forth
Consensual solidarity	Degree of agreement on values, attitudes, and beliefs among family members	• Intrafamilial concordance among individual measures of specific values, attitudes, and beliefs • Ratings of perceived similarity with other family members in values, attitudes, and beliefs	• Connections with Afrocentric values and practices (that is, respect for elders, special care for children and elders, kinship ties, spirituality, collectivism, and so forth) • Generational values, similarities, and differences
Functional solidarity	Degree of helping and exchanges of resources—giving and receiving support across generations	• Frequency of intergenerational exchanges of assistance (for example, financial, physical, emotional) • Ratings of reciprocity in the intergenerational exchange of resources	• Supportive behaviors and traditions (that is, role of children, parents, grandparents, extended family, the church, lodges and fraternal orders, and so forth in providing support and care)
Normative solidarity	Strength of commitment to performance of familial roles and familial obligations	• Ratings of importance of family and intergenerational roles • Ratings of strength of filial obligations	• Afrocentric holistic, collectivist orientation • Filial beliefs and responsibilities (that is, intergenerational support for at-risk youths, young families, and dependent elders) • Availability of aunts, uncles, children, extended family, church family, and other supports
Structural solidarity	Opportunity structure for intergenerational relationships reflected in number, type, and geographic proximity of family member	• Residential propinquity of family members • Number of family members • Health of family members	• Location of family and extended family members • Migration history • Transportation and travel distances and resources

Source: Bengtson, V. L. & Roberts, R E L. (1991). Intergenerational solidarity in aging families: An example of formal theory construction. *Journal of Marriage and the Family, 53,* 856–870.

Afrocentric worldviews expand this element so that migration patterns, transportation issues, and travel distances are included. Th e empowerment strategy focuses on helping families rethink how to address structural proximity barriers. Th is could take the form of family members organizing and sharing transportation resources or establishing a family "home place" or location where family members can gather for respite, celebrations, and support.

Using This Model

Th is model is not complicated and can be used in harmony with other empowerment-oriented approaches. A culturally appropriate assessment of intergenerational issues and resources is conducted. Practitioners are directed to explore each of the intergenerational solidarity elements with family members using the practice strategies outlined in Table 2.

Associational solidarity is explored by asking family members questions about their family traditions and how they communicate and keep in touch with each other. Family solidarity is enhanced when there are traditions, activities, and history that serve to keep family members connected—for example, Sunday dinners at a relative's home, regular phone calls, church or religious service attendance, family reunions, birthday celebrations, or Christmas or other holiday activities. Th e practitioner can work with family members to use a variety of practice strategies (outlined in Table 2) to help family members improve their associational solidarity. Th is might include encouraging family members to plan and or participate in family events. Participation in family events can lead to more cross-generational communication and contact.

Aff ectional solidarity questions are posed to family members by fi rst exploring whom they feel particularly close to and why. Helping family members understand their traditions regarding family roles and relationships and how they infl uence aff ectional solidarity is an important practice strategy. Aff ectional solidarity can be nurtured by encouraging a sense of intergenerational kinship—that is, aff ection for family and extended family members. It encompasses cultivation of intergenerational relationships. Th e practitioner role is to aid family members in identifying and developing closer ties.

Consensual solidarity is also important and can be explored by discussing family values and by affi rming a shared vision for family life. Exploring family members' perceptions and generation differences and similarities provides information regarding family solidarity. Gauging the family's sense of cultural pride and their African American identify is also pertinent. Cultural pride can serve as a unifying force for family solidarity. History reminding to facilitate appreciation of family cultural strengths is appropriate as a practice strategy and might include providing information about cultural history, supporting family opportunities to share thoughts and information about cultural values and beliefs, and engaging family members in activities that will enhance cultural pride. Communities oft en have Kwanzaa celebrations, concerts, and religious-related programs; watch movies and videos; read books; or engage in culturally inspired storytelling activities. Th ese resources can serve as activities and information that connect the generations and facilitate consensual solidarity.

Functional solidarity is assessed by identifi cation of the "go-to" family members when someone needs assistance. It is also important to identify family roles and resources and how support and care are exchanged across the family and the generations. Th e practice strategy is to create or restore the family helping network and involves helping family members to embrace shared responsibility and intergenerational support and care for all family members.

Normative solidarity is assessed by exploring expectations regarding family roles. It is also crucial to discuss what happens when someone is not able to perform the designated role. What are the family norms for who should step in? The practice strategy is to affirm, strengthen, and formalize the family members' commitment to one another. This may take the form of encouraging the development of

Table 2: Afrocentric Intergenerational Solidarity Model—Questions and Practice Strategies

Associational Solidarity Questions

- Tell me about your family's traditions (holiday celebrations, Sunday dinners, family reunions, special events, and so forth).
- How do you participate?
- How does your family keep in touch? How do you keep in touch?

Practice Strategies

- Encourage cross-generation communication, and contact.
- Help family consider methods to communicate and to support each other.
- Encourage family members to participate in family events (family reunions, and so forth) and efforts to remain connected.

Affectional Solidarity Questions

- Tell me about the family members you feel close to.
- What makes you feel particularly close to this person?
- Tell me about your extended family and others who are like family. Do you feel close to them?
- Are their certain relationships or duties that you must honor and respect?

Practice Strategies

- Nurture relationship building, intergenerational kinship, and equable care.
- Encourage supportive family and extended family closeness.

Consensual Solidarity Questions

- Tell me about your family's history—your grandparents, great grandparents, and so forth.
- What were/are important values, beliefs, and traditions in your family?
- Do you and family members have similar values and beliefs regarding __(sex, religion, education, drugs, etc.)?
- Do you feel a connection and pride with the African American community? What type of cultural activities do you and your family participate in?

Practice Strategies

- Engage family in history reminding to facilitate an understanding of cultural and family strengths.
- Facilitate healing by engaging family in activities that will enhance cultural pride and self-esteem.
- Encourage intergenerational respect and help family members acknowledge their shared visions.
- Help family recognize intergenerational resources and strengths.

Functional Solidarity Questions

- How does your family respond when one of its members needs assistance?
- Who are the family members with resources (good, steady job; a home; savings; and so forth) in your family? Are they obligated to help out others in the family? Is there an exchange of resources?
- Do older family members feel obligated to help out younger family members, and is this help reciprocal?

Practice Strategies

- Support flexible family roles and intergenerational kinship.
- Encourage reciprocal intergenerational support and care.
- Assist family in using informal (extended family, church or faith based, and so forth) and formal support systems and recourses.

Normative Solidarity Questions

- What roles do parents, grandparents, children, adult daughters and sons, aunts, uncles, and so forth play in your family?
- In your family, what happens when someone is not able to function in his or her role as parent, son, daughter, caregiver, and so forth?

Practice Strategies

- Encourage and support caregiving and other family commitments.
- Develop multigenerational family support programs for grandparents, and other kin, raising children and for children caring for dependent elders.
- Encourage the development of an extended family support systems.

Structural Solidarity Questions

- Where do your family members live?
- What led them to move to _____? Do you visit?
- How do family members travel when they visit one another? Are there any barriers to visiting?
- Does your family have a "home place," a residence where family members gather for special occasions?

Practice Strategies

- Help family overcome travel- and visiting-related barriers.
- Help family members identify a plan for staying connected.
- Develop community intergenerational programs.

multigenerational networks where children, parents, grandparents, aunts, and uncles all play a role in supporting and caring for family members. Because this responsibility can be demanding, connecting families with community resources such as family support programs, support groups for caregivers, and other programs that serve to strengthen families and extended family helping is crucial.

Structural solidarity is explored by assessing family proximity. Some families use the home of a family member to gather for celebrations or other rituals: It is their home place. Other families do not have a central location, and some family members may live great distances from the family core of the home place. Th e role of the practitioner is to help family members explore proximity issues and overcome barriers to traveling and visiting with relatives. Th is help might include pooling of resources so that all family members can attend the family reunions, church or religious services, and health and wellness care. Providing assistance to families in the use of strategies to support involvement in family and extended family activities could help family members to visit and stay connected.

Use of this model involves the exploration of all solidarity elements. Family members and families may show strengths in a specifi c area. If not, the practitioner can then use one or all of the strategies suggested in the Practice Strategy sections of Table 2. To follow are three vignettes that present contemporary family issues and suggested strategies.

Vignette One. Denise is a 32-year-old African American single, divorced mother who is trying to cope with caregiving for both her son and her grandmother. Denise's nine-year-old son, David, has been referred to the school social worker due to excessive absences from school. Her 69-year-old grandmother had a stroke, six months ago, and is now residing with Denise and her son David and her 14-year-old daughter. Denise is distraught because her maternal grandmother was "the strong one in the family." All solidarity elements must be assessed. However, there is a pressing need for support and assistance for Denise and her family. Th is calls for focusing fi rst on normative and functional solidarity. Th e worker can help Denise examine her current caregiving roles. It is also important for the worker to discuss Denise's decision to care for her grandmother—What is her sense of obligation and commitment to this role? Once Denise has explored her caregiving values, beliefs, the realities of her situation, and her intentions, she and the practitioner can develop a plan. Th is might include exploring family resources, the availability of other family and extended family members for support and caregiving, and more formal resources.

Vignette Two. Mr. Brown is an 84-year-old African American, retired Navy civilian dock worker. His wife of 47 years died 14 years ago aft er a battling cancer for four years. His only son died in an accident 22 years ago. Mr. Brown has two granddaughters, ages 30 and 32, and one great-grandson, age 9. Th ey talk on the phone occasionally, but his granddaughters and great-grandson live 2,000 miles away, and he has not been able to visit them. Mr. Brown reports that he is "lonely" and is considering moving into an assisted-living facility. He wants to reconnect with his family before he moves. All the solidarity elements must be assessed. Immediate issues appear to be Mr. Brown's expressed loneliness and his infrequent contact with his granddaughters and great-grandson. Th is calls for focusing on associational, aff ectional, and structural solidarity. Th e worker can help Mr. Brown make contact with his granddaughters and with other family members, especially those family members who have been supportive in the past. Mechanism to maintain communication should also be explored. Th is may consist of organizing regular visiting, where transportation is arranged for Mr. Brown. It could also mean arranging regular phone contact, sharing pictures, and sending cards. Mr. Brown may also benefi t from more contact with other family, extended family, and friends from church or any groups that he has participated in over his life course (for example, lodges, fraternal orders, church clubs, civic groups). Also, intergenerational programs, if available, may also be a good resource.

Vignette Th ree. Joan, a 41-year-old African American woman, is incarcerated because of a drugrelated charge. She is in the second year of a three-year sentence and is now drug free. She has three sons, ages 19, 12, and 10. Th e two youngest sons reside with their paternal grandmother. Joan's oldest son has lived with her mother most of his life. Joan has not seen her sons in two years. Th e younger children's father died in a car accident; he was driving while impaired. Joan is very concerned about her sons and wants to provide a better life for them. She hopes to arrange visitation, and, so far, her younger son's grandmother has been uncooperative. Her 19-year-old son has refused to visit.

Although all solidarity elements should be assessed fi rst, this situation points to aff ectional and consensual solidarity problems. Joan must be aware that her addiction and past behaviors may have caused apprehension and skepticism on the part of her family. As the practitioner helps Joan to make contact with her children, it will be important for him or her to engage the family in forgiveness, relationship building, and reaffi rming of a shared vision across generations for the health and well-being of the children and family. Th e kinship bonds are in need of revitalization.

CONCLUSION

In view of contemporary issues facing families and the signifi cance of multigenerational families, culturally relevant models of practice are called for. African American multigenerational families have a legacy of resilience, spirituality, and hope that has served to fortify vulnerable members. As our society ages, the number of multigenerational families will increase, and intergenerational cohesion issues will move to the forefront. Th is demographic shift , and the opportunity for shared lives, can be an asset for families. An empowerment-oriented framework that provides a mechanism to build on cultural strengths, intergenerational kinship, and support processes by which generations can provide mutual assistance and care during times of need is indicated. Th is model is a good step in that direction. Many aspects of this model have been a part of culturally responsive work with African American families.

Th e Afrocentric intergenerational sodality model is a strengths-based approach that works to empower multigenerational families and intergenerational relationships. In this regard, there is an assumption that families and extended families have strengths and that some form of intergenerational kinship can be nurtured. A shortcoming of this model is that the full application of each solidarity component has not been systematically tested. I plan to apply this model to practice interventions and intergenerational programming.

Th e Afrocentric intergenerational practice model shows promise. Building on Bengtson and others' intergenerational solidarity construct, infused with an Afrocentric worldview, this model provides a culturally relevant approach for work with African American multigenerational families. It facilitates an understanding of how intergenerational relationships can be supported and provides multidimensional guidance regarding intergenerational relationships and multigenerational families. Th e intergenerational model considers generational transmission from a strengths perspective, looking not only at problems, but also at the assets that multiple generations may provide. It is a framework that taps into the power, resilience, and capital from past and current traditions and relationships. Th e three vignettes provide examples of how this model might be used. To fully examine this model, additional applications should be studied.

Application of the Afrocentric intergenerational practice model, in conjunction with other empowerment-oriented approaches, is a best practice method. Social workers are called on to work with African American and other families. Th is work is especially relevant for work with vulnerable African American families in need of nurturance and care. As our society ages, it will be increasing important to understand intergenerational issues and develop resources that help multigenerational families navigate the complex and changing relationships and problems in our contemporary society. As we move through this century, this model may prove to be very relevant to the changing demographics of our aging society.

REFERENCES

Bagley, C. A., & Carroll, J. (1998). Healing forces in African-American families. In H. I. McCubbin, E. A. Th ompson, A. I. Th ompson, & J. A. Farrell (Eds.), *Resiliency in African-American families* (pp. 117–143). London: Sage Publications.

Barnes, S. (2001). Stressors and strengths: A theoretical and practical examination of nuclear single parent, and augmented African American families. *Families in Society, 85*, 449–460.

Bengtson, V. L. (2001). Beyond the nuclear family: Th e increasing importance of multi-generational bonds. *Journal of Marriage and the Family, 63*, 1–16.

Bengtson, V. L, & Mangen, D. J. (1988). Family intergenerational solidarity, revisited. In D. J. Mangen, V. L. Bengtson, & P. H. Landry (Eds.), *Measurement of intergenerational relationship* (pp. 222–238). Newbury Park, CA: Sage Publications.

Bengtson, V. L, & Roberts, R. E. L. (1991). Intergenerational solidarity in aging families: An example of formal theory construction. *Journal of Marriage and the Family, 53*, 856–870.

Bengtson, V. L., Rosenthal, C.J., & Burton, L. M., (1990). Paradoxes of families and aging. In R. H. Binstock & L. K. George (Eds.), *Handbook of aging and the social sciences* (4th ed., pp. 253–282). San Diego: Academic Press.

Bengtson, V. L., & Schrader, S., S. (1982). Parent-child relationships. In D. Mangen & W. Peterson (Eds.), *Handbook of research instruments in social gerontology* (Vol. 2, pp. 115–185). Minneapolis: University of Minnesota Press.

Billingsley, A. (1992). *Climbing Jacob's ladder: Th e enduring legacy of African-American families*. New York: Simon & Schuster.

Billingsley, A., & Morrison-Rodriguez, B. (1998).Th e black family in the 21st century and the church as an action system: A macro perspective. *Journal of Human Behavior in the Social Environment, 1*(2–3), 31–47.

Carter, B., & McGoldrick, M. (1999). *Th e expanded family life* (3rd ed.). Boston: Allyn & Bacon.

Christian, C. M. (1995). *Black saga: Th e African American experience*. Boston: Houghton Miffl in.

Denby, R. W. (1996). Resiliency and the African American family: Model of family preservation. In S. L. Logan (Ed.), *Th e black family: Strengths, self-help, and positive change* (pp. 144-163). Boulder, CO: Westview Press.

Freeman, E. M., & Logan, S. L. (Eds.). (2004). *Reconceptualizing the strengths and common heritage of black families: Practice, research and policy issues*. Springfi eld, IL: Charles C. Th omas.

Hagestad, G. O. (1996). On-time, off -time, out of time? Refl ections on continuity and discontinuity from an illness process. In V. L. Bengtson (Ed.), *Adulthood and aging: Research on continuities and discontinuities* (pp. 204–222). New York: Springer.

Hill, R. (1971). *Th e strength of black families*. New York: Emerson-Hall.

Hill, R. B. (1993). *Research on the African-American family: A holistic perspective*. London: Auburn House.

Hill, R. B. (1998). Understanding black family functioning: A holistic perspective. *Journal of Comparative Family Studies, 29*, 1–11.

Hill, R. B. (1999). *Th e strengths of African American families: Twenty-fi ve years later*. New York: University Press of America.

King, V. (1994) .Variation in the consequences of nonresident father involvement for children's well-being. *Journal of Marriage and the Family, 56*, 963–972.

Logan, S. L. (Ed.). (2001). *Th e black family: Strengths, self-help, and positive change* (2nd ed.). Boulder, CO: Westview Press.

Martin, J., & Martin, E. (1985). *Th e helping tradition in the black family and community*. Washington, DC: NASW Press.

McAdoo, H. P. (1998). African-American families: Strengths and realities. In H. I. McCubbin, E. A. Th ompson, A. I. Th ompson, & J. A. Futrell (Eds.), *Resiliency in African-American families* (pp. 17–30). London: Sage Publications.

McCullough-Chavis, A., & Waites, C. (2004). Genograms with African American families: Considering cultural context. *Journal of Family Social Work, 8*(2), 1–19.

McPhatter, A. R. (1997). Cultural competence in child welfare: What is it? How do we achieve it? What happens without it? *Child Welfare, 16*, 255–278.

Miles, T. P. (1999). Living with chronic disease and the policies that bind. In T. P. Miles (Ed.), *Full-color aging: Facts, goals, and recommendations for America's diverse elders* (pp. 53–63). Washington, DC: Gerontological Society of America.

Riley, M. W. (1987). On the signifi cance of age in sociology. *American Sociological Review, 52*, 1–14.

Roberts, R. E. L., Richards, L. N., & Bengtson.V. L. (1991). Intergenerational solidarity in families: Untangling the ties that bind. *Marriage & Family Review, 16*, 11–46.

Ruiz, D., & Carlton-LaNey, I, (1999).Th e increase in intergenerational African American families headed by grandmothers. *Journal of Sociology & Social Welfare, 26*(4), 71–86.

Schiele. J. H. (1996). Afi ocentricity: An emerging paradigm in social work practice. *Social Work, 41*, 284–294.

Schiele. J. H. (2000). *Human services and theAfrocentric paradigm.* Binghamton, NY: Haworth Press.

Silverstein, M., Parrott.T. M., & BengtsonV. L. (1995). Factors that predispose middle-aged sons and daughters to provide social support to older parents. *Journal of Marriage and the Family, 57*, 465–476.

Staples, R. (1999). *Th e black family: Essays and studies.* Belmont, CA: Wadsworth.

U.S. Census Bureau. (2004). *People and households.* Retrieved February 20, 2008, from http://www.census.gov/ population/www/projections/usinterimproj/natprojtab02a.pdf

Waites, C. (2008). *Social work practice with African-American families: An intergenerational perspective.* New York: Routledge.

Waites, C., Macgowan, M. J., Pennell, J., Carlton-LaNey, I., & Weil, M. (2004). Increasing the cultural responsiveness of family group conferencing. *Social Work, 49*, 291–300.

Parental Infl uence, School Readiness and Early Academic Achievement of African American Boys

Emanique M. Joe and James Earl Davis

Th is study examined the relationship between parental infl uence and the school readiness of African American boys, using data from the Early Childhood Longitudinal Study: ECLS-K. Parents' infl uence, via their academic beliefs and behaviors, was associated with the cognitive performance of African American boys during kindergarten. While previous research has produced similar results, the present study indicates there are diff erences in which academic beliefs and parenting behaviors are most eff ective in facilitating school readiness and early achievement. Emphasizing the importance of academic skills for African American boys was associated with higher reading and mathematics achievement as well as prior enrollment in center-based child care. Parenting behaviors, such as discussing science topics, reading books, and discussing family racial and ethnic heritage, diff ered in their signifi cance in predicting cognitive outcomes. Implications for diff erences in the kinds of parental involvement in the education of African American boys are discussed.

Recently there has been a signifi cant amount of attention from researchers, educators, parents, and policymakers on the academic achievement gap and the disproportionate number of African American males who are represented among underachievers (Davis, 2008; Mickelson & Greene, 2006). Th is increased interest in the academic performance of young African American males in particular is oft en linked to negative consequences for future educational and social opportunities. Certainly, lags in early achievement particularly in reading and mathematics become more diffi cult to overcome for students who are located in under-resourced schools with limited access to high quality instructional and learning activities (Brown, Dancy, & Davis, 2007; Ferguson, 2003). Evidence also suggests that diff erences in early academic achievement among children begins prior to their school entry, and is signifi cantly infl uenced by families' race/ethnicity, poverty status, parental educational attainment, and children's health and living environments (Currie, 2005; Reichman, 2005).

Empirical investigations of the influence of family characteristics on children's academic outcomes emphasize the role of parent as an important mediating factor in children's academic achievement, and this is particularly true for African American boys (Boyd-Franklin & Franklin, 2000; Ferguson, 2000). Research has also been conducted concerning the educational experiences of African American boys (Entwisle, Alexander, & Olson, 2007; Ferguson, 2003) and the roles parents play in preparing their children for success in school (Brook-Gunn & Markman, 2005; Hill & Craft , 2003; Jeynes, 2005). While a few studies indicate that parental involvement and several aspects of parenting are associated with academic achievement among African American boys (Mandara, 2006; Toldson, 2008), research is unclear regarding how early schooling experiences and social contexts affect school readiness and the early academic achievement of African American boys (Davis, 2003).

Educational policy initiatives such as *No Child Left Behind* (NCLB, 2002) has increased accountability among institutions, educators, and parents to better prepare children to succeed academically. However, there is little empirical evidence regarding the extent to which parents' roles (within the home and their children's schools) influences the school readiness and early academic achievement of African American boys.

This study presents a unique examination of parental involvement in its use of a nationally representative sample, Early Childhood Longitudinal Study (ECLS-K). With such an increased emphasis on children's academic performance, in addition to the disproportionate number of African American males entering elementary schools at an academic disadvantage, the collaboration among those actors (i.e., teachers, parents), factors (i.e., socioeconomic status), and institutions (i.e., early childhood centers, schools) is critical. To this end, the purpose of this study is to address the question of whether, and to what extent, different parental beliefs and behaviors are associated with cognitive outcomes of African American boys in kindergarten? This study provides recommendations for policy and early intervention initiatives that seek to address the academic disparities among young African American males.

Review of Literature

Education research has consistently indicated the underachievement of African American males throughout their academic trajectories (from elementary to post-secondary school; Fan & Chen, 2001; Polite & Davis, 1999). These existing academic disparities are seen as early as kindergarten; thereby suggesting that differences among children's school readiness begins prior to school entry (Entwisle & Alexander, 1993; Lewit & Schuurmann-Baker, 1995). Failure to resolve these early academic inequities, especially among children from low-income families and ethnic minorities, can adversely affect children's academic trajectories, limiting their opportunities thereafter (American Educational Research Association, 2005; Entwisle, Alexander, Cadigan, & Pallas, 1987; Entwisle & Alexander, 1993). The national education reform initiative, NCLB, has increased accountability among schools and parents to focus on achievement outcomes. However, an unintended consequence of NCLB's mandating nationwide standardized testing of grades three through eight is that many younger children (e.g., preschoolers and kindergartners) are expected to exhibit certain measurable academic and social skills as being indicative of their "readiness" for school.

Various attempts at conceptualizing "school readiness" have emphasized the following dimensions: physical and motor development, physical health and well-being; social and emotional development; approaches to learning (i.e., initiative, attitudes toward learning, task mastery); cognition, language and general knowledge capabilities with certain academic skills (e.g., letter and number recognition); and social skills (e.g., ability to share and communicate; Kagan, Moore, & Bredekamp, 1995; Miedel & Reynolds, 1999; National Association for the Education of Young Children, NAEYC, 1995). Several perspectives of readiness and early academic achievement have acknowledged the influence of various social and parental factors (i.e., parental educational attainment, income, poverty status); school conditions and practices (i.e., instructional resources, school dropout, and segregation), and student characteristics and behaviors (i.e., student motivation and effort for learning, drug usage, crime) that are associated with the achievement gap among children (Broffenbrenner, 1979; Currie, 2005; Grissmer, Flanagan, & Williamson, 1998; Lee & Burkam, 2002; Mashburn & Pianta, 2006; Rimm-Kaufman & Pianta, 2000).

Research indicates that there are differences in parents' academic beliefs by families' socioeconomic status and race/ethnicity. For example, research shows that working and middle class families have higher expectations for their school-age children's achievement (Huttman, 1991; Willie, 1986) than their less affluent peers. However, research of ethnic minority parents' academic beliefs presents somewhat inconsistent findings. When compared to their Caucasian peers, racial and ethnic minority parents often have higher expectations of their older school-age children's academic performance (Slaughter-Defoe, Nakagawa, Takanishi, & Johnson, 1990; Stevenson, Chen, & Uttal, 1990). However, a study conducted with a sample of African American families suggests that parents (and teachers) often report lower expectations for African American boys (ages 6-16) than for girls (Wood, Kaplan, & McLoyd, 2007).

Additionally, with increased attention to school readiness, investigations regarding those school readiness skills (e.g., knowing the letters of the alphabet, being able to sit still) parents generally prioritize for their children; have been conducted with large samples. This research indicates that those parents with less educational attainment prioritized social and emotional behaviors, while their more educated peers prioritized academic-related skills as indicators of their children's school readiness (West, Denton, & Germino-Hausken, 2000). However, Diamond and colleagues (2000) found that ethnic minority parents were significantly more likely to place equal value on their preschool children's possession of both academic and social behavioral skills than Caucasians. Evidence suggests that parents' expectations for their children are associated with both short-term and long-term academic achievement regardless of race, ethnicity and social class (Fan, 2001; Fuligini, Galinsky, & Poris, 1995; Halle, Kurtz-Costes, & Mahoney, 1997; Hess, Kashiwagi, Azuma, Price, & Dickson, 1980). However, much of the existing research focuses on those parents' academic beliefs of older school age children and not on the association between parents' academic beliefs and the early academic performance of young African American boys.

There are various significant benefits of parents being involved in their children's schooling: higher academic achievement, reduced absenteeism better socio-emotional behavior, increased achievement, and more positive attitudes toward school (Cole-Henderson, 2000; Grolnick, Benjet, Kurowski, & Apostoleris, 1997; Reynolds, 1989; Taylor, Hinton, & Wilson, 1995). Existing research also shows that there are differences in parental involvement within homes or schools according to various parental and social factors. For example, research suggests that African American parents are more involved in educational activities within the home while their Caucasian peers are more likely to be involved in school settings (Eccles & Harold, 1996). Early studies regarding the involvement of African American families' in their children's schooling have found a positive association between these behaviors and academic outcomes of African American school age boys (Reynolds, 1989, 1992).

The home environment of families is thought to be a crucial setting for academically preparing children for school and for fostering their academic achievement (Marchant, Paulson, & Rothlisberg, 2001; Slaughter-Defoe, 2000). Some of the more common educational and social activities that many parents engage in with their children at home include assisting with homework and school-related projects, reading books with their children, visiting libraries and museums and other cultural activities, ensuring that children are prepared for school, and having school-related rules within the home (Epstein & Dauber, 1991; Pomerantz, Moorman, & Litwack, 2007; Stone & McKay, 2000). However, it has been argued that racial/ethnic diff erences indicated in existing research regarding parental home involvement do not adequately represent the full extent of involvement of ethnic minority parents in their children's lives (Epstein & Dauber, 1991; Stone & McKay, 2000).

Previous fi ndings also suggest parents' personal literacy behaviors (e.g., frequency of reading for pleasure) and the types of reading materials within the home are associated with child outcomes, such as development of literacy skills, learning to read at earlier ages, and higher reading scores on readiness assessments (Elliot & Hewison, 1994; Farver, Yiyuan, Eppe, & Lonigan, 2006; Senechal & LeFevre, 2002). However, empirical research is limited in its specifi c focus on the impact of literacy behaviors within the home on various outcomes for African American males (Tatum, 2005). Other results show that parents who actively engage their children in certain social (e.g., sports/clubs, performing arts) and cultural activities (e.g., engaging in ethnic/cultural activities) have a signifi cant infl uence on their children's readiness and academic performance (Beasley, 2002; Demo & Hughes, 1990; Farkas & Hibel, 2008). Also, although much of existing research has not been conducted with younger children, the parenting behavior of racial socialization (i.e, parents transmitting information regarding ethnicity and race) has been associated with cognitive functioning and academic achievement (Caughy, O'Campo,; Marshall, 1995; Randolph, & Nickerson, 2002). However, again the research discussed is limited in its focus on how such parenting behaviors can impact academic outcomes specifi cally for African American boys.

Additionally, parents' school-related involvement typically includes such behaviors as attending school events, workshops, and academic conferences; volunteering for certain events or activities within the school; or participating in various school committees or boards. Research indicates that such school-related involvement is associated with students' general measures of academic achievement (Fan & Chen, 2001; Hill & Craft , 2003; Jeynes, 2005). Once again there are social class diff erences in parents' school involvement. For example, when compared with their less affl uent peers, parents from affl uent socioeconomic backgrounds with higher educational attainment are signifi cantly more likely to be involved in their children's schools (Pomerantz et al., 2007). Research is still limited in individual studies that have considered both forms of parental involvement (home and school) and the infl uence of these factors on children's academic outcomes, particularly for African American males.

Purpose

Th e discussion of the literature and the school readiness framework indicates the importance of investigating the association of parental academic beliefs and parenting behaviors on academic outcomes for African American boys. Current investigations of school readiness are limited in that most examinations of parental involvement have either focused on parents' school-related involvement *or* home involvement; have used older longitudinal data sets; or have conducted research with small samples of school-age children (Diamond, Reagan, & Bandyk, 2000; Halle, Kurtz-Costes, & Mahoney, 1997; Jeynes, 2005; Stevenson, Chen, & Uttal, 1990). Moreover, empirical research is also limited in its investigations of the various factors, in addition to the infl uential "role" of parents (through parenting beliefs and behaviors) on the academic achievement among young African American males (Davis, 2003; Mandara, 2006). Th is study advances a comprehensive approach in its investigation of various parental and social factors that are associated with cognitive outcomes in the early schooling of young African American males.

Methods

Sample

Th e present study used the Early Childhood Longitudinal Study-Kindergarten Class (ECLS-K) Public Use Data, a nationally representative study, with an original kindergarten sample of approximately 22,000 children enrolled in 1,277 kindergarten programs throughout the country during the 1998–1999 academic year (West, Denton, & Germino-Hausken, 2000).

Th is investigation was conducted with a subsample of African American boys ($N = 1,616$) and their parents, utilizing data collected from parents' for the fall and spring, and cognitive outcome measures during kindergarten. Th e decision to use the preceding data points was based on a theoretical consideration of school readiness and the availability of variables used for this study. Conceptually, children's early transitional period to school has considered the importance of kindergarten in preparing children for elementary school (La Paro, Pianta, & Cox, 2000; Rimm-Kaufman & Pianta, 2000). Th is study adopts the preceding perspective and examines children's kindergarten outcomes. Descriptive analyses of this subsample of boys indicate that the majority (78.3%) attended full-day kindergarten programs, within public schools (88.9%), and that 53.5% of these boys were from single-parent households.

Measures

Because mothers were typically the selected parent respondent for the parent interviews, variables for mothers' characteristics (i.e., age, education level) were used for this study (National Center for Educational Statistics, 1999). In addition, the composite socioeconomic status (SES) variable was used for the multivariate analyses, whereas the categorical SES and poverty composite variables were used for descriptive analyses. Th e composite SES variables were derived from parents' education level, occupation, and household income. In addition, child center variables for this study included the recoding of prior child care experiences (i.e, type of child care) and the characteristics of their current school (i.e., public or private school) variables.

Six variables indicating those skills parents' believed were important for their children to have prior to school entry were selected to indicate parents' academic beliefs (Likert scale, 1 = *essential* to 5 = *not important*). Confi rmatory factor and reliability analyses were employed to determine the grouping of the six school readiness variables, and resulted in two factors, academic skills ($a = .72$) and social emotional skills ($a = .67$); mean scores were then computed to create these two variables.

Parenting behaviors variables for this study consisted of the frequency in which parents engaged in the following with their children:

- Reading books with children (1-*not at all*–4-*everyday*);
- Discussing ethnic heritage (1-*never*–5-*several times a week*);
- Discussing nature or engaging in science projects (1-*not at all*–4-*everyday*); and • Attending parent-teacher conferences (1-*one time*–5-*fi ve or more times*).

It is important to note that typically the investigations of parents' school-related involvement behaviors have examined parents volunteering within their children's school (Epstein & Lee, 1995).

However, due to the high number of missing cases (49.4% of parents reported this behavior was "not applicable") the frequency of parents' volunteering in schools was not examined in this study.

Finally, the Direct Cognitive Assessment outcome measures for kindergartners contained items measuring children's competence in the three following areas: (a) Reading: measuring basic skills (e.g., letter recognition, print familiarity, sounds); (b) Math: measuring skills in problem-solving and conceptual and procedural knowledge; and (c) General Knowledge: measuring knowledge of the natural sciences and social studies. A longitudinal weight specifi ed as appropriate by ECLS-K (National Center for Educational Statistics, 1999) was used in the multivariate analyses to answer whether, and to what extent, diff erent parental beliefs and behaviors are associated with cognitive outcomes of young African American boys.

Results

As shown in Table 1, the mean age for African American boys in this sample was a little over fi ve (5.44) years old. Descriptive analyses also indicate that 26.5% of these boys had attended a center-based child care program at least a year prior to entering kindergarten. Approximately half (50.3%) of the mothers in this sample had received a high school diploma or less, and approximately 40% of the household incomes for these families were below the poverty level.

Multivariate analyses were conducted, as shown in Table 2, to determine which parental factors predicted cognitive outcomes of African American boys in kindergarten aft er accounting for the eff ects of various independent (background) variables. According to the fi ndings, the three regression models explained approximately 16% of the variance in reading, 14% of the math, and 15% of the general knowledge assessments of these boys in kindergarten.

An additional parenting behavior (of which approximately one-third of the sample engaged in with their sons) that was modestly signifi cant for boys' performance on the math measure was the frequency in which parents discussed nature or engaged in doing science projects. When parents involve their sons in some type of science-based discussion, they potentially increase problem-solving skills that are essential to performing well on cognitive assessments. Further investigations regarding the potential link between parents engaging in this type of behavior and the math achievement of African American boys should continue to be explored.

Th e results of these analyses indicate that the parental factors, academic beliefs, and behaviors examined do infl uence African American boys' performance. First, whether young African American males were from more affl uent families was a highly signifi cant predictor of how well they performed on reading (β 0.23, p = .001), math (β 0.21, p = .001) and general knowledge (β 0.23, p = .001) assessments. Also, it appears that those boys enrolled in some type of center-based child care (not including Head Start) was modestly signifi cant in their reading (β 0.07, p = .05), math (β 0.09, p = .01), and general knowledge (β 0.07, p = .05) outcomes. Th e type of school African American boys were currently enrolled in during kindergarten was also signifi cant, albeit inversely associated, with how well they performed in reading (β -0.06, p = .001); math (β -0.13, p = .001); and general knowledge (β -0.08, p = .01); thus indicating that boys in public schools did not perform as well as their peers in private schools for these domains.

Additionally, the priority parents place on their children having academic and social-emotional skills prior to entering school varied in its signifi cance in predicting the cognitive outcomes of young African American males. For example, although modestly signifi cant, placing a higher level of importance on their sons having academic school readiness skills was a signifi cant predictor for performance on reading (β -0.12, p = .05) and math (β -0.10, p = .05) assessments. Although, for those parents who valued social-emotional skills, this variable was modestly signifi cant for African American boy's general knowledge outcome measure (β -0.08, p = .05).

Th e results indicate that parenting behaviors have diff ering aff ects on the cognitive outcome for African American males in kindergarten. For example, frequently reading books was only modestly signifi cant in predicting boys' reading assessment scores (β 0.01, p = .05). Whereas, the frequency in

Table 1

Family Characteristics and Social Factors of Sample of Black Boys in Kindergarten

Characteristics	(N)	%
Former Child Care [a]		
None	187	11.6
Home-based childcare	280	17.4
Head Start	263	16.3
Center-based	428	26.5
Other types of care	102	6.4
Kindergarten Programs [b]		
Half Day	311	19.2
Full Day	1183	73.2
Type of School		
Private	205	12.7
Public	1411	87.3
Poverty Threshold		
At or Above Poverty Level	573	60.1
Below Poverty Level	381	39.9
Family Composition [c]		
Single Parent Household	733	45.4
Dual Parent Household	539	33.4
Mother's Education Level [d]		
Less than High School Diploma	271	16.8
High School Diploma	541	33.5
Some College experience	395	24.4
Bachelor's Degree	112	6.9
Master's Degree	29	1.8
PhD or other Professional Degree	0	0.6
Other types of schooling	99	6.1
Average age of Child (in months)	68.32	(SD) 4.44
Average age of Mother	31.88	(SD) 8.12

Note. [a] Unweighted Total Sample (N = 1616) due to missing values (N = 356) the sum of the percentages may not equal 100; [b] Unweighted Total Sample (N = 1616) due to missing values (N = 122) the sum of the percentages may not equal 100; [c] Unweighted Total Sample (N = 1616) due to missing values (N = 344) the sum of the percentages may not equal 100; d. Unweighted Total Sample (N = 1616) due to missing values (N = 160) the sum of the percentages may not equal 100. *SD* – Standard Deviation

which parents' discussed nature or engaged in science projects with their sons was a modest signifi cant predictor for how well these kindergarteners performed on the math assessment (β 0.07, p = .05), but was more of a signifi cant predictor of how well boys performed on general knowledge readiness assessments (β 0.13, p = .001). Interestingly, the parenting behavior that was signifi cant for all three cognitive measures (Reading: β. 0.10, p = .01; Math: β. 0.07, p = .05; and General Knowledge: β. 0.10, p = .01) was how frequently parents discussed their families' ethnic heritage with their sons. Finally, it appears that whether parents participated in parent-teacher conferences was negatively correlated with boys' reading (β -0.02, p = .05) and general knowledge (β -0.09, p = .01) outcomes. Such a fi nding implies that those parents who attended parent-teacher conferences more frequently had sons who had lower levels of performance on cognitive assessments.

Contextual Information Regarding Parenting Behaviors

In order to examine the association between parent characteristics and their parenting behaviors ANOVA and chi-square analyses were conducted for the four behaviors: (a) reading books to child, (b) discussing racial/ethnic heritage, (c) discussing nature, engaging in science projects, and (d) attending parent-teacher conferences. According to the results from the ANOVA (shown in Table 3), there were no signifi cant diff erences between the mother's age, education level, and family socioeconomic status and whether these parents frequently attended parent-teacher conferences throughout the school year. However, mean scores indicate that mothers who were older than 30 years of age (M = 2.20) and those families whose household incomes were low (Low SES, M = 2.38 and Low medium SES, M = 2.12), attended parent-teacher conferences more frequently than their peers.

Chi square analyses were conducted to investigate the relationships between parent characteristics and the remaining three parenting behaviors. A summary of these statistical associations is shown in Table 4. Th e results of these analyses indicate that there are highly signifi cant relationships between parents reading books to their young sons and parents' education level, X^2 (18, 84.31), p = .001; and socioeconomic status, X^2 (12, 75.84), p = .001. According to the means, in general, the higher a mother's education level and socioeconomic status the more frequently books are read to her son at home. Similarly, there were signifi cant associations between the mother's education level X^2 (24, 53.86), p = .01, family' s socioeconomic status X^2 (16, 47.95), p = .001, and parents' discussing their family's ethnic heritage with their sons. Further examination revealed that as families' socioeconomic status and the mother's education level increased, parents (approximately 25% of the sample) discussed their family's ethnic heritage with their children more oft en. Finally, there was an association between the mother's education level (X^2 (18, 40.77), p = .01) and socioeconomic status (X^2 (12, 39.06), p = .001) and how oft en parents talked to their children about nature or engaged in science projects with them. Interestingly, it appears that approximately one-third of the parents in this sample engaged in this behavior with their sons at least once or twice a week.

Discussion

Th e purpose of this study is to examine parental infl uence, through their academic beliefs and parenting behaviors, on African American boys during their kindergarten year. Th e multivariate analyses provide evidence that specifi c parental factors, beliefs and parenting behaviors do relate to the cognitive performance of African American boys. In general, the results of this study support prior research that parents are infl uential actors in their children's academic development (Brooks-Gunn & Markman, 2005; Slaughter, 1987). However, this study contributes to existing research by suggesting that the parental infl uence (specifi cally the parenting behaviors discussed here) have diff ering aff ects on the cognitive outcomes for African American males in kindergarten.

Findings from this study support existing research regarding the strong infl uence of socioeconomic status on children's school readiness, which indicates that those children from less affl uent families are less likely to be "ready" when entering school in kindergarten (Zill, Collins, & West, 1995). Although, the research of Davis-Kean (2005) emphasizes the importance of parents' engaging in academic activities with their children at home to off set some of the negative eff ects of socioeconomic status on children's academic performance, further investigations of parents' behaviors within the home could prove benefi cial to research on parental involvement. Another signifi cant predictor of reading, math, and general knowledge measures worth mentioning is whether African American boys were enrolled in some type of center-based child care prior to school entry. Although this study does not test for the

Table 2

Black Males Cognitive Outcomes for the Spring of Kindergarten

Variables	Reading N = 816			Mathematics N = 816			General Knowledge N = 816		
	β 1	SE	β 2	β 1	SE	β 2	β 1	SE	β 2
Socioeconomic Status	3.13	0.48	0.23***	2.38	0.41	0.21***	2.33	0.36	0.23***
Center-based Child Care before kindergarten	1.50	0.69	0.07*	1.56	0.59	0.09**	1.12	0.53	0.07*
Kindergarten Program Public School	-5.84	1.21	0.16***	-3.82	1.03	-0.13***	-2.28	0.92	-0.08**
Academic School Readiness Beliefs	0.43	0.22	-0.08*	-0.46	0.19	-0.10*	0.04	0.17	0.00
Social Emotional School Readiness Beliefs	-0.15	0.30	-0.02	0.13	0.25	-0.02	-0.45	0.22	-0.08*
Read Books to Child	0.81	0.39	0.07*	0.52	0.33	0.05	0.36	0.29	0.04
Discuss Racial/Ethnic Heritage	0.78	0.25	0.10**	0.47	0.22	0.07*	0.56	0.19	0.10**
Discuss Nature / Engage in Science Projects	-0.05	0.35	-0.00	0.59	0.30	0.07*	0.99	0.27	0.13***
Attend Parent-teacher Conference	-0.44	0.21	-0.07*	-0.31	0.18	-0.06	0.41	0.16	-0.09**
Intercept	0.41			0.39			0.40		
R^2	0.17			0.15			0.16		
Adjusted R^2	0.16			0.14			0.15		

Note: * = $p < .05$; ** = $p < .01$; *** = $p < .001$
β 1 - unstandardized Beta coefficient   β 2 - standardized Beta coefficient

117

Table 3

Frequency of Parents Attending Parent-Teacher Conferences by Parent Characteristics

Characteristics	*M*	*SD*
Mother's Age		
19-30	2.12	1.61
Older than 30	2.20	1.94
F	0.47	
Mother's Education Level		
Less than High School	2.10	1.31
High School Diploma	2.30	1.94
Some College	2.12	1.42
Bachelor's Degree	1.94	1.36
Master's Degree	2.17	2.06
PhD/Professional Degree	1.71	1.11
Other Schooling	2.09	1.28
F	0.86	
Socioeconomic Status		
Low SES	2.38	1.77
Low Medium SES	2.12	1.76
Medium SES	2.06	1.41
Medium High SES	2.08	1.16
High SES	2.02	1.63
F	1.92	

Note. $* = p < .05$; $** = p < .01$; $*** = p < .001$; SES – Socioeconomic Status.

Table 4

Associations between Frequency of Parenting Behaviors and Parent Characteristics

	Reading Books to Children [a]	Discussing Ethnic Heritage [b]	Discussing Nature / Science [c]
Mother's Age	$X^2(3)7.98*$	$X^2(4)4.19$	$X^2(3)0.30$
19-30			
Older than 30			
Mother's Education Level	$X^2(18)84.31***$	$X^2(24)53.86***$	$X^2(18)40.77***$
Less than High school			
HS Diploma			
Some college			
BA Degree			
Master's Degree			
PhD/Prof. Degree			
Other types of schooling			
Family's Socioeconomic Status	$X^2(12)75.84***$	$X^2(16)47.95***$	$X^2(12)39.06***$
Low SES			
Low Medium SES			
Medium SES			
Medium High SES			
High SES			

Note. Total Sample $N = 1616$; [a] Unweighted Sample for Reading Books: Mother's Age ($N = 1152$), Mother's Ed. Level ($N = 1291$), Family SES ($N = 1310$); [b] Unweighted Sample for Discussing Ethnic Heritage: Mother's Age ($N = 1312$), Mother's Ed. Level ($N = 1323$), Family SES ($N = 1350$); [c] Unweighted Sample N for Discussing Nature/Science: Mother's Age ($N = 1152$), Mother's Ed. Level ($N = 1290$), Family SES ($N = 1308$); $* = p < .05$; $** = p < .01$; $*** = p < .001$. SES – Socioeconomic Status.

quality of their preschool experiences, these results confi rm prior research on school readiness that emphasize the importance of socioeconomically disadvantaged children involvement in some type of quality preschool/child care program as a means of increasing their school readiness (Barnett, 2002; Peisner-Feinberg et al., 1999).

Although this study does not investigate a causal relationship between parents' academic beliefs and their resulting behaviors, the results do indicate that parents' beliefs regarding the importance of academic or social-emotional skills is modestly signifi cant in predicting outcomes for African American boys. For example, parents who emphasize the importance of academic skills for their sons were more concerned with how well their sons perform on academically oriented measures (i.e., reading, math). Further research investigating the relationship between the priority parents place on certain skills for African American boys' and how these beliefs aff ect their parenting behaviors could better inform the development of parent-education interventions.

Findings from this study also reveal that the frequency of parents' engagement in certain behaviors has diff ering eff ects on reading, math, and general knowledge outcomes for African American boys. For example, the frequency in which parents read books to their sons was signifi cantly related to how well these young boys performed on the reading assessment in kindergarten. Such a fi nding confi rms the importance of literacy activities on student academic achievement and the specifi c involvement of parents (Hair, Halle, Terry-Humen, Lavelle, & Calkins, 2006; Halsall & Green, 1995).

Interestingly, the behavior that appeared to be infl uential on all outcomes for boys in this study was how frequently parents' discussed the racial and ethnic heritage of their family with their sons. Approximately 25% of this sample engaged in this behavior several times a month with their children. Such a fi nding supports existing evidence that indicate the importance of developing a positive ethnic identity for higher cognitive scores in reading among high-risk students (Beasley, 2002), for greater factual knowledge and better problem-solving skills (Caughy, O'Campo, Randolph, & Nickerson, 2002), and for higher levels of academic orientation and outcomes for African American youth (Chavous et al., 2003). Th is study highlights the considerable importance of parents' racial/ethnic socialization eff orts specifi cally for young African American males who are oft en burdened with identity issues connected to racial stereotypes and low academic expectations (Davis, 2008; Mickelson & Greene, 2006).

Finally, the fi ndings indicate there is an inverse association between those parents who attended parent-teacher conferences and African American boys' performance on the three outcome measures. Such fi ndings suggests that parents who attend parent-teacher conferences may be doing so as an intervention for some type of problem, academic or otherwise, their boys are having at school. Unfortunately, ECLS-K does not provide data that allowed investigators to examine the purpose for having scheduled conferences between parents and teachers. Further exploration of why special meetings or conferences are needed between parents and teachers could provide a better understanding of the inverse association between this behavior and children's outcomes.

Implications and Recommendations for Research, Policy and Practice

Research Implications

As indicated in this study, parental attitudes and parenting practices have diff ering infl uence on the cognitive outcomes of young African American boys. Such fi ndings regarding the infl uential role of parents in children's school readiness and early achievement have implications for future research. A potential direction for research would be empirical investigations of within-group diff erences of parents (i.e., comparing African American boys from diff erent socioeconomic backgrounds). Such research on social class diff erences could be useful in determining whether, and which, specifi c parenting behaviors are more infl uential for increasing African American boys' early academic achievement. Also, including more recent waves of data collected for ECLS-K (kindergarten through eighth grade), further research would allow investigators to examine whether parents' academic views and goals for their children mirror those parenting behaviors that facilitate academic achievement of African American boys throughout elementary school. Future research should also investigate fathers' role, specifi cally as it pertains to parenting behavior and its infl uence on the academic achievement of African American males. Currently, there is a growing body of literature that points to the relationship between fathers' involvement and children's academic and social-emotional school readiness (Downer & Mendez, 2005; Jayakody & Kalil, 2002). However, additional research on the infl uence of fathers' role in the academic experiences and outcomes of African American boys could provide insight into this critical parent-child relationship.

Practice and Policy Implications

It is important to operate from the perspective that parents are children's "fi rst teachers." Although parents are important actors in the early schooling of African American boys, they are not solely responsible for their education and development. Findings from this study suggest that policy and program initiatives consider adopting a conceptualization of "school readiness" that considers the importance of social context (e.g., parents, teachers, family background, educational settings) on the early schooling of African American males. To this end, it is extremely important that interventions are developed through a collaboration of policymakers, local schools, communities, and families. Th is would encourage the translation of these fi ndings into the development of educational resources (i.e., parenting programs, teacher professional development programs) that seek to advance African American males' school readiness and academic achievement. Adopting such a collaborative perspective, as it pertains to this study, acknowledges the importance of certain parenting behaviors (i.e., discussing ethnic heritage, frequency in reading books, engaging in science/nature discussions and projects) on the positive academic outcomes for young African American boys.

One potential direction would model a recent intervention (i.e., "Th e Th ree Year Old Journey") implemented by the Harlem Children's Zone, an initiative that seeks to provide a range of support services targeting the social, health, educational, and educational needs of African American families (Dobbie & Fryer, 2009). "Th e Th ree Year Old Journey" program seeks to inform parents' knowledge regarding their child's development, language skills, and their parenting skills. Developing such family-based interventions could potentially provide the necessary resources and supports for families via various parenting programs and parent-child workshops. For example, this study indicates a signifi cant association between the frequency in which parents read books with their children and reading outcomes for African American boys. Such a fi nding supports the development of a family-based program that adopts a literacy component. A literacy workshop could stress the importance of parents frequently reading to their children and also provide them with diff erent strategies and literacy activities to engage in with their sons.

Th e fi nding indicating that the frequency in which parents engaged their sons in discussions of their family's ethnic heritage was a signifi cant predictor of all three academic outcomes suggests that this particular behavior may serve as protective factor for young African American boys. Given the positive infl uence of this parenting behavior, similar to the preceding discussion of literacy, a racial socialization component could also be integrated into support programs for African American families. Such a program could provide parents with strategies and resources to foster a strong sense of cultural pride among their sons and help them begin to view their academic achievement as an important part of their racial/ ethnic identity (Oyserman, Harrison, & Bybee, 2001; Smith, Atkins, & Connell, 2003). Such exposure, especially in the earlier years, could be an eff ective device in increasing children's problem-solving skills, self-esteem, and academic achievement (Caughy, O'Campo, Randolph, & Nickerson, 2002).

Young children are intrinsically interested in science, discovery, and exploration; and daily question their social environment and the causes and processes involved in their physical world (Brown, 1997). Recent research fi nds that in general those young children, who were frequently involved in a variety of science activities within schools and engaged in various scientifi c inquiry, enjoyed science more and also felt more competent in their abilities (Mantzicopoulos, Patrick, & Samarapungavan, 2008). Findings from this study refl ect the theme of the importance of young children's exposure to science. Specifi cally, the more parents discussed nature and scientifi c discovery or engaged in science projects during out-of-school time, the higher their sons performed in math and general knowledge measures. Broadening the perspective of science and scientifi c activities to include other areas (e.g., nutrition and health, environmental issues, weather and climate change, technology) and encouraging the collaboration between science educators and parents in early schooling could potentially infl uence young African American males' sense of self-effi cacy in these areas.

Finally, there are directions for polices that could better serve the academic needs of young African American males. First, school district level policies could expand existing professional development interventions available to teachers and administrators to include trainings that address the importance of increasing their academic expectations for their African American male students, in addition to and providing instruction on a diverse range of activities and resources to use with African American boys (Morgan & Bhola, 2006). Also, the Obama administration's proposed education reform includes an increase in funding for early childhood education programs for preschoolers, in addition to providing fi rst-time parents with regular visits from trained health care providers to assist with issues regarding children's health and preparation for school. Such reform eff orts could pave the way for the development of more family-based programs, some of which were discussed in this research that could impact the development and school readiness of young African American boys.

Limitations of the Study

Although this study is important in providing contextual information regarding parental infl uence on the academic outcome of young African American boys, it does present several limitations. First, performing secondary analysis of ECLS-K data collected from parents and teachers required the selection of variables that best represented certain concepts (proxies) of parents' beliefs and behaviors. Also, given the large amount of missing variables for those school-related involvement behaviors, this study is constrained in its empirical investigation of parents' school-related involvement on boys' outcomes. Another methodological issue involves the use of one item for the racial socialization construct, which presents a challenge when comparing this fi nding with some of the existing research on racial/ethnic socialization (Hughes et al., 2006). Restricting this sample to African American males in kindergarten also does not allow for a comparison of how various forms of parental involvement impact diff erent racial/ethnic subgroups of boys. Nevertheless, this study provides empirical evidence to support the claim that the academic behaviors and beliefs of parents are potentially important in school readiness and achievement outcomes.

Conclusion

Th e mandates of NCLB have created assessment-centered school environments where parents are too oft en seen as spectators. Parents have an important role in school readiness and achievement outcomes of young children as illustrated in the fi ndings from this study. Educators must work with parents to assure that the most academically vulnerable students, such as African American boys, are nurtured and supported to actualize their academic potential.

When conceptualizing "school readiness" currently there is no consensus on a single defi nition (Graue, 2006; Saluga, Scott-Little, & Cliff ord, 2000). Graue's research (1992) proposes that children's school readiness should be viewed as ideas or meanings constructed by communities, families, and schools. Furthermore, Mashbum and Pianta's (2006) perspective of school readiness acknowledges that children acquire school-related competencies through social relationships with their peers, their teachers, and their families. Th rough its fi ndings this study supports the perspectives proposed by Graue (2006) and Mashburn and Pianta, but seeks to advance the defi nition of school readiness and future research to acknowledge the infl uence of social and parental factors, academic beliefs, and parenting behaviors on the early schooling of children. Doing so gives promise for the development of policies and interventions that may reduce the achievement disparities that exist among ethnic minority children, particularly young African American boys.

References

American Educational Research Association. (2005). Early childhood education: Investing in quality makes sense, *Research Points 3.* Retrieved from http://www.aera.net/uploadedFiles/Journals_and_Publications/Research_Points/RPFall05.pdf

Barnett, W. S. (2002). Early childhood education. In A. Molnar (Ed.), *School reform proposals: the research evidence* (pp. 1–26). Greenwich, CT: Information Age.

Beasley, T. (2002). Infl uence of culture-related experiences and socio-demographic risk factors on cognitive readiness among preschoolers. *Journal of Education for Students Placed At Risk, 7,* 3–23.

Boyd-Franklin, N., & Franklin, A. J. (2000). *Boys into men: Raising our African American teenage sons.* Rutherford, NJ: Penguin Putnam.

Broff enbrenner, U. (1979). *Th e ecology of human development. Experiments by nature and design.* Cambridge, MA: Harvard University Press.

Brooks-Gunn, J., & Markman, L. (2005). Th e contribution of parenting to ethnic and racial gaps in school readiness. *Th e Future of Children, 13,* 139–168.

Brown, A. L. (1997). Transforming schools into communities of thinking and learning about serious matters. *American Psychologist, 32,* 399–413.

Brown, M. C., Dancy, T. E., & Davis, J. E. (2007). *Th e children Hurricane Katrina left behind: Schooling context, professional preparation, and community politics.* New York: Peter Lang.

Caughy, M. O., O'Campo, P. J., Randolph, S. M., & Nickerson, K. (2002). Th e infl uence of racial socialization practices on the cognitive and behavioral competence of African American preschoolers. *Child Development, 73,* 1611–1625.

Chavous, T. M., Benat, D. H., Schmeelk-Cone, J., Caldwell, C. H., Kohn-Wood, L., & Zimmerman, M. A. (2003). Racial identity and academic attainment among African American adolescent. *Child Development, 74,* 1076–1090.

Cole-Henderson, B. (2000). Organizational characteristics of schools that successfully serve low-income urban African American students. *Journal of Education for Students Placed at Risk, 5,* 77–91.

Currie, J. (2005). Health disparities and gaps in school readiness. *Th e Future of Children 15,* 117–138.

Davis, J. E. (2003). Early schooling and academic achievement of African American males. *Urban Education, 38,* 515.

Davis, J. E. (2008). Toward understanding African American males in K–12 education. In L. Tillman (Ed.), *Handbook on African American education,* (pp. 399–416). Th ousand Oaks, CA: Sage.

Davis-Kean, P. E. (2005). Th e infl uence of parent education and family income on child achievement: Th e indirect role of parental expectations and the home environment. *Journal of Family Psychology, 19,* 294–304.

Demo, D. H., & Hughes, M. (1990). Socialization and racial identity among Black Americans. *Social Psychology Quarterly, 53*, 364–374.

Diamond, K., Reagan, A., & Bandyk, J. (2000). Parents' conceptions of kindergarten readiness: Relationships with race, ethnicity, and development. *Th e Journal of Educational Research 94*, 93–100.

Dobbie, W., & Fryer, R. G. (2009). Are high-quality schools enough to close the achievement gap? *Evidence from a Bold Social Experiment in Harlem.* Harvard University. Retrieved from http://www.economics.harvard.edu/ faculty/fryer/fi les/hcz%204.15.2009.pdf

Downer, J. T., & Mendez, J. L. (2005). African American father involvement and preschool children's school readiness. *Early Education & Development, 16*, 317–340.

Eccles, J. S., & Harold, R. D. (1996). Family involvement in children's and adolescents' schooling. In A.B.J.R. Dunn (Ed.), *Family school links: How do they aff ect educational outcomes?* (pp. 3–34). Mahwah, NJ: Erlbaum.

Elliot, J. A., & Hewison, J. (1994). Comprehension and interest in home reading. *British Journal of Educational Psychology, 64*, 203–220.

Entwisle, D., Alexander, K., Cadigan, D., & Pallas, A. (1987). Kindergarten experience: Cognitive eff ects or socialization? *American Educational Research Journal, 24*, 337–364.

Entwisle, D. R, & Alexander, K. L. (1993). Entry into school: Th e beginning school transition and educational stratifi cation in the United States. *Annual Review of Sociology, 19*, 401–423.

Entwisle, D. R., Alexander, K. L, & Olson, L. S. (2007). Early schooling: Th e handicap of being poor and male. *Sociology of Education, 80*, 114–138.

Epstein, J., & Lee, S. (1995). National patterns of school and family connections in the middle grades. In B. Ryan, G. Adams, T. Gullotta, R. Weissberg & R. Hampton (Eds.), *Th e family-school connection: theory, research and practice* (vol. 2, pp. 108–154). Th ousand Oaks: Sage.

Epstein, J. L., & Dauber, S. (1991). School programs and teacher practices of parent involvement in inner-city elementary and middle schools. *Th e Elementary School Journal, 91*, 289.

Fan, X. (2001). Parental involvement and students' academic achievement: A growth modeling analysis. *Journal of Experimental Education, 70*, 27–61.

Fan, X., & Chen, M. (2001). Parental involvement and students academic achievement: A meta anlaysis. *Educational Psychology Review, 13*, 1–22.

Farkas, G., & Hibel, J. (2008). Disparities in school readiness. In A. C. Booth, Ann (Ed.), *Being unready for school: Factors aff ecting risk and resilience* (pp. 3–28). New York: Erlbaum, Taylor & Francis.

Farver, J. M., Yiyuan, X., Eppe, S., & Lonigan, C. J. (2006). Home environments and young Latino children's school readiness. *Early Childhood Research Quarterly, 21*, 196–212.

Ferguson, A. A. (2000). *Bad boys: Public schools in the making of Black masculinity*. Ann Arbor: University of Michigan Press.

Ferguson, R. F. (2003). Teachers' perceptions and expectations and the Black-White test score gap. In O. S. Fashola (Ed.), *Educating African American males: Voices from the fi eld* (pp. 79–128). Th ousand Oaks, CA: Corwin Press.

Fuligini, A. S., Galinsky, E., & Poris, M. (1995). *Th e impact of parental employment on children.* (Unpublished manuscript.)

Graue, M. E. (1992). Social interpretations of readiness for kindergarten. *Early Childhood Research Quarterly, 7*, 225–243.

Graue, M. E. (2006). Th e Answer Is Readiness—Now, What is the Question? *Early Education and Development, 17*, 43–56.

Grissmer, D., Flanagan, A., & Williamson, S. (1998). Why did the Black-White score gap narrow in the 1970s and 1980s? In C. Jencks & M. Phillips (Eds.) *Th e Black-White test score gap* (pp 182–228). Washington, DC: Brookings Institution.

Grolnick, W. S., Benjet, C., Kurowski, C. O., & Apostoleris, N. H. (1997). Predictors of parental involvement in children's schooling. *Journal of Educational Psychology, 89*, 538–548.

Hair, E., Halle, T., Terry-Humen, E., Lavelle, B., & Calkins, J. (2006). Children's school readiness in the ECLS-K: Predictions to academic, health, and social outcomes in fi rst grade. *Early Childhood Research Quarterly, 21*, 431–454.

Halle, T., Kurtz-Costes, B., & Mahoney, J. (1997). Family infl uences on school achievement in low-income African American families. *Journal of Educational Psychology, 89*, 527–537.

Halsall, S., & Green, C. (1995). Reading aloud: A way for parents to support their children's growth in literacy. *Early Childhood Education Journal, 23*, 27–31.

Hess, R. D., Kashiwagi, K., Azuma, H., Price, G. G., & Dickson, W. (1980). Maternal expectations for mastery of developmental tasks in Japan and the United States. *International Journal of Psychology, 15*, 259–271.

Hill, N. E., & Craft, S. A. (2003). Parent school involvement and school performance: Mediated pathways among socioeconomically comparable African American and Euro American families. *Journal of Educational Psychology, 95*, 74–83.

Hughes, D., Rodriguez, J., Smith, E. P., Johnson, D. J., Stevenson, H. C., & Spicer, P. (2006). Parents' ethnic-racial socialization practices: A review of research and directions for future study. *Developmental Psychology, 42*, 747–769.

Huttman, E. (1991). A Research note on dreams and aspirations of Black families. *Journal of Comparative Family Studies, 22*, 147–158.

Jayakody, R., & Kalil, A. (2002). Social fathering in low-income, African American families with preschool children. *Journal of Marriage and Family, 64*, 504–516.

Jeynes, W. (2005). A meta-analysis of the relation of parental involvement to urban elementary school student academic achievement. *Urban Education, 40*, 237–269.

Kagan, S. L., Moore, E., & Bredekamp, S. (Eds.) (1995). *Reconsidering children's early learning and development: Toward shared beliefs and vocabulary.* Washington, DC: National Education Goals Panel.

La Paro, K., Pianta R. C., & Cox, M. J. (2000). Kindergarten teachers' reported use of kindergarten to fi rst grade transition practices. *Th e Elementary School Journal, 101*, 63–78.

Lee, V., & Burkam, D. (2002). *Inequality at the starting gate: Social background diff erences in achievement as children begin school.* Washington, DC: Economic Policy Institute.

Lewit, E. M., & Schuurmann-Baker, L. (1995). School readiness. *Th e Future of Children, 5*, 128–139.

Mandara, J. (2006). Th e impact of family functioning on African American males' academic achievement: A review and clarifi cation of the empirical literature. *Teachers College Record, 108*, 206–223.

Mantzicopoulos, P., Patrick, H., & Samarapungavan, A. (2008). Young children's motivational beliefs about learning science. *Early Childhood Research Quarterly, 23*, 378–394.

Marchant, G. J., Paulson, S. E., & Rothlisberg, B. A. (2001). Relations of middle school students' perceptions of family and school contexts with academic achievement. *Psychology in the Schools, 38*, 505–519.

Marshall, S. (1995). Ethnic socialization of African American children: Implications for parenting, identity development, and academic achievement. *Journal of Youth and Adolescence, 24*, 377–396.

Mashburn, A. J., & Pianta R. C. (2006). Social relationships and school readiness. *Early Education and Development, 17*, 151–176.

Mickelson, R. A., & Greene, A. D. (2006). Connecting pieces of the puzzle: Gender diff erences in Black middle school students' achievement. *Th e Journal of Negro Education, 75*, 34–48.

Miedel, W. T., & Reynolds, A. J. (1999). Parent involvement in early intervention for disadvantaged children: Does it matter? *Journal of School Psychology, 37*, 379–402.

Morgan, L. P., & Bhola, S. (2006). *Creating a culture of success: Black men-steps toward success.* New York: Th e Children's Aid Society.

NAEYC. (1995). *NAEYC position statement on school readiness.* Retrieved from http://www.naeyc.org/resources/ position_statements/psredy98.htm

National Center for Educational Statistics. (1999). *ECLS-K base year data fi les and electronic codebook.* Retrieved from http://nces.ed.gov/pubs2001/2001029.pdf

No Child Left Behind Act of 2001. Pub. L. No. 107–110, 115 Stat. 1425. (2002).

Oyserman, D., Harrison, K., & Bybee, D. (2001). Can racial identity be promotive of academic effi cacy? *International Journal of Behavioral Development, 25*, 379–385.

Peisner-Feinberg, E., Burchinal, M. R., Cliff ord, R. M, Yazejian, N., Culkin, M. L., Zelazo, J., et al. (1999). *Th e children of the cost, quality, and outcomes study go to school* (Technical Report). Executive summary. Chapel Hill: University of North Carolina at Chapel Hill, Frank Porter Graham Child Development Center.

Polite, V. C., & Davis, J. E. (1999). *African American males in school and society: Practices and policies for eff ective education.* Williston, VT: Teachers College.

Pomerantz, E. M., Moorman, E. A., & Litwack, S. D. (2007). Th e how, whom, and why of parents' involvement in children's academic lives: More is not always better. *Review of Educational Research, 77*, 373–410.

Reichman, N. E. (2005). Low birth weight and school readiness. *Future of Children, 15*, 91–116.

Reynolds, A. J. (1989). A structural model of fi rst-grade outcomes for an urban, low socioeconomic status, minority population. *Journal of Educational Psychology, 81*, 594–603.

Reynolds, A. J. (1992). Comparing measures of parental involvement and their eff ects on academic achievement. *Early Childhood Research Quarterly, 7*, 441–462.

Rimm-Kaufman, S. E., & Pianta, R. C. (2000). An ecological perspective on the transition to kindergarten: A theoretical framework to guide empirical research. *Journal of Applied Developmental Psychology, 21*, 491 – 511.

Saluga, G., Scott-Little, C., & Cliff ord, R. (2000). Readiness for school: A survey of state policies and defi nitions. *Early Childhood Research and Practice, 2.* Retrieved from http://ecrp.uiuc.edu.proxy.lib.umich.edu/v2n2/ saluja.html

Senechal, M., & LeFevre, J. (2002). Parental involvement in the development of children's reading skill: A fi ve-year longitudinal study. *Child Development, 73*, 445–460.

Slaughter-Defoe, D. (2000, September). Early childhood development and school readiness: Some observations about "homework" for new century working parents. Paper presented at the Annual Meeting of the Voices for Illinois Children. Chicago, IL.

Slaughter-Defoe, D. T., Nakagawa, K., Takanishi, R., & Johnson, D. J. (1990). Toward cultural/ecological perspectives on schooling and achievement in African- and Asian-American children. *Child Development, 61*, 363–383.

Slaughter, D. T. (1987). Th e home environment and academic achievement of Black American children and youth: An overview. *Th e Journal of Negro Education, 56*, 3–20.

Smith, E. P., Atkins, J., & Connell, C. M. (2003). Family, school, and community factors and relationships to racialethnic attitudes and academic achievement. *American Journal of Community Psychology, 32*, 159–173.

Stevenson, H. W., Chen, C., & Uttal, D. H. (1990). Beliefs and achievement: A study of Black, White, and Hispanic children. *Child Development, 61*, 508–523.

Stone, S., & McKay, M. (2000). Predictors of urban parent involvement. *School Social Work Journal, 15*, 12–28.

Tatum, A. W. (2005). *Teaching reading to Black adolescent males: Closing the achievement gap.* Portland, ME: Stenhouse.

Taylor, L. C., Hinton, I. D., & Wilson, M. N. (1995). Parental infl uences on academic performance in AfricanAmerican students, *Journal of Child and Family Studies, 4*, 293–302.

Toldson, I. A. (2008). *Breaking barriers: Plotting the path to academic success for school-age African-American males.* Washington, DC: Congressional Black Caucus Foundation, Inc.

West, J., Denton, K., & Germino-Hausken, E. (2000). *America's kindergartners: Findings from the Early Childhood Longitudinal Study, kindergarten class of 1998–99, fall 1998.* Washington, DC: U. S. Department of Education, National Center for Education Statistics. Document Number 2000–070)

Willie, C. V. (1986). Th e Black family and social class. In R. Staples (Ed.), *Th e Black families: Essays and studies* (3rd ed., pp. 99–106). Belmont, CA: Wadsworth.

Wood, D., Kaplan, R., & McLoyd, V. C. (2007). Gender diff erences in the educational expectations of urban, low-income African American youth: Th e role of parents and the school. *Journal of Youth and Adolescence, 36*, 417–427.

Zill, N., Collins, M., & West, J. (1995). Approaching kindergarten. A look at preschoolers in the United States. *Young Children, 51*, 35–38.

Authors

EMANIQUE M. JOE is Postdoctoral Fellow in Combined Program in Education and Psychology, School of Education, at the University of Michigan, in Ann Arbor.

JAMES EARL DAVIS is Professor, Department of Educational Leadership & Policy Studies at Temple University in Philadelphia.

Perceptions of Teacher Expectations by African American High School Students

Beverly E. Pringle, James E. Lyons and Keonya C. Booker

African American high school students are performing behind their White classmates regardless of whether they are in majority or minority populations at school. Teacher expectations, among school-related factors that can impact the academic achievement of African American high school students, are the focus of this study. Interviews were conducted with 48 African American students in two high schools of dissimilar racial makeup. Th is study revealed two major themes denoting the importance of teacher expectations and quality of instruction. Implications of this study for the education of African American students are addressed.

The educating of African American children in the United States has historically endured challenges. Today, fi ft y-six years aft er the *Brown* decision (1954), public school educators continue to seek understanding and solutions to the persistent achievement gap between White and Black students. Such unforeseen changes as the infl ux of middle-class White females becoming the primary teachers for children of color in public education led researchers to closely examine the role of the teacher and the impact that teacher expectations have on the academic success of African American students as well as all children.

Among the primary racial and ethnic groups in this country, African American students particularly, record poor academic performance (Pennerman, 2003). Th is Black-White achievement gap is a persistent, pervasive, and signifi cant disparity in educational achievement and attainment among groups of students as determined by a standardized measure. Since it is normally analyzed according to race and ethnicity, achievement disparities negatively refl ect educational outcomes for poor children and children of color on a consistent basis.

A new emphasis on suburban districts is especially compelling given 2000 Census data that show one-third of all Black children and roughly half of all Hispanic, Asian, and White children live in suburban communities (Th ernstrom & Th ernstrom, 2003). Although some of these schools are poor and segregated like many in urban districts, others are racially integrated in upscale neighborhoods where resources are relatively bountiful and the schools are reputedly excellent. An achievement gap does exist

Beverley E. Pringle, James E. Lyons, & Keonya C. Booker, "Perceptions of Teacher Expectations by African American High School Students," *Th e Journal of Negro Education*, vol. 79, no. 1, pp. 33–40. Copyright © 2010 by Howard University.

even in some of the well-resourced, middle-class school districts in the nation (Steele, 1997). Th ese African American students have similar preschool educational experiences as well as parent expectations. For example, in Shaker Heights, Ohio where most of the African American students are middle or upper middle class, this problem was perceived to be so prevalent that Black parents, community leaders, and school offi cials invited Dr. John Ogbu to conduct a study of this phenomenon to try to determine the causes. Ogbu concluded that Black students were not only disengaged from academic work, but the reasons for Black student disengagement stemmed from factors in both the societal and school system and from community forces from which the students were not immune (Ogbu, 2003). Th ese factors included school race relations, internalized White beliefs, levels of discipline, collective identity, culture, language, and peer pressure (Ogbu, 2003).

Statement of the Problem

Student achievement is aff ected by many variables that can be categorized as either school-related factors or outside forces. School-related variables, or system factors, as described by Ogbu (2003), include pre-school experiences, school practices, and home-school relations. Outside forces such as parental expectations and education, socioeconomic status, and societal discriminatory practices among others make up the second category.

Even when researchers' control for socioeconomic status, level of parental education, and other factors contributing to scholastic achievement, the score gap between White and African American students persists (Brown, 2002). Rather than focusing solely on test scores, studies show that administrators and teachers need to consider schools in a much broader context. School offi cials are also investigating African American and White diff erences in discipline referrals, dropout rates, educational aspirations, and perceptions of the school climate in addition to identifying and applying successful instructional methods. Th e gap is also found in course level enrollment, performance in specifi c courses, rates of participation in gift ed programs and in special education placement (Ogbu, 2003). Th us, some practices by schools and teachers, as duly witnessed, are counterproductive to the academic achievement of certain minority students, particularly African American students.

Although many school-related factors have been identifi ed and, to some extent, used in developing policy and change, the highlight of this study focuses on one particular school practice among several factors. School practices that have been identifi ed as aff ecting academic achievement are school climate, teacher expectations, and instructional methods (Brown, 2002). Th e focus of this study is teacher expectations. Since researchers have not been able to fully explain why African American students underachieve, and since the research suggests that teacher expectations are oft en one factor, this study sought to ask the students themselves. Specifi cally, the research question of interest is: *What are African American high school students' perceptions of teacher expectations?*

Method

Th e research design in this study was qualitative. Qualitative research requires sensitivity to underlying meaning when gathering and interpreting data because it focuses on meaning in context (Glesne, 2006). Th is study was interpretive—the researchers' key concern was to understand the eff ects of teacher expectations on the academic achievement of African American students as perceived by the students themselves.

Participants

All African American graduating seniors at two high schools in the Southeast, Wheeler, and Mission High Schools (pseudonyms), were asked to participate in this study. Wheeler High's student population is 91.9% White and 8.1% minority, which includes 3.2% African American students. Mission High's student population is 27.9% White and 72.1% minority, which includes 27.9% African American students, 21.8% Hispanic students, and 22.4% other minorities. Study participants included 10 (3.2%) African American senior students out of 307 seniors from Wheeler High and 38 (28.3%) African American students out of 134 seniors from Mission High.

Data Collection

Th e research methodology employed was descriptive, allowing the researchers to gather information objectively as well as acknowledging subjective nuances that may have occurred during the course of data collection (Merriam, 2002). Of particular focus in the current study was the interview data that spoke to student perceptions. As aforementioned, the interviewees were African American seniors enrolled in Wheeler and Mission High Schools. Th ese students were selected by an affi rmative response to a question on a survey (in another part of a larger study) requesting student participation in face-to-face interviews.

A semi-structured interview protocol was used which incorporated a series of 15 questions to guide the discussions in the interviews. Students were asked general questions about their relationships with teachers, grading and instructional policies, and personal interactions. Th is type of interview enabled the researchers to conduct qualitative investigations in an open-ended format. It also allowed participants to expound on responses in their own way. Th ese question types elicited positive and negative responses about teacher expectations as the students saw them. Students were able to express opinions and feelings without reservations. All information received from participants was confi dential, and the researchers agreed not to reveal names.

Data Analysis

Th e authors used fi eld notes to interpret the interview results. Data gathered from these interviews were transcribed within days of the interviews to increase accuracy. Subsequently, the transcriptions were analyzed to determine common themes in the students' responses (Marshall & Rossman, 2006). Th is process was ongoing throughout the semester because the interviews were held with students from diff erent schools and at diff erent times over a period of three months. Th rough an iterative process of incorporating new information with existing information, the authors were able to develop themes that emerged from the students' voices. Th e analysis began with a cursory review of transcriptions, then moved into a stage of reducing codes to more specifi c units of analysis and, fi nally, into a selective phase showing associations between themes. A word should be added about our roles as researchers and issues of trustworthiness and credibility. Th e information in this research study underwent a rigorous analytical process as well as the constant discussion of fi ndings among the researchers. Th e work was triangulated by interviewing multiple sources (i.e., students) and relying on many people (i.e., research team) to review the fi ndings and develop themes.

By documenting the process that was used in this study, the authors explained decisions made, how data were collected, and categories and themes that emerged. External validity refers to the extent to which the fi ndings of one study can be applied to other situations (Merriam, 2002), which is diffi cult in qualitative research. However, one way to increase trustworthiness is to use more than one site within a study. Th e participants in this study were students from two diff erent high schools within the participating school district. Findings that were consistent between participating sites increased the ability of the results to be transferred to other situations and contexts.

Findings

From the iterative data analysis, student responses revealed two primary themes of *teacher expectations*, with an emphasis on race and race relations within the high schools, and *qualities of teacher instruction*, with an attention to issues of course diffi culty. Th e themes are detailed with illustrative quotations.

Teacher Expectations

African American students that were interviewed for this study tied teacher expectations to whether or not their teachers genuinely cared about them or even liked them. For example, one female student stated that an English teacher did not like her; therefore, she did not encourage her. Another student who had also been a student in that class reiterated that the teacher had not been fair to the fi rst student.

Student: I believe [Subject] teacher hated me. He hated giving me an A but he knew that 1 had documented everything in his class. He told me that I had a "Ghetto Black Girl Mentality" because of the way I shook my head, moved my hands in front of the class, but he said my speech was good.

Interviewer: Did you ask him what is the Ghetto Black Girl Mentality?

Student: He said, 'you know what I mean; you just a little snappy with things.' I said ok and sat down … I have one classmate who had 0s on her progress report; she found her work in the trash can. We had African Americans with absences on days that they had been in class because they had work that was dated; whereas, White kids could come to school, and they didn't have absences. Me and [another student] in that class contacted the NAACP.

Students participating in the interviews did, however, believe that their teachers expected them to graduate from high school and go on to college. Generally speaking, the students perceived that "teachers knew who was going to graduate [from high school], but the ones that they were not sure of, they did not encourage them or pull them to the side to help them." Th is was a common fi nding in the study, with over three-fourths of the students reporting a perception of lower expectations for them or the other students with whom they identifi ed. Th ese students described having feelings of dread at attending the class, low morale, and a lack of motivation. Th e most outspoken students on this issue perceived a direct association between the negatively charged interpersonal relationships with certain teachers that had decreased their feelings of belongingness in the classroom setting. A feeling of belongingness is oft en the fi rst step to increasing student interest and activity in the life of the class (Sirin & Rogers-Sirin, 2004).

Over one-half of the African American students that were interviewed believed that race or ethnicity was a factor in the way that their teachers viewed them. Th ese students were from both high schools and had few, if any, ethnic minority teachers. Th e following are excerpts from their conversations with the researchers.

Student: Yeah, like in the classroom, as far as like work assignments, sometimes some of the teachers didn't expect much [from me] so like I would sometimes use that to my advantage because I felt like I didn't have to do as much … So like I was making a poster. My poster didn't have to look as good as the White person's … I felt like I would still get the same grade … it usually fl ip fl ops both ways!

Student: I know one student, a White student … real smart and all; really crazy … usually suspended like every week … Th e teachers really care for him … like keep him on track, like he'll walk out of class; they'll let him go … sometimes I don't think that they would do that for a Black student … I have a fear of sleeping in class because I would get in more trouble than versus like a White student.

Student: Th ere were only two African Americans in AP [Subject] … so you already feel sorta out of place. So you [the teacher] are making absurd remarks, trying to make them funny, like when he was making a comment about MLK. All of these Whites are making so-call funny remarks about Black people; we're the only Blacks in there.

With regard to a student's socioeconomic background and its infl uence on teacher interactions, the student interviewees diff ered to some degree in their opinions. African American students from Mission High (the predominantly African American school) thought that this issue was minor although one student noted, "sometimes students were treated as a charity case that they could not do for themselves … they (teachers) go by judgment and not by what is really happening with that person." Th is was not the circumstance as described by African American students from Wheeler High School (the predominantly White school).

Student 1: I think they think everyone is rich in this school … stuck up, snotty kids and are spoiled.
Interviewer: Do you agree?
Students: No!
Student 1: It's like the outside looking in; that's how we're viewed, even from other schools … It's not our fault. It's our parents who want to make our lives better. … It should not be taken out on us.
Interviewer: Are you treated badly?
Student 1: I think it is just some teachers that think we're all spoiled brats.
Researcher: Are you saying that this is more of a socio-economic confl ict versus a racial confl ict?
Student 1: Defi nitely!

Student 2: Some teachers are shocked or surprised that you have these nice things. It was awkward; very strained. A teacher could not grasp that concept that you as a Black student came from an affl uent family and can do as well.

Qualities of Teacher Instruction

According to student interview data, over 60% of students reported having adequate teacher instruction. For instance, two students interviewed at diff erent times described the same English teacher below:

Student 1: White English IV teacher—he encouraged me; he took the time and really got on my level; he called me and helped me with my writing … because I was graduating early and couldn't take honors, he made sure that I stayed on the honors level.
Student 2: Th ere were no race barriers; no academic barriers. He stopped the whole class, not just pulling you aside and goes over information. He would make sure you understand. I really do like writing. I applied for many scholarships and he helped me.

Th ere were, however, instances in which students at both schools described teachers who did not off er assistance, showed favoritism toward certain groups of students such as athletes, and had poor classroom management. Th e following student detailed a need for parental intervention aft er her teacher was not assisting her.

Student: English is my favorite subject. One time when I was in the danger zone … C, D, and F and I told my teacher, 'You're not doing what you're supposed to do.' I've never made below a B in English. I said, 'Look Miss So-and-so, I need your help and you tell me that this is all you're going to do, that I will have to do this on my own time?' Th en this is when I had to step out, and this is when my mother had to speak on my behalf to the administration …

Th e additional remarks in the interviews revealed students responded well to teachers who were most challenging, but fair. Th ese teachers were oft en an English, mathematics, or science teacher. Student comments about their best teachers ranged from "cool," "not boring," "accepts you for who you are; keeps you in check," "made class fun; talked to you," "s/he got on my level," "she makes us relax; has patience," "goes the extra mile and tutors others," to "he knew our names." Spanish teachers, described as "those teachers treated all students equal," were also highly rated by the Mission High group while students from Wheeler High described their entire math department as "strong."

Just as students were quick to discuss their best teachers, they also expressed their defi nition of a bad teacher. Aside from students referring to this type of teacher as being "boring," a bad teacher was described as one who "lectured for one and one-half hours and didn't answer your questions," "showed favoritism to football players," "does not provide help," and "gives us work without explaining it" among other comments. A few students described teachers with unfavorable attitudes—"not wanting to be here; only here because of the bonus money," or telling the students "I've got a degree, you get yours." Th e following comments are from two students sharing their views on lackadaisical teachers.

Mission High Student: It was the teacher's mentality. She said 'Ya'll ain't going to do nothing but show out and cut up. Friday's not a day of teaching so like y'all don't want to do nothing, so we're not going to.' How she know that? You gotta teach every day. I mean, just cause it's Friday, you still gotta teach.

Wheeler High Student: To me, the quality of a good teacher is someone who does not sit at their desk and doodle on their notepad. Not someone who'll give you work and have you stranded not knowing. I'm not saying that you have to go step by step and baby me, but let me know exactly what you want from this. How can I give you a productive paper; how can I do well on this thing if you're not being clear on what you want? A good teacher provides assistance, doesn't just give out assignments … I like to be challenged, but when you leave me out here stranded and now I'm making failing grades, that is not ok with me. … But you can go back to your desk and work on your coloring … work on your scrapbook while instructional time is going on … Test-taking skills … I can't do that when you put on a transparency and say here, do this and go back to your desk.

In the interviews with African American students, responses varied when the researchers asked if they had been encouraged to take honors and AP classes. Nearly all of the students interviewed at both schools had taken at least one honors class in high school. One female student had been in the gift ed program in elementary school and continued taking honors classes throughout high school. Another student commented that a 9th grade teacher did encourage her to take honors classes. She took Honors English I–IV, Spanish III, and Computerized Accounting which was considered an honors course in her school. However, several students from both schools expressed dismay about comments made to them by particular teachers in either their 9th or 10th grade year or that a counselor had either dissuaded them or neglected to provide them with vital information concerning honors or AP courses.

Student: I was never discouraged … well I would say one time in my 10th grade year I was told that I shouldn't take an AP class. I said 'Ok, whatever.' I made an A in this person's class, so at the end of the year when they sign you up and you go to get your [teacher's] initial, she said that she didn't think that that [AP] was right for me. I said ok. I'll just take honors … I thought about it later. My GPA was a 3.8 but it could have been a 4.0 if I had taken that AP class.

One male student felt like his counselor tried to discourage him, since he had moved to this school district from another state. He shared that he and his mother made the decision for him to continue with honors classes. Similarly, another young man stated that his counselor did not tell him about the fee waiver for college exams when he moved into the district in 10th grade. When asked by the researchers if he had any regrets the student replied, "Yeah. Because of some of the requirements for college, I would have taken it [the waiver] with biology, anatomy/physiology and more classes."

Student: It was self-motivation, parental motivation, and support from some of my teachers. … But in my senior year before school really began, I went to my counselor and said 'I think I want to do AP [Subject].' She replied 'I just don't think you're ready for all that workload.' Th at really hurt me. … Th e counselor did not base her answer on anything, even aft er I told her to pull up my record and get some of my teachers' comments about my attitude towards class and what I do … I'm a good student.

One young lady was so dissuaded by her 10th grade English teacher that she did not take an honors or AP class. Th is discouragement was also refl ected in the response of another student who stated that neither she nor any other Blacks took a math course beyond pre-Calculus.

Discussion

Th e fi ndings of this study led to three conclusions. First, the majority of the 48 students in this study believed that race or ethnicity was a factor in the way that teachers treated them. Second, many of the respondents indicated they perceived that some of their teachers have lower expectations for African American students. In particular, many students reported that they were either not encouraged or blatantly discouraged from taking advanced or honors classes. Also, they reported that some teachers had demonstrated, by word or deed, not expecting as much in terms of high quality work from African American students in comparison to what they expected from White students. Th ird, many of the students indicated that the most challenging and fair teachers tended to be in the disciplines of the languages and mathematics.

Conclusion

Th e fundamental purpose of this study was to explore the relationship between teacher expectations and the interpersonal perceptions of African American high school students. Research indicates that teacher expectations are one of many factors that strongly infl uence students' academic success. Th is assessment applies to many African American children in K–12 schools across the United States. Furthermore, the level of performance of many African American youth has created a serious achievement gap between them and White students in public schools. Teacher expectations can mean diff erent things to diff erent people. Th erefore, it is important to understand that the teacher can be the most infl uential factor in a student's academic success. "Anything a child feels is diff erent about himself which cannot be referred to spontaneously, casually, naturally, and uncritically by the teacher can become a cause for anxiety and an obstacle to learning" (Paley, 2000, p. xv).

Th is poses yet another concern about the teachers of African American children. Because children must feel a sense of belonging in schools and that their teachers do care about them, student-teacher relationships are also important. Th e power of that relationship is what determines how instrumental the classroom teacher is in creating conditions in which a student can be successful. He or she must be able to emotionally connect with students because that is what makes it possible for the child to identify with and internalize the teacher's disposition toward learning (Comer, Joyner, & Ben-Avie, 2004). Without that emotional contact, students may reject school and become ambivalent or reluctant to get involved (Parsons, 2005). High expectations breed high performance.

Th e fi ndings and conclusions of this study must be viewed with some caution, however, since this was a qualitative study done with a relatively small sample and was based principally on the perceptions of the respondents. Nevertheless, the study does accurately present the feelings of the participants, expressed through their own voices and words, of how they perceive their school experiences with teachers. Th erefore, the fi ndings can be used as lens through which researchers and educational practitioners might more eff ectively assess and address the daily interactions between high school teachers and African American students in the classroom.

REFERENCES

Brown, K. E. (2002). Th e infl uence of school climate, teacher expectations, and instructional methods on academic achievement of low SES African American elementary students: A case study. *Dissertation Abstract International, 63*(07B), 3512.

Brown v. Th e Board of Education Topeka Kansas, 347 U.S. 483 (1954).

Comer, J., Joyner, E. T., & Ben-Avie, M. (2004). *Six pathways to healthy child development and academic success: Th e fi eld guide to Comer schools in action.* Th ousand Oaks, CA: Corwin.

Glesne, C. (2006). *Becoming qualitative researchers* (3rd ed.). New York: Allyn & Bacon.

Marshall, C., & Rossman, G. (2006). *Designing qualitative research* (4th ed.). Th ousand Oaks, CA: Sage.

Merriam, S. B. (2002). *Qualitative research in practice: Examples for discussion and analysis.* San Francisco, CA: Jossey-Bass.

Ogbu, J. U. (2003). *Black American students in an affl uent suburb: A study of academic disengagement.* Mahwah, NJ: Erlbaum.

Paley, V. G. (2000). *White teacher.* Cambridge, MA: Harvard University Press.

Parsons, E. C. (2005). From caring as a relation to a culturally relevant caring: A White teacher's bridge to Black students. *Equity & Excellence in Education, 38*, 25–34.

Pennerman, A. J. (2003). An investigation of perceived factors that contribute to the achievement gap: A comparison of Black and White students. *Dissertation Abstracts International, 64*(09), 4649.

Sirin, S. R., & Rogers-Sirin, L. (2004). Exploring school engagement of middle class African-American adolescents. *Youth & Society, 35*, 323–340.

Steele, C. M. (1997). A threat in the air. How stereotypes shape intellectual identity and performance. *American Psychologist, 52*, 613–629.

Th ernstrom, A., & Th ernstrom, S. (2003). *No excuses: Closing the racial gap in learning.* New York: Simon & Schuster.

Authors

BEVERLEY E. PRINGLE is a public school administrator in the Rochester City School District in Rochester, New York.

JAMES E. LYONS is Professor in the Department of Educational Leadership at the University of North Carolina at Charlotte.

KEONYA C. BOOKER is Director of Continuing Education at Johnson C. Smith University in Charlotte, North Carolina.

Operationalizing Style

Quantifying the Use of Style Shift in the Speech of African American Adolescents

Jennifer Renn and J. Michael Terry

Th e vast majority of research to date on African American Vernacular English style shift has taken the form of qualitative analyses of individual case studies; however, despite its great success, in focusing on individual rather than group style and style shift ing, such work by itself is unable to answer key questions about style and style shift at the level of social groups, communities of practice, and broader based communities. Recent quantitative analyses, such as Craig and Washington's (2006) Dialect Density Measure (DDM), have sought to capture stylistic variation at the group level by analyzing dozens of linguistic features meant to represent a dialect, but use of such large numbers of features severely restricts the types of statistical analyses that can be applied to a given data set and therefore limits the utility of the technique. To test whether a smaller subset of features can be used to quantify stylistic variation, we analyzed a sample of 108 sixth-grade students observed in two conditions that diff ered in formality. Th ree measures were used to track changes in style, two large-scale DDMs constructed from a set of more than 40 variables and a subset measure that used only 6 variables. Analyses indicate that the larger DDMs were highly correlated with the subset measure, thus indicating that a small number of features can be used to reliably refl ect shift ing styles.

The goal of this article is to add to the current understanding of how African American Vernacular English (AAVE) speakers shift their speech styles in relation to situational context. We wish to make explicit the underlying assumption that AAVE speakers are oft en thought of and, more importantly, oft en think of themselves as a group. Th us, we expect that AAVE speakers share to some degree a set of common practices when it comes to their style-shift ing. In light of this assumption, we propose a set of quantitative methods controlled for and applied to groups to capture these practices.

In focusing on group rather than individual style shift ing, this work shares the aims of many of the earliest studies of stylistic variation, which themselves sought to identify and to some degree explain group rather than individual patterns of variation (Labov 1966; Guy 1980). Operating in this tradition, the present study is meant to complement more recent research on style which has, in contrast, focused almost exclusively on single case studies. Th ere are at least two reasons for the current trend toward studying style qualitatively at the level of the individual. First, quantitative methods, like those advocated here, are admittedly limited in what they can reveal. For instance, they have little to say in current

Jennifer Renn & J. Michael Terry, "Operationalizing Style: Quantifying the Use of Style Shift in the Speech of African American Adolescents," *American Speech*, vol. 84, no. 4, pp. 367–390. Copyright © 2009 by Duke University Press. Reprinted with permission.

debates over whether style shift ing is mostly a reactive phenomenon, conditioned by and not just related to diff erences in context, or whether, as numerous authors maintain, it is a more proactive craft ing of identity. Coupland (forthcoming) and others (Schilling-Estes 2004; Moore and Podesva 2009) argue that answers to such questions concerning why people style shift can be found only through the detailed analysis of how people use linguistic features in unfolding discourse; therefore, style shift ing should be studied through the qualitative analysis of case studies.

While they undoubtedly provide invaluable information, case studies fail to answer key questions about style shift in populations, questions that not only have theoretical interest, but also aff ect practical matters. One reason for the increased interest in style shift among AAVE speakers is that it has been suggested that the ability to style shift from AAVE to the educational standard is an important academic skill for African American students and that the inability of many African American students to do so may contribute to the current black-white academic achievement gap. To investigate this and other possible ramifi cations of style shift , one must be able to examine style shift at the level of social groups, communities of practice, and broader based communities. Th eir limitations notwithstanding, here more quantitative methods are particularly useful. In the end, both methodologies contribute something important to the study of style shift .

A second reason that current methods of studying style shift have been largely limited to studying individuals rather than entire groups stems from the diffi culty involved in individuating dialects such as AAVE. Th e basic problem is this: if dialects are not (and perhaps cannot) be clearly defi ned, which linguistic features should be observed to identify dialectal shift s? Monitoring too large a number of features only muddies the waters, rendering most statistical techniques ineff ectual. While we do not advance any new defi nition of AAVE in this paper, we outline how the issue of defi nition has shaped the study of AAVE style shift and infl uences the design of the methods we put forward. Th us, this study unites two traditionally elusive themes in the study of AAVE, namely, its operational defi nition and contextually based shift s in its use.

Despite the countless descriptions of the linguistic traits associated with African American speech, there has been little discussion of what the precise linguistic parameters defi ne AAVE as a variety. Operationally, it appears feasible to simply describe features associated with African American speakers and to assume that these features are integral to the defi nition of a largely unitary variety. Th e question of defi ning the essential and/or exclusive sets of AAVE traits is, however, a much more challenging pursuit, both descriptively and theoretically. Th is defi nitional issue has haunted AAVE for as long as linguists have attempted to describe it. However, the defi nitional dilemma in determining the parameters of a language variety is hardly unique to AAVE; in fact, it is relatively common to confront defi nitional ambiguity and vagueness in delimiting languages and varieties.

Within the fi eld of linguistics, there is a long tradition of discussion and debate over the seemingly fundamental question of what exactly constitutes a language or a dialect of a language. A signifi cant part of the American structuralist program, for example, involved attempting to rework traditional notions of these terms into sets of theoretically defensible defi nitions and, wherever possible, going further by providing an operational basis for using those defi nitions. Th e lack of success of these and other eff orts to fi nd workable defi nitions, however, has led the majority of linguists to conclude, along with Chambers and Trudgill (1980, 5), that the concept of "a 'language' is not a particularly linguistic notion at all."

Building on the work of German linguist Heinz Kloss (1967) and his distinction between *Ausbau* languages (closely related languages that are oft en mutually intelligible) and *Abstand* languages (language structurally so dissimilar that they are not mutually intelligible), Fasold (2004) highlights what is generally seen as the chief impediment to arriving at strict defi nitions of language and associated terms: the "commonsense," everyday notion of a language that we would wish to refi ne is a mixed bag. It is partly structural and partly sociopolitical, each arena (the *Ausbau* and the *Abstand* in Kloss's terminology) prescribing its own criteria for defi ning languages, with the two diff erent types of criteria failing to converge on any one "thing" that one might call a language or dialect. Not even the commonly used criterion of mutual intelligibility is able to reveal a common ground and reliably individuate languages. Th e well-known cases of German and the Scandinavian languages, among others, show that intelligibility between language varieties is not always mutual and that oft en sociopolitical considerations are at odds with structural similarities, creating asymmetries in understanding.

In response to this heterogeneous mixture of language-defi ning criteria, one branch of linguistics has focused on the formal properties of language, adopting the stance advocated by Chomsky (1980, 1986) that linguistics is not the study of languages but the study of grammars, the sets of organizing principles that govern language structure. Another branch of linguistics spearheaded by Labov (1966, 2001) has, with a diff erent set of goals, focused on language in society, acknowledging the epiphenomenal nature of languages and dialects, while simultaneously recognizing that as speakers communicate on these and more fi ne-grained sociolinguistic levels, examining the interactions among the formal and more sociocultural properties of language is necessary to understand many important aspects of language variation and change.

Because it calls attention to potentially important correlations between variation in linguistic structures and changes in sociocultural conditions, the study of style (i.e., speakers' conscious and unconscious use of linguistic structures to situate themselves with respect to others and to express identity) plays an important role in sociolinguistic research. Like languages and dialects, individual styles also resist clear defi nition. Rather than focus on defi ning styles, researchers have instead focused on identifying style shift , noting changes in linguistic features that speakers use in response to various social conditions that are thought to determine style. While this focus on style shift avoids directly defi ning styles, it does not evade the issue completely. Th e question of which linguistic features to look to as indicators of a shift remains a practical research matter. Initial notions of what defi nes a style (or dialect or language) play an important role in guiding research on intraspeaker language variation though it may not be explicitly recognized. For example, the study of style shift among speakers of AAVE demands some sense of what constitutes AAVE and how the selected linguistic variations for measuring variation are representative of this variety.

In the face of this defi nitional challenge, researchers have tended to cast their nets broadly, examining large numbers of linguistic features that are thought to be a part of AAVE. Th is has, in turn, led to other methodological consequences, including limiting the range of statistical options available for studying patterns of variation at the level of the dialect. Instead, most work on AAVE style shift ing, like most work on style shift generally, has focused on case studies or small numbers of speakers in relatively uncontrolled, natural situations rather than under experimental conditions. Typically, a single AAVEspeaking subject is monitored for possible changes among a large number of features (e.g., Rickford and McNair-Knox 1994; Weldon 2004; Kendall and Wolfram 2009). Th is is despite great interest in AAVE speakers as a group.

As noted, in this study we use quantitative methods controlled for and applied to groups rather than the individual to better ascertain how AAVE speakers shift their speech styles related to situational context. Th e method we employ identifi es style shift by tracking the use or nonuse of a carefully selected subset of AAVE features in the speech of a group of African American youth in diff erent situations. Two separate measures, both made up of a broad-based inventory of AAVE structures, are used for comparison and to establish the effi cacy of the subset measure, rather than as a single summary variable meant to identify shift by capturing any feature that could arguably be considered characteristic of AAVE. Building on knowledge acquired through methods like Craig and Washington's (2006) Dialect Density Measure that look at a large set of AAVE linguistic features, this approach provides researchers with an opportunity to better describe and understand style shift ing at the population level by widening the range of statistical analysis methods that can be applied to the endeavor. At the same time, it allows for a narrower, more detailed focus on the subsets and individual features that seem to be included in that shift .

ISSUES IN CHARACTERIZING AAVE

In many respects, the steadily increasing interest in AAVE has helped fuel the growth of sociolinguistics.

One reason for this interest is a growing awareness of the role that vernacular plays in the African American community. Not only is AAVE an important indicator of identity and group membership, but, oft en as a result, it fi gures prominently in discussions of social and educational issues such as employment and academic achievement. As alluded to earlier, research shows high AAVE use is correlated with low academic achievement (e.g., Craig, Connor, and Washington 2003; Craig and Washington 2004), and it has been suggested that speakers' use of AAVE may play a role in the academic achievement gap between African American students and their white peers. Th e relative eff ect of social demographic factors versus structural linguistic factors is a matter of great debate. What is clear, however, is that as researchers attempt to better understand these and other issues regarding AAVE, current methods of studying populations of speakers must continue to be refi ned and expanded. To further the investigation of the many issues surrounding AAVE, a number of more fundamental matters fi rst must be addressed, including the best way to characterize AAVE and, given a characterization, how to accurately and reliably measure a speaker's level of dialect use.

It is well documented that speech patterns in African American communities tend to diff er from those of European American communities. Early descriptive work by Labov et al. (1968) and Fasold and Wolfram (1970) noted that despite regional diff erences these patterns tend to share enough of a resemblance in terms of both linguistic structure and social use to be included under the rubric of African American English in the socio-linguistic literature.[1] More recent work by Rickford (1999) provides a list of phonological, morphological, and syntactic features that are common to AAVE, and an even more detailed account of the attributes typical of AAVE speakers is provided by Green (2002). Green gives in-depth specifi cations of lexical, semantic, syntactic, morphosyntactic, and phonological properties characteristic of AAVE. Despite the work of these and other linguists, like any other language or dialect, AAVE resists strict defi nition. Th ere is a great deal of truth in the words of Strang (1970, 227), who stated that "dialects are artifacts, fi ctitious entities invented by speakers, in which, for limited purposes, linguists suspend disbelief." Th is is not to say that the concept of a dialect is not a useful or important one; it is only to say that linguists must be clear about the purposes to which they put it.

One problem of distinguishing and analyzing AAVE as its own entity is that most of an AAVE speaker's speech overlaps greatly with that of speakers of standard American English and other varieties of English. In Craig and Washington's (2004) study of school-age children, for instance, the child with the most vernacular speech style used only one AAVE feature per 2.3 words.[2] Th us, more than half of that child's speech consisted of forms that are shared with other English varieties. In their 1981 study, Seymour and Seymour report noticeable phonological contrasts in these two dialect groups. Th ey note, however, that many diff erences could be attributed to incomplete language development rather than dialect diff erences, since "unique error types were not exclusively characteristic of either group" (274). Although obvious contrasts in these studies show that for various purposes AAVE and standard English may be thought of as discrete varieties of English, they also highlight the considerable overlap between them.

Additionally, many distinguishing features of AAVE are characteristic of other regionalized or socially stratifi ed varieties of English. Comparisons with European Americans who utilize a regional Southern dialect are of particular interest, as the degree of similarity between "black speech" and "white speech" is greatest in the Southern United States. For example, double modals such as *might could* and the use of an auxiliary like the preverbal *done* construction in sentences such as *John done gone to the store* are common to Southern vernaculars and AAVE (Wolfram and Schilling-Estes 2006). Most of these "shared" features, however, are found more frequently in AAVE or occur in a wider range of linguistic environments in the speech of African Americans (Rickford 1999).

Another problem is that although in practice AAVE is oft en treated as a unitary dialect, it is well known that, like any other language or dialect, it varies depending on region, age, gender, and individual speaker characteristics. While a core set of features may distinguish AAVE from other language varieties, AAVE speakers can oft en be identifi ed as hailing from certain areas of the United States based on regional infl uences. For example, Wolfram and Schilling-Estes (2006) note the existence of regional AAVE varieties such as Northern metropolitan, Southern rural, South Atlantic coastal, and Gulf region.

Other factors, such as gender, have been found to aff ect variability in AAVE use. Most investigations of AAVE, such as Wolfram (1969), suggest that men use higher levels of AAVE features than women. His study of third-person singular -*s* absence in Detroit, for example, indicated that working-class men tended to use the vernacular form signifi cantly more frequently than women. Th ere is, however, a great deal of individual variation, as shown by Rickford (1992), who found higher incidences of this feature in the speech of two women in East Palo Alto than any of their male counterparts, demonstrating the unpredictability of language use.

Still other studies show the importance of membership in social networks and communities of practice in a speaker's level of AAVE use. Mallinson and Childs (2007) examined a rural Appalachian community where African American women were divided into two social groups, the "porch sitters" and the "church ladies." Each group used a particular speech style that indicated their social ties, their group and individual identities, and their orientation toward their local community. Th e language of the fi rst group, the "porch sitters," contained a large proportion of AAVE features, while the "church ladies" utilized more standard and regional Appalachian characteristics in their speech. Th ese diff erences demonstrate the importance of social associations in the amount and type of vernacular employed by a speaker. If there is indeed a homogeneous core in AAVE, it obviously is highly nuanced and more of a convenient, politically based fi ction than a rigorous linguistic construct. In fact, in line with Lippi-Green (1997), Wolfram (2007) observes that the notion of a unitary, homogeneous variety of AAVE is a bit of sociolinguistic folklore: it is a kind of strategic essentialism in the sense of Spivak (1988). Th at is, African Americans temporarily forgo variation to highlight their commonality, as well as to combat popular interpretations of their speech patterns in terms of the principle of linguistic subordination, whereby language varieties associated with socially subordinate groups are viewed as linguistic defi cits rather than neutral linguistic diff erences (Lippi-Green 1997).

THE STUDY OF STYLE

Against a backdrop of studies on dialectal diff erence and its meaning, many scholars have worked to develop a better understanding of intraspeaker style and its role in language variation. Th e Attention to Speech model (Labov 1972), the Audience Design model (Bell 1984), and the Speaker Design approach (e.g., Schilling-Estes 1998; Eckert 2000; Coupland 2007) are three major theories that have been used to explain self-stylization. While these theories all off er useful insight into speakers' use of style, they are not meant as models of style itself, but of the underlying conditions and attitudes that produce style shift . For example, the works of Bell (1984, 2001) and Preston (1991) looked at the infl uence of social diff erences on language use, fi nding that range of linguistic variation in style within a given social group was smaller than the scope of their social diff erences. By focusing on the more concrete behavior of style shift ing, it is possible to avoid the potentially impossible task of defi ning and explaining style while still seeing it at work.

Th e Attention to Speech model proposed by Labov (1966) marked the fi rst major account of speakers' ability to modify their speech styles. Originally intended to identify conditions under which speakers produce their most vernacular style, this model contrasts speakers' use of "casual" and "careful" speech. In his model, Labov defi nes casual speech as "the everyday speech used in informal situations where no attention is directed to language" (92), while careful speech is more self-conscious, oft en altered as a result of the presence of an interviewer or for some other reason (100). Th ese two speech types are revealed by paralinguistic cues such as diff erences in tempo, pitch, volume, and breathing as well as by the use of laughter in conversation. Labov's initial investigations of style were conducted using sociolinguistic interviews, which specifi cally attempted to elicit the two speech types by eff ecting particular speech conditions during the interview. A key fi nding of that work was that in a more formal situation like an interview, speakers use fewer vernacular features presumably because they are paying closer attention to their speech. Labov's original intent notwithstanding, the Attention to Speech model has long served as the basis for a great deal of work that focuses on the process of style shift ing itself. Th e relative formality of circumstances of speech is oft en viewed as a primary trigger for style shift ing.

A diff erent explanation of style shift ing was proposed by Bell (1984). Building upon Street and Giles's (1982) notion of a speech accommodation model, he suggested that speakers adjust their speech to win the approval of other members of the conversation. Unlike Labov's model, this Audience Design approach focuses on others, both participants and nonparticipants (e.g., auditors or eavesdroppers) in the conversation, as the principal catalyst of style shift ing. In this view, both the speaker and the interlocutor play an integral role in contributing to style.

More recent work has continued to build on the notion of speech conditions (which include the participants involved) as an impetus for style shift ing. Finegan and Biber (1994) found "systematic patterns of register variation and social dialect variation," which were related to the linguistic environment, speaker demographics and characteristics, and the situation of use (315). Ervin-Tripp (2001) adds to their work, indicating that particular circumstances, such as speech versus writing, planned versus unplanned speech, and face-to-face conversation versus a speech presented to a group of people, trigger style shift s among all monolinguals. For example, style shift has been noted to occur in response to a speaker's conversational partner. Speakers tend be less self-conscious and therefore use more "regular" or vernacular speech with addressees whom they consider peers or who are familiar to them.[3] Reminiscent of Labov's Attention to Speech model and his distinction between formal and informal context, Rickford and McNair-Knox (1994) argue that these signifi cant shift s are not due to accommodation alone because they refl ect the social characteristics of addressees rather than their linguistic behavior. In addition to infl uences, discussion topic may impact speech style. Using an interview situation to hold the speech conditions constant, studies by Labov (2001) looked at how the interviewer's manipulation of topic resulted in changes in the interviewees' vernacular use. In response to more typical interview questions about the interviewee's background, subjects used more careful speech; when the interviewer directed the conversation toward topics that were of "maximal interest and emotional involvement" to the subject, more casual speech was used.

A still more recent attempt at explaining style is the Speaker Design approach, which successfully addresses factors not fully brought to the fore by the Attention to Speech and Audience Design scenarios. While researchers like Bell (1997), using the notion of initiative style shift , have long recognized that speakers can and do shift styles to alter existing situations through the craft ing of their own identities, proponents of the Speaker Design model (e.g., Schilling-Estes 2004; Coupland 2007) believe that the speaker's identity and relationships with interlocutors are the prime motivators of shift s in speech style.

Unlike the other theories, the Speaker Design approach focuses on the speakers themselves rather than outside infl uences as the reason for change. Th is model hypothesizes that in choosing to use or exclude certain linguistic features, speakers indicate group membership and personal identity. Th us, a speaker's style is the consequence of his or her own choices in seeking to promote a particular persona. For example, Coupland's (1984) case study of a Welsh travel assistant found that she closely matched her clients' use of several phonological variables, in spite of the fact that her interlocutors varied widely in their degree of standardness. Rather than attributing this merely to accommodation, he argues that she is asserting an identity, stating:

> Sue is NOT attempting to reproduce the actual levels of standardness for particular variables that she detects in the speech of her interlocutors; rather she is attempting to convey via her pronunciation and presumably other behaviors, verbal and nonverbal, a *persona* which is similar to that conveyed by her interlocutors. [1984, 65]

Similarly, Schilling-Estes's (2004) North Carolina study compares how African Americans and Lumbee Indians vary their use of certain linguistic markers in response to the ethnic identity they are putting forth. Both the Lumbee speaker and the African American speaker she analyzed used features that highlighted their ethnicity when discussing topics like race relations, but used such features considerably less frequently when discussing more impersonal topics. Th us, each speaker used language as a way of refl ecting his personal identity.

Each of these theories illustrates a major tack that has been taken in the study of style shift . Although each contributes important ideas about style shift that are neglected by its competitors, no one theory seems to completely capture the full richness of the phenomenon. Rather than indicating a weakness in any of the core ideas these theories are built on, this perhaps suggests that no single theory is capable of capturing the complex nature of style and style shift . It is certainly clear that the context, the audience, and the speaker's individual, interpersonal, and group identities all have an impact on stylistic choices. It is equally clear that by noting when and how speakers change their speech, linguists have been able to better understand style, despite the fact that individual styles are elusive if one attempts to defi ne them in a rigorous, unitary, and theoretically defensible way.

QUANTIFYING THE USE OF A LANGUAGE VARIETY

Although the application of quantitative analysis techniques to the study of language variation and style has been extensive, it has largely been restricted to a focus on individual variables rather than composite metrics of dialect use. Th e literature consists mainly of case studies of individuals and analysis of individual variables. While these approaches identify important linguistic behaviors, conclusions are diffi cult to extrapolate to composite dialects for larger populations. If we want to capture generalizations about AAVE speakers as a group and not simply as individuals, then some sort of composite measure is needed as way of identifying that group.

Historically, there have been three primary methods applied to the assessment of composite dialect use (Oetting and McDonald 2002). Th e fi rst is the use of listener judgments to assess dialect. Th is method provides listeners, either expert sociolinguistic judges or naive language judges from representative populations of speakers, with speech samples and asks them to assess speaker characteristics such as age, ethnicity, region, and community. Despite minimal training and oft en very short speech samples, listeners' responses tend to be quite reliable using this technique. A second quantitative approach is a type-based method, where researchers look for language patterns that they consider characteristic of a given language variety; if a given speaker utilizes a predetermined number of the selected patterns, he or she is classifi ed as a speaker of that dialect. For example, Smith, Lee, and McDade (2001, 150) classifi ed subjects as AAVE speakers if they produced at least fi ve nonmainstream AAVE patterns. Finally, token-based methods have been used to attain information about a speaker's dialect type and degree of use. Th ese approaches involve counting the number of utterances or words that contain a nonstandard feature and dividing them by the total number of utterances or words in the speech sample; thus, researchers are able to look at dialect as a continuum ranging from light to heavy use, rather than merely specifying a cutoff value that categorizes speakers as dialect using or not.

One of the more prevalent token-based methods used in the fi eld of speech-language pathology is the Dialect Density Measure (DDM) (Craig, Washington, and Th ompson-Porter 1998; Craig and Washington 2004). Th is instrument was developed specifi cally to gauge a speaker's composite use of AAVE. Th e Craig and Washington (2006) DDM uses a predetermined list of features based on the descriptive literature of AAVE (e.g. Fasold and Wolfram 1970; Labov 1972; Rickford 1999; Green 2002), calculates the total number of features that occur in a speech sample, and divides that total by the number of utterances in the sample.4 In this way it accounts for the fact that an utterance may contain more than one AAVE feature. Because young children's utterances are much shorter than those of older children and adults, they also compute the total number of features divided by the total number of words.

A number of patterns in the vernacular use of African Americans have been identifi ed using Craig and Washington's DDM. In Craig and Washington's (2004) study of school-age children, there were two very clear changes in vernacular use based upon age. Comparisons of diff erent community types also demonstrated signifi cant diff erences. Studies found that African Americans in a "mid-size central city" utilized AAVE features half as oft en as those from an "urban-fringe community"[5] (Craig and Washington 2004; Th ompson, Craig, and Washington 2004). Finally, diff erences in AAVE use due to situational context have been revealed using a DDM. In studies of younger children, it was determined that AAVE features were used much more frequently in situations where the children spontaneously described pictures versus when they either read standard English text aloud or wrote a story (Craig and Washington 2004; Th ompson, Craig, and Washington 2004). Th ese examples illustrate the assorted ways that DDMs have been used to quantify AAVE production.

Such measures, however, have numerous restrictions as well, restrictions that challenge their defi nitional and operational effi cacy. First, the justifi cation for including or excluding structures from a comprehensive measure is not always straightforward and consensual. As discussed above, there is much debate and little consensus about which features best characterize AAVE and if all features are equally weighted in the defi nition of AAVE, to say nothing of the overlap between many features of AAVE and other vernacular varieties. Th us, it is not clear that the Craig and Washington DDM nor any similar measure could truly be considered all inclusive or effi ciently predictive. Additionally, the kinds of statistical analyses that can be undertaken with a measure containing dozens of features are extremely limited. Performing an exploratory factor analysis on a large number of features can easily require such large sample sizes as to make a linguistic study impractical. Although there is much debate in the fi eld of statistics regarding the minimal sample size required for an exploratory factor analysis, MacCallum et al. (2001) suggest that when the amount of variance explained by common factors is low, a subjects-to-variables ratio as large as 20:1 might be necessary for a stable solution. Th us, a study that uses only 30 linguistic variables, would call for a sample size of 600 participants, a number that would be extremely diffi cult to recruit for any kind of in-depth or longitudinal language study. Finally, measures that confl ate an assortment of features calculate a unitary score that pays attention only to the speaker's overall vernacular use. While this methodology might indicate that a shift has taken place, combining all the vernacular features glosses over the disproportionately larger role that certain features have during style shift . In the process, a great deal of information about language and style use, as well as how particular features are used strategically in interaction, is missed with such measures.

One way to combat the diffi culties that accompany such large-scale quantitative measures is to take a more narrow approach and focus on only a few linguistic features. By choosing a subset of features, measures like the six-feature subset AAVE measure advocated, developed, and used in this study, it may be possible to avoid some of the diffi culties of trying to defi ne AAVE as a language variety while increasing the operational statistical possibilities for studying style. By focusing on a handful of features culled from a larger set, there is less need to argue over how AAVE should be characterized as a dialect. Instead of dealing with this problematic objective, one can focus only on the features that are the most responsive to context, gender, and other factors. Also, a measure utilizing a smaller number of features greatly increases one's analytical options. Th e reduced number of variables allows for the application of factor analysis and other types of structural equation modeling techniques. Measures that include dozens of features are oft en limited to rudimentary analysis methodologies such as t-tests and chi-square tests, thereby limiting the information that can be attained. Additionally, this subset method can be used to highlight those particular features that shift under particular conditions. If one is interested in which features shift as a result of the formality of a given situation, the researcher might identify several features that potentially play a prominent role in this linguistic behavior by noting those that seem to exhibit the greatest variation in usage across contexts.

Importantly, this technique builds on the information provided by large-scale instruments like the DDM. In the case study presented in this article, the DDM is used to suggest which features are worth considering, and its feature list is subsequently pared down to a minimally adequate subset. A close examination of what such subset features have in common may result in a better understanding of what speakers are doing linguistically when they engage in style shift ing. By paying closer attention to how speakers use features within sets, it may be possible to attain a better understanding of style. Additionally, large-scale measures like the DDM are important as a way to test the validity of a selected subset. A high correlation between a large-scale measure and a subset of features would lend credence to the use of the selected features. Th e remainder of this article describes how the DDM and the subset technique were used in a study of contextual style shift ing among African American adolescents.

STYLE SHIFTING AND AAVE

Th is analysis uses data from a study of 108 typically developing African American boys and girls from lower and middle socioeconomic status homes who were 11–13 years of age at the time of observation (Renn 2007). Half of the study participants were enrolled as infants and have since participated in a longitudinal study of AAVE and its relation to literacy skills in early adolescence (Roberts et al. 1995); the other half were recruited at grade 6 as friends of current study subjects, specifi cally to create a peerto-peer environment. Th e study examines the use of AAVE structures in two formal and two informal peer contexts to determine which features are most aff ected by the formality of the situation. Th e formal contexts included two speeches, one in which the youth were asked to simulate a speech to a group of parents about their school and one in which they presented a "kids-only" vacation plan to an imaginary audience. Th e informal contexts involved a discussion between the subjects about problems or issues they selected and a free talk period while eating a snack.

For each subject, 50 utterances from each context were analyzed in terms of 40 morphosyntactic and 3 phonological features. Th e list of morphosyntactic features includes all of those listed in Craig and Washington's (2006) DDM as well as six additional features. We thus have two types of DDM measures, the one off ered by Craig and Washington (2006) and a revised and extended DDM constructed by Wolfram and Terry. Morphosyntactic features used by Craig and Washington (2006) included copula absence (e.g., *He nice* for *He is nice*), invariant be (e.g., *Th ey be messing up* indicating a habitual behavior or occurrence), and third-person singular -*s* absence (e.g., *She like me* for *She likes me)*. Additional morphosyntactic features were selected through consultation with various sources, including Rickford (1999), Green (2002), and Wolfram and Adger's (1993) Dialect Profi le Form from the Baltimore city school district.[6] Only three of the phonological features from the DDM were retained in this study. Th e selected phonological features were nasal fronting, in which /n/ is used for /ŋ/ in unstressed -*ing* forms (e.g,. *swimmin'* for *swimming*); prevocalic cluster reduction, where a word-fi nal consonant cluster is reduced when followed by a vowel (e.g., *bes' apple* for *best apple)*; and labialization, where /f/ is substituted for /θ/ (e.g., /maʊf/ for *mouth*) or /v/ is substituted for /ð/ (e.g., /ɔvɚ/ for *other*). Th ese particular phonological features were chosen because they have been shown in various studies to be particularly prevalent in style shift ing (Rickford and McNair-Knox 1994; Labov 2001). By the same token, the preponderance of morphosyntactic variables over phonological ones in the dialect profi le is justifi ed by the observation that morphosyntactic features generally play a more salient role in distinguishing standard from nonstandard dialect forms (Wolfram 1970; Wolfram and Fasold 1974).

Additionally, some features that are combined in the Craig and Washington DDM were separated into individual features in these analyses. For example, while the Craig and Washington measure combines all forms of subject-verb agreement, the extended DDM measure separates this feature into four specifi c categories: addition of infl ectional -*s* on non-third-person singular subjects, absence of thirdperson singular -*s*, generalization of *is* and *was*, and diff erence in number between the subject and the modal auxiliaries *do* and *have*. Separating certain features into more specifi c classes allows one to better understand what exactly occurs during style shift ing.[7] Additionally, some of the features that are confl ated by Craig and Washington may be diff erent enough to show very dissimilar patterning in their distribution. For example, the absence of the possessive marker -'*s* on a noun is a very diff erent process from substituting a nominative or objective case pronoun for a possessive pronoun (e.g., *kids just going to walk to THEY school*). Variables can also be examined in terms of diff erential social marking. Nasal -*ing* fronting (e.g., *runnin'* for *running*), for instance, is a generic diagnostic feature of all varieties of American English, whereas third-person -*s* absence (e.g., *go* for *goes*) is largely restricted to AAVE in the United States. By separating such features, we are then not only able to look at them individually, but also have the option of confl ating them if desired.

Th ree summary measures were used and compared in this study. For each measure, the total number of instances of certain AAVE features was counted. As previously noted, the features that were studied in this project were initially based on those that were used by Craig and Washington (2006). Each of the measures, however, diff ered from the others in important and conscientiously designed ways.

Th e fi rst of the summary measures was the reduced version of the Craig and Washington measure (CW measure). Th is measure had the advantage of being the closest match to the Craig and Washington method, which is currently used regularly in dialect research in speech-language pathology. Th us, it was considered the "benchmark" measure against which to compare the other measures. Drawbacks to this measure included the exclusion of other potentially relevant vernacular features and the limitations on statistical analysis that accompany such a large number of variables. Th e second measure (full measure) was thus created to include other potentially relevant AAVE, while the third measure (subset measure) attended to the statistical limitations.

Th e full measure included all of the features of the CW measure as well as the six additional morphosyntactic features. Th is measure was created in order to look at the possible contributions of certain morphosyntactic features that were not included by Craig and Washington. Th e hope was that if any of these additional vernacular features did play a role in style shift , this measure would unearth them. Th us, this was the most comprehensive measure of the three and the one considered to have more content validity. Including even more variables in this measure, however, exacerbated the problem of reducing the number of available statistical analysis techniques.

Th e subset measure consisted of a subset of six AAVE features. Th e six features were selected because they seemed to be the most sensitive to changes in formal-informal context change used in the experiment. Th is determination was made based on data comparing the means of each AAVE feature by context. Table 1 lists the six features used in this measure, as well as examples of each.

Each of these measures was calculated in two ways: once as a proportion of AAVE features over the total number of words and once as a proportion of features over the total number of utterances. Both calculations were performed because each method was imperfect but had its advantages. Th e total number of words was used in the fi rst approach because there was a context-based imbalance in the number of words per utterance; the mean number of words per utterance was 10.02 in the formal contexts and 5.92 in the informal contexts. Th is discrepancy meant that in each formal utterance there were nearly twice as many opportunities for a vernacular feature to occur. Some features, like multiple negation or negative concord, require the existence of a multiword utterance to be realized, however. Th us, the total number of utterances was used as the other calculation method. Th is method is also the standard system used by researchers like Craig and Washington (2006). Th erefore, calculating the summary variables in this way allowed for more opportunity for direct comparison with other measures.

Using both methods allowed for the detection of patterns that were strong enough to be seen using all of the summary variables.

TABLE
!!6% &EATURES #OMPRISING 3UBSET -EASURE

6 Êi>ÌÕÀiÊ	Ý>"« □i
.ASAL FRONTING	ÃÜˆ""""~½FORÃÜˆ""""˜}
#OPULA ABSENCE	iÊ˜ViFORi½ÃÊ˜Vi
-ODAL AUXILIARY ABSENCE	œÜÊÞœÕÊ`œÊÌ…ˆÃ¶FORœÜÊ`œÊÞœÕÊ`œÊÌ…ˆÃ¶
4HIRD PERSON SINGULAR ‡ÃABSENCE-…iÊ□ˆ□iÊ…˜FOR-…iÊ□ˆ□iÃÊ…˜
-ULTIPLE NEGATION	/…iÞÊˆˆˆ½ÌÊœÊ˜œÌ…˜}
˜½ÌFORÃÊ˜œÌ	/…iÊV>ÀÃÊ˜½ÌÊ}œ˜>Ê"œÛi

Correlations among the three measures were calculated to determine how they compared to one another, using the Pearson *r* test. Th is was done both for the measures that were calculated as a proportion of the total number of utterances (see table 2) and for those calculated as a proportion of the total number of words (see table 3). Interestingly, the correlations in tables 2 and 3 were essentially identical, suggesting that the method of calculation is fairly inconsequential.

Th e near-perfect correlation ($r = .99$) between the full and CW measures supports the validity of the CW instrument as an indicator of AAVE use. Although the full measure might arguably be considered a more accurate rendering of AAVE in terms of its linguistic validity, the additional features and reclassifi cation of features have little eff ect on the overall assessment of speakers' vernacular use. Th is suggests that not only is the Craig and Washington DDM a reasonable measure of AAVE use, but the eff ect of reducing the number of vernacular features included in a summary variable has a surprisingly small eff ect on its effi cacy as well.

Correlations between the subset measure and the more comprehensive measure support the utility of using a carefully selected subset of features. As shown in both cases, there was a very strong positive correlation between the subset measure and the larger measures ($r = .94$). Th is means that despite the fact that the subset measure contains a small fraction of the features included in formulating the other measures, it did a very good job of capturing the degree to which subjects used AAVE forms. Given the drawbacks of using a measure with a large number of variables, this fi nding is extremely promising.

TABLE
#ORRELATIONS OF 3UMMARY -EASURES #ALCULATED AS A 0ROPORTION OF 4OTAL
5TTERANCES

-Õ""">ÀÞÊi>ÃÕÀiÊ -ÕLÃiÌÊi>ÃiÕÕÊ□□Êi>ÃÕÀiÊ 7Êi>ÃÕÀi
3UBSET MEASURE
&ULL MEASURE
#7 MEASURE

TABLE
#ORRELATIONS OF 3UMMARY -EASURES #ALCULATED AS A 0ROPORTION OF 4OTAL 7ORDS

-Õ""">ÀÞÊi>ÃÕÀiÊ -ÕLÃiÌÊi>ÃiÕÕÊ□□Êi>ÃÕÀiÊ 7Êi>ÃÕÀi
3UBSET MEASURE

#7 MEASURE

Finally, it is important to reiterate that the measure put forth in this study is tailored to identify style shift ing based on diff erences in the formality of a given situation; thus, the features that were selected for the subset measure were chosen because of their apparent sensitivity to context. Th is technique might be implemented to address other questions, like diff erences based on gender and socioeconomic status. As discussed earlier, numerous factors can play a role in language use. Th e literature on language variation suggests that diff erent features vary due to these factors. Th us, distinct subsets might be created for use with these diff erent factors. Th is view contrasts with the objectives of many conducting vernacular research in the fi eld of speech pathology, where the focus is oft en on trying to fi nd one statistical measure to account for all vernacular use. Th ere is no reason, however, to be limited to one overall diagnostic measure. Indeed, because of its inherent limitations, an all-compassing measure may not provide the same quality of information that could be garnered from measures that are carefully designed for specifi c purposes.

Th ese three summary variables were subsequently used to compare speakers' overall vernacular use in the two diff erent contexts. A repeated measures analysis using the general linear model was performed to account for the dependency between the observations within each child. As table 4 shows, the diff erence between contexts was statistically signifi cant using all three summary variables and regardless of how the measures were calculated (i.e., by words or by utterances).

Th us, speakers used signifi cantly more AAVE features in the informal contexts than in the formal contexts. Figure 1 illustrates AAVE feature use by context for the summary measures calculated as a proportion of total utterances. Figure 2 depicts the same results for measures calculated as a proportion of the total number of words. All of these comparisons demonstrated statistically signifi cant diff erences, regardless of the measure used.

As the literature on AAVE and on style shift in general cites context formality as a common source of style shift , the resultant shift found in these analyses was expected. Th e most interesting outcome of these analyses was that all of the summary measures were very consistent and reliable. Specifi cally, the success of the subset measure indicated that a measure containing a small number of features can be eff ectively used to identify style shift in AAVE. Th e next step, then, was to directly compare this measure to the two larger measures. To more eff ectively assess the measures' success at capturing the subjects' style shift ing, a third method of comparison was applied. In this method, a proportion of the formal summary score to the informal summary score was computed for each measure, allowing for a better opportunity to distinguish the diff erence between formal and informal linguistic behavior. Figure 3 illustrates the relationship among these measures by context. As fi gure 3 indicates, the values of the three summary measures were all very close in both the formal and informal cases.

TABLE

4EST OF $IFFERENCE #ONTEXT   FOR %ACH 3UMMARY -EASURE

-Õ""> ÀÞÊi>ÃÕÀiÊ	‡Û> ÕÕÊ	«‡Û> ÕÕı
#7 MEASURE COMMUNICATION UNITS		
#7 MEASURE WORDS		
&ULL MEASURE COMMUNICATION UNITS		
&ULL MEASURE WORDS		
3UBSET MEASURE COMMUNICATION UNITS		

3UBSET MEASURE WORDS

FIGURE
#OMPARISON BY #ONTEXT 5SING 4OTAL 5TTERANCES IN 3UMMARY -EASURE #ALCULATIONS

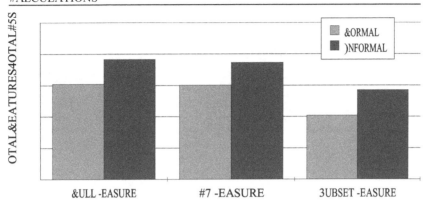

4

FIGURE
#OMPARISON BY #ONTEXT 5SING 4OTAL 7ORDS IN 3UMMARY -EASURE #ALCULATIONS

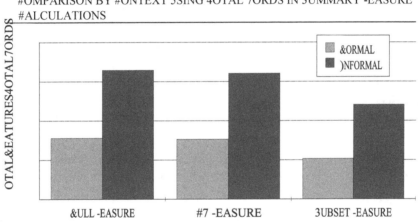

4

CONCLUSION

Building on previous studies of style and previous uses of composite language measures like the Craig and Washington DDM, the approach to studying style shift advocated in this article allows researchers to go beyond the examination of individuals' style shift ing and examine it at the group level. What is

FIGURE
#OMPARISON OF !LL 3UMMARY -EASURES #ALCULATED IN #OMMUNICATION 5NITS

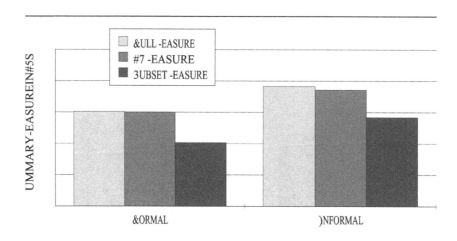

off ered here is not meant to replace more standard methods of investigation, that is, those that rely on the detailed analysis of case studies. Such studies are uniquely able to answer a range of important questions concerning both the nature of style shift and the reasons why speakers engage in it. Instead, the methods introduced here are meant to work in concert with and complement these more traditional techniques, and in doing so, to expand the possibilities for understanding the use of style and its broader implications for speakers. Tracking style shift using a subset of features culled from a larger composite dialect measure increases the number and kinds of relevant statistical techniques and thus allows researchers to capture generalizations about groups of speakers in order to better understand the use of language in society.

Our study illustrates one such opportunity by investigating style shift ing among 108 African American adolescents. Th e subset measure used indicated a statistically signifi cant increase in speakers' use of AAVE forms in informal situations as compared to formal contexts. Comparison of these results with those of two larger composite measures, including the Craig and Washington DDM, supports its validity. Not only did the large measures detect the same result as the subset with regard to shift ing styles, but a direct comparison between the subset and the composite measures indicated an extremely large positive correlation ($r = .94$), which further supports the effi cacy of a measure consisting of a small set of features. Knowing how this group of AAVE speakers performs as style shift ers adds important information to their educational profi les. Th e tool is now being used with this same group to investigate possible correlations between style shift ing and literacy, as well as to answer such questions as whether students who begin as frequent style shift ers continue that behavior.

Th e fi ndings reported here validate the subset measure as an eff ective method of identifying and quantifying style use in groups of speakers. Its utility is not restricted, however, to the study of AAVE. Appropriate subsets of features could be created and applied to other populations as well, resulting in new possibilities for the study of style. Admittedly, the attempt to capture group patterns using a composite measure takes us considerably beyond the standard approach in which independent, isolated linguistic features are correlated with social factors and style is viewed more as an individualistic rather than group phenomenon. It is, however, consistent with early variationist views, such as that of Labov (1966), that treat stylistic variation as a group phenomenon and, by giving those who hold those views new tools, we believe, constitutes a signifi cant step in attempting to examine the authentic interplay of individual and group behavior.

NOTES

We gratefully acknowledge funding support from National Science Foundation grants BCS-0544744 and BCS-0843865 and Maternal and Child Health Bureau grants MCJ-370599, MCJ-379154, MCJ-370649, and R40MC-00343. We thank Walt Wolfram, Joanne Roberts, and Susan Zeisel for their feedback on this article.

1. Much of this early work used labels such as *Nonstandard Negro English* and later *Black English Vernacular,* a term coined by William Labov to refer to the variety we are calling *African American Vernacular English.* For further discussion and a more exhaustive list of the names that have been given to this variety, see Green (2002, 5–8).
2. To some extent, these fi ndings are also a product of defi nitional issues. Th e Craig and Washington (2004) inventory is largely grammatical, ignoring vowels and other phonological traits in favor of morphosyntactic features, which aff ects the outcome of these investigations.
3. See Milroy and Gordon (2003) for a discussion of the various attempts researchers have made to defi ne *vernacular* in the literature.
4. Utterances were determined based on the criteria set in Craig and Washington (2006) and Loban (1976), in which they were defi ned as "an independent clause plus its modifi ers."
5. Th e "mid-size central city" was Ann Arbor, Michigan, a college town where 16% of the students in the public schools are African American; the "urban-fringe community" was in Detroit, Michigan, where 86% of the student body was African American (Standard and Poor's School Evaluation Services).
6. Th e added morphosyntactic features were past form for participle, regularization of irregular past tense form, zero relative pronoun, uninverted direct question, inverted question without *if/whether,* and regularized *mines.*
7. Other features that are divided in our proposed measure are the use of *ain't* (into *ain't* meaning *did + not* versus *are + not, is + not,* or *have + not);* undiff erentiated pronoun case (into the use of nominative and objective pronouns used interchangeably versus the use of the objective form for the demonstrative); double marking (into multiple agreement on irregular plural nouns versus pronouns versus irregular verbs); zero possessive (into deletion of the possessive - *'s* marker versus the use of the nominative or objective pronominal form rather than the possessive pronoun); and double copula/auxiliary/modal (into double copula or auxiliary versus double modal).

REFERENCES

Bell, Allan. 1984. "Language Style as Audience Design." *Language in Society* 13: 145–204.

___. 1997. "[Language] Style as Audience Design." In *Sociolinguistics: A Reader and Coursebook,* ed. Nikolas Coupland and Adam Jaworski, 240–50. Basingstoke: Macmillan.

___. 2001. "Back in Style: Reworking Audience Design." In *Style and Sociolinguistic Variation,* ed. Penelope Eckert and John R. Rickford, 139–69. Cambridge: Cambridge Univ. Press.

Chambers, J. K., and Peter Trudgill. 1980. *Dialectology.* Cambridge: Cambridge Univ. Press.

Chomsky, Noam. 1980. *Rules and Representations.* New York: Columbia Univ. Press.

___. 1986. *Knowledge of Language: Its Nature, Origin, and Use.* New York: Praeger.

Coupland, Nikolas. 1984. "Accommodation at Work: Some Phonological Data and Th eir Implications." *International Journal of the Sociology of Language* 46: 49–70.

___. 2007. *Style: Language Variation and Identity. Cambridge:* Cambridge Univ. Press.

___. Forthcoming. "Th e Sociolinguistics of Style." In *Th e Cambridge Handbook of Sociolinguistics,* ed. Rajend Mesthrie and Walt Wolfram. New York: Cambridge Univ. Press.

Craig, Holly K., Carol M. Connor, and Julie A. Washington. 2003. "Early Positive Predictors of Later Reading Comprehension for African American Students: A Preliminary Investigation." *Language, Speech, and Hearing Services in the Schools* 34: 31–43.

Craig, Holly K., and Julie A. Washington. 2004. "Grade-Related Changes in the Production of African American English." *Journal of Speech, Language, and Hearing Research* 47: 87–93.

———. 2006. *Malik Goes to School: Examining the Language Skills of African American Students from Preschool–5th Grade.* Mahwah, N.J.: Erlbaum.

Craig, Holly K., Julie A. Washington, and Connie Thompson-Porter. 1998. "Performances of Young African American Children on Two Comprehension Tasks." *Journal of Speech, Language, and Hearing Research* 41: 445–57.

Eckert, Penelope. 2000. *Linguistic Variation as Social Practice: The Linguistic Construction of Identity in Belten High.* Malden, Mass.: Blackwell.

Ervin-Tripp, Susan. 2001. "Variety, Style-Switching, and Ideology." In *Style and Sociolinguistic Variation,* ed. Penelope Eckert and John R. Rickford, 44–56. Cambridge: Cambridge Univ. Press.

Fasold, Ralph W. 2004. "Making Languages." In *ISB4: Proceedings of the 4th International Symposium on Bilingualism,* ed. James Cohen, Kara T. McAlister, Kellie Rolstad, and Jeff MacSwan, 697–702. Somerville, Mass.: Cascadilla.

Fasold, R. W., and Walter A. Wolfram. 1970. "Some Linguistic Features of Negro Dialect." In *Teaching Standard English in the Inner City,* ed. Ralph W. Fasold and Roger W. Shuy, 41–86. Washington, D.C.: Center for Applied Linguistics.

Finegan, Edward, and Douglas Biber. 1994. "Register and Social Dialect Variation: An Integrated Approach." In *Sociolinguistic Perspectives on Register,* ed. Douglas Biber and Edward Finegan, 315–47. Oxford: Oxford Univ. Press.

Green, Lisa J. 2002. *African American English: A Linguistic Introduction.* Cambridge: Cambridge Univ. Press.

Guy, Gregory R. 1980. "Variation in the Group and the Individual: The Case of Final Stop Deletion." In *Locating Language in Time and Space,* ed. William Labov, 1–36. New York: Academic Press.

Kendall, Tyler, and Walt Wolfram. 2009. "Local and External Standards in African American English." *Journal of English Linguistics* 37: 305–30.

Kloss, Heinz. 1967. "Abstand Languages and Ausbau Languages." *Anthropological Linguistics* 9: 29–41.

Labov, William. 1966. *The Social Stratification of English in New York City.* Washington, D.C.: Center for Applied Linguistics.

———. 1972. *Language in the Inner City: Studies in the Black English Vernacular.* Philadelphia: Univ. of Pennsylvania Press.

———. 2001. *Studies in Sociolinguistics: Selected Papers by William Labov.* Beijing: Beijing Language and Culture Univ. Press.

Labov, William, Paul Cohen, Clarence Robins, and John Lewis. 1968. *A Study of the Non-standard English of Negro and Puerto Rican Speakers in New York City.* Vols. 1 and 2. Cooperative Research Report 3288. Philadelphia: U.S. Regional Survey.

Lippi-Green, Rosina. 1997. *English with an Accent: Language, Ideology, and Discrimination in the United States.* London: Routledge.

Loban, Walter. 1976. *Language Development: Kindergarten through Grade Twelve.* NCTE Committee on Research Report No. 18. Urbana, Ill.: National Council of Teachers.

MacCallum, Robert C., Keith F. Widaman, Kristopher J. Preacher, and Sehee Hong. 2001. "Sample Size in Factor Analysis: The Role of Model Error." *Multivariate Behavioral Research* 36: 611–37.

Mallinson, Christine, and Becky Childs. 2007. "Communities of Practice in Sociolinguistic Description: Analyzing Language and Identity Practices among Black Women in Appalachia." *Gender and Language* 1: 173–206.

Milroy, Lesley, and Matthew Gordon. 2003. *Sociolinguistics: Method and Interpretation.* Malden, Mass.: Blackwell.

Moore, Emma, and Robert Podesva. 2009. "Style, Indexicality, and the Social Meaning of Tag Questions." *Language in Society* 38: 447–85.

Oetting, Janna B., and Janet L. McDonald. 2002. "Methods for Characterizing Participants' Nonmainstream Dialect Use in Child Language Research." *Journal of Speech, Language, and Hearing Research* 45: 505–18.

Preston, Dennis R. 1991. "Sorting Out the Variables in Sociolinguistic Th eory." *American Speech* 66: 33–56.

Renn, Jennifer. 2007. "Measuring Style Shift : A Quantitative Analysis of African American English." Master's thesis, Univ. of North Carolina at Chapel Hill.

Rickford, John R. 1992. "Grammatical Variation and Divergence in Vernacular Black English." In *Internal and External Factors in Syntactic Change,* ed. Marinel Gerritsen and Dieter Stein, 175–200. Berlin: Mouton de Gruyter.

___. 1999. *African American Vernacular English: Features, Evolution, Educational Implications.* Oxford: Blackwell.

Rickford, John R., and Faye McNair-Knox. 1994. "Addressee- and Topic-Infl uenced Style Shift : A Quantitative Sociolinguistic Study." In *Perspectives on Register: Situating Register Variation Within Sociolinguistics,* ed. Douglas Biber and Edward Finegan, 235–76. New York: Oxford Univ. Press.

Roberts, Joanne Erwick, Margaret R. Burchinal, Lynn P. Medley, Susan A. Zeisel, Martha Mundy, Jackson Roush, Stephen Hooper, Donna Bryant, and Frederick W. Henderson. 1995. "Otitis Media, Hearing Sensitivity, and Maternal Responsiveness in Relation to Language during Infancy." *Journal of Pediatrics* 126: 481–89.

Schilling-Estes, Natalie. 1998. "Investigating 'Self-Conscious' Speech: Th e Performance Register in Ocracoke English." *Language in Society* 27: 53–83.

___. 2004. "Constructing Ethnicity in Interaction." *Journal of Sociolinguistics* 8: 163–95.

Seymour, Harry N., and Charlena M. Seymour. 1981. "Black English and Standard American English Contrasts in
Consonantal Development of Four and Five-Year Old Children." *Journal of Speech and Hearing Disorders* 46: 274–80.

Smith, Tina T., Evan Lee, and Hiram L. McDade. 2001. "An Investigation of T-Units in African American EnglishSpeaking and Standard American English-Speaking Fourth-Grade Children." *Communication Disorders Quarterly* 22: 148–57.

Spivak, Gayatri Chakravorty. 1988. "Can the Subaltern Speak?" In *Marxism and the Interpretation of Culture,* ed.
Cary Nelson and Lawrence Grossberg, 271–313. Urbana: Univ. of Illinois Press.

Strang, Barbara M. H. 1970. *A History of English.* London: Methuen.

Street, Richard L., Jr., and Howard Giles. 1982. "Speech Accommodation Th eory: A Social Cognitive
Approach to Language and Speech Behavior." In *Social Cognition and Communication,* ed. Michael E. Roloff and Charles R. Berger, 193–226. Beverly Hills, Calif.: Sage.

Th ompson, Connie A., Holly K. Craig, and Julie A. Washington. 2004. "Variable Production of African American English across Oracy and Literacy Contexts." *Language, Speech and Hearing Services in Schools* 35: 269–82.

Weldon, Tracey. 2004. "African American English in the Middle Classes: Exploring the Other End of the Continuum." Paper presented at the 33rd annual conference on New Ways of Analyzing Variation (NWAV 33), Ann Arbor, Sept. 30–Oct. 3.

Wolfram, Walt. 1969. *A Sociolinguistic Description of Detroit Negro Speech.* Washington, D.C.: Center for Applied Linguistics.

___. 1970. "Sociolinguistic Implications for Educational Sequencing." In *Teaching Standard English in the Inner City,* ed. Ralph W. Fasold and Roger W. Shuy, 105–19. Washington, D.C.: Center for Applied Linguistics.

___. 2007. "Sociolinguistic Folklore in the Study of African American English." *Language and Linguistic Compass* 1: 292–313.

Wolfram, Walt, and Carolyn Adger. 1993. *Handbook on Language Diff erences and Speech and Language Pathology: Baltimore City Public Schools*. Washington, D.C.: Center for Applied Linguistics.

Wolfram, Walt, and Ralph W. Fasold. 1974. *Th e Study of Social Dialects in American English*. Englewood Cliff s, NJ.: Prentice Hall.

Wolfram, Walt, and Natalie Schilling-Estes. 2006. *American English: Dialects and Variation*. 2nd ed. Cambridge: Blackwell.

Cultural Considerations in the Development of School-Based Interventions for African American Adolescent Boys with Emotional and Behavioral Disorders

Zewelanji Serpell, Charlayne C. Hayling,
Howard Stevenson, and Lee Kern

African American males are overrepresented among youth in special education identifi ed as having emotional and behavioral disorders. Compared to other youth in special education, they have the least access to needed services and the worst social and academic outcomes. Little empirically supported guidance exists to inform the development of eff ective and culturally responsive interventions for these youth. Th is article addresses this gap in the literature by reviewing existing research, and highlighting problems with current approaches to identifi cation, referral, and treatment. Th e authors provide specifi c examples about ways to harness African American adolescents' strengths when developing culturally responsive, school-based interventions and discuss implications for educational policy.

African American adolescent males are disproportionally represented among students in special education identifi ed as having emotional and behavioral disorders (EBD; Osher, Woodruff , & Sims, 2002). Students identifi ed as having EBD demonstrate the poorest educational, behavioral, and social outcomes of any disability group, with no documented improvements over the past several decades (Bradley, Dolittle, & Bartolotta, 2008; Wagner, Newman, & Cameto, 2004). Frank, Sitlington, and Carson (1995) found that students with EBD have lower grades, more course failures, higher retention, and lower rates of passing minimum competency tests compared to students in all other disability groups. Only about 28% of African American students with EBD graduate from high school, and as many as 50% drop out of school (Blackorby & Wagner, 1996). Post-school outcomes are similarly poor. Fift y-eight percent of students with EBD are arrested within 3 to 5 years of leaving school; this fi gure rises to 73% for students who drop out (Wagner, 1995). Challenges among this group persist into

Zewelanji Serpell, Charlayne C. Hayling, Howard Stevenson, & Lee Kern, "Cultural Considerations in the Development of School-Based Interventions for African American Adolescent Boys with Emotional and Behavioral Disorders," *Th e Journal of Negro Education*, vol. 78, no. 3, pp. 321–332. Copyright © 2009 by Howard University. Reprinted with permission. Provided by ProQuest LLC. All rights reserved.

adulthood, typifi ed by diffi culties with obtaining and maintaining employment, poor interpersonal relationships, and high rates of substance abuse (Bullis & Cheney, 1999; Greenbaum et al., 1996).

Finding ways to eff ectively meet the needs of African American males with EBD is therefore critical. Eff ective intervention for these youth will depend on the extent to which we understand their characteristics and needs, in tandem with available systems of care, particularly schools. Th is article reviews previous research on the school experiences of African American males with EBD, and discusses implications for developing culturally responsive interventions and educational policy.

Defining the Problem

Issues Contributing to Overrepresentation

Th e overrepresentation of African American males in EBD is a problem that has persisted for many decades, and trends in the data indicate that this problem is getting worse (Zhang & Katsiyannis, 2002). Th is is partially because behaviors that classify a student as EBD are ill-defi ned, and school systems are left to determine what student behaviors align with the categorical criteria.

Classifi cation begins with the federal defi nition of EBD articulated in the Individuals with Disabilities Education Act (IDEA-P. L. 101-476) under the term "emotional disturbance." IDEA defi nes emotional disturbance of EBD as:

> … a condition exhibiting one or more of the following characteristics over a long period of time and to a marked degree which adversely aff ects school performance: (a) an inability to learn which cannot be explained by intellectual, sensory, or health factors; (b) an inability to build or maintain satisfactory relationships with peers and teachers; (c) inappropriate types of behaviors or feelings under normal circumstances; (d) a general mood of unhappiness or depression; (e) a tendency to develop physical symptoms or fears associated with personal or school problems.

Students with schizophrenia are included in this classifi cation, whereas students with social maladjustment are not, unless it is determined that they also are emotionally disturbed. States interpret the clause about excluding students with social maladjustment very diff erently; some states exclude all students with characteristics of oppositional defi ant or conduct disorders, while others include these students (Gresham & Kern, 2004). States also vary widely in their rates of identifi cation (Ysseldyke, Algozzine, & Th urlow, 1995).

Part of this variation is due to the fact that the federal defi nition of EBD encompasses a great deal of ambiguity. For example, the eligibility characteristics include three limiting criteria: *severity* ("to a marked degree"), *duration* ("for a long period of time"), and *impact on school performance* ("adversely aff ects educational performance"), but these criteria are highly subjective and typically left for school personnel to decide.

Diff ering rates of identifi cation can be found in schools with diverse student populations. Little overrepresentation of African American students in EBD programs is evident in school districts where African Americans comprise between 13%–33% of the student body. In contrast, school districts with less than 13% African Americans have more overrepresentation, particularly if they are located in low-poverty areas (Oswald, Coutino, Best, & Singh, 1999). Oswald and colleagues suggested that these diff erences may be lessened by teaching staff in wealthy districts with lower percentages of African

Americans how they may be being less tolerant of diff erences, especially behaviors exhibited by students of diff erent ethnic and cultural backgrounds. Approximately 90% of teachers in America are Caucasian (Ferri & Connor, 2005) and very few teachers receive training to recognize cultural diff erences among their students. Some suggest that this lack of training may infl uence the EBD over-identifi cation of racial minority children (Skiba & Rausch, 2006). A lack of cultural competence has been shown to be related to a higher likelihood of teachers attributing overrepresentation to characteristics of the students or their families (Kearns, Ford, & Linney, 2005).

Race appears to play a central role in teachers' appraisals of students and related expectations. For example, in a study by Neal, McCray, Webb-Johnson, and Bridgest (2003); 136 middle school teachers in a suburban school district in the Southwest were shown videos depicting an African American and a Caucasian student engaging in diff erent types of movement patterns (e.g., walking styles) with other physical variables held constant (e.g., height and weight). Th e fi ndings showed that teachers rated students who were engaged in culture-related movement styles as lower-achieving, more aggressive, and more likely to require special education services than students engaged in 'standard' movement styles.

Several studies also showed that racial or cultural factors infl uence teachers' appraisal of students even when they are using standardized scales. For example, teacher ratings of African American students using standard attention defi cit hyperactivity disorder (ADHD) rating scales are consistently elevated (DuPaul et al., 1997; Epstein, March, Conners, & Jackson, 1998; Reid et al., 1998) and show little congruence with ratings by African American parents or the youth themselves (Youngstrom, Loeber, & Stouthamer-Loeber, 2000). Other studies using standardized rating scales highlighted a bias that Caucasian teachers in particular have toward African American youth (Pigott & Cowen, 2000; Zimmerman, Khoury, Vega, Gil, & Warheit, 1995). Researchers have also expressed concerns that the standardized tests frequently used during assessment of behavioral problems refl ect the values and experiences of Caucasian middle class students, rendering them culturally and linguistically biased in both content and norms (Ferri & Connor, 2005).

Placement, Practices, and Related Outcomes

Fierros and Conroy (2002) reported two trends in their analysis of data from studies by the Offi ce of Special Education Placement, the Offi ce of Civil Rights, and statewide studies: (a) once identifi ed, minority students from all major racial groups are more likely than Caucasian students with disabilities to be removed from general education classrooms for some or all of the school day; and (b) African American students are most oft en over-identifi ed in disability categories that have the highest correlation with isolation from general education settings. Th ey also reported that in some states, disproportionality in both identifi cation and placement in separate classrooms is high for African American males. Although overall more students with disabilities are being mainstreamed in general education classes, students with EBD continue to be segregated in special needs classes. Additionally, African American males are excluded from regular education classes at two to three times the rate of other students (Landrum, Katsiyannis, & Archwamety, 2004).

Students classifi ed as EBD and assigned to a special classroom are not guaranteed access to more intensive interventions, nor does separate placement appear to improve their general academic functioning. Hendrickson, Smith, Frank, and Merical (1998) conducted record reviews and interviews to identify services received by 99 students with EBD and placed either in self-contained classrooms within regular schools (n = 49) or in segregated schools (n = 50). Fift y-fi ve percent of the students in the study received no supplemental or related services. When data were examined by placement, 49% of students in regular schools and 60% of those in segregated schools did not receive additional services. Th ese data contradict the premise that students in more restrictive environments receive services not available in less restrictive settings. Hendrickson and colleagues also report that students served in self-contained classrooms in public schools had greater decreases in problem behavior and more gains in appropriate behavior than those in the segregated school settings, raising additional concerns about placement patterns and practices.

Despite legal protections (IDEA, 2004), students with EBD are expelled at more than double the rate of any other disability group (Wagner, Newman, & Cameto, 2004). Students with EBD also receive more punitive disciplinary practices, such as corporal punishment and suspension. Studies by Skiba and colleagues (2006) demonstrate that the use of more punitive measures (expulsion and suspension) is more common with African American males, despite the fact that there is no evidence that these students exhibit higher rates of disruptive behavior (Townsend, 2000). Furthermore, the reasons teachers provide for disciplinary actions are far more subjective for African American males than they are for their Caucasian counterparts. Th at is, teachers frequently cite "intimidating/disrespectful behavior" as the reason for referring African American youth, whereas reasons cited for Caucasian youth are "bringing weapons to school" or "smoking on school premises" (Skiba, Michael, Nardo, & Peterson, 2002).

Punitive disciplinary measures oft en used with African American males are not only contraindicated, but also can exacerbate existing problems. Restrictive and punitive disciplinary measures contribute to an increase in problem behaviors, such as aggression and school vandalism (e.g. Mayer, 1995) and result in lost opportunities for instruction, further widening the achievement gap (Garibaldi, 1992). Finally, students who are suspended or expelled from school are at higher risk of having encounters with the legal system (Townsend, 2000). In all, the disciplinary procedures commonly used with students with EBD, and African American males in particular, are likely to perpetuate their academic diffi culties and aggravate their problem behaviors.

Evidence-based Interventions for Adolescents with EBD

Few studies on interventions for adolescents with EBD exist. A recent review of school-based intervention programs for EBD by Reddy and colleagues (2009) noted that most studies include children below 12 years of age, and only 3 of the 29 studies identifi ed dealt exclusively with adolescents. Existing evidence-based interventions for children (even if modifi ed) may not be eff ective for adolescents. Developmental and contextual shift s in adolescence likely warrant very diff erent approaches to assessment and intervention to address problem behavior (Wolraich et al, 2005). For example, interventionists must consider the fact that not only are expectations for independence higher, the risks associated with not meeting academic and social expectations are worse for adolescents than for younger students. Furthermore, measures of risk and outcome in adolescence need to be expanded to include several variables that are not as relevant in childhood, such as identity development, commitment to a vocation, skill in a wider variety of personal relationships (e.g., relationships with employers, romantic partners), ethnic group identifi cation, risky sexual behaviors, and substance abuse.

One program that targets adolescents with EBD and that has demonstrated positive outcomes is the "check and connect" intervention, designed to increase student engagement and prevent school dropout among urban high school students with EBD (Sinclair, Christenson, & Th urlow, 2005). Sinclair and colleagues found that students who received the check and connect intervention had lower rates of dropout and mobility; higher rates of school persistence and completion; and received more special education transition program services compared to students who did not receive the intervention. Th e other two studies on adolescents that Reddy and colleagues (2009) described were limited by small ($N < 5$) and non-diverse samples. Th us, there is an absence of research on eff ective and comprehensive interventions, particularly for African American youth.

Another gap in the existing literature on EBD interventions that is important for adolescent research is the lack of attention paid to race and ethnicity as potential moderators of intervention outcome.

Intervention studies of children with EBD oft en include a relatively large sample of African Americans, but results are rarely disaggregated by race or ethnicity. To the authors' knowledge, no studies of evidence-based programs for EBD have included an assessment of culture- or race-specifi c variables (e.g. racial identity or perceptions of racial climate), which might serve as mediating factors in how recipients respond to interventions. A recent review of over 40 journals examining intervention outcomes for adolescents with EBD (Center for Adolescent Research in the Schools, 2009), yielded 160 studies, none of which included measures related to racial or ethnic identity, in spite of the fact that 72 studies reported having African American adolescents in the sample.

Th is fi nding is not surprising since most interventions designed to address EBD target behavior and academic problems, and not issues related to race or the social interactions that contribute to a racially tense climate (Stevenson, 2008). For example, although stress is increasingly recognized as a factor in youth emotional and behavioral problems, rarely is *racial* stress considered relevant. Racial stress may pose signifi cant challenges to African American students and teachers within school classrooms (Kellow & Jones, 2008) and youth appraisal of this type of stress can exacerbate or reduce relational tensions between these students and their teachers and their peers. One correlate of racial stress is the perception of a racial climate. Mattison and Aber (2007) studied racial climate and achievement and found that compared to their European American counterparts, African American high schoolers perceived their schooling experiences as less racially fair. Furthermore, perceptions of racial unfairness for both African American and European American students were associated with poor student academic and behavioral outcomes.

The Case for Culturally Responsive School-Based Interventions

A framework to guide the process of developing culturally responsive interventions is not without challenges. First, there is the problem of defi ning what is meant by culture and how to accomplish cultural responsiveness in school contexts. Approaches that focus simply on matching personnel and students by racial characteristics are inadequate. Cultural responsiveness entails focusing not only on understanding student behaviors and well-being, but also on the person-in-environment contextual reality and treating racial/ethnic factors as primary and appropriate targets for intervention (Stevenson, 2009). Previous sections of this article have summarized research that suggests specifi c racial/ethnic dynamics may arise between teachers and African American males that have implications for the mislabeling, misinterpretation, referral, treatment, and school-related outcomes of these students. Th e infl uence of the interpersonal dynamics between these students and their teachers must therefore be considered early in the intervention development process.

Contextual Processes Influencing Vulnerability

Ecological risk factors have long been cited as having direct eff ects on the psychosocial development of youth. African American families are disproportionately aff ected by poverty and the literature is replete with examples of the ways they are further disadvantaged by racism, discrimination, and segregation (Brody et al., 2006; Nyborg & Curry, 2003). At a very young age, children begin to experience the deleterious eff ects of these circumstances. Garcia-Coll and colleagues' (1996) integrative model posits that the developmental processes of children from racial/ethnic minority groups are aff ected fi rst by social position variables, such as race, social class, and gender. Th ese social position variables operate through the mechanisms of racism, discrimination and segregation. Such contextual factors induce vulnerability and create a cyclical dynamic wherein African American males grow up in suboptimal environments, develop maladaptive behaviors, and are ultimately disenfranchised.

Research suggests that teachers are less competent in working with African American students compared to Caucasian students (Chang & Sue, 2003; Decker, Dona, & Christenson, 2007). A few studies provide empirical support for these diff erences. Murray, Waas, and Murray (2008) examined whether there was an association between teacher-student interactions and school adjustment among African American, Latino, and Caucasian students in low-income urban school settings. Th ey found that race moderated teacher-student relationships and African American students were more likely to express a dislike for school when teacher confl ict was high and closeness was low. Another study by Brody and colleagues (2006) examined the role of perceived racial discrimination in the adjustment of African American youth. Th e results indicated that conduct problems and depressive symptoms among African American students were linked to increases in perceived discriminatory encounters.

Few studies have examined racial dynamics between African American students and their teachers, and how these contribute to school disengagement and failure (Th omas, Coard & Stevenson, Bentley, & Zamel, 2009). Nonetheless, the research indicates that race plays a signifi cant role in teacher-student interactions and school adjustment. Furthermore, the negative impact of discrimination is particularly pernicious for African American youth in school settings, although racial socialization may serve as a mediator of perceptions of discrimination and the development of racial identity (Stevenson & Arlington, 2009). It is therefore critical that interventions, supports, and services address both sociodemographic factors and contextual variables in order to adequately address the needs of African American males with EBD.

Cultural Processes Influencing Protection

Many African American youth continue to exhibit resilience despite the academic, physical, and psychological challenges they face in their schools and communities. African American youth navigate their environments with competencies that result from unique personal characteristics, adaptive culture, and family processes. Brondolo and colleagues (2008) posited three types of individual-level coping with racial discrimination: (a) racial identity development, (b) social support seeking, and (c) anger suppression and expression. Th ese individual-level coping strategies are important, but are functionally related to family and community infl uences. A good example is racial/ethnic socialization, which involves messages that contribute to African American youth acquiring a racial/ethnic identity and help them make meaning of racial/ethnic confl ict they may regularly encounter. A wealth of research has established that racial/ethnic socialization processes serve a protective function by buff ering the eff ects of racism on well-being and identity (Sellers, 2009; Stevenson & Arrington, 2009); promoting racial identity maturation (Th omas, Townsend, & Belgrave, 2003); mitigating and promoting youth emotional functioning (Davis & Stevenson, 2006), promoting academic engagement, achievement, expectations, and success (Murry, Berkel, Brody, Miller, & Chen, 2009); and mitigating the negative perceptions teachers have about the behavior of African American boys (Th omas et al., 2009).

Acknowledging that individual diff erences exist, what can be gleaned from the literature is that as a whole, African American adolescent boys with EBD will face signifi cant challenges in school. Some of these challenges will be associated with biases inherent in school personnel's assessments, placement, and intervention practices. As such, schools constitute a distinctive sociocultural context for African American males and staff within this context can undermine the possibility of positive outcomes for these students. An important fi rst step toward ameliorating this problem is acknowledging the importance of racial issues in the classroom and being more culturally responsive in eff orts to ensure these student's needs are adequately met.

A growing body of work exists targeting the behavioral and emotional challenges of African American youth using culturally relevant in-school and aft er-school programs (Ghee, Walker, & Younger, 1998; Th omas, Davidson, & McAdoo, 2008; Watts, Abdul-Adil, & Pratt, 2002). Th ese programs share a focus on improving African American youths' self-esteem, racial/ethnic identity, racial discrimination awareness, sociopolitical consciousness, and emotional and behavioral literacy. Educational research testing innovative instructual strategies with low-income African American students demonstrates that capitalizing on a specifi c set of cultural themes and associated values and behavioral repertoires can improve African American students' acquisition of academic competencies and underlying intellectual skills (Boykin & Bailey, 2000). Such studies show that optimal learning environments for African American students are those imbued with or structured to capitalize on themes that are part of African American people's meaning system (Boykin & Bailey, 2000). Such themes include movement expressiveness, orality, and communalism. Empirical studies emanating from this paradigm demonstrate that African American students perform better aft er learning in culturally congruent contexts than they do in traditional school contexts (Boykin & Cunningham, 2004; Boykin, Lilja, & Tyler, 2004; Serpell, Boykin, Madhere, & Nasim, 2007; Serpell & Cole, 2008).

Harnessing the aforementioned cultural themes in the development of interventions may prove particularly useful for promoting positive outcomes among African American males with EBD. A program targeting a similar subpopulation of African American males provides some insight into how this might be done. Th e Preventing Long-term Anger and Aggression in Youth (PLAAY) program (Stevenson, 2003) designed to reduce anger and aggression in African American males, targets the interactions between students and teachers. Trained professionals help students reframe their appraisal of confl icts and reposition their coping and agency within particular contexts. Program components and assessments refl ect cultural styles (the conceptualization of which is congruent with the aforementioned cultural themes), such as the dynamic use of language. Preliminary results indicate that PLAAY signifi cantly reduces anger and aggression among adolescents with a previous history of aggressive behavior. Additionally, students who participated in the program demonstrated a reduced sensitivity to rejection which oft en precipitates aggressive outbursts (Davis, Zamel, Hall, Espin, & Williams, 2003).

Few evidence-based interventions exist for adolescents with EBD and the eff ort to develop evidencebased interventions for all adolescents will likely also benefi t African American males with EBD. However, the review of research on African American youth suggests that it is also critical to consider variables related to these students' unique values, beliefs, and behavioral repertoires, as well as the beliefs and practices inherent in the school system. Culturally responsive interventions should encompass programmatic or curricular adjustments that consider culturally relevant pedagogy and/or culturally responsive environments (Gay, 2000; Ladson-Billings & Tate, 2006). While limited, emerging research is delineating the ways in which a variety of culturally specifi c protective factors, such as racial socialization, can be harnessed in treatment development eff orts. As the specifi city of our understanding of such factors improves, so too does the promise for successfully incorporating them into school-based interventions and improving student outcomes.

Psychologists, educators, and researchers will need to work collaboratively to determine appropriate theoretical frameworks to ensure that treatment development eff orts are culturally responsive. Relevant research examining the vulnerabilities and strengths of African American males with EBD are extremely sparse and this must be addressed if these students' needs are to be met in schools. Th e social science fi eld requires more thoughtful approaches that can answer specifi c questions relevant to treatment development eff orts. For example, studies need to be suffi ciently powered to unyoke race and poverty and to examine race as a potential moderator of treatment outcome. It also is critical that studies assess the degree to which contextual factors, such as racial tension in the classroom, inhibit the eff ectiveness of interventions. Lastly, assessment and measurement are important issues that must be addressed. For example, research must examine how outcomes are assessed in a group for whom rater bias exists, racial/ethnic variables need to be considered, and few culturally relevant assessments with established psychometric properties are available.

Policy Recommendations

Shift s in policy are contingent on adequate knowledge about what is likely to work with African American adolescent boys with EBD. Recommendations that follow from this review therefore center on acknowledging gaps in the research literature and existing practice; and extracting general guidelines to inform eff orts to develop culturally responsive school-based interventions and improve educational policies. Th ese recommendations can be summarized under the following:

- improving student-teacher interactions, particularly among teachers and students with diff ering racial/ethnic backgrounds;
- adopting culturally responsive assessment and treatment development practices;
- meaningfully engaging families from racial/ethnic minority groups; and
- reconceptualizing the role of schools and school-based professionals, with an increased focus on students' mental health.

Policies that support practices fostering strong and positive student-teacher relationships must become a priority if the needs of African American students with EBD are to be adequately met. Emphasizing quality student-teacher relationships highlights the importance of culturally responsive approaches that can be bolstered by appropriate mandates for teacher preparation and training. Cultural competence among teachers can be remediated through engagement in self-awareness and self-refl ection processes developed through guided and supervised exposure to racially stressful situations (Stevenson, Winn, Walker-Barnes, & Coard, 2005). Teachers' self-appraisal of their teaching and racial negotiation competence can elucidate how African American male students' emotional and behavioral expressions are interpreted, managed, or mismanaged.

Th e role of teachers also must be redefi ned to include addressing mental health concerns. Such a mandate would transform teacher training and evaluation, ensuring that attention is paid to the social and emotional needs of students. Additionally, policies that foster the meaningful and early engagement of racial/ethnic minority parents in schools' processes of identifi cation and intervention will help bring in culturally appropriate appraisals of students' actual needs (Serpell, Clauss-Ehlers, & Lindsay, 2007). An important caveat to each of these recommendations is that teacher eff orts to more eff ectively meet the needs of African American adolescent boys must be supported by the school and this will likely entail systemic changes in the expectations, training, and support provided to teachers (Adelman & Taylor, 2004). One way school systems can improve the support provided to teachers is to capitalize on the expertise of the oft en underutilized school-based mental health professionals in order to train teachers. Th ese recommendations are intended to serve as catalysts for change and are geared towards ultimately improving the awareness, knowledge, and skills of professionals charged with the responsibility of serving African American boys in educational settings.

Th e preparation of this article was supported by the Institute of Education Sciences, U.S. Department of Education, Grant R324C080011. Th e work was conducted through the Center for Adolescent Research in Schools (CARS). Th e opinions expressed are those of the authors and do not represent views of the U.S.
Department of Education.

References

Adelman, H. S., & Taylor, L. (2004). Mental health in schools: A shared agenda. *Report on Emotional & Behavioral Disorder in Youth, 4,* 59–78.

Blackorby, J., & Wagner, M. (1996). Longitudinal postschool outcomes of youth with disabilities: Findings from the National Longitudinal Transition Study. *Exceptional Children, 62,* 399–413.

Boykin, A. W., & Bailey, C. (2000). *Th e role of cultural factors in school relevant cognitive functioning: Synthesis of fi ndings on cultural contexts, cultural orientations and individual diff erences* (Report 42). Washington, DC, and Baltimore, MD: Howard University & Johns Hopkins University, CRESPAR.

Boykin, A. W., & Cunningham, R. (2004). Enhancing cognitive performance in African American children through multiple contexts: Infusing Afro-cultural ethos. In R. Jones (Ed.), *Black psychology* (4th ed.) (pp.487–508). Hampton, VA: Cobb & Henry.

Boykin, A. W., Lilja, A, & Tyler, K. M. (2004). Th e infl uence of communal vs. individual learning context on the academic performance in social studies of African American 4th and 5th grade children. *Learning Environments Research Journal, 7,* 227–244.

Bradley, R., Dolittle, J., & Bartolotta, R. (2008). Building on the data and adding to the discussion: Th e experiences and outcomes of students with EBD. *Journal of Behavioral Education, 17,* 4–23.

Brody, G. H., Chen, Y., Murry, V. B., Ge, X, Simons, R. L., Gibbons, F. X., Gerrard, M., & Cutrona, C. E. (2006). Perceived discrimination and the adjustment of African American youths: A fi ve-year longitudinal analysis with contextual moderation eff ects. *Child Development, 77,* 1170–1189.

Brondolo, E., Brady, N., Th ompson, S., Contrada, R. J., Cassells, A., Tobin, J., & Sweeney, M. (2008). Perceived racism and negative aff ect: Analyses of trait and state measures of aff ect in a community sample. *Journal of Social and Clinical Psychology, 27,* 150–173.

Bullis, M., & Cheney, D. (1999). Vocational and transition interventions for adolescents and young adults with emotional or behavioral disorders. *Focus on Exceptional Children, 31,* 1–24.

Center for Adolescent Research in Schools (CARS) assessment core literature review (2009). Retrieved May 30, 2009, from http://www.ies-cars.org/

Chang, D. F., & Sue, S. (2003). Th e eff ects of race and problem type on teachers' assessments of student behavior. *Journal of Consulting and Clinical Psychology, 71,* 235–242.

Davis, G. Y., & Stevenson, H. C. (2006). Racial socialization experiences and symptoms of depression among Black youth. *Journal of Child and Family Studies, 15,* 293–307.

Davis, G. Y., Zamel, P. C., Hall, D., Espin, E., & Williams, V. R. (2003). Life aft er PLAAY: Alumni group and rites of passage empowerment. In H. C. Stevenson (Ed.) *Playing with anger: Teaching coping skills to African American boys through athletics and culture* (pp. 169–182). Westport, CT: Greenwood Praeger.

Decker, D. M., Dona, D. P., & Christenson, S. L. (2007). Behaviorally at-risk African American students: Th e importance of student-teacher relationships for student outcomes. *Journal of School Psychology, 45,* 83–109.

DuPaul, G. J., Power, T. J., Anastopoulos, A. D., Reid, R., McGoey, K. E., & Ikeda, M. J. (1997). Teacher ratings of attention-defi cit/hyperactivity disorder symptoms: Factor structure, normative data, and psychometric properties. *Psychological Assessment, 9,* 436–444.

Epstein, J. N., March, J. S., Conners, K., & Jackson, D. L. (1998). Racial diff erences on the Conners teacher rating scale. *Journal of Abnormal Child Psychology, 26,* 109–118.

Ferri, B. A., & Connor, D. J. (2005). In the shadow of *Brown:* Special education and overrepresentation of students of color. *Remedial and Special Education, 26,* 93–100.

Fierros, E. G., & Conroy, J. W. (2002). Double jeopardy: An exploration of restrictiveness and race in special education. In D. Losen & G. Orfi eld (Eds.), *Racial inequity in special education* (pp. 39–70). Cambridge, MA: Harvard Education.

Frank, A. R., Sitlington, P. L., & Carson, R. R. (1995). Young adults with behavioral disorders: A comparison with peers with mild disabilities. *Journal of Emotional and Behavioral Disorders, 3,* 156–164.

Garcia-Coll, C., Lamberty, G., Jenkins, R., McAdoo, H., Crnic, K., Wasik, B., & Vazquez Garcia, H. (1996). An integrative model for the study of developmental competencies in minority children. *Child Development, 67,* 1891–1914.

Garibaldi, A. M. (1992). Educating and motivating African American males to succeed. *Th e Journal of Negro Education, 61,* 12–18.

Gay, G. (2000). *Culturally responsive teaching: Th eory, research, and practice.* New York: Teachers College.

Ghee, K., Walker, J., & Younger, A. (1998). Th e raamus academy. *Journal of Prevention & Intervention in the Community, 16,* 87–102.

Greenbaum, P. E., Dedrick, R. F., Friedman, R. M., Kutash, K., Brown, E. C., & Lardieri, S. (1996). National adolescent and child treatment study (NACTS): Outcomes for children with serious emotional and behavioral disturbance. *Journal of Emotional and Behavioral Disorders, 4,* 130–146.

Gresham, F. M., & Kern, L. (2004). Internalizing behavior problems in children and adolescents. In R. Rutherford, M. Quinn, & S. Mathur (Eds.), *Handbook of research in behavior disorders* (pp. 262–281). New York: Guilford.

Hendrickson, J. M., Smith, C. R., Frank, A. R., & Merical, C. (1998). Decision making factors associated with placement of students with emotional and behavioral disorders in restrictive educational settings. *Education and Treatment of Children, 21,* 275–302.

Hilliard, A. G., III. (1992). Th e pitfalls and promises of special education practice. *Exceptional Children, 59,* 168–172.

Individuals with Disabilities Education Act Reauthorization (IDEA) of 2004, 20 U.S.C. § 1400 *et seq.*

Kearns, T., Ford, L., & Linney, J. A. (2005). African American student representation in special education programs. *Th e Journal of Negro Education, 74,* 297–310.

Kellow, J. T., & Jones, B. D. (2008). Th e eff ects of stereotypes on the achievement gap: Reexamining the academic performance of African American high school students. *Journal of Black Psychology, 34,* 94–120.

Landrum, T., Katsiyannis, A., & Archwamety, T. (2004). An analysis of placement and exit patterns of students with emotional or behavioral disorders. *Behavioral Disorders, 29,* 140–153.

Ladson-Billings, G. J., & Tate, W. (2006). *Education research in the public interest: Social justice, action, and policy.* New York: Teachers College Press.

Mayer, G. R. (1995). Preventing antisocial behavior in the schools. *Journal of Applied Behavior Analysis, 28,* 467–478.

Murray, C., Waas, G. A., & Murray, K. M. (2008). Child race and gender as moderators of the association between teacher-child relationships and school adjustment. *Psychology in the Schools, 45,* 562–578.

Murry, V. M., Berkel, C., Brody, G. H., Miller, S. J., & Chen, Y. (2009). Linking parental socialization to interpersonal protective processes, academic self-presentation, and expectations among rural African American youth. *Cultural Diversity and Ethnic Mental Health, 15,* 1–10.

Neal, L. V. I., McCray, A. D., Webb-Johnson, G., & Bridgest, S. T. (2003). Th e eff ects of African American movement styles on teachers' perceptions and reactions. *Journal of Special Education, 37,* 49–57.

Nyborg, V. M., & Curry, J. F., 2003. Th e impact of perceived racism: Psychological symptoms among African American boys. *Journal of Clinical Child & Adolescent Psychology, 32,* 258–266.

Osher, D., Woodruff, D., & Sims, A. E. (2002). *Schools make a diff erence: Th e overrepresentation of African American youth in special education and the juvenile justice system.* In D. Losen & G. Orfi eld (Eds.), *Racial inequity in special education* (pp. 93–115). Cambridge, MA: Harvard Education.

Oswald, D. P., Coutinho, M. J., Best, A. M., & Singh, N. N. (1999). Ethnic representation in special education: Th e role of school related economic and demographic variables. *Journal of Special Education, 32,* 194–206.

Pigott, R. L., & Cowen, E. L. (2000). Teacher race, child race, racial congruence, and teacher ratings of children's school adjustment. *Journal of School Psychology, 38,* 177–196.

Reddy, L., Th omas, C., Newman, E., & Chen, V. (2009). School-based prevent and intervention programs for children with emotional disturbance: A review of treatment components and methodology. *Psychology in the Schools, 46,* 132–152.

Reid, R., DuPaul, G. J., Power, T. J., Anastopolous, A. D., Rogers-Adkinson, D., Noll, M. B., et al. (1998). Assessing cultural diff erent students for attention defi cit hyperactivity disorder using behavior rating scales. *Journal of Abnormal Child Psychology, 26,* 187–198.

Sellers, R. (2009, April). *Racial Identity in African American Adolescent Development.* Paper presented at the Black Caucus Preconference Meeting during the annual convention of the Society of Research in Child Development, Denver, CO.

Serpell, Z., Boykin, A. W., Madhere, S., & Nasim, A. (2007). Th e signifi cance of contextual factors on African American student's transfer of learning. *Journal of Black Psychology, 32,* 418–441.

Serpell, Z., Clauss-Ehlers, C., & Lindsey, M. A. (2007). Schools' provision of information regarding mental health and associated services to culturally diverse families. In S. W. Evans, M. Weist, & Z. Serpell (Eds.), *Advances in school-based mental health interventions* (vol. 2, pp.18-1–18-17). Kingston, NJ: Civic Research Institute, Inc.

Serpell, Z., & Cole, J. (2008). Move to learn: Enhancing story recall among urban African American children. *Journal of Urban Learning, Teaching, and Research, 4, 73–85.*

Skiba, R. J., Michael, R. S., Nardo, A. C., & Peterson, R. L. (2002). Th e color of discipline: Sources of racial and gender disproportionality in school punishment. *Th e Urban Review, 34,* 317–342.

Skiba, R. J., & Rausch, M. K. (2006). Zero tolerance, suspension, and expulsion: Questions of equity and eff ectiveness. In C. M. Evertson & C. S. Weinstein (Eds.), *Handbook of classroom management (pp.* 1063–1092). Mahwah, NJ: Erlbaum.

Sinclair, M. F., Christenson, S. L., & Th urlow, M. L. (2005). Promoting school completion of urban secondary youth with emotional or behavioral disabilities. *Exceptional Children, 71,* 465–482.

Stevenson, H. C. (2003). *Playing with anger: Teaching coping skills to African American boys through athletics and culture.* Westport, CT: Greenwood Praeger.

Stevenson, H. C. (2008). Fluttering around the racial tension of trust: Proximal approaches to suspended Black student-teacher relationships. *School Psychology Review, 37,* 354–358.

Stevenson, H. C. (2009). *Recasting racially anxious encounters: Th eorizing racial/ethnic coping and agency socialization.* (Manuscript submitted for publication.)

Stevenson, H. C., & Arrington, E. G. (2009). Racial/ethnic socialization mediates perceived racism and identity experiences of African American students. *Cultural Diversity and Ethnic Mental Health, 15,* 125–136.

Stevenson, H. C., Winn, D., Walker-Barnes, C., Coard, S. (2005). Style matters: Towards a culturally relevant framework for interventions with African American families. In V. McLoyd, K. Dodge, & N. Hill (Eds.), *Emerging issues in African-American family life: Context, adaptation, and policy* (pp. 311–334). Duke Series in Child Development and Public Policy. New York: Guilford Press.

Th omas, D. E., Coard, S. I., Stevenson, H. C., Bentley, K., & Zamel, P. (2009). Racial and emotional factors predicting teachers' perceptions of classroom behavioral maladjustment for urban African American male youth. *Psychology in the Schools, 46,* 184–196.

Th omas, D. E., Townsend, T. G., & Belgrave, F. Z. (2003). Th e infl uence of cultural and racial identifi cation on the psychosocial adjustment of inner-city African American children in school. *American Journal of Community Psychology, 32,* 217–228.

Th omas, O., Davidson, W., & Mcadoo, H. (2008). An evaluation study of the Young Empowered Sisters (YES!) program: Promoting cultural assets among African American adolescent girls through a culturally relevant school-based intervention. *Journal of Black Psychology, 34,* 281–308.

Townsend, B. (2000). Th e disproportionate discipline of African American learners: Reducing school suspensions and expulsions. *Exceptional Children, 66,* 382–391.

Wagner, M. (1995). Outcomes for youths with serious emotional disturbance in secondary school and early adulthood: Critical issues for children and youths. *Th e Future of Children, 5,* 90–112.

Wagner, M., Newman, L., & Cameto, R. (2004). *Changes over time in the secondary school experience of students with disabilities: A special topic report of fi ndings from the National Longitudinal Transition Study-2 (NLTS2).* Menlo Park, CA: SRI International.

Watts, R. J., Abdul-Adil, J. K., & Pratt, T. (2002). Enhancing critical consciousness in young African American men: A psychoeducational approach. *Psychology of Men & Masculinity, 3,* 41–50.

Wolraich, M. L., Wibbelsman, C. J., Brown, T. E., Evans, S. W., Gotlieb, E. M., Knight, J. R., et al. (2005). Attentiondefi cit/hyperactivity disorder among adolescents: A review of the diagnosis, treatment, and clinical implications. *Pediatrics, 115,* 1734–1746.

Youngstrom, E. Loeber, R., & Stouthamer-Loeber, M. (2000). Patterns and correlates of agreement between parent, teacher, and male adolescent ratings of externalizing and internalizing problems. *Journal of Consulting and Clinical Psychology, 68,* 1038–1050.

Ysseldyke, J. E., Algozzine, B., & Th urlow, M. L. (1995). *Critical issues in special education* (2nd ed.). Boston: Houghton Miffl in.

Zhang, D., & Katsiyannis, A. (2002). Minority representation in special education a persistent challenge. *Remedial and Special Education, 23, 180–187.*

Zimmerman, R. S., Khoury, E. L., Vega, W. A., Gila A. G., & Warheit, G. J. (1995). Teacher and parent perceptions of behavior problems among a sample of African American, Hispanic, and Non-Hispanice students. *American Journal of Community Psychology, 23,* 181–197.

Authors

ZEWELANJI SERPELL is Assistant Professor in the Psychology Department at Virginia State University in Petersburg. CHARLAYNE C. HAYLING is a doctoral student in Counseling Psychology at Lehigh University in Bethlehem, Pennsylvania. HOWARD C. STEVENSON is Associate Professor and Chair, Applied Psychology and Human Development, Graduate School of Education, University of Pennsylvania in Philadelphia. LEE KERN is Professor in the College of Education at Lehigh Univerity.

Low-Income African American Male Youth with ADHD Symptoms in the United States

Recommendations for Clinical Mental Health Counselors Catherine Tucker and Andrea L. Dixon

African-American males living in poverty are among the least likely children and adolescents to receive mental health services in the United States, even though they are the most likely to be referred to mental health agencies for services. In this article the authors explore current problems facing impoverished African American youth who exhibit symptoms of attention defi cit hyperactivity disorder (ADHD), their need for mental health services, and the barriers to services that they face, and off er recommendations for mental health counselors.

There are strategies for working with at-risk populations (Bemak & Chung, 2005; Carter, 2003; Diemer, 2007; Santa Lucia, 2004). Well-prepared counselors in both schools and mental health settings can be powerful allies for clients who are impoverished and marginalized and who experience barriers to mental health services. Perhaps no group is in greater need than are young, African American males (DayVines & Day-Hairston, 2005; Noguera, 2003), especially those diagnosed with learning, emotional, and behavioral disorders.

Currently, African American males lead all other race and gender groups in incarceration rates, new HIV infections, homicide deaths, poverty rates, and diagnosed learning disorders (Center for Disease Control and Prevention, 2006; Noguera, 2003). Oft en the complex pathways that lead African American young men to negative outcomes include missed opportunities by both schools and community agencies to intervene with problematic behaviors at earlier ages (Logan, 2001; Monroe, 2005; Noguera, 2003). Th erefore, when young, low-income African American males and their caregivers arrive in mental health agencies, counselors need specifi c skills and strategies to help the clients attain specifi c goals in counseling, overcome barriers to treatment, and begin to quell the negative life outcomes common among African American males (Day-Vines & Day-Hairston, 2005; Logan). In this article we explore some of the challenges facing contemporary African American low-income male youth who have symptoms of attention defi cit hyperactivity disorder (ADHD) and the barriers to mental health services that they experience. We also off er recommendations for mental health counselors.

AFRICAN AMERICAN MALES AND ADHD

In 2006 in the United States there were 4.5 million children between the ages of 5 and 17 who had been diagnosed with ADHD (Pastor & Reuben, 2008). Th e number of these children has risen steadily over the past decade, as has the proportion of children in the U.S. who are taking psychotropic medications (Pastor & Reuben). Projections about the economic impact of educational and medical services for children diagnosed with ADHD fall conservatively at \$36–\$52 billion a year as of 2005, making ADHD an important economic as well as social issue (Pelham, Foster, & Robb, 2007).

Th e impact of this upward trend in diagnosis is not evenly distributed by race, social class, or gender. Boys are diagnosed with ADHD almost twice as oft en as girls across all races, and those who are nonwhite (both Hispanic and African American) are the most oft en diagnosed of all groups (Cuff e, Moore, & McKeown, 2005). Th ere is no clear reason for the large gender and race discrepancies in the prevalence of ADHD (Cuff e et al.; Miller, Nigg, & Miller, 2009; Pastor & Reuben, 2008). However, recent research on the impact of genetic inheritance on ADHD, along with other research focused on gender and ethnic diff erences in the expression of ADHD symptoms, may help resolve these questions (Miller et al.).

One area of disparity that is somewhat better understood is social class. Th ere is a large, signifi cant, and long-standing gap in diagnosis rates between children who are privately insured, those who have Medicaid coverage, and those with no insurance. Children with Medicaid coverage are the most likely to be diagnosed with ADHD, closely followed by those with private insurance; those with no coverage at all lag far behind (Pastor & Reuben, 2008).

When the risk factors associated with being African American, male, and living in poverty are combined with the inattentive and hyperactive symptoms of ADHD, the risk of academic failure and punishment for disruptive school behavior escalates dramatically (Angold et al., 2002). African American male youths have a disproportionately high rate of ADHD, with an estimated prevalence rate of 5.56%, compared to 4.33% for Euro American boys, and 1.77% for females of all races (Cuff e, Moore, & McLeown, 2005). Th us, African American males are uniquely vulnerable in both communities and schools.

Th e possible reasons for higher ADHD prevalence rates among African American males are multifaceted and complex. Increased exposure to risk factors among low-income African American males, including high rates of poverty and exposure to environmental toxins, such as lead, may increase the likelihood of developing symptoms of ADHD (Arnold et al., 2003; Miller, Nigg, & Miller, 2009). Almost twice as many African American children live below the poverty line as Euro American children (U.S. Census Bureau, 2006). In addition, inner-city African American children have far greater exposure to dangerous levels of lead (36%) than the overall U.S. child population (4%) (CDC, 2006). Also, issues of accurate assessment and diagnosis for African Americans, cultural diff erences in perceptions of children's behavior, the impact of poverty on children's access to care, and possible bias and discrimination among referring school and mental health personnel may impact variations in ADHD among ethnic and gender groups (Cuff e, Moore, & McKeown, 2005; Miller, Nigg, & Miller).

African American males are overrepresented in most categories of learning, emotional, and behavioral disabilities. Th ey are most severely overrepresented in areas of disability that are descriptive of disruptive and inappropriate behavior at school compared to categories of disability that describe specifi c learning problems (Colpe, 2000). Although they comprised only 15% of the U.S. population in 2001, African American children were overrepresented in specifi c learning disabilities (18%), mental retardation (34%), and emotional disturbance categories (28%) (Offi ce of Special Education Programs, 2005). African American males also make up a majority of the students identifi ed as emotionally disturbed in the U.S. (Colpe) and are far more likely than their Euro American or female peers to be suspended, expelled, or subjected to corporal punishment (National Center for Education Statistics, 2001). Adams, Benshoff , and Harrington (2007) found in a review of National Educational Longitudinal Study (NELS) data from the 1990s likely than their Euro American or Hispanic peers to be referred to school counselors and more likely to be referred for classroom behavior than for academic issues. African American males are also disproportionately absent from advanced courses and college campuses (Noguera, 2003). Although not all the African American boys who comprise the statistics on school failure and special education placement have ADHD, many of them may, and many others may be exhibiting some of the disruptive or inattentive symptoms of the disorder (Miller, Nigg, & Miller, 2009). The high stakes involved for African American youth should compel both school and clinical mental health counselors to understand the dynamics involved in assessment, diagnosis, and referral for these children.

Issues of Diagnosis and Assessment

Once African Americans boys are enrolled in clinical mental health services, the next barrier to effective treatment presented is the potential for bias in assessment. Miller, Nigg, and Miller (2009) note that higher symptom scores based on race seem to exist across most of the popular teacher rating scales for ADHD, including the Connors Scale (1997) and the SNAP-IV (Swanson, 1992), although not the Child Behavior Check List (Achenbach, 1991). A confirmatory study by Epstein, Willoughby, Valenica, Tonev, Abikoff, and Arnold (2005) using classroom observations found that the higher ratings were not due to teacher rating bias but to the apparently higher rate of classroom behavior problems among African American boys. This may be due either to a different manifestation of ADHD among African American boys or to a difference in overall classroom structure in schools with larger numbers of minority students (Miller et al.). More research is needed to clarify this point. There is some evidence to support the theory that the use of a structured diagnostic interview by a clinical mental health counselor may help correct for possible bias (Miller et al.). Using multiple methods of assessment and involving several people with varying relationships to the child may currently be the most effective way to reduce bias (Foy & Earls, 2005; Miller et al.). Informal interviews and methods of assessment seem to also bias assessment toward more ADHD diagnosis in this population (Whaley & Geller, 2007).

Also, because African American youth can experience significant delays between symptom onset and initiation of services, the array of ADHD symptoms seems to be more severe than in other race and gender groups (Arnold et al., 2003; Bussing, Zima, Gary, & Garvan, 2003). Other possible barriers to accurate diagnosis, including exposure to environmental toxins like lead, psychosocial stress in poor urban neighborhoods, and lower birth weights for African Americans than for Euro Americans all need to be investigated to determine the accuracy of current diagnostic methods for ADHD (Arnold et al.; Bussing et al.; Miller et al.).

One possible model for accurately assessing African American boys for ADHD may be the collaborative process instituted in Guilford County, North Carolina, in the early 1990s (Foy & Earls, 2005). This model utilizes collaborative communication between pediatricians, school nurses, and educators from the local school system; mental health clinicians; and family advocates. They drafted a clear protocol for assessment of children with possible symptoms of ADHD across the entire county, so that every child seen for an ADHD screening visit at the physician's office would have the same assessment protocol before the appointment. Besides providing the physician with a packet of information before diagnosis that included several rating scales, brief intelligence and achievement screen scores, classroom observation data, and the student's grades and discipline history, the plan provides for school nurses to assist families with medication management and follow-up with behavioral interventions (Foy & Earls). Although no data are available on outcomes from this effort, it seems to follow guidelines suggested by health policy and mental health experts to achieve more culturally sensitive assessments of African Americans and to achieve better overall parity in mental health care (Arnold et al., 2003; Bussing et al., 2003; Howell, 2004; Richardson, Anderson, Flaherty,

& Bell, 2003). Th e Guilford model is also a compelling example of a collaborative approach following clear assessment protocols that can be used as the basis for future models that might help reduce the disparities African Americans experience in assessment and diagnosis.

DISPARITIES IN MENTAL HEALTH CARE FOR AFRICAN AMERICANS

As the numbers of African American children and adolescents referred for mental health services because of disruptive school behaviors increases, the impact of poverty and unequal access to mental health care on their well-being becomes more apparent. Chow, Jaff ee, and Snowden (2003) found that African American children in high-poverty neighborhoods were signifi cantly more likely than their middle-class peers, or than Euro American, Hispanic, or Asian children in poverty, to be referred for early mental health intervention services—yet they were less likely to receive them.

Rates for receiving an evaluation for suspected ADHD also diff er by race. Only 28% of African American boys, compared to 51 % of Euro American boys, who are reported as exhibiting some symptoms of ADHD are ever formally evaluated (Ellison et al., 2002). Even when socioeconomic status is controlled for, African American boys have much higher reported rates of problem behaviors than do Euro American boys (Cohen's d = .045, p < .001) but are far less likely to receive a diagnosis of ADHD (OR = .66, p < .001) (Miller et al., 2009). Th ese confl icting rates of symptom history and diagnosis may be due to inaccessibility of mental health care, parent perceptions of mental health treatment, and higher risk factors (Miller et al.). African American children were found to be more likely to be referred to mental health agencies at much younger ages than their Euro American peers and far more likely to have been referred for services by a social service or criminal justice agency. Th is result held true even when income variables were controlled.

When African Americans do receive mental health care, they are more likely to use emergency services, less likely to continue with outpatient therapy (Chow et al., 2003), and more likely to be prescribed atypical antipsychotic medications and assigned to intensive case management (Kuno & Rothbard, 2005). Th e reasons behind this divide between racial groups in numbers of children referred for services, likelihood of receiving service, and quality of services received are not understood entirely. However, there are data to support the possibility of race-based bias among helping professionals, minority distrust of service-providing agencies, and economic and structural barriers to services.

Policy and Structural Barriers to Mental Health Care for African Americans
According to the U.S. Surgeon General's Report on Children's Mental Health (1999), the two major types of barriers to mental health services for low-income children of all races are (1) service delivery issues, including state and federal policies; and (2) family diffi culties. For African American youth, issues of race along with those of social class and access need to be considered. It is likely that all these issues combine to create barriers, and they are oft en diffi cult to delineate.

Service delivery issues in mental health care are broad-ranging and complex. Th e ability to design their own children's health insurance programs gives state lawmakers fl exibility but also means that there are no national standards for care or coverage (Howell, 2004). And although federal law requires that children who receive mental health screenings be granted access to needed follow-up care, stateadministered health care programs may limit access to such services (Children's Defense Fund, 2005). Current trends toward capitation of state public mental health services further jeopardize the likelihood that people in poverty, especially those of color, will receive adequate mental health care (Snowden, Wallace, Kang, Cheng, & Bloom, 2007).

In addition, more than 40 years aft er the beginning of the American Civil Rights Movement, African American children are still more likely than children of all other racial groups to be removed from their homes due to abuse or neglect and are more likely not to be returned to their families by social service agencies (U.S. General Accounting Offi ce [GAO], 2007). African American children made up only 15% of the entire child population of the U.S. in 2004 yet constituted 27% of children living in foster care (USGAO). Even though African American children have far more contact with social service agencies than Euro American children, they are far less likely to receive adequate mental health care (Angold et al., 2002).

Perhaps the most insidious trend in the reluctance of low-income African American families to seek out mental health services for their children is highlighted in a report from the USGAO (2003). Th e GAO report outlines the phenomenon of parents of all races having to give up custody of their children to the state in order to access mental health care for serious chronic problems. Th e GAO estimated that in 2001 more than 12,700 children were placed in the custody of state agencies solely to make them eligible for expensive mental health treatments, primarily in residential care facilities. Obviously, families with fewer fi nancial resources are more likely to have to make drastic custody decisions to receive treatment for their children. However, with residential treatment for mental health problems sometimes costing in excess of $250,000 annually, this is an issue that extends to middle-class families as well.

African American Family Concerns and Mental Health Care

In addition to state and federal regulations and diffi culties with aligning policies, families who live in poverty face more quotidian barriers to accessing mental health care. Cultural-contextual issues, such as a stigma against help-seeking, negative expectations, fi nancial barriers, and a lack of perceived need for services, hinder some families from receiving care, as Bussing et al. (2003) found in their study of help-seeking behavior for families with children diagnosed with ADHD. Lack of information about how to access services and what services are available and denial of the severity of a child's need for help are also common among low-income mothers (Arcia, Fernandez, Marisela, Castillo, & Ruiz, 2004). Families in rural areas may have diffi culty fi nding transportation to appointments (Myers & Gill, 2004). Homeless families oft en face the additional diffi culty of having no address or telephone number where heath care providers can reach them (French, Reardon, & Smith, 2003).

Some authors have theorized that living in poverty generates higher stress, which can lead to higher levels of child abuse, depression, drug use, anxiety, and behavior problems (McKay, Lynn, & Bannon, 2005). Furthermore, families living in poverty oft en lack access to or knowledge about professional helpers. Arcia et al. (2004) found that out of 62 Latina mothers interviewed, about half (32) reached the mental health clinic's door "almost by happenstance … the mother's search looked like a pinball in a game" (p. 1225). Tucker (2009) found that low-income African American caregivers oft en feel frustrated and powerless when trying to navigate systems of care, and that counselors can be very helpful in reducing those feelings by acknowledging the diffi culties they face and working collaboratively with them.

African American caregivers may also experience concerns about cultural stigma surrounding mental health care and about racially motivated discrimination by mental health care personnel (Ayalon & Alvidrez, 2007). Logan (2001) pointed out that African Americans oft en view emotional issues as private matters to be dealt with by the family or informal helping networks and that seeking formal mental health care is sometimes perceived as violating family and community privacy. Th is reluctance to seek formal help may be based on historical abuses by the U.S. government; changing the perceptions of agencies will likely take concerted, well-planned eff orts if African American youth are to receive the services they need (Logan).

RECOMMENDATIONS FOR MENTAL HEALTH COUNSELORS

Th e cultural disconnections between low-income African Americans and the nation's mental health care facilities not only skew communications but also limit young peoples' life options (Carter, 2003; Lee, 2005; Noguera, 2003). Since children in need of mental health care must be brought to services by their caregivers, one critical step in closing the treatment gap for low-income African American males with mental health needs is to create better working alliances with their families. To create strong relationships with families, counselors need to understand the unique challenges facing African Americans living in poverty and be skilled in fostering collaborative relationships with them.

Th e cultural dissonance between predominantly middle-class Euro American counselors and lowincome African American families may cause clients to feel disrespected and unwelcome in the social system of mental health centers (Applebaum, 2002; Day-Vines & Day-Hairston, 2005; Monroe, 2005; Noguera, 2003; Tucker, 2009; Winters, 1993). While this disconnection is most likely unintentional, to improve communication and bridge the distance between the Euro American middle-class world of the mental health center and the low-income African American world of some families needs to be examined intentionally and directly. Streamlining referral processes to require fewer trips to the clinic, shortening waiting times for services, and providing clear information about what to expect might help bring more families in.

Complex sociocultural issues are as prominent inside the counseling room as in society at large. Youth, parents, and counselors of all races oft en have diff ering goals and expectations of counseling (Garland, Lewczyk-Boxmeyer, Gabayan, & Hawley, 2004). Young people also have expressed a desire to be involved in decision-making about services (Dogra, 2005). Th is may be a particularly salient point in light of the fi nding of Garland et al. that of 170 adolescents interviewed, only about one-third agreed with their caregivers about the goals of treatment.

Eff ective communication is not a one-size-fi ts-all structure. Counselors must consider the racial, ethnic, economic, and cultural backgrounds of the families they serve so as to create appropriate programs of communication (Applebaum, 2002; Comer, 1989). To reach low-income African American families eff ectively counselors should draw from the literature to inform their practices for engaging these families. For example, African American parents oft en prefer more directive, concrete approaches to problem-solving than do some other racial groups (Miller et al., 2009). Counselors should also be aware that a large study from the National Institutes of Mental Health found that African American boys with ADHD improved more with a combination of stimulant medication and behavioral therapies (Arnold et al., 2003) than with either treatment alone.

Counselors can begin to shift the family-agency communications paradigm from one of pathology and need to one of collaboration by instituting the following changes:

- Acknowledge and build on the wisdom already present in the family. Ask what strategies have worked in helping the child complete tasks, get organized, and behave appropriately in the past. If nothing comes to mind, ask caregivers about eff ective strategies used with their other children or by their friends or family members (Logan, 2001).
- Make sure caregivers feel involved in all stages of diagnosis and treatment planning. Be alert to the "don't make waves" response that can come from caregivers who feel blamed and powerless (Erford, 2003).

- Avoid blaming the caregiver for the child's diffi culties. Th is is particularly salient for counselors in schools, where caregivers frequently report feeling blamed for their children's misbehavior (Tucker, 2009).
- Be aware of possible racial and gender bias in formal and informal assessments. Use multiple methods of assessment, including feedback from parents, teachers, and other signifi cant adults in the child's life (Foy & Earls, 2005; Miller et al., 2009). Do not rely on any single measure of a child's behavior to make a diagnosis. Be sure to include the child in this process.
- Be aware of possible challenges to accessing care, and if necessary help the family navigate the system. Ask about transportation, cost, and time issues and problem-solve about them to remove barriers to treatment compliance. Barriers related to perceptions about stigma and cultural norms about privacy should also be discussed openly (Ayalon & Alvidrez, 2007).
- Especially when there has been a long delay between the onset of the problem and the fi rst appointment, counselors should work to insure that caregivers feel that they are leaving the session with some useful ideas. Caregivers can become frustrated if intake sessions do not involve any problem-solving or psychoeducation and may not return if they feel the eff ort to attend was not worthwhile (Logan, 2001).

By engaging families in a mutual sharing model of communication instead of a more traditional one-way, counselor-as-expert mode, counselors can begin to overcome the negative expectations about counseling held by some low-income and minority parents (Logan).

Recalling Liu's intrapsychic model of classism (2001), counselors are encouraged to be aware of possible internalized classism when working with low-income or minority parents. Liu's premise is that social class is not defi ned so much by income as by a person's subjective experience of where he or she fi ts within the social class hierarchy (Liu, Pickett, & Ivey, 2007). Oft en people's subjective experience of social class matches their current economic situation, but not always. Mental health counselors should be aware of this possibility and be watchful for possible class bias in their approach to clients. Internalized classism may lead lower-income caregivers to have low expectations of counseling, low self-effi cacy regarding treatment compliance and success, or both (Liu et al., 2007). Low-income or minority individuals may have diffi culty "reading" social cues common in middle-class environments like mental health care settings. Counselors should take care to fully explain all mental health care issues and avoid professional jargon so that caregivers can clearly understand all possible interventions and alternatives. Th e reality is that many cultural groups in the U.S. have negative, stereotypical beliefs about mental health care that may prevent counselors from providing eff ective treatment (Ayalon & Alvidrez, 2007; Logan, 2001; Tucker, 2009). Counselors who are prepared to address issues of stigma, shame, and fear with their clients might have better chances of serving clients for more sessions and experience greater investment from their clients.

Sharing power and giving caregivers more voice would also help reduce what Erford (2003) calls the "don't make waves" role parents sometimes play when they feel they do not have equal power in decision making (p. 197). Th is role, in which for fear of negative consequences caregivers will agree to anything suggested by professionals, may feature prominently in families where other children may have been treated coercively or remanded to state care. Creating collaborative communication with low-income and African American families is not a one-time exercise (Comer, 1989; Winters 1993). Mental health counselors need to spend time intentionally creating and fostering relationships over time so as to make a real impact on the alienation and disenfranchisement felt by many parents in that population. Lott (2001, p. 255) suggested the following steps for working more eff ectively with low-income families (we have added details pertinent to intervention with clients diagnosed with ADHD):
- Take the initiative in creating relationships with caregivers of young clients. Caregivers oft en have negative expectations of mental health care. Taking extra time to answer questions and

explain processes, forms, and procedures can be very helpful in initiating collaborative relationships.

- Find ways to involve low-income caregivers other than as "consent-givers." Invite them to participate as collaborators, innovators, and critics. Be especially sensitive to how caregivers may perceive pharmacotherapies. Ask them what they have heard about medications for ADHD and what worries they may have about specifi c drugs. Also, be aware that some caregivers may harbor feelings of stigma about being seen at the agency offi ce. Exploring how they feel about mental health care in general and the agency in particular can alleviate anxieties about treatment.

- Act as an advocate for the client and the family with other agencies and personnel. Also, unfortunately, barriers to treatment can exist within agencies. If the caregiver is having trouble scheduling appointments for other services, getting accurate bills, etc., the counselor can help the caregiver fi nd solutions to the problems before they sabotage treatment.

- Coordinate services among community agencies to reduce miscommunication and confusion. Children with ADHD sometimes receive services from multiple agencies, and caregivers can quickly become overwhelmed and frustrated. Counselors can be instrumental in forming teams in the community to help sort out details of treatment and can also help caregivers better understand systems of care by simply explaining the role of each agency and person in the child's treatment plan.

CONCLUSION

It is apparent that impoverished African American males with ADHD are not receiving just or fair treatment in many systems of care in the U.S. As counselors it is our responsibility to work to close the treatment gap for this and other marginalized and oppressed populations. By becoming conscious of the issues involved in the assessment, diagnosis, and treatment of ADHD, counselors take the fi rst steps toward creating a more just system of care. If further progress is to be made, counselors need to systematically learn and incorporate more inclusive methods of reaching marginalized clients and act as advocates for them within systems of care. Th is is a call to all current and future mental health counselors to address the barriers and injustices clients living in poverty and diagnosed with ADHD and other mental health issues experience every day of their lives.

REFERENCES

Achenbach, T. (1991). *Manual for the Child Behavior Checklist/4–18 and 1991 profi le.* Burlington, VT: University of Vermont Department of Psychiatry.

Adams, J., Benshoff , J., & Harrington, S. (2007). An examination of referrals to the school counselor by race, gender, and family structure. *Professional School Counselor, 10,* 389–399.

Alegria, M., Canino, G., Rios, R., Vera, M., Calderon, J., Rusch, D., & Ortega, A. (2002). Inequalities in use of specialty mental health services among Latinos, African Americans, and non-Latino Whites. *Psychiatric Services, 53,* 1547–1555.

Angold, A., Erkanli, A., Farmer, E., Fairbank. J., Bums, B., Keeler, G., & Costello, E. (2002). Psychiatric disorder, impairment, and service use in rural African American and White adolescents. *Archives of General Psychiatry, 59,* 893–901.

Applebaum, P. (2002). *Multicultural and diversity education.* Santa Barbara, CA: ABC-CLIO.

Arcia, E., Fernandez, M., Marisela, J., Castillo, H., & Ruiz, M. (2004). Modes of entry into services for young children with disruptive behaviors. *Qualitative Health Research, 14,* 1211–1226.

Arnold, L., Elliot, M., Sachs, L., Bird, H., Kraemer, H. C., & Wells, K. C. (2003). Eff ects of ethnicity on treatment attendance, stimulant response/dose, and 14-month outcome in ADHD. *Journal of Clinical and Consulting Psychology, 71,* 713–727.

Ayalon, L., & Alvidrez, J. (2007) Th e experience of Black consumers in the mental health system: Identifying barriers to and facilitators of mental health treatment using the consumer's perspective. *Issues in Mental Health Nursing, 28,* 1323–1340.

Bemak, F., & Chi-Ying Chung, R. (2005). Advocacy as a critical role for urban school counselors: Working towards equity and social justice. *Professional School Counseling, 8,* 196–202.

Breda, C. (2003). Off ender ethnicity and mental health service referrals from juvenile court. *Criminal Justice and Behavior, 30,* 644–667.

Bussing, R., Zima, B., Gary, F., & Garvan, C. (2003). Barriers to detection, help-seeking, and service use for children with ADHD symptoms. *Journal of Behavioral Health Services & Research, 30,* 176–189.

Carter, P. (2003). "Black" cultural capital, status positioning, and schooling confl icts for low-income African American youth. *Social Problems, 50,* 136–155.

Center for Disease Control and Prevention. (2006). Racial and ethnic disparities in the diagnosis of HIV/AIDS— 33 states, 2001–2004. *Morbidity and Mortality Weekly Report, 55,* 121–125.

Children's Defense Fund (2005). Children's Mental Health Resource Kit. Retrieved September 1, 2006, from http:// www.childrensdefense.org/site/DocServer/cmh_resource.pdf?docID=1361

Chow, J., Jafee, K., & Snowden, L. (2003). Racial/ethnic disparities in the use of mental health services in poverty areas. *American Journal of Public Health, 93,* 792–797.

Colpe, L. (2000). Estimates of mental and emotional problems, functional impairments, and associated disability outcomes for the U. S. child population in households. In R. Manderscheid & M. Henderson (Eds.), *Mental health, United States, 2000* (pp. 269–278). Washington, DC: USDHHS.

Comer, J. (1989). Th e school development program: A psychosocial model of school intervention. In G. L. Berry & J. K. Asamen, (Eds.), *Black students: Psychosocial issues and academic achievement.* Th ousand Oaks, CA: Sage.

Conners, C. K. (1997). *Conners' Rating Scale, revised: Technical manual.* North Tonawanda, NY: Multi-Health Systems.

Cuff e, S., Moore, C., & McKeown, R. (2005). Prevalence and correlates of ADHD symptoms in the National Health Interview Survey. *Journal of Attention Disorders, 9,* 392–401.

Davison, J., & Ford, D. (2002). Perceptions of attention defi cit hyperactivity disorder in one African American community. *Journal of Negro Education, 70,* 264–274.

Day-Vines, N., & Day-Hairston, B. (2005). Culturally congruent strategies for addressing the behavioral needs of urban, African American adolescents. *Professional School Counseling, 8,* 236–243.

Department of Health and Human Services. (2000, June). *Report of the Surgeon Generals conference on children's mental health: A national action agenda* (S. Olin, Ed.). Retrieved August 5, 2008, from http://surgeongeneral. gov/topics/cmh/childreport.htm

Dogra, N. (2005, July/August). What do children and young people want from mental health services? *Current Opinion in Psychiatry, 18,* 370–373.

Diemer, M. (2007). Two worlds: African American men's negotiation of predominately White educational and occupational worlds. *Journal of Multicultural Counseling and Development, 35, 3–14.*

Ellison, A., Pottick, K., Zito, J., Jensen, P., Katz, L., Safer, D., Nadeau, K., Robin, A., Warner, L., & Ross, E. C. (2002). Identifi cation and treatment of ADHD: A lifespan perspective. In R. Manderscheid, & M. Henderson (Eds.). *Mental health, United States, 2002.* Washington, DC: USDHHS.

Epstein, J. N., Willoughby, M., Valenica, E. Y., Tonev, S., Abikoff , H., & Arnold, L. (2005). Th e role of children's ethnicity in the relationship between teacher ratings of ADHD and observed classroom behavior. *Journal of Consulting & Clinical Psychology, 73,* 424–434.

Erford, B. (2003). *Transforming the school counseling profession.* Upper Saddle River, NJ: Pearson.

Foy, J., & Earls, M., (2005). A process for developing community consensus regarding the diagnosis and management of attention defi cit hyperactivity disorder, *Pediatrics, Vol. 115,* January.

French, R., Reardon. M., & Smith, P. (2003). Engaging with a mental health service: Perspectives of at-risk youth. *Child & Adolescent Social Work, 20,* 529–548.

Garland, A., Lewczyk-Boxmeyer, C., Gabayan, E., & Hawley, K. (2004). Multiple stakeholder agreement on desired outcomes for adolescents' mental health services. *Psychiatric Services, 55,* 671–676.

Howell, E. (2004). *Access to childrens mental health services under Medicaid and SCHIP* (Series B, No. B–60) (New Federalism: National Survey of America's families) (Th e Urban Institute, Ed.). Retrieved August 5, 2008, from http://www.urban.org

Kuno, E., & Rothbard, E. (2005). Th e eff ect of income and race on quality of psychiatric care in community mental health centers. *Community Mental Health Journal, 41,* 613–622.

Liu, W., Pickett, T., & Ivey, A. (2007). White middle-class privilege: Social class bias and implications for training and practice. *Journal of Multicultural Counseling and Development, 35,* 194–207.

Liu, W. (2001). Expanding our understanding of multiculturalism: Developing a social class world-view model. In D. Pope-Davis & H. L. K. Coleman (Eds.), *Th e intersection of race, class, and gender in counseling psychology* (pp. 127–170). Th ousand Oaks, CA: Sage.

Logan, S. (2001). *Th e Black family: Strengths, self-help, and positive change.* Boulder, CO: Westview.

Lott, B. (2001). Low-income parents and the public schools. *Journal of Social Issues, 57,* 247–259.

McKay, M., Lynn, C., & Bannon, W. (2005). Understanding inner city child mental health needs and trauma exposure: Implications for preparing urban service providers. *Journal of Orthopsychiatry, 75,* 201–210.

McMiller, M., & Weisz, J. (1996). Help-seeking preceding mental health clinic intake among African American, Latino, and Caucasian youths. *Journal of the American Academy of Child and Adolescent Psychiatry, 35,* 1086–1095.

Miller, T., Nigg, J., & Miller, R. (2009). Attention defi cit hyperactivity disorder in African American children: What can be concluded from the past ten years? *Clinical Psychology Review, 29,* 77–86.

Monroe, C. (2005). Why are "bad boys" always Black? Causes of disproportionality in school discipline and recommendations for change. *Th e Clearing House* (September/October), 45–52.

Myers, J. E., & Gill, C. (2004). Poor, rural, and female: Under-studied, under-counseled, more at-risk. *Journal of Mental Health Counseling, 26(3),* 225–242.

National Center for Education Statistics. (2006). *Th e condition of education 2006.* Washington, DC: US Department of Education. (NCES-2006).

Noguera, P. (2003). Th e trouble with Black boys: Th e role and infl uence of environmental and cultural factors on the academic performance of African American males. *Urban Education, 38,* 431–459.

Offi ce of Special Education Programs. (2005). *Twenty-fi ft h annual report to Congress on Special Education Programs.* Retrieved February 20, 2009, from www.ed.gov/about/reports/annual/osep/2003/25th-vol-1-sec-2.pdf

Pastor, P. N., & Reuben, C. A. (2008). Diagnosed attention defi cit hyperactivity disorder and learning disability: United States, 2004–2006. National Center for Health Statistics. *Vital Health Statistics, 10* (237).

Pelham W. E., Foster M., & Robb, J. A. (2007).Th e economic impact of attention-defi cit/hyperactivity disorder in children and adolescents. *Journal of Pediatric Psychology, 32,* 711–27.

Richardson, J., Anderson, T., Flaherty, J., & Bell, C. (2003, December). Th e quality of mental health care for African Americans. *Culture, Medicine, & Psychiatry, 27,* 487–498.

Santa-Lucia, R. (2004). Connections: Understanding gender and race diff erences in school-based problem behavior during adolescence (doctoral dissertation, University of South Florida, 2004). *DAI AA131132455, 65B, 2649.*

Snowden, L., Masland, M., Libby, A., Wallace, N., & Fawley, K. (2008). Racial/ethnic minority-children's use of psychiatric emergency care in California's mental health system. *American Journal of Public Health, 98,* 118–124.

Snowden, L., Wallace, N., Kang, S., Cheng, J., & Bloom, J. (2007). Capitation and racial and ethnic diff erences in use and cost of mental health services. *Administration and Policy in Mental Health and Mental Health Services Research, 34,* 456–464.

Stevens, J., Harman, J., & Kelleher, K. (2005). Race and ethnicity and insurance status as factors associated with ADHD treatment patterns. *Journal of Child and Adolescent Psychopharmacology, 15,* 88–96.

Swanson, J. M. (1992). *School-based assessments and interventions for ADD students.* Irvine, CA: KC Publishing.

Takeuchi, D., Bui, K., & Kim, L. (1993). Th e referral of minority adolescents to community mental health centers. *Journal of Social Behavior, 34,* 153–164.

Tucker, C. (2009). Low-income African-American caregivers' experiences of being referred to mental health services by the school counselor. *Professional School Counselor, 12,* 240–252.

U.S. Census Bureau (2006). *Historical poverty tables.* Retrieved May 7, 2009, from http://www.census.gov/hhes/www/poverty/histpov/hstpov4.html

U.S. Department of Health and Human Services. (1999) *Mental health: A report of the Surgeon General—Executive summary.* Rockville, MD: U.S. Department of Health and Human Services, Substance Abuse and Mental Health Services Administration, Center for Mental Health Services, National Institute of Mental Health.

U.S. Department of Justice. (2006, December 31). *Bureau of Justice statistics—prison statistics.* Retrieved January 23, 2008, from http://www.ojp.usdoj.gov/bjs/prisons.htm

U.S. General Accounting Offi ce. (2003). *Report. Child welfare and juvenile justice: Federal agencies could play a stronger role in helping states reduce the number of children placed solely to obtain mental health services.* (Washington, DC: Author).

U.S. Government Accountability Offi ce. (2007). *African American children in foster care: Additional HHS assistance needed to help states reduce the proportion in care.* Retrieved September 10, 2008, from http://www.gao. gov/new.items/d07816.pdf

Whaley, A. L., & Gellar, P. A. (2003). Ethnic/racial diff erences in psychiatric disorders: A test of four hypotheses. *Ethnicity & Disease, 13,* 499–512.

Winters, W. (1993). *African American mothers and urban schools.* New York: Lexington Books.

What African American Male Adolescents Are Telling Us about HIV Infection among Their Peers

Cultural Approaches for HIV Prevention

Dexter R. Voisin and Jason D. P. Bird

Th is study explored the beliefs of African American male adolescents concerning the high rates of HIV infection among their peers and their reasons for those beliefs. In-depth interviews were conducted with a sample of 16 male African Americans, and a thematic analysis of the data was conducted. Half of the participants believed that peers were not becoming infected at higher rates than white youths and reported high rates of sexual risk taking. Conspiracy beliefs and high rates of sexual adventurism for all teenagers were among the reasons off ered to support this belief. Participants who believed the uneven incidence rates reported low levels of sexual risk taking. Th ese participants identifi ed early and unsafe sexual activity—in conjunction with social factors such as negative peer and media infl uences, poor parental supervision, and dangerous neighborhood environments—as contributing reasons for these disparate rates. Sexual behaviors were markedly diff erent among both groups. Th e implications of these fi ndings are discussed in the context of culturally relevant approaches to prevention of HIV infection among this group.

In the United States, African American male adolescents are at signifi cant risk of HIV infection. For instance, male African Americans between the ages of 14 and 24 years comprise approximately 16.8 percent of the adolescent population (U.S. Census Bureau, 2000), but they account for more than 55 percent of all new adolescent HIV infections (Centers for Disease Control and Prevention, 2006a). Consequently, more research is needed to obtain a clearer understanding of the factors associated with sexual risk behaviors within this group. Such research is critical if we are to develop culturally relevant approaches to curtailing the spread of HIV infection among African American male adolescents. Conspiracy theories in relation to health have long been present among some segments of the African American populace. According to Turner's (1993) classic study *I Heard It Th rough the Grapevine: Rumor in African-American Culture*, there is a distinction between malicious intent theories and benign neglect theories. Malicious intent theories refer to deliberate attempts by the government to "undermine" the African American population. An example would be the belief that AIDS was created by white America to eliminate the African American population (see Towns, 1995). As evidence, believers point to the disease's rapid spread in their community and the government's nonresponsiveness to African American health care needs (Parsons, Simmons, Shinhoster, & Kilburn, 1999). Benign neglect theories involve a government that does little to solve problems in the African American community because the well-being of African Americans is a low priority (Turner, 1993). A contemporary example of this theory, some would argue, is represented by Hurricane Katrina and the government's delayed and deplorably inadequate response to the disaster in New Orleans. It is believed that conspiracy beliefs stem from chronic experiences of discrimination (Bird & Bogart, 2005).

Some of these beliefs also have historical origins. For instance, the Tuskegee Experiment, in which African American men were deliberately left untreated for syphilis in the name of "science," has undermined trust in public health offi cials and spawned a number of prominent conspiracy theories. For reviews of conspiracy theories among African Americans, see Parsons et al. (1999).

However, only recently have studies examined the role of conspiracy theories about the origin of HIV and its relationship to sexual risk behaviors among African Americans. For example, Bogart and Th ornburn (2005) in a random telephone sample of 500 African Americans between the ages of 15 and 44 found that 59 percent of the sample believed that signifi cant information about AIDS is being held back from the public, 53 percent believed that a cure for AIDS was being withheld from the public, and 43 percent believed that the government was using people who take new medications as guinea pigs. For men—with sociodemographic variables, partner characteristics, sexually transmitted disease history, perception of risk, and psychological factors controlled for—stronger conspiracy beliefs were signifi cantly associated with more negative condom attitudes and inconsistent condom usage (Bogart & Th ornburn, 2005).

Another study using a community-based sample of 1,494 men and women (ages 18 to 50 and over) from four racial or ethnic groups (African American, Latino, non-Hispanic white, and Asian) found that the highest levels of belief in conspiracy theories (for example, AIDS being an agent of genocide created by the U.S. government to kill minority populations) were reported among women, African Americans, and Latinos. In addition, for African American men only, higher levels of belief in conspiracy theories were associated with lower rates of condom use (Ross, Essien, & Torres, 2006).

Collectively, the earlier-mentioned studies have begun to document associations between conspiracy beliefs and low condom usage among male African Americans. However, additional research is warranted. Almost no research has examined the relationship between conspiracy beliefs and sexual risk among a cohort of solely African American male adolescents. Th is is unfortunate given that boys oft en have greater sexual decision-making power than girls in sexual encounters (Amaro, Fried, Cabral, & Zuckerman, 1990). Insights into factors infl uencing risk behaviors among boys may enable us to design more eff ective intervention programs, which may benefi t boys and their sexual partners. In addition, prior researchers have focused on samples of male and female African Americans spanning wide age ranges (that is, 15 to 50 years and older) (Bogart & Th ornburn, 2005; Ross et al., 2006).Th is is problematic, because conspiracy theories may have strong origins in generational cohorts at particular moments in history and may evolve over time. Also, gender diff erences are likely very signifi cant. Furthermore, conspiracy theories may exist in conjunction with other social factors (for example, hopelessness among African American youths, media infl uences) that are perceived to have bearing on why rates of HIV infection may be especially high among specifi c vulnerable populations. Moreover, additional insights into such conspiracy beliefs may have important implications for culturally pertinent adolescent HIV intervention programs. Finally, according to the information-motivation-behavioral skills (1MB) model (Fisher & Fisher, 1992; Fisher, Fisher, Williams, & Malloy,

182

1994), access to accurate information is believed to have direct eff ects on adolescents' sexual behavior. Th erefore, it is important to explore how accurate information versus conspiracy beliefs may be associated with sexual risk behaviors among

African American male youths. More specifi cally, in this study we examined whether male youths who believe that their peers are becoming infected with HIV at higher rates than white youths are engaging in diff erent sexual behaviors than are those who do not believe in such disparate rates.

Th erefore, the purpose of the current study was to focus on one of the most vulnerable and underresearched groups—African American male adolescents—using a qualitative approach to generate knowledge that may prove important to the design of more eff ective culture- and gender- specifi c HIV prevention approaches.

METHOD

As part of a larger investigation into the relationship between community-level factors and HIV sexual risk behaviors among African American youths in a large urban area, we queried participants about their perception of the uneven rates of HIV infection among their peers. Th e study question was intended to test for the existence of conspiracy beliefs within this cohort and to solicit participants' opinions about why rates of HIV infection might be higher among their peers. We asked participants to respond to a specifi c statement: "Some people say that African American teens are becoming infected with HIV much faster than white teens. What do you think about this?" Th is question, which was created as a stand-alone inquiry into participants' beliefs about the impact of HIV on African American adolescents, was intentionally worded to elicit information about whether a participant believed that HIV rates were higher for African American youths and the reasons for that belief.

A small convenience sample of participants was recruited using three approaches: (1) passive recruiment in which fl yers were posted on the community boards at local YMCAs, supermarkets, and housing developments throughout Chicago's South Side; (2) active recruitment, in which two African American recruiters (one male, one female) distributed fl yers outside public venues frequented by adolescents and parents on Chicago's South Side; and (3) snowball sampling methods, with referrals from study participants. Five participants each were recruited through passive and active recruitment strategies, and six were recruited through snowball sampling. Participants were eligible if they were currently attending regular high school, self-identifi ed as an African American born in the United States, were between the ages of 14 and 17, obtained written parental permission, and provided informed assent prior to being interviewed.

Individual one-on-one, face-to-face semistructured interviews were conducted with 16 male African Americans. All interviews were conducted in 2005 at the University of Chicago, in a private offi ce, and were led by Dexter R. Voisin, who is also a male African American. Interviews were recorded on audiotape and transcribed verbatim. On completion of the in-depth interview, each participant completed a brief questionnaire that assessed demographics (for instance, age; grade level; living arrangements; number of people in the household [including the participant]; parents' educational level; and household receipt of welfare benefi ts, which was used as a proxy for socioeconomic status) .Th ese demographic variables were selected because previous research has shown that they are related to the sexual risk behaviors being assessed in this study (Canterbury et al., 1995;Voisin, 2003,Voisin, DiCle- mente, Salazar, Crosby, & Yarber, 2006).Th e sexual behaviors assessed were age at sexual debut, number of sexual partners, number of times having had sex in the past 12 months, and condom usage during the past 12 months. Th is mixed-methods approach, or triangulation, was used to strengthen study validity by providing a secondary mechanism by which to collect information, confi rm data, and inform analysis and interpretation (Golafshani, 2003).

Overall, interviews lasted between 35 and 70 minutes. Participants were off ered $10 for participation. All names were changed to protect the identity of participants. Study protocols were approved by the Institutional Review Boards at the University of Chicago and the University of California, San Francisco.

Using standard qualitative data analysis techniques, we organized participants' responses to the research question by means of a raw pattern analysis (Coff ey &Atkinson, 1996; Miles & Huberman, 1994), which entailed condensing raw data into a brief summary format to establish links between the question and fi ndings derived from the data. Coding was used to summarize segments of data into a smaller number of subsets, themes, or constructs. Two researchers doubled-checked transcriptions to ensure accuracy, and they reviewed and discussed the fi nal codes and emergent themes to ensure interrater reliability of at least 85 percent. When applicable, descriptive numerical data were analyzed using SPSS version 13.0. Fictitious names are used for all participants in this study.

RESULTS

Sixteen male adolescents were interviewed, and 15 responded to the study question. One participant self-identifi ed as bisexual, and given that the dynamics around sexual risk taking may be diff erent for bisexual male adolescents, his data were omitted from the analyses. Th e fi nal sample comprised 14 participants, ranging in age from 14 to 17 years, with the mean age being 16.14 *(SD ± 0.95)* years.

Th e majority of participants (79 percent) lived in households headed by single women, and 21 percent lived in households with two parents. Half of the participants had mothers who had completed "some college" or "had a college degree" and "lived in households with 4 to 6 persons." About one-third (29 percent) of respondents reported that they received or would qualify for free school lunches, and 21 percent reported that someone in their household had received welfare assistance during the past 12 months. Th ese data suggest that the majority of participants were not from lower socioeconomic households. Seventy-one percent of the sample reported "ever having had sexual intercourse," defi ned as having vaginally penetrated a girl; 29 percent of these adolescent male African Americans reported "not yet having had sexual intercourse."

Participants' beliefs in the statement that African American youths were becoming infected with HIV at higher rates than their white peers could generally be assigned to one of two categories. Th e sample was evenly split between those who agreed either wholeheartedly (four of 14) or with some minor qualifi cations (three of 14) and those who completely disagreed (seven of 14) with this statement. Across each grouping, participants off ered various reasons to support their perceptions. Th e demographic and sexual activity data for all participants, by category of acceptance of the statement, are presented in Table 1.

Perceived Reasons for High Rates of HIV Infection

As illustrated in Table 1, among the group that agreed with the research statement, 57 percent reported having had sex. Th eir mean age was 16.14 years, and the mean age at sexual debut was 14.25 years. Among the sexually active participants from this group, none reported having had unprotected sex. In this category, four participants fully agreed with the statement and three generally agreed with the statement. Th e latter participants, when off ering reasons why they believed rates of infection were higher among their peers than among white youths, all went on to qualify their responses by indicating three primary beliefs: sexual risk taking is related to adolescence in general; white teenagers are as likely as African American teenagers to engage in sexual activity and make the same mistakes; and all adolescents, regardless of race, are similar with regard to wanting to have sex.

Th e cohort of participants who agreed that African American youths were contracting HIV at higher rates than their white peers off ered several reasons why they believed this statement was accurate. Th ere were generally four perceived reasons why they believed their peers were becoming infected with HIV:

Table 1: Profile of Participants			
Variable	Total Sample (N = 14)	Agree Group (n = 7)	Disagree Group (n = 7)
Demographic data			
Age (years) (M ± SD)	16.14 ± 0.95	16.14 ± 0.90	16.14 ± 1.07
Education (grade)	10	10	10
No. in household			
1–3	29 (4)	14 (1)	43 (3)
4–6	50 (7)	71 (5)	29 (2)
7–9	14 (2)	15 (1)	14 (1)
10+	7 (1)	0 (0)	14 (1)
Household composition			
Woman head	79 (11)	57 (4)	100 (7)
Both parents present	21 (3)	43 (3)	0 (0)
Mother's education			
Don't know	43 (6)	29 (2)	57 (4)
High school	7 (1)	14 (1)	0 (0)
Some college	43 (6)	43 (3)	43 (3)
College degree	7 (1)	14 (1)	0 (0)
Father's education			
Don't know	58 (8)	44 (3)	71 (5)
<Ninth grade	7 (1)	14 (1)	0 (0)
High school	7 (1)	14 (1)	0 (0)
Some college	21 (3)	14 (1)	29 (2)
College degree	7 (1)	14 (1)	0 (0)
Qualify for free school lunch	29 (4)	29 (2)	29 (2)
Receive welfare	21 (3)	29 (2)	14 (1)
Sexual dynamics			
Sexually active	71 (10)	57 (4)	86 (6)
Sexually active last 12 mo.	57 (8)	29 (2)	86 (6)
Age at sexual debut (years)	13.20	14.25	12.50
Sexual partners over lifetime (n)	5.8	2.0	8.3
Sexual encounters past 12 mo. (n)	53.73	21.00	64.70
Consistent condom use	50 (5)	100 (4)	17 (1)

Note: Except where noted otherwise, values represent percentages (with number of participants given in parentheses).

(1) a general increase in sexual activity and risk for African American youths, (2) negative peer infl uences, (3) lack of parental monitoring, and (4) media infl uences. Responses were not mutually exclusive, and choices were not rank ordered. All percentages were driven by the data.

Increased Sexual Activity and HIV Risk Behavior. Th e majority of respondents (57 percent) believed that African American youths were engaging in sexual risk behaviors that were placing them at heightened risk of becoming HIV positive, with one participant indicating that HIV risk was higher because "black youth have more sex than white youth." In addition, having an early sexual debut and having sex without condoms were identifi ed as specifi c high-risk sexual behaviors. Earlier exposure to sexually explicit information and materials and entering puberty at increasingly younger ages were viewed as contributing factors to some of these high-risk behaviors. An example of these themes is illustrated here: "Black teens are less likely to engage in safer sex. … Out of the people that I know … who are pregnant, none of them say they got pregnant because a condom broke, it was because they were having unprotected sex" (Antwan, 17 years old).

Th e Role of Negative Peer Infl uences. Peer infl uences were also viewed by 43 percent of these participants as a contributing factor to the higher rates of HIV infection among African American youths. Th ese respondents believed that teenagers wanted to have sex because they believed their peers were also sexually active. Along similar lines, gang involvement was also believed to be a signifi cant underlying peer factor promoting early and unsafe sex. One respondent maintained that "black teens are exposed to more gangs, violence, and sex … than white teens." Th is respondent further highlighted the belief that gang members engaged in more risky sexual activities and had more girls wanting to have sex with them because of their bad boy image, stating that "some girls like that mentality."

Lack of Parental Monitoring. Twenty-nine percent of these respondents identifi ed lack of adequate parental monitoring as another important contributing factor to high rates of HIV infection among their peers. Th ey believed that African American teenagers were not monitored suffi ciently by their parents in comparison with their white peers. Being allowed to have later curfews was identifi ed as one example of this lack of satisfactory monitoring and supervision. For example, Antwan stated, "my mom, she bring me condoms, she tell me, you know, 'Don't ever, you know, without a condom'," but he implied that not all African American adolescents may be getting the same message from their parents. A certain level of despair and "living in the now" was identifi ed by one participant as a signifi cant factor leading to increased HIV infection rates among peers:

> Th ey don't really care … they just want to live in the now. … Th ey're just ready to have sex with a girl but they don't think about what if I get this girl pregnant or what if I catch something … what could happen. … Black youth end up joining gangs and not thinking about the future when their lives don't work out as planned and because they have no opportunities, no education, no job. Joining a gang is the last hope. (Tyrone, 16 years old)

Media Infl uences. Media infl uences were identifi ed as signifi cant factors promoting early and frequent sexual activity. Twenty-nine percent of these participants believed that some African American artists were infl uencing adolescents through their music and videos to engage in sex. An example of these themes is illustrated here:

> For those black youth at more risk, it's because … of TV … now sex is in everything, like in commercials, in movies, it's just shown, no editing … it's just out there. We are being exposed to it, especially in like music videos and we've been exposed to it … like maybe more than a white teen. (Jimmy, 17 years old)

Reasons for the Belief that African American Youths Are not at Greater HIV Risk

In contrast, an equal percentage of respondents upheld the viewpoint that African American youths were not becoming infected with HIV at higher rates than their white peers. Among this group, 86 percent reported having had sex. Th eir mean age was 16.14 years, and their mean age at sexual debut was 12.50 years. Among the sexually active participants from this group, 83 percent reported having had unprotected sex one or more times in the past 12 months.

In general, the majority of these participants identifi ed some conspiratorial beliefs related to intentional misrepresentation of HIV rates among African American and white youths. For instance, almost half (43 percent) expressed beliefs supporting the viewpoint that statistics were purposely skewed or misleading and that African American youths were not contracting HIV at higher rates than their white peers. One respondent, Dennis (16 years old), expressed the belief that white youths were contracting HIV at rates similar to those of African American youths. However, he believed that wealthy white youths were able to use private doctors, which allowed them to conceal their HIV diagnoses, and therefore the available statistics were misleading. He stated:

> I think that's a lie. I think that white teens are coming with it, also their parents just got a lot of money so they're keeping theirs under wraps. … Th e black teens come out with it, they tell people, white teens don't tell that many people and if they do they tell their private doctors.

Another participant, Jimmy (16 years old), reported that the statistics were inaccurate because of racism:

> I am going to tell you the honest to God truth … how I feel. I think that it's just a number. … I hate to say it like this, I'm not a racist person, but sometimes I feel like that … that they say things … they claim that, you know, that slavery is over, or … no more segregation. But there's always … some form of it. … So basically … I think it's things like they just saying … to put us down.

Jimmy also stated that the lack of widespread HIV testing resulted in inaccurate statistics, arguing that

> every single person that have AIDS aren't accounted for. … Like, as I say, it's some people that have AIDS that don't know they have AIDS … a lot of people my age, like I said, they're not thinking about AIDS. So if they have sex, they're not going to run in and get tested right away. So I'm … I'm thinking like it's a lot of people that's … that's walking around with AIDS that don't know it right now.

Finally, Jimmy also reported that he believed a cure for AIDS was being withheld from some segments of the population:

> I believe it is a cure for AIDS that they just not sharing with the res[t] like Magic Johnson, he claimed to have AIDS in what, 92? … 90? … But he's still alive. And, you know, he's on TV and you don't see him sick. A couple times, well, when you're sick and you've got AIDS, you know, you can't … you can't really know how to get well. Like so that makes me wonder, like is there really a cure for AIDS … or are they just … saying that you know to put us down. … I hate to say … the United States have hide … a lot of things from, you know. … It was this thing about September 11th, like … [they] didn't take it serious. Like I believe there's a lot of things that they just not telling.

Twenty-nine percent of the participants believed that HIV transmission was related to wild, drugcrazed sex. Consequently, they believed that a higher proportion of white peers were actually infected with HIV because they were engaging in more sexual adventurism than African American youths. Th is theme is illustrated by the following statement:

> No, I think it's false, I think whites become, have HIV, because they're just wild with it, everything they do is just wild, and they just think that black people are bringing our country down, but they just don't know that it's a lot of white people who are being reckless. Th e white people are getting the drugs in here, the black people sell them but the white people are bringing them over … a lot of white teenagers sniff coke, smoke rocks, do ecstasy, all types of other diff erent drugs that we, a lot of black people don't even know about, so, I think it's just drugs. (Walter,
> 17 years old)

DISCUSSION

Th is study provided mixed support for the existence of conspiracy beliefs among African American male adolescents. Half of the participants upheld the view that African Americans are becoming infected with HIV at higher rates than white Americans; half of the participants disagreed with this assertion. For participants who agreed with the statement, behavioral factors such as early sexual activity, greater sexual activity, and sex without condoms were identifi ed as signifi cant risk factors that could account for these uneven HIV infection rates. In addition, social factors such as media infl uences promoting sex, the perception that peers were having sex, gang infl uences, and inadequate parental supervision were also perceived to be factors infl uencing HIV sexual risk behaviors (DiClemente, Salazar, Crosby, & Rosenthal, 2005; Voisin et al., 2006; Wingood et al., 2001.) All of these social factors have been empirically documented in prior research as being associated with adolescent sexual risk behaviors. Recognition by participants of the earlier-mentioned social infl uences underscores the importance of considering these correlates when designing eff ective HIV education and prevention approaches for this population.

It is interesting to note that participants who believed that members of their peer group were at higher risk of HIV infection than their white peers reported having fewer lifetime sexual encounters than those who disagreed with this statement. Th ose who believed the statement and were sexually active reported a later age at sexual debut and consistent condom usage. Consistent with the IMB model (Fisher & Fisher, 1992; Fisher et al., 1994), participants who believed the accuracy of prevention messages may have been more inclined to engage in self-protective behaviors such as abstinence or consistent condom usage.

Half of the study participants subscribed in some degree to conspiracy beliefs or had a general mistrust of the dominant social order related to reported HIV statistics. Such beliefs were associated with earlier sexual debut, a higher number of sexual partners, and inconsistent use of condoms during sexual activity. It is not surprising that several researchers have argued that conspiracy theories pose real barriers to HIV prevention. A deep distrust of government will increase the likelihood that some African Americans will reject certain public policy "solutions" off ered by the government (Parsons et al., 1999.) Another explanation is that teenagers who engage in unsafe sexual behaviors are more likely to justify such risky practices by subscribing to conspiracy beliefs.

However, like those of any study, the present fi ndings must be interpreted in the context of the study's methodological limitations. Th is study used a small convenience sample that was geographically limited and not very diverse socioeconomically. In addition, convenience sampling may have resulted in some degree of self-selection bias. For example, whereas African American men who have sex with men (MSM) continue to be one of the groups at highest risk of HIV infection (Centers for Disease Control and Prevention, 2006b; Cohen, Bell, & Ifatunji, 2005), the present study's focus on heterosexually identifi ed youths was driven by the type of respondents who self-selected into the study. Although this study was not able to address the specifi c barriers experienced by African American MSM, we did have the opportunity to address another population that is oft en overlooked— heterosexually identifi ed African American youths—and the data gathered suggest avenues of future research with heterosexual youths. Specifi c studies would need to be conducted with African American MSM youths, given that these people oft en face double discrimination because of their racial and sexual minority status within the larger society and discrimination within segments of the black community and church.

Despite these limitations, the major perceptions expressed in this study are robust, given the degree of agreement that existed among the half of the sample subscribing to the research statement (that is, data saturation was achieved). A larger sample size might be used in future studies to uncover a more expanded set of reasons for these perceptions. An important future study might investigate how teenagers of other racial and ethnic groups would answer the same question, with regard to African Americans or members of their own racial or ethnic group, and whether their answers were also framed in the context of conspiracy theories. Ethnic matching between participants and interviewer was used in the present study to reduce participants' tendency to produce socially desirable responses. However, this approach may have also triggered more conspiracy beliefs than objective responses, for some respondents, given their increased comfort level. Acceptance of some statements about HIV may also vary by region across the United States, as do the prevalence of HIV infection, the availability of services, the surrounding community's tolerance for people infected with HIV, and the emphasis of HIV education or prevention eff orts in schools and other community settings (Voisin et al., 2006). Finally, it is also not clear what role the adolescent female partners of the population studied are playing in establishing or supporting these youths' sexual habits (such as condom usage or early sexual debut) or viewpoints. It is important to explore this issue further, because some research has shown that African American boys, in particular, may experience perceived pressure from their female partners to engage in sex (Voisin, Salazar, Crosby, DiClemente, & Yarber, 2007).

Cultural Approaches for HIV Prevention

Th is study extends prior research in several important ways. First, it targeted a specifi c subsample of African Americans within a particular age range—boys between the ages of 14 and 17. Many of these male adolescents may be removed from historical events revealing the existence of discrimination in health care, such as the Tuskegee Experiment, and they did not express particular conspiracy beliefs related to condom usage (for example, doctors put HIV in condoms; condoms are a genocidal project, intended to eliminate the African American population) (Bogart & Th orburn, 2005). Some participants did, however, express a certain level of belief in conspiracy theories or mistrust regarding reported incidence and prevalence rates of HIV infection among peers (for example, fi gures are made up or deliberately skewed to blame or discriminate against minority populations). According to Bogart and Th orton, many conspiracy beliefs may stem from a general mistrust of the health care system or the government. Th erefore, interventions that encourage candid discussions of conspiracy beliefs within the context of societal and structural discrimination in relation to health may have the greatest chances of promoting HIV awareness and prevention among African American male youths. Along these lines, fi ndings may suggest the need for more HIV prevention messages to be delivered by people within the African American community who are considered by these youths to be credible sources (for example, music artists, HIV-infected peers, celebrities, parents). Th ese broad approaches to delivering HIV messages may be especially important given that people in many disadvantaged communities may lack access to adequate and traditional health care services through which they might normally receive such information (Centers for Disease Control and Prevention, 2002).

Second, these data suggest that some of the participants minimized the seriousness of HIV infection for African American male adolescents. Most of these participants were sexually active and had reported one or more incidents of sexual intercourse without condoms within the past 12 months. For these youths, minimizing the high incidence rates among members of their peer group may have been one way of controlling anxiety about possible HIV infection or of intellectually justifying risky sexual behavior. Candid discussions of this sensitive topic facilitated by social work practitioners, or trained peer facilitators in nontraditional settings (for example, barber shops, athletic courts, social clubs, fraternities), may be one approach that could reach this high-risk segment of the youth population.

Th ird, some responses seemed to refl ect misunderstandings about what constitutes HIV risk, focusing on "wild, unusual sex" versus merely unprotected sex. In addition, there appears to be a persistent perception that HIV-positive individuals remain noticeably sick, suggesting a lack of information about current HIV treatments and fueling misperceptions regarding the health of HIV-infected individuals.

As noted earlier, this was illustrated by one respondent who remarked, "Magic Johnson, he claimed to have AIDS in what, 92? … 90? … But he's still alive. And, you know, he's on TV and you don't see him sick. … When you're sick and you've got AIDS … you can't really know how to get well." Th is belief may underscore the need for further HIV education among members of this population—education that openly addresses longstanding myths and stereotypes about HIV infection and infected individuals.

Th e present fi ndings have signifi cant implications for social work practice. According to Bird and Bogart (2005), given the current and historical treatment of African Americans by the health care system, conspiracy theories should not be ignored. It is important for social work practitioners to both acknowledge these oppressive histories and recognize their own positions of power as agents of social and individual change. Th ese positions of power can sometimes obscure the ways in which particular types of knowledge are taken for granted as "correct" whereas others are discounted as "incorrect." Likewise, social work practitioners working with marginalized populations need to not only be aware of issues of distrust and oppression, but also provide the clinical space for clients to openly discuss such beliefs. One method would be to ask more open-ended questions about a clients' HIV beliefs and concerns about media and community messages regarding HIV risk and infection rates. Th is approach would also provide an opportunity for practitioners to assess the impact of conspiracy theories on HIV risk behavior and identify ways to affi rm clients.

Another way to acknowledge this power diff erential is to use known and trusted individuals within communities to disseminate more fact-based information about HIV. According to the Henry J. Kaiser Family Foundation, African Americans are more likely than white Americans to rely on family, friends, acquaintances, and religious organizations for information about HIV (Aragon, Kates, & Green, 2001). Furthermore, many misunderstandings about HIV prevention stem directly from stigmatizing, prejudicial, and discriminatory attitudes toward HIV-infected individuals (Beatty, Wheeler, & Gaiter, 2004). For example, homophobia, as expressed through religious beliefs in some black churches, has served to perpetuate negative attitudes and beliefs about people infected with HIV (Brooks, Etzel, Hinojos, Henry, & Perez, 2005). Th erefore, use of key informants or stakeholders is important, because it not only helps to educate important people in the community about the facts of HIV infection, but also uses known mechanisms by which individuals in predominantly black communities access information about HIV.

As indicated by the participants in this study, misinformation and conspiracy theories about HIV among African American male youths is a very real phenomenon. Th is misinformation is likely to result in a poor understanding of HIV risk, denials of the prevalence of HIV infection within the African American population, and increased HIV transmission. Acknowledging issues of power, providing opportunities for clients to discuss their personal beliefs about HIV, and using community stakeholders to disseminate HIV-prevention messages will ultimately increase the fl ow of information, decrease these misunderstandings about HIV, and generate new prevention opportunities for African American male youths.

REFERENCES

Amaro, H., Fried, L., Cabral, H., & Zuckerman, B. (1990). Violence during pregnancy and substance use. *American Journal of Public Health, 80,* 575–579.

Aragon, R., Kates, J., & Green L. (2001). *African American's views of the HIV/AIDS epidemic at 20 years: Findings from a national survey.* Retrieved April 1, 2007, from http://www.kff .org/hivaids/loader.cfm?url=/commonspot/ security/getfi le.cfm&PageID= 13866

Beatty, L. A.,Wheeler, D., & Gaiter, J. (2004). HIV prevention research for African Americans: Current and future directions. *Journal of Black Psychology, 30,* 40–58.

Bird, S., & Bogart, L. (2005). Conspiracy beliefs about HIV/AIDS and birth control among African Americans: Implications for the prevention of HIV, and other STIs, and unintended pregnancy. *Journal of Social Issues, 61,* 109–126.

Bogart, L., & Th ornburn, S. (2005). Are HIV/AIDS conspiracy beliefs a barrier to HIV prevention among African Americans? *Journal of Acquired Immune Defi ciency Syndrome, 38,* 213–218.

Brooks, R. A., Etzel, M. A., Hinojos, E., Henry, C. L., & Perez, M. (2005). Preventing HIV among Latino and African American gay and bisexual men in a context of HIV-related stigma, discrimination, and homophobia: Perspectives of providers. *AIDS Patient Care and STDs, 19,* 737–744.

Canterbury, R., McGarvey, E., Sheldon-Keller, A.,Waite, D., Reams, P., & Koopman, C. (1995). Prevalence of HIVrelated risk behaviors and STDs among incarcerated adolescents. *Journal of Adolescent Health, 17,* 173–177.

Centers for Disease Control and Prevention. (2002, July). Update: AIDS United States. *Morbidity and Mortality Weekly Report, 5,* 592–595.

Centers for Disease Control and Prevention. (2006a, February). *Fact sheet: HIV/AIDS among African Americans.* Retrieved April 1, 2007, Year, from http://www.cdc.gov/hiv/topics/aa/resources/factsheets/aa.htm

Centers for Disease Control and Prevention. (2006b, June). *Fact sheet: HIV/AIDS among youth.* Retrieved April 1, 2007, from http://www.cdc.gov/hiv/resources/factsheets/youth.htm

Coff ey, A., & Atkinson, P. (1996). *Making sense of qualitative data.* Th ousand Oaks, CA: Sage Publications.

Cohen, C.J., Bell, A., & Ifatunji, M. (2005). *Reclaiming our future: Th e state of AIDS among black youth in America.* Retrieved April 1, 2007, from http://www.blackaids. org/ShowArticle.aspx?pagename=ShowArticle& articletype=RESOURCE&articleid= 139&pagenumber=1

DiClemente, R.J., Salazar, L. F., Crosby, R. A., & Rosenthal, S. L. (2005). Prevention and control of sexually transmitted infections among adolescents: Th e importance of a socio-ecological perspective. *Public Health, 119,* 825–836.

Fisher, J. D., & Fisher, W. A. (1992). Changing AIDS-risk behavior. *Psychological Bulletin, 111,* 455–474.

Fisher, J. D., Fisher, W. A., Williams, S. S., & Malloy.T. E. (1994). Empirical tests of an information-motivationbehavioral skills model of AIDS-preventive behavior with gay men and heterosexual university students. *Health Psychology, 13,* 238–250.

Golafshani, N. (2003). Understanding reliability and validity in qualitative research. *Qualitative Report, 8,* 597–607.

Miles, M., & Huberman, A. (1994). *Qualitative data analysis: An expanded sourcebook* (2nd ed.). Th ousand Oaks, CA: Sage Publications.

Parsons, S., Simmons, W., Shinhoster, F., & Kilburn, J. (1999). A test of the grapevine: An empirical examination of conspiracy theories among African Americans. *Social Spectrum, 19,* 201–222.

Ross, M., Essien, J., & Torres, I. (2006). Conspiracy beliefs about the origin of HIV/AIDS in four racial/ethnic groups. *Journal of Acquired Immune Defi ciency Syndrome, 41,* 342–344.

Towns, E. (1995). *Testimony in AIDS and HIV infection in the African American community.* Washington, DC: U.S. Government Printing Offi ce.

Turner, P. (1993). *I heard it through the grapevine: Rumor in African-American culture.* Berkeley: University of California Press.

U.S. Census Bureau. (2000). *March current population survey.* Washington, DC: U.S. Government Printing Offi ce.

Voisin, D. (2003).Victims of community violence and HIV sexual risk behaviors among African American adolescent males. *Journal of HIV/AIDS Prevention & Education for Adolescents & Children,* 5(3/4), 87–110.

Voisin, D. R., DiClemente, R.J., Salazar, L. F., Crosby, R. A., & Yarber, W. L. (2006). Ecological factors associated with STD risk behaviors among detained female adolescents. *Social Work, 51,* 71–79.

Voisin, D., Salazar, L., Crosby, R., DiClemente, R., & Yarber.W. (2007). Understanding motivations for having sex among detained youth: Implications for HIV prevention programs. *Journal of HIV/AIDS and Social Services, 6,* 29–41.

Voisin, D., Salazar, L., Crosby, R., DiClemente, R., Yarber, W., & Staples-Home, M. (2006). HIV testing among detained youth. *Journal of HIV/AIDS Prevention in Children and Youth,* 6(2), 83–96.

Wingood, G. M., DiClemente, R. J., Harrington, K., Davies, S., Hook, E. W., III, & Oh, M. K. (2001). Exposure to X-rated movies and adolescents' sexual and contraceptive-related attitudes and behaviors. *Pediatrics, 107,* 1116–1119.

Dexter R. Voisin, PhD, *is associate professor, School of Sodal Service Administration, University of Chicago, 969 East 60th Street, Chicago, IL 60637; e-mail: d-voisin@uchicago.edu.*

Jason D. P. Bird, MSW *is a graduate student, School of Social Service Administration, University of Chicago. Th e research reported in this article was supported, in part, by National Institutes of Health Grant R25 HD045810–02 to the Center for AIDS Prevention Studies.*

Eating Disorders in African American Girls

Implications for Counselors

Regine M. Tallyrand

Given the recent focus on eating disorders in children, it is imperative that counselors consider eating concerns that aff ect children of all racial and ethnic groups and hence are eff ective in working with this population. Th e author discusses risk factors that potentially contribute to eating disorders in African American girls given their unique socialization experiences as racial and ethnic minorities. Also, the author provides strategies for developing eff ective and culturally responsive counseling interventions to work with this population.

E ating disorders were once considered disorders that occurred most frequently among college-age, European American women of middle- and upper-class backgrounds (Smolak & Striegel-Moore, 2001; J. K. Th ompson & Smolak, 2001). Recently, however, more attention has been directed toward children and their eating disorder prevalence rates (Bardick et al., 2004; Reijonen, Pratt, Patel, & Greydanus, 2003; Robinson, Chang, Haydel, & Killen, 2001; J. K. Th ompson & Smolak, 2001). In fact, it is estimated that girls as young as 9 years experience body dissatisfaction and dieting behaviors, which are two major risk factors associated with anorexia and bulimia (Reijonen et al., 2003; Robinson et al., 2001; J. K. Th ompson & Smolak, 2001; S. H. Th ompson, Rafi roiu, & Sargent, 2003). Moreover, prevalence rates for obesity in children and adolescents have increased signifi cantly in recent years, with African American and Latino American children exhibiting signifi cantly higher rates in comparison with their European American counterparts (Dounchis, Hayden, & Wilfl ey, 2001; Th orpe et al., 2004).

Despite the recent focus on eating disorders in school-age youth, empirical evidence of eating disorders among children of color is lacking, with only a few studies emphasizing risks for this population. Furthermore, potential risk factors in the development of eating disorders may be diff erent for children of color than for European American children (Dounchis et al., 2001; Smolak & Striegel-Moore, 2001). For example, children of color may experience additional contextual stressors (e.g., acculturation and racism) that are unique to their socialization experiences as racial and ethnic minorities (Dounchis et al., 2001; Logio, 2003). Given the prevalence of obesity in ethnically diverse children, it is imperative that counselors consider eating concerns that aff ect children of all racial and ethnic groups and hence are eff ective in working with this population. Furthermore, because eating disorder attitudes and behaviors can have serious short- and long-term academic, physical, and psychosocial consequences, the development of community and school-based programs focused on the prevention of eating disorders in children is essential (Bardick et al., 2004; Moreno & Th elen, 1993; Robinson et al., 2001; Rome et al., 2003; Th orpe et al., 2004).

Th e purpose of this article is to outline risk factors that potentially contribute to eating disorder symptoms in African American girls and to provide recommendations for counselors on the prevention and identifi cation of eating disorders in African American girls. First, risk factors related to the development of eating disorders in African American girls are provided. Second, implications for counselors are discussed. Finally, the need to develop culturally responsive prevention programs is discussed. Although this article focuses on risk factors specifi c to the socialization experiences of African American girls, these risk factors can be applied to other girls who identify with oppressed racial or cultural groups.

Risk Factors for African American Girls

According to the *Diagnostic and Statistical Manual of Mental Disorders* (4th ed., text rev.; American Psychiatric Association, 2000), *anorexia* is characterized by a person's refusal to maintain her or his body weight through use of excessive dieting and inaccurate perceptions of her or his body image on the basis of an obsessive fear of becoming fat. *Bulimia* is characterized by a person's excessive rapid bingeing followed by purging through use of self-induced vomiting, misuse of laxatives or diuretics, restrained eating, or excessive exercise. *Binge-eating disorder* is described by recurrent episodes of binge eating that occur in the absence of regular use of compensatory behaviors such as purging (Striegel-Moore et al., 2005) and is oft en associated with obesity. *Obesity* is defi ned by having a body mass index of 30 or greater and/or weighing more than 20% above the upper limit for one's height (Davis, Clance, & Gailis, 1999).

Within the past 20 years, a growing body of empirical evidence supporting a relationship between race, ethnicity, and eating disorders has emerged. In general, research concerning eating disorder symptomatology has suggested that African American girls demonstrate fewer eating disorder symptoms (e.g., severe dieting behaviors, body dissatisfaction) than do their European American counterparts (Dounchis et al., 2001; Logio, 2003; Lynch, Eppers, & Sherrodd, 2004; Pernick et al., 2006; S. H. Th ompson et al., 2003). Nevertheless, diff erences in prevalence rates of eating disorder symptoms for African American girls may refl ect cultural diff erences in manifestations of their symptoms rather than the lack of them (Dounchis et al., 2001; Smolak & Striegel-Moore, 2001).

Although African American girls, in general, may be at a lower risk for engaging in severe dieting behaviors or experiencing body dissatisfaction compared with European American girls, they may be at a greater risk for developing unhealthy eating practices that can lead to obesity and obesity-related health concerns, including diabetes (Dounchis et al., 2001; Logio, 2003; Robinson et al., 2001; S. H. Th ompson et al., 2003). For example, Logio (2003) surveyed European American and African American female and male adolescents and found that African American female adolescents, in comparison with their European American counterparts, were at greater risk for overweight body size and behaviors (e.g., bingeing behaviors) consistent with gaining weight. For African American girls, this risk may be related to the fact that within African American culture, heavier body ideals are accepted and social pressures concerning thinness may not exist (Logio, 2003; Robinson et al., 2001;

Smolak & Striegel-Moore, 2001; J. K. Th ompson & Smolak, 2001). Furthermore, societal factors such as racism and socioeconomic status (SES) may contribute to emotional overeating or bingeing behaviors, as well as exposure to poor food choices and malnutrition, which may eventually lead to becoming overweight or obese (Dounchis et al., 2001; Logio, 2003; B. Th ompson, 1994, 1997). In the following sections, I outline risk factors that may be unique to African American girls.

Acculturation

Acculturation refers to the process of adopting the cultural norms of the majority culture, including adjusting to a new language, customs, and rituals (Helms & Cook, 1999; Kim & Abreu, 2001). Acculturation has been suggested to play a role in the development of eating disorders such that African American girls who value European American cultural norms of thinness may exhibit severe dieting behaviors and body dissatisfaction that are consistent with anorexia and bulimia (Dounchis et al., 2001; Smolak & Striegel-Moore, 2001). Furthermore, researchers have found that high levels of acculturative stress may result in a greater number of bulimic symptoms and body dissatisfaction (Perez, Voelz, Pettit, & Joiner, 2002). On the contrary, maintaining African American cultural values may protect African American girls from endorsing eating behaviors and attitudes characteristic of anorexia and bulimia given that social pressures regarding thinness may not exist within African American culture (Abrams, Allen, & Gray, 1993; Logio, 2003; Smolak & Striegel-Moore, 2001; B. Th ompson, 1994). Furthermore, obesity may not be stigmatized in African American culture as it is in the dominant European American culture (Davis et al., 1999; Smolak & Striegel-Moore, 2001; S. H. Th ompson et al., 2003). Finally, belonging to a collectivistic culture (i.e., African American culture) may result in less focus on individual body size and more focus on using larger ethnic group body norms as a reference point (Fernandez, Malacrne, Wilfl ey, & McQuaid, 2006). It is important to note, however, that adopting African American cultural norms may be related to higher levels of other unhealthy eating practices (e.g., compulsive overeating) because this mode of coping with emotions is acceptable within the African American community and does not necessarily violate cultural standards of beauty of the African American cultural group (D. J. Harris & Kuba, 1997; B. Th ompson, 1994).

Although prior research has found that African American girls are less concerned with weight, dieting behaviors, or being thin compared with their European American counterparts (Dalton et al., 2007; Dounchis et al., 2001; Logio, 2003; Lynch et al., 2004; Pernick et al., 2006; S. H. Th ompson, Corwin, & Sargent, 1997), some researchers have suggested that this trend may soon be changing in this population. Specifi cally, several researchers have asserted that African American cultural factors may no longer protect African American girls because African American role models portrayed in the media seem to value the European American cultural norms of thinness (Franko et al., 2004; Granberg, Simons, Gibbons, & Melby, 2008; Robinson et al., 2001). For example, Robinson et al. (2001) conducted a study of overweight concerns and body dissatisfaction among ethnically diverse third-grade children and found that African American girls had signifi cantly more overweight concerns than did Asian American and Filipino American girls. In addition, Granberg et al. (2008) surveyed African American female adolescents, and the authors found support for a relationship between weight and depression and also found that cultural and ethnic factors did not moderate this relationship. Th e results from these two studies suggest that African American cultural factors may no longer protect African American girls and adolescents from the dominant European American culture's emphasis on thinness. Given this potential change in trends, it seems that evaluating cultural values regarding food and body image in ethnically diverse children may be a valuable tool in understanding the development of eating disorders in this population.

Racial Identity

Whereas *acculturation* refers to how individuals adopt the cultural values of the majority group, *racial identity* refers to how individuals understand themselves as racial beings. There are several models of racial identity that have been discussed and researched in the counseling and psychological literature, including Cross's (1971) original Nigrescence model, Helms's (1995) Black Racial Identity Model, and Sue and Sue's (1999) Racial/Cultural Identity Development model. Central to most racial identity theories is the belief that commitment to one's racial group is necessary for healthy psychological functioning (Helms & Cook, 1999). In this section, I use Helms's Black Racial Identity Model to describe the process of understanding oneself as a racial being. Helms's Black Racial Identity Model consists of four schemas that determine what cognitive and affective processes individuals undergo when presented with racerelated events (e.g., being called a derogatory name because of one's racial group membership). These four schemas are (a) Preencounter (perceiving Whites and White culture as superior), (b) Encounter (experiencing confusion about how to respond to racial cues), (c) Immersion/Emersion (idealizing Blackness and denigrating Whiteness), and (d) Internalization (treating Blacks as one's primary, but not exclusive, reference group; Helms, 1995). The schemas are considered to be developmental, active processes in which individuals may move back and forth from more simplistic (e.g., self-hatred, denial of racial group membership) to more sophisticated (e.g., healthy acceptance of racial group membership) forms of racial identity development, depending on the racial events to which they are exposed. According to Helms, the ultimate goal of these developmental processes is for an individual to abandon her or his feelings of internalized racism and to achieve a positive and healthy collective group (i.e. Black) identity.

Very few studies have explored the relationships between racial identity and eating disorder symptoms in African Americans. Results from these studies have shown that African American women who idealize Whiteness tend to engage in restrictive forms of eating disorder attitudes and behaviors (e.g., dietary restraint, body dissatisfaction; Abrams et al., 1993; Bessellieu, 1997; S. M. Harris, 1994; Talleyrand, 1998). Although no studies to date have looked at the relationships between racial identity and eating disorder symptoms in African American girls, it can be assumed that these results may be applicable to a younger population because African American children may also be exposed to discrimination, racism, and race-related events (Constantine & Blackmon, 2002; Day-Vines, Patton, & Baytops, 2003; Holcomb-McCoy, 2005). Therefore, understanding how African American girls respond to or internalize racism or race-related events may provide crucial information related to how they may manifest their eating disorder symptoms.

SES

One cannot study racial issues in children without addressing issues of class because there is a complex intersection between class and race (Constantine, 2002; Day-Vines et al., 2003). Empirical research supporting the relationship between poverty and obesity has been plagued with inconsistencies. Some researchers have contended that lower SES African American women are at a higher risk for becoming obese than are higher SES African American women (O'Neill, 2003). Other researchers have found that, although there is a strong inverse relationship between obesity and SES in European American women, the same does not hold true for African American women (Zhang & Wang, 2004). For example, Zang and Wang (2004) found that income inequality did not affect the rates of obesity among African American women. Nonetheless, researchers have found that poor families may experience malnutrition or consume food diets high in fats and sugars (Dounchis et al., 2001; Paul, 2003). Given that ethnic minority families' SES is likely to be lower than that of European American families (Dounchis et al., 2001; Paul, 2003) and that obesity is a problem among this population, it is important to consider that children who come from working or lower class African American families may be at risk for becoming overweight or obese.

In contrast, although African American children from middle-class families may be protected from poverty and malnutrition (Day-Vines et al., 2003), they still may experience eating disorder attitudes and behaviors that are related to majority cultural values. Indeed, Robinson et al. (2001) found that higher SES was associated with more dieting behaviors, weight preoccupation, and thinner desired body shape in a sample of African American schoolchildren. Given the inconsistencies and limited empirical fi ndings in this area, counselors should be aware of the potential implications of SES on the presentation of eating behaviors and attitudes in African American girls.

Summary

It seems that risk factors for African American girls may include sociocultural factors that go beyond traditional eating disorder risk factors. Th at is, acculturation, racism, and SES may aff ect why and how African American girls may manifest their eating attitudes and behaviors. For example, African American girls who have less access to nutritional food choices because of their SES may be prone to engaging in unhealthy, weight-gaining food practices. In addition, African American girls who adopt African American cultural values and norms regarding food and body size may also be at risk for becoming overweight or obese. In contrast, African American girls who have been socialized to adopt European American cultural values regarding thinness may be prone to engaging in more dieting behaviors and experiencing body dissatisfaction. For that reason, counselors should be aware of risk factors and eating concerns that aff ect children of all racial and ethnic groups and develop culturally appropriate interventions when working with these populations. In addition, given the lack of research conducted in this area, more empirical information is needed to better understand the infl uence of race, culture, and SES on eating attitudes and behaviors among young children.

Implications for Counselors

Given the increasing numbers of African American children experiencing high prevalence rates of overweight and obesity, it is imperative that counselors are aware, acknowledge, and understand how race, culture, and SES contribute to children's academic, personal, and physical well-being. Th erefore, assessing clients' racial and cultural socialization processes may be benefi cial in determining if, how, and why African American girls manifest their eating disorder symptoms. Th e following are specifi c recommendations for counselors working with African American girls.

First, according to the American Counseling Association's Multicultural Counseling Competencies (Sue, Arredondo, & McDavis, 1992), it is important for counselors to acknowledge their own racial and cultural stereotypes, biases, and privilege; to understand how culture and race have infl uenced their clients' worldviews; and to develop culturally appropriate counseling strategies and interventions when working with clients who are culturally diff erent. Th at is, counselors must be aware and respectful of their clients' personal and cross-cultural socialization experiences to provide a safe psychological space for their clients who may have eating concerns.

Second, understanding how a client's level of acculturation to her or his own African American culture or the majority European American culture infl uences her or his beliefs regarding food and physical appearance is critical. For example, an African American girl who internalizes the cultural norms of European American culture may exhibit attitudes and behaviors that are consistent with a pursuit for thinness and body dissatisfaction (Abrams et al., 1993; Smolak & Striegel-Moore, 2001). Consequently, she may be more at risk for displaying eating disorder symptoms (e.g., severe dieting, body dissatisfaction) that are consistent with anorexia or bulimia (Robinson et al., 2001). Conversely, an African American girl who has adopted African American cultural norms may be less tempted to engage in severe dieting behaviors or experience body dissatisfaction (Abrams et al., 1993; Robinson et al., 2001; Smolak & Striegel-Moore, 2001; B. Th ompson, 1994; S. H. Th ompson et al., 2003) but may engage in other unhealthy eating practices (e.g., poor food choices, overeating) that could potentially lead to becoming overweight or obese (Dounchis et al., 2001; Logio, 2003; S. H. Th ompson et al., 2003).

Counselors should consider fi nding out what cultural values their clients have adopted by having them discuss the messages they have received from their families or peers regarding physical appearance and eating behaviors. One exercise to consider is a cultural values exercise called the *Coat of Arms exercise* (adapted from Simon, 1976). Th is exercise asks participants to draw a shield shape in preparation for making a personal coat of arms. Th e shield is then divided into sections, and participants are asked to respond to several questions that assist them in identifying the cultural rituals and values (e.g., foods, religious beliefs, languages) that they experience in their families of origin. Questions such as "What foods remind you of your family of origin?" and "What are your family's beliefs about religion?" can be posed to clients to have them refl ect on their family experiences and how these messages have shaped their views toward race, culture, food, and body image. Responses to the Coat of Arms questions can then be used to generate discussion in an individual or group counseling setting.

Th ird, in addition to assessing levels of acculturation, counselors should assess the degree to which African American girls understand and internalize the oppressive forces in their lives. For example, how do African American girls cope with the psychological ramifi cations of being African American and female in the United States? Helping clients identify how they respond to racism and sexism could provide valuable information concerning their presenting eating concerns (D. J. Harris & Kuba, 1997; B. Th ompson, 1994, 1997). Some informal racial identity assessments may include inquiring about an African American client's racial socialization processes. For example, if a counselor is working with an African American girl who is distressed about her weight and body image and identifi es with various identity groups (i.e., gender and race), the counselor may want to explore which group membership is most salient for the client in her current life (Sue & Sue, 1999). What racial socialization agents (e.g., parents, peers, religion) are present in her life? What messages does she receive about being African American or female? Understanding the saliency of each of these group memberships may be essential to understanding how her group membership aff ects her eating problems (Salazar & Abrams, 2005). Furthermore, counselors may want to consider fostering positive racial and gender identity development in their clients by portraying African American women as positive role models.

Finally, given that African American families may be aware that they could be victimized by acts of racism and prejudice because of their sociopolitical histories (Terrell & Terrell, 1981; Th omas, Witherspoon, & Speight, 2004), they may be less likely to seek access to mental and physical health services. Consequently, counselors should consider developing culturally responsive health-promoting workshops for African Americans in their local schools and communities. Recently, several researchers developed a multicenter research project called the *Girls Health Enrichment Multi-Site Studies* (Story et al., 2003). Th is project consisted of several aft er-school, short-term intervention programs for African American girls focusing on increasing physical activity and healthy eating through the use of recruitment and intervention strategies that were consistent with African American cultural values, traditions, and customs. Story et al. (2003) found that the most eff ective recruitment strategies were media promotions targeting radio stations with African American audiences and school and community presentations with support from community leaders and school leaders. Furthermore, the most eff ective intervention strategies included aft er-school dance classes, a family-based intervention to reduce television viewing, and psychoeducational materials targeting the development of healthy eating and activity skills for youth. Th ese strategies did not focus on obesity prevention, but rather on a holistic concept of health that included high self-esteem, spirituality, and cultural awareness as well as physical health.

Considering the fact that African American girls ages 5 to 17 years are at risk for being overweight or obese (Dounchis et al., 2001), counselors should consider targeting African American female adolescents with eating disorder prevention programs that include culturally relevant activities. For example, developing a program that consists of activities including dancing, family, and community involvement and psychoeducational programs emphasizing a holistic approach to health could be eff ective among African American female populations. Use of such intervention programs may contribute to treating the widespread problem of obesity among African American girls (Davis et al., 1999; Story et al., 2003). In addition, given the lack of empirical, theoretical, and diagnostic research that adequately captures eating disorders among ethnically diverse children (Wonderlich, Joiner, Keel, Williamson, & Crosby, 2007), it is important for counselors to engage in qualitative and quantitative research that examines risk factors related to eating behaviors in African American girls. Use of qualitative research may be extremely benefi cial given the potential for interaction among contextual factors in the manifestation of eating disorders in racially and ethnically diverse children. Ultimately, use of qualitative and quantitative research could assist with the development of culturally relevant measures and theories of eating disorders. Finally, the growing concern regarding eating disorders among African American children and the lack of research in this area underscore the need to educate counseling professionals at training seminars or at national or international conferences about the risks that are presented to this population.

References

Abrams, K. K., Allen, L. R., & Gray, J. J. (1993). Disordered eating attitudes and behaviors, psychological adjustment, and ethnic identity: A comparison of Black and White female college students. *International Journal of Eating Disorders, 14,* 49–57.

American Psychiatric Association. (2000). *Diagnostic and statistical manual of mental disorders* (4th ed., text rev.). Washington, DC: Author.

Bardick, A. D., Bernes, K. B., McCulloch, A. R. M., Witko, K. D., Spriddle, J. W., & Roest, A. R. (2004). Eating disorder intervention, prevention, and treatment: Recommendations for school counselors. *Professional School Counseling, 8,* 168–174.

Bessellieu, L. D. (1997). Th e meaning of weight and body image in African-American women. *Dissertation Abstracts International: Section B. Sciences and Engineering, 58*(03), 1520.

Constantine, M. G. (2002). Th e intersection of race, ethnicity, gender, and social class in counseling: Examining selves in cultural contexts. *Journal of Multicultural Counseling and Development, 30,* 210–215.

Constantine, M. G., & Blackmon, S. M. (2002). Black adolescents' racial socialization experiences: Th eir relations to home, school, and peer self-esteem. *Journal of Black Studies, 32,* 322–335.

Cross, W. E. (1971). Th e Negro-to-Black conversion experience: Towards a psychology of Black liberation. *Black World, 20,* 13–27.

Dalton, W. T., Klesges, L. M., Beech, B. M., Kitzmann, K. M., Kent, A. E., & Veazey Morris, K. D. (2007). Comparisons between African American girls' and parents' perceptions of girls' weight concerns and weight control behaviors. *Eating Disorders, 15,* 231–246.

Davis, N. L., Clance, P. R., & Gailis, A. T. (1999). Treatment approaches for obese and overweight African American women: A consideration of cultural dimensions. *Psychotherapy, 36,* 27–35.

Day-Vines, N. L., Patton, J. M., & Baytops, J. L. (2003). Counseling African American adolescents: Th e impact of race, culture, and middle class status. *Professional School Counseling, 7,* 40–51.

Dounchis, J. Z., Hayden, H. A., & Wilfl ey, D. E. (2001). Obesity, body image, and eating disorders in ethnically diverse children and adolescents. In J. K. Th ompson & L. Smolak (Eds.), *Body image, eating disorders, and obesity in youth* (pp. 67–91). Washington, DC: American Psychological Association.

Fernandez, S., Malacrne, V. L., Wilfl ey, D. E., & McQuaid, J. (2006). Factor structure of the Bulimia Test-Revised in college women from four ethnic groups. *Cultural Diversity and Ethnic Minority Psychology, 12,* 403–419.

Franko, D. L., Striegel-Moore, R. H., Barton, B. A., Schumann, B. C., Garner, D. M., Daniels, S. R, … Crawford, P. B. (2004). Measuring eating concerns in Black and White adolescent girls. *International Journal of Eating Disorders, 35,* 179–189.

Granberg, E. M., Simons, R. L., Gibbons, F. X., & Melby, J. N. (2008). Th e relationship between body size and depressed mood: Findings from a sample of African American middle school girls. *Youth & Society, 39,* 294–315.

Harris, D. J., & Kuba, S. A. (1997). Ethnocultural identity and eating disorders in women of color. *Professional Psychology: Research and Practice, 28,* 341–347.

Harris, S. M. (1994). Racial diff erences in predictors of college women's body image attitudes. *Women & Health, 21,* 89–104.

Helms, J. E. (1995). An update of Helms's White and People of Color Racial Identity models. In J. G. Ponterotto, J. M. Casas, L. A. Suzuki, & C. M. Alexander (Eds.), *Handbook of multicultural counseling* (pp. 181–198). Th ousand Oaks, CA: Sage.

Helms, J. E., & Cook, D. A. (1999). *Using race and culture in counseling and psychotherapy: Th eory and process.* Boston, MA: Allyn & Bacon.

Holcomb-McCoy, C. C. (2005). Empowerment groups for urban African American girls: A response. *Professional School Counseling, 8,* 390–392.

Kim, B. S. K., & Abreu, J. M. (2001). Acculturation measurement: Th eory, current instruments, and future directions. In J. G. Ponterotto, J. M. Casas, L. A. Suzuki, & C. M. Alexander (Eds.), *Handbook of multicultural counseling* (2nd ed., pp. 394–424). Th ousand Oaks, CA: Sage.

Logio, K. A. (2003). Gender, race, childhood abuse, and body image among adolescents. *Violence Against Women, 9,* 931–954.

Lynch, W. C., Eppers, K. D., & Sherrodd, J. R. (2004). Eating attitudes of Native Americans and White female adolescents: A comparison of BMI- and age-matched groups. *Ethnicity & Health, 9,* 253–266.

Moreno, A. B., & Th elen, M. H. (1993). A preliminary prevention program for eating disorders in a junior high school population. *Journal of Youth and Adolescence, 22,* 109–124.

O'Neill, S. K. (2003). African American women and eating disturbances: A meta-analysis. *Journal of Black Psychology, 29,* 3–16.

Paul, D. G. (2003). *Talkin' back.* Westport, CT: Praeger.

Perez, M., Voelz, Z. R., Pettit, J. W., & Joiner, T. E. (2002). Th e role of acculturated stress and body dissatisfaction in predicting bulimic symptomatology across ethnic groups. *International Journal of Eating Disorders, 31,* 442–454.

Pernick, Y., Nichols, J. F., Rauh, M. J., Kern, M., Ji, M., Lawson, M. J., & Wilfl ey, D. (2006). Disordered eating among a multiracial/ethnic sample of female high-school athletes. *Journal of Adolescent Health, 38,* 689–695.

Reijonen, J. H., Pratt, H. D., Patel, D. R., & Greydanus, D. E. (2003). Eating disorders in the adolescent population: An overview. *Journal of Adolescent Research, 18,* 209–222.

Robinson, T. N., Chang, J. Y., Haydel, K. F., & Killen, J. D. (2001). Overweight concerns and body dissatisfaction among third-grade children: Th e impacts of ethnicity and socioeconomic status. *Th e Journal of Pediatrics, 138,* 181–187.

Rome, E. S., Ammerman, S., Rosen, D. S., Keller, R. J., Lock, J., Mammel, K. A., ... Silber, T. J. (2003). Children and adolescents with eating disorders: Th e state of the art. *Pediatrics, 111,* 98–108.

Salazar, C. F., & Abrams, L. P. (2005). Conceptualizing identity development in members of marginalized groups. *Journal of Professional Counseling: Practice, Th eory, and Research, 35,* 47–59.

Simon, S. B. (1976). Values clarifi cation vs. indoctrination. In D. Purpel & K. Ryan (Eds.), *Moral education: It comes with the territory* (pp. 130–131). Berkeley, CA: McCutchin.

Smolak, L., & Striegel-Moore, R. H. (2001). Challenging the myth of the golden girl: Ethnicity and eating disorders. In R. H. Striegel-Moore & L. Smolak (Eds.), *Eating disorders: Innovative directions in research and practice* (pp. 111–132). Washington, DC: American Psychological Association.

Story, M., Sherwood, N. E., Obarzanek, E., Beech, B. M., Baranowski, J. C., Th ompson, N. S., ... Rochon, J. (2003). Recruitment of African-American pre-adolescent girls into an obesity prevention trial: Th e GEMS pilot studies. *Ethnicity and Disease, 13,* 78–87.

Striegel-Moore, R. H., Fairburn, C. G., Wilfl ey, D. E., Pike, K. M., Dohm, F., & Kraemer, H. C. (2005). Toward an understanding of risk factors for binge-eating disorder in Black and White women: A community-based case-control study. *Psychological Medicine, 35,* 907–917.

Sue, D. W., Arredondo, P., & McDavis, R. J. (1992). Multicultural counseling competencies and standards: A call to the profession. *Journal of Counseling & Development, 70,* 477–486.

Sue, D. W., & Sue, D. (1999). *Counseling the culturally diverse: Th eory and practice* (3rd ed.). New York, NY: Wiley.

Talleyrand, R. M. (1998). *Acculturation and racial identity as predictors of eating disorder symptomatology in African American college women* (Unpublished master's thesis). University of Maryland, College Park.

Terrell, F. N., & Terrell, S. (1981). An inventory to measure cultural mistrust among Blacks. *Th e Western Journal of Black Studies, 5,* 180–184.

Th omas, A. J., Witherspoon, K. M., & Speight, S. L. (2004). Toward the development of the Stereotypic Roles for Black Women Scale. *Journal of Black Psychology, 30,* 426–442.

Th ompson, B. (1994). *A hunger so wide and so deep.* Minneapolis: University of Minnesota Press.

Th ompson, B. (1997). Multiracial feminist theorizing about eating: Refusing to rank oppressions. *Eating Disorders: Th e Journal of Treatment & Prevention, 4,* 104–114.

Th ompson, J. K., & Smolak, L. (Eds.). (2001). *Body image, eating disorders, and obesity in youth: Assessment, prevention and treatment.* Washington, DC: American Psychological Association.

Th ompson, S. H., Corwin, S. J., & Sargent, R. G. (1997). Ideal body size beliefs and weight concerns of fourth-grade children. *International Journal of Eating Disorders, 21,* 279–284.

Th ompson, S. H., Rafi roiu, A. C., & Sargent, R. G. (2003). Examining gender, racial, and age diff erences in weight concerns among third, fi ft h, eighth, and eleventh graders. *Eating Behaviors, 3,* 307–323.

Th orpe, L. E., List, D. G., Marx, T., May, L., Helgerson, S. D., & Frieden, T. R. (2004). Childhood obesity in New York City elementary school students. *American Journal of Public Health, 94,* 1496–1500.

Wonderlich, S. A., Joiner, T. E., Keel, P. K., Williamson, D. A., & Crosby, R. D. (2007). Eating disorder diagnoses: Empirical approaches to classifi cation. *American Psychologist, 62,* 167–180.

Zhang, Q., & Wang, Y. (2004). Trends in the association between obesity and socioeconomic status in U.S. adults: 1971–2000. *Obesity Research, 12,* 1622–1632.

Differences between European Americans and African Americans in the Association between Child Obesity and Disrupted Parenting

Leslie Gordon Simons et al.

INTRODUCTION

T he rate of obesity among children has more than doubled the past 30 years (Berkowitz and Stunkard 2002) increasing concern about its physical and emotional health consequences (Braet, Mervielde, and Vandereycken 1997; DeJong and Kleck 1986). Th is increase has been especially marked among African-American children; rates of overweight and obesity among African American girls, for example, are nearly twice those of European American girls (Baskin, Ard, Franklin, and Allison 2005). Awareness of these trends has contributed to a growing interest in the social psychological causes and consequences of childhood obesity. One of the most active areas of research has emphasized the association between childhood obesity and dysfunctional family relationships. While this line of research has produced a number of important results (Favaro and Santonastaso 1995; Fulkerson, McGuire, Neumark-Sztainer, Story, French, and Perry 2002; Mendelson, White, and Schliecker 1995; Renman, Engstrom, Silfverdal, and Aman 1999; Steinberg and Phares 2001), we argue that it has also been limited in ways that refl ect the medical and psychiatric perspectives long dominant in this fi eld. In particular, there tends to be an assumption about causal direction-that poor parenting tends to make children overweight.

In this paper, we draw from the family stress model developed by Conger and colleagues (Conger and Conger 2002) to propose an alternative perspective for understanding this relationship. According to this model, hardship and negative events create family stress. Th e emotional distress that results disrupts parenting which then leads to child and adolescent maladjustment. Th e model indicates that the stressor produces emotions and behaviors in parents that create problematic outcomes for children because they disrupt the parents' ability to engage in high quality parenting. Support for this model has been demonstrated in other studies using the same two samples utilized in the present study.

Leslie Gordon Simons, Gene R. Brody, Velma M. Murry, Ellen Granberg, Yi-Fu Chen, Ronald L. Simons, Rand D. Conger, & Fredrick X. Gibbons, "Diff erences between European Americans and African Americans in the Association between Child Obesity and Disrupted Parenting," *Journal of Comparative Family Studies*, vol. 39, no. 2, pp. 207–228.

We argue that, among European American parents, child overweight and obesity disrupts the quality of parenting children receive because the stigma associated with obesity acts as a stressor, making effective parenting more difficult. Theory and research on determinants of parenting have established that a child's characteristics do impact the parenting practices of mothers and fathers (Belsky 1984; Vondra and Belsky 1989). To date, this work has largely been limited to consideration of the effects of a child's temperament and has shown that parents are often less involved when their children have difficult temperaments (Lytton 1990; Sampson and Laub 1993; Simons, Johnson, Conger, and Elder 1998). Drawing from both Conger's (Conger, Wallace, Sun, Simons, McLoyd, and Brody 2002; Conger and Conger 2002) family stress model and research on the impact of stigma as a parental stressor, we argue that obesity is another child characteristic that is likely to have a disruptive effect on quality of involvement for some parents.

STRESS AND THE STIGMA OF CHILDHOOD OBESITY

Parenting an overweight child may be stressful for a number of reasons. Fears about obesity's health consequences may be a significant stressor. Parents may feel guilty or frustrated by their inability to influence their child's weight trajectory. This may, in turn, exacerbate parents' worries about their children's physical and emotional well-being. Parents may also be embarrassed about having an obese child. Such feelings may have been exacerbated by negative comments from family members, school officials, or health care providers. All of these experiences may result in the feeling of stigma: a discrediting characteristic that influences both how people perceive themselves and how they are perceived and treated by others (Goffman 1963). In particular, stigma tends to evoke assessments of incompetence and lack of moral trustworthiness and is accompanied by status loss, negative treatment, and strained interactions for both the stigmatized person and his or her intimate associates (Jones, Farina, Hastorf, Markus, Miller, and Scott 1984; Link and Phelan 2001); we argue that such assessments may be particularly salient sources of stress for parents of overweight children.

Obesity is a stigmatized status in much of western culture (Schwartz 1986: Stearns 1999), particularly among whites and members of the middle class (Adams, Sargent, Thompson, and Richter 2000) and there is ample evidence that being heavy results in status loss for both children and adults (Adams, Smith, Wilbut, and Grady 1993; Benson, Severs, Tatgenhorst, and Loddengaard 1980; DeJong 1980; DeJong 1993; Garn, Sullivan, and Hawthorne 1989; Gortmaker, Must, Perrin, Sobal, and Dietz 1993; Neumark-Sztainer, Story, and Faibisch 1998; Ritchey and Fishbein 2001; Sobal, Nicolopoulos, and Lee 1995). The small amount of empirical work that has examined the impact of children's obesity on parental behavior suggests parents are not immune to this devaluing impulse (Crandall 1991; Crandall 1995). In addition, research considering parental responses to other forms of stigma in their children suggests stigma increases the amount of stress parents' experience.

First, awareness that one's child may be seen by others as deviant is, in itself, distressing and parents must find ways to cope with their own negative feelings. This is particularly difficult when parents shared the views of others before learning of their own child's stigma (Fields 2001). Additionally, parents may internalize a sense of shame as a result of having a stigmatized child and this may, in turn, influence their attitudes and behaviors toward that child (Green 2003; Schneider and Conrad 1983).

Parents may also find others judge them negatively because they have an overweight child. This effect, which Goffman (1963) called "courtesy stigma," occurs when one is stigmatized because of an association with a marked person, rather than being marked oneself. In the case of raising an overweight child, parents may find their abilities or effectiveness as parents are questioned by friends, family, or service providers such as physicians, teachers, or social workers. Further, parents may internalize such judgments, directing them towards themselves. Such a response may be particularly likely if parents are worried about the negative health consequences of obesity. Interactions such as these may be quite stressful for the parent, contributing to small behavioral changes that add up to a decline in the quality of parenting (Ambert 2001).

Although there is ample evidence suggesting that stigma can interrupt relations between parents and children, concern about specifi c types of stigma varies by culture and subculture (Link and Phelan 2001). African Americans, for example, hold more weight-tolerant attitudes than European Americans (Crago, Shisslak, and Estes 1996; Nichter 2000) and are, in general, less concerned about body weight as a stigmatizing characteristic. For example, despite being heavier than whites, black women have higher self esteem and a more positive body image-patterns that have also been documented among adolescents (Cash and Henry 1995; Rucker and Cash 1992; Siegel 2002). African American girls are also more likely to receive positive feedback from family members about their appearance, regardless of their weight (Crago, Shisslak, and Estes 1996; Nichter 2000). Further, overweight is more common among children and adults in African-American communities, a pattern that may contribute to these more moderate attitudes (Swallen, Reither, Haas, and Meier 2005). Th ese fi ndings suggest that, while not unconcerned[1], members of the African American community are less anxious about issues of being overweight. Consequently, we anticipate that African-American parents will be better equipped to cope with obesity as a stressor and thus that the association between child body weight and parental behavior will be signifi cantly weaker among African American families than among European American families.

CHILD OBESITY AND PARENT BEHAVIORS

Considering the argument that obesity in one's child makes high quality parenting more stressful and diffi cult can best be accomplished by assessing specifi c parenting practices of both mothers and fathers. Past research looking at parents and their overweight children has used global measures of family function which we argue may have obscured the impact of stigma on these relationships. In particular, we believe that a reliance on family function perspectives as the predominant theoretical orientation has led to a focus on parental behaviors as contributors to children's weight gain (Kinston, Loader, and Miller 1987; Mendelson, White, and Schliecker 1995; Steinberg and Phares 2001).

If stigma does interrupt the relationship between parents and children then its infl uence should be most clearly seen in the actions parents take (or fail to take) with respect to their children. In addition, our focus on specifi c parenting practices is more consistent with contemporary family sociology and developmental psychology approaches to understanding the role of parents in child development. Further, by emphasizing parenting practices rather than global family functioning, we are able to isolate the actions of each parent. Fathers are rarely included in research on parent-child relationships, including that focused on obesity. Examining specifi c parental behaviors, rather than family environment, permits clear distinctions to be made between mothers and fathers. We expect that the cultural diff erences in the eff ect of child obesity on parenting will hold for both mothers and fathers. Focusing on specifi c parental behaviors of mothers and fathers will also facilitate our ability to specify the role played by diff erences in weight attitudes among African-Americans as opposed to European-Americans. If sensitivity to obesity stigma is indeed an infl uential stressor, we would then expect to see a pattern in which the association between child's weight and

---

[1] As a group, African Americans should not be characterized as "fat friendly" or approving of overweight or obesity (Rucker and Cash 1992). When asked to assess ideal body sizes, for example, both African Americans and European Americans tend to prefer fi gures that fall within the range of clinical normality with African Americans selecting ideals at the higher end and European Americans selecting ideals at the lower end (Th ompson, Sargent, and Kemper 1996).

parent's behaviors, whether by mothers or fathers, will be stronger among European-Americans than African American parents. Including both mothers and fathers provides a stronger test of our hypotheses because it allows us to demonstrate that cultural diff erences exist regardless of the sex of the parent.

In this analysis, we examine four dimensions of parenting behavior: warmth, monitoring, use of inductive reasoning, and problem solving as reported by the children in our samples. We chose these elements of parenting because of their well documented relationship to positive child outcomes such as well being and emotional health (Conger, Conger, Elder, Lorenz, Simons, and L. B. 1992; Conger and Elder 1994; Conger and Conger 2002; Conger, Cui, Bryant, and Elder 2000; Simons 1996; Simons, Chao, Conger, and Elder Jr. 2001; Simons, Murry, McLoyd, Lin, Cutrona, and Conger 2002b). Also, prior focus group research has determined that these dimensions are meaningful to both European-American and African American parents and capture what they consider to be important dimensions of eff ective parenting (Simons et al., 2002b).

Both warmth and monitoring have been examined in previous work on the relationship between family environment and child overweight status. A warm family environment is associated with lower levels of binge eating disorder, healthier eating behavior, and lower levels of obesity among girls (Archibald, Graber, and Brooks-Gunn 1999; Archibald, Linver, Graber, and Brooks-Gunn 2002; Byely, Archibald, Graber, and Brooks-Gunn 1995; Hodges, Cochrane, and Brewerton 1998; Mellin, Neumark-Sztainer, Story, Ireland, and Resnick 2002; Mendelson, White, and Schliecker 1995). In this analysis, we consider the application of warm and caring behavior by both mothers and fathers toward their children and we anticipate that European American parents will display less warmth toward their overweight children. We anticipate weaker or insignifi cant relationships for African American parents.

Monitoring among parents of overweight children has been indirectly assessed in studies looking at parental pressure to diet. In general, moderate levels of monitoring show the strongest association between with healthy eating and exercise behaviors (Fulkerson et al., 2002; Mellin et al., 2002). Parents, particularly mothers, actively comment on their children's weight, providing feedback and encouraging or discouraging weight loss (Adams, Sargent, Th ompson, and Richter 2000; Mellin et al., 2002; Vincent and McCabe 2000).

On the surface, these results suggest parents, especially mothers, would respond to their overweight children with increased monitoring. However, an important diff erence between these studies and the present investigation is that previous work has focused on parental monitoring of diet and physical activity whereas this study will examine the degree to which parents are aware of a wider range of their children's day to day activities and patterns. We use Body Mass Index (BMI) as a measure of obesity. BMI is a relationship with weight and height that is associated with body fat and health risk. For European American parents, we expect to fi nd a negative relationship between child BMI and parents' general level of monitoring. Although, parents who are particularly concerned about weight may closely track behaviors they perceive to be relevant to this arena, we expect that they pay less attention to nonweight related activities. Th is lower degree of monitoring would be consistent with the general pattern of withdrawal predicted by a negative response to obesity stigma. As with warmth, we do not expect this pattern among African-American parents.

We also examine parental use of inductive reasoning and problem solving. Parents display inductive reasoning when they provide the reasons and justifi cations behind rules and decisions they make regarding their children. Problem solving entails forming a collaborative relationship with the child in order to help him or her overcome challenges and diffi culties. We included these dimensions in our parenting measures because they are indicative of parental concern and involvement in the life of their child, and past research has shown them to be a part of an eff ective approach to parenting. For our European American sample only, we expect that a child's weight will be inversely related to both of these dimensions of parenting.

THE QUESTION OF CAUSAL ORDER

Previous work on the relationship between family environment and childhood obesity has presumed a causal order in which dysfunctional family systems promoted unhealthy eating in children, leading to weight gain and obesity. Working from the family stress model, we off er an argument in which the primary direction of the association moves in the opposite direction. Of course, the ideal circumstance for testing this argument is one in which longitudinal panel data are available that can support a direct analysis of causal priority. Unfortunately, it is quite diffi cult to establish causal priority directly, as most longitudinal studies incorporating both parenting behaviors and body weight begin collecting data during late childhood or early adolescence. Both quality of parenting and BMI tend to be very stable during these years and the association between BMI and parenting is apt to be modest. Hence methods such as cross-lagged analysis or reciprocal eff ect structural equation modeling are likely to generate insignifi cant paths between child BMI and quality of parenting. Ideally, a prospective study would need to begin when children are quite young and neither weight trajectories nor parenting behaviors have stabilized.

In the absence of such data, we cannot defi nitively establish the direction of this relationship. However, by comparing these associations in two community samples, one in which concern about obesity stigma is known to be elevated and another in which it is more moderate, we believe we can suggest something about the likely direction of these eff ects. If the results turn out as we have hypothesized, and only the European American parents show a negative association between child weight and parental behaviors, it would suggest that at least some of the association extends from child weight to parental behavior, rather than solely the reverse. Were this not the case, the relationship should hold across both ethnic groups since there is no reason to expect that African American children would respond diff erently to poor quality parenting than would European American children raised in similar structural conditions.

THE PRESENT STUDY

In the present study, we test two hypotheses. First, we expect that child obesity will be inversely related to quality of parenting for European American mothers and fathers. Second, we expect that this relationship will not be evident for African American mothers and fathers. To test these predictions, we examine the association between children's body weight and four specifi c parenting behaviors: warmth, monitoring, inductive reasoning, and problem solving. In contrast to past studies, we assess the BMI of both boys and girls and we consider the parenting practices of both mothers and fathers. We also examine this association in two community samples, one European American and the other African American. In line with our argument that obesity stigma represents a form of parental stress, we expect to fi nd a consistent association between child weight and disrupted parenting only for the European American sample, given its cultural concern with being thin.

In order to explore this comparison further, we also consider the potential that diff erences between African-American and European-American parents may result from class status rather than racial group membership. In general European-American families have higher household incomes than do AfricanAmerican families and obesity is generally more common among persons of lower socio-economic status (Schoenborn, Adams, and Barnes 2002). Consequently, it is possible that the more moderate attitudes towards obesity found among African-American families refl ects this social class diff erence. In order to account for this possibility, we control for socio-economic status in these analyses.

Also, as noted earlier, while African-Americans hold more moderate attitudes about weight than do European-Americans, this does not mean they are unconcerned about weight, particularly as a threat to health and well being (Kumanyika, Wilson, and Guilford-Davenport 1993; Rucker and Cash 1992). Rather, the possibility exists that African-American parents simply have a higher threshold for weight stigma and that among the most obese children similar patterns resulting from parental distress will be evident. For this reason, we also test for non-linear relationships between child BMI and parent behaviors.

METHODS

Samples

Families from the Iowa Youth and Families Project (IYFP) and the Family and Community Health Study (FACHS) were used to test the study hypotheses. All of the families in the IYFP sample are European American, whereas all of those in the FACHS sample are African American. Th e advantage of using these two samples is that they have utilized similar parenting measures and data collection procedures.

Th e IYFP was designed to assess the processes involved in the transition from childhood to adolescence, as well as to understand the broader socioeconomic stress created by economic hardship in the family of origin. Th e IYFP sample consists of 451 White, two-parent families recruited through the cohort of all seventh-grade students, boys and girls, in eight counties in North Central Iowa who were enrolled in school during winter and spring of 1989. An additional criterion for inclusion in the study was the presence of a sibling within 4 years of age of the seventh grader. Slightly less than half of the cohort of seventh graders had families who met these criteria. Seventy-eight percent of the eligible families agreed to participate in the study. Th e study families were mostly working class and lived on farms (about one third) or in small towns. Median income was $29,642 and average education was 13.5 years for both mothers and fathers. Additional information regarding the sample is available in Conger et al., (1992).

Our analyses are based on wave 2 of the study when the target children were roughly 13.5 years of age. In order to maximize the N, both the targets and their siblings were included in our analyses. We selected wave 2 as we wanted to ensure that the younger siblings were at least approaching, if they had not yet entered, the teen years. Th is was important as cultural norms regarding weight are generally seen as less applicable to young children (Smolak and Levine 2001). Th ey become relevant, however, and might be expected to infl uence parental behavior, as the child enters the teen years. Our sample of girls consisted of 224 targets and 219 siblings. Th e average age for the girls was 13.6, with over 80% being between the ages of 12 and 15. Our sample of boys consisted of 200 targets and 204 siblings, with an average age of 13.8. Again, over 80% were between the ages of 12 and 15. Standard errors and signifi cance levels for analyses involving the IYFP sample were adjusted for dependence between targets and siblings using the STATA statistical program.

FACHS is a multi-site investigation of neighborhood and family eff ects on the health and development of African American children. Th e sample consists of 867 African American families, 467 in Iowa and 400 in Georgia. Families were recruited from a pool of all eligible 5th graders enrolled in school. Most study families were recruited by telephone. However, aft er repeated unsuccessful attempts to make telephone contact, or if a potential participant did not have a telephone, a staff member attempted to make face-to-face contact. If the potential participant was no longer at the address, we asked neighbors for information regarding their new address. Th e sample yielded respondents from neighborhoods that are ethnically (10% or higher African American) and economically diverse (10% to 100% below poverty). Th e response rate was approximately 80%. Median income was $20,803 and the average education level of primary caregivers was a high school diploma. Th ere was no signifi cant diff erence in income or education of the primary caregiver between the Iowa and Georgia subsamples. Additional information regarding the sample is available in Simons, Lin, Gordon, Brody, Murry, and Conger (2002a).

Our analyses are based upon data collected at wave 2 of FACHS when the target children were roughly 13 years of age. Th us the IYFP and FACHS children included in our analysis were of approximately the same age. We included all boys and girls in the FACHS sample who had a mother or father who participated as either a primary or secondary caregiver. Th is consisted of 329 girls who had a mother and 114 who had a father who participated in the study. Two-hundred-eighty-eight boys had a mother and 104 a father who participated in the study.

Procedures

At each wave, both projects used two home interviews to collect data from family members. Th e second visit occurred within 7 days of the fi rst visit. At each home visit self-report questionnaires were administered to the caregiver and the child in an interview format. Each interview was conducted privately between one participant and one researcher, with no other family members present. Th e instruments were presented on laptop computers. Questions appeared in sequence on the screen, which both the researcher and participant could see. Th e researcher read each question aloud and the respondent entered a response using a personal keypad. All IYFP interviewers were European American whereas all FACHS interviewers were African American. Interviewers cannot see respondent's answers as they are entered.

Measures

Body Mass Index

Adolescents in both the IFYP and FACHS samples were asked to report their height and weight, and this information was used to calculate a Body Mass Index (BMI) score for each individual.[2] BMI is an assessment generally used by physicians and health experts to determine if a person is underweight, overweight, or within a healthy weight range and has the advantage of being comparable across persons of both genders and of diff ering stature. An individual's BMI score is calculated according to the following formula: weight/height in inches[2] x .703 (Centers for Disease Control 2004) and assessments of weight and overweight among children were made using BMI-for-age growth charts that have been adapted for use with culturally diverse groups of respondents (Cole, Bellizzi, Flegal, and Dietz 2000; National Center for Health Statistics 2000).

Parental Behavior

Past research has established that eff ective parents show warmth and support, help their children solve problems, monitor their behavior, and use inductive reasoning to explain parental decisions and consequences when behavioral infractions occur (Gray and Steinberg 1999; Maccoby and Martin 1983; Maccoby 1992). As part of IYFP, scales were developed to assess each of these dimensions of parenting (Conger and Elder 1994). Th ese scales have been shown to have strong reliability and validity (Conger et al., 1992; Simons 1996). With only minor modifi cations, these same scales were incorporated into the instruments used for FACHS. Focus group feedback prior to data collection indicated that the scale items are meaningful to African American parents and capture what they consider to be the important dimensions of eff ective parenting.

---

[2] Adolescents' self-reported height and weight do diff er slightly from objectively measured height and weight, with correlations of about .9 (Brener, McManus, Galluska, Lowry, and Wechsler 2003). However, when used for non-clinical purposes, BMI based on self-report measures have acceptable reliability and validity (Brener et al., 2003).

Th e scales ask the children to report how oft en (1 = never, 5 = always) during the past year that their mother and father engaged in various parenting activities. Th e 8-item parental warmth scale consists of items such as "How oft en does your mom (dad) act loving and aff ectionate toward you?" Coeffi cient alpha for the scale was .92 for IYFP and .90 for FACHS. Th e child monitoring scale consists of fi ve questions (e.g., "How oft en does your mom (dad) know who you are with when you are away from home?"). Coeffi cient alpha was .66 for IYFP and .74 for FACHS. Th e inductive reasoning scale is comprised of six items (e.g., "How oft en does your mom (dad) discipline you by reasoning, explaining, or talking to you?"), and coeffi cient alpha was .85 for IYFP and .72 for FACHS. Finally, the problem solving scale consists of 4-items (e.g., "When you and your mom (dad) have a problem, how oft en can the two of you fi gure out how to deal with it?"), and had alpha coeffi cient of .91 for IYFP and .62 for FACHS, respectively.

Family Socioeconomic Status

For both samples, family SES was assessed by fi rst summing mother and father's education. Th is variable was then standardized and added to a standardized measure of per capita income in dollars. Th is approach provided equal weight to both education and income in determining family SES.

RESULTS

Among adults, both the Center for Disease Control and the World Health Organization defi ne a BMI of 25–30 to be overweight and a BMI of over 30 as very overweight or obese (Centers for Disease Control 2004), defi nitions which apply equally to men and women. In contrast, children's body fatness tends to vary by age and gender and consequently there is far less consensus regarding the cutoff s that should be used for children and adolescents. One of the most widely accepted standards for establishing overweight status among children are the "Body mass index-for-age percentiles" (a.k.a. BMI-for-age) developed by the National Center for Health Statistics and the National Center for Chronic Disease Prevention and Health Promotion (National Center for Health Statistics 2000). Additional work has attempted to generalize the BMI-for-age standards across culturally and nationally diverse data sets; these results conclude that at age 13 the criteria for being either overweight or obese should be 21.91 and 26.84, respectively, for boys and 22.58 and 27.76, respectively, for girls (Cole, Bellizzi, Flegal, and Dietz 2000). Table 1 reports the mean BMI scores for the boys and girls in each of our samples, as well as the percentage in each group who are classifi ed as overweight or obese using the criteria recommended by Cole et al., (2000).

Consistent with the fi ndings of previous reports, the table shows that the African American children in our study are more likely to be overweight than the European American children. Compared to the

Table 1.

Means and Standard Deviations for BMI and Percent Overweight and Obese by Race of Child.

	European American		African American	
	Girls	Boys	Girls	Boys
Mean	20.42	20.94	23.98	22.68
s.d.	3.52	3.50	5.99	5.09
overweight	23%	23%	50%	42%
obese	4%	7%	22%	14%

European Americans, the African Americans have higher average BMI scores and are more likely to be both overweight and obese. T-test and chi square analyses showed these differences to be statistically significant (p < .01). The differences are especially large for girls. For example, although the proportion of obese African American boys in this sample is twice that of European American boys (14% versus 7%), African American girls are over five times more likely than European American girls to be obese (22% versus 4%).

Tables 2 and 3 present analyses designed to test the hypothesis that child's BMI will be related to quality of parenting for European American parents but not for African American parents. We began our analyses by regressing the various dimensions of parenting on BMI while controlling for SES. As shown in columns 1 and 4 in Table 2, these models revealed an inverse relationship between daughters' BMI and the parenting behaviors of the European American parents. The beta coefficients are modest but statistically significant for both mothers and fathers. This finding suggests that among white girls higher weight is associated with less monitoring, warmth, inductive reasoning, and problem solving by both mothers and fathers. A similar pattern is evident in column 10 for European American fathers of sons. There is a significant inverse relationship between a boy's BMI and a father's display of each of the four parenting practices. The results are less consistent, however, for mothers. As shown in column 7, son's BMI is related to less monitoring and inductive reasoning, but the coefficients for warmth and problem solving fail to reach statistical significance.

Table 3 shows a very different pattern of findings for the African American parents. As shown in columns 1, 4, 7, and 10, there are no significant standardized regression coefficients between BMI and parental behavior. In many cases these insignificant coefficients are also positive. Thus they are not even in a direction consistent with the idea that BMI disrupts parenting. This is true for mothers and fathers, and regardless of the gender of the child.

It might be the case, however, that these coefficients fail to detect a negative association between BMI and parenting because they assume a linear relationship between the two constructs. For example, African American parents may have a higher threshold for defining a child as overweight so that a child must approach extreme obesity before his or her weight has a disruptive effect on parenting. If this is the case, the relationship between BMI and quality of parenting would be curvilinear, with the inverse association between the two variables only becoming evident at very high levels of BMI.

To test this possibility, each of the parenting practices was regressed on BMI and BMI squared. The results of these regressions are presented in columns 2, 5, 8, and 11 of Table 3. The table shows that in almost every case the quadratic term is not significant for either African American fathers or mothers. The only exception is fathers' warmth towards African American daughters. In this case, however, the quadratic term is positive whereas a negative association would be expected if the disruptive effect of weight on parenting is most evident at higher levels of BMI. A positive quadratic term suggests that BMI is associated with greater warmth from fathers among the most obese girls in the sample. It is

Table 2.

Regression of Parenting of European Mothers and Fathers Upon Child's BMI.

						Daughters					
Sons											
				Mothers				Fathers			
Mothers			Fathers								
				1	**2**	**3**		**4**	**5**	**6**	**7**
8		**9**		**10**	**11**	**12**					
Monitoring											
BMI				-.134*	-.115*	-.158*		-.171*	-.192*	-.186*	-
.113*	-.114*			-.113*	-.143*	-.123*		-.142*			
SES				-.028	-.027	-.073		-.022	-.023	-.051	
.018				.018	.017		-.051	-.050	.044		
BMI²				—	-.036	—		—	.040	—	—
-	.003	—		—	-.049	—					
BMI x SES				—	—	-.109		—	—	-.069	—
	-	.004		—	—	.041					
Inductive Reasoning											
BMI				-.115*	-.118*	-.134*		-.100	-.129*	-.122*	-
.109*		-.128*	-.111*		-.114*	-.123*	-.115*				
SES				.025	.025	-.011		.144*	.143*	.102	
.066		.066	.056		.090	.090	.085				
BMI²				—	.006	—		—	-.054	—	—
-	.044	—		—	.022	—					
BMI x SES				—	—	-.086		—	—	-.100	—
-	—	.058		—	—	.033					
Warmth											
BMI				-.116*	-.153*	-.133*		-.124*	-.173*	-.147*	-.069
	-.106	-.070		-.140*	-.185*	-.141*					
SES				-.034	-.035	.065		.077	.075	.034	
.033		.032	.028		.048	.046	.046				
BMI²				—	.065	—		—	.091	—	
-	.088	—		—	.107	—					
BMI x SES				—	—	-.076		—	—	-.104	—
-	—	.027		—	—	.010					
Problem Solving											
BMI				-.175*	-.213*	-.191*		-.187*	-.235*	-.198*	-.069
	-.084	-.068		-.144*	-.179*	-.144*					
SES				-.045	-.047	-.075		.070	.068	.049	
.040		.040	.030		.031	.030	.027				
BMI²				—	-.070	—		—	.089	—	—
-	.042	—		—	.086	—					
BMI x SES				—	—	-.071		—	—	-.052	—
-	—	.060		—	—	.024					

* indicates significance at .05 levels

Table 3.

Regression of Parenting of African American Mothers and Fathers Upon Child's BMI.

					Daughters						
Sons											
				Mothers				Fathers			
Mothers			Fathers								
				1	**2**	**3**		**4**	**5**	**6**	**7**
8		**9**		**10**	**11**	**12**					
Monitoring											
BMI				-.022	-.058	-.021		-.113	-.040	-.115	-.100
.096				.102	-.036	-.023		-.020			
SES				-.091	-.089	.090		.186*	.187*	.145	.005
.008				.006		.250*	.047	.037			
BMI²				—	.059	—		—	-.148	—	—
-	.012	—		—	-.020	—					
BMI x SES				—	—	-.010		—	—	-.100	—
-	—	.009		—	—	.055					
Inductive Reasoning											
BMI				-.023	-.020	-.027		.084	.010	.088	-.029
	-.027	-.044		-.021	-.022	-.043					
SES				.016	.016	.021		.074	.073	.157	.041
.040		.037		.239*	.239*	.257*					
BMI²				—	-.005	—		—	.150	—	—
-	-.007	—		—	.002	—					
BMI x SES			—	—		.038	—	—	.	203*	—
-	—	-.062		—	—	-.076					
Warmth											
BMI				-.014	-.065	-.023		-.124	-.229*	-.119	.016
	.026	.011		-.022	-.018	.005					
SES				.051	.048	.061		098	.097	.189	
.023		.018	.021		.031	.029	.008				
BMI²				—	.084	—		—	.212*	—	
-	-.029	—		—	-.008	—					
BMI x SES				—	—	.085		—	—	.223*	—
-	—	-.022		—	—	.094					
Problem Solving											
BMI				-.001	-.018	-.007		-.054	-.055	-.052	.012
.033		.068		.1037	.051	.040					
SES				.035	.034	.043		.098	.098	.140	
.037		.026	.035		.113	.109	.11				
BMI²				—	.028	—		—	.002	—	—
-	-.058	—		—	.023	—					
BMI x SES			—	—	.066		—	—	.102		—
-	—	-.022		—	—	.010					

* indicates significance at .05 levels

interesting to note that the quadratic terms are also insignifi cant in the regressions for the European American mothers and fathers (see Table 2). Th is indicates that the association between BMI and quality of parenting for this group is linear, rather than being largely limited to parents of very heavy children.

In an eff ort to further explore the lack of eff ect among African American families, we considered whether the relationship between BMI and quality of parenting is moderated by social class. It may be that lower class persons are less infl uenced by the popular cultural emphasis upon being thin. Th e European American sample used in our analysis is largely working class, whereas the African American sample contains a large proportion of very disadvantaged families. Although there may not be an inverse relationship between BMI and quality of parenting for these low SES families, such a relationship may exist for the higher status families in our African American sample. To assess this possibility, we regressed each of the dimensions of parenting behavior upon BMI, family SES, and the interaction term formed by multiplying BMI and family SES. Table 3 shows that in every case BMI remains unrelated to parenting, and in only two instances (viz., fathers' monitoring of daughters and fathers' inductive reasoning with sons) is family SES related to parenting. More importantly, in only two cases—fathers' warmth towards daughters and fathers' inductive reasoning with daughters—is there an interaction between social class and BMI. In both cases, the interaction term is positive suggesting that African American fathers show the highest levels of warmth and inductive reasoning when they are of high SES with an obese daughter. Th us the table provides no support for the idea that BMI has a more disruptive eff ect upon African American parents as they enter the middle class. As can be seen in Table 2, there is also no evidence that social class moderates the association between BMI and parenting in the European American sample. In no case was the interaction of class and BMI signifi cant.

Th e results reported in Tables 2 and 3 suggest that BMI has a negative association with the parenting practices of European American parents, but that this eff ect is not evident for African American parents.

Figure 1. Structural Equation Model to be tested.

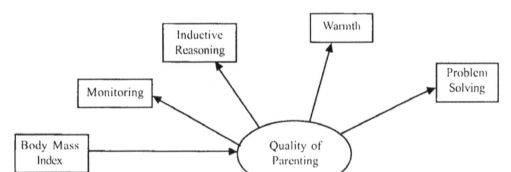

None of the associations between BMI and parental behavior is signifi cant for African American parents, whereas the eff ect for European American parents holds across a wide variety of parenting practices, regardless of the gender of the parent or child. Th e fi nal step in our analysis was to establish that the diff erences between European American and African American parents in the association between BMI and parenting are statistically signifi cant. Structural equation modeling (SEM) was used to perform this test. Th e model to be tested is depicted in Figure 1.

SEM allows one to use confi rmatory factor analysis with a set of correlated indicators to form a latent construct. For both European American and African American parents, the four measures of parenting were highly correlated. Th is allowed us to use the four measures as indicators of a latent construct that we labeled quality of parenting. Th e four parenting measures showed high loadings on this quality of parenting factor regardless of the parent's sex or ethnicity. Th e loadings ranged from .68 to .89 for warmth, from .75 to .87 for inductive reasoning, from .78 to .85 for problem solving, and from .43 to 58 for monitoring. We ran a series of SEM models to assess the association between child's body mass index and the latent construct quality of parenting. In every case the various fi t indices (e.g., chi square, CFI, IFI, etc.) indicated that the model provided a good fi t to the data. Table 4 shows the results obtained in these analyses. Th e coeffi cients are standardized.

Beginning with mothers' parenting of daughters, the table shows that the association between BMI and quality of parenting is statistically signifi cant (-.16) for European American mothers and statistically insignifi cant (-.02) for African American mothers. To test whether these coeffi cients were signifi cantly diff erent from one another, we compared the baseline model, in which these paths were constrained to be equal for the two groups of mothers, with the alternative model that allowed the paths to diff er. Th e diff erence in χ^2 between the baseline and the alternative model was 5.77. With one degree of freedom, this χ^2 has a p-value of .016, indicating that that there is a signifi cant diff erence in the magnitude of the association between BMI and quality of parenting for the two groups of mothers.

Table 4.

Results of Structural Equation Models Assessing the Association between Child's BMI and the Latent Construct Quality of Parenting.

Daughters				Sons			
Mothers		Fathers		Mothers		Fathers	
European American	African American	European American	African American	European American	African American	European American	African American
-.16*	-.02	-.09*	-.04	-.10*	-.02	-.16*	-.00

Next, the table shows the association for father of girls. Th e coeffi cient between BMI and quality of parenting is a statistically signifi cant -.19 for the European American fathers but an insignifi cant -.04 for the African American fathers. Th e diff erence in χ^2 between the baseline that constrained these two paths to be equal and the alternative that freed them to diff er was 7.30. With one degree of freedom, this change in χ^2 has a p-value of .007. Th us, there is a highly signifi cant diff erence between the coeffi cients for the two groups of fathers.

Turning to mothers of sons, the coeffi cient between BMI and quality of parenting is a statistically signifi cant -.10 for the European American mothers whereas the coeffi cient for African American mothers is an insignifi cant .02. Th e diff erence in χ^2 between the baseline model and the depicted model that freed them to diff er was 2.917. With one degree of freedom, this change in χ^2 only approaches signifi cance with a p-value of .0877. Finally, for fathers of boys there is a signifi cant coeffi cient of -.16 for European American fathers and an insignifi cant coeffi cient of .00 for the African American fathers. Freeing the paths to diff er produced an improvement in χ^2 of 4.024. With one degree of freedom, a χ^2 of this magnitude has a p-value of .045, indicating a signifi cant diff erence between the paths for the two groups of fathers. Th us the SEM analysis provided further support for our hypotheses.

DISCUSSION

Th is analysis examined a relatively under researched question in the literature on childhood obesity and parenting—the potential that a child's weight may infl uence the quality of parenting he or she receives. Past research has shown an association between child weight and family environment; these studies rarely addressed causal priority explicitly and typically assumed that the direction of infl uence moved from family interactions to child weight. We do not dispute the potential that such an association exists but, equally, we argue there are numerous reasons to expect children's weight status may infl uence the quality of the parenting they receive. In general, child characteristics have been shown to be a determinant of parenting behaviors. With respect to obesity in particular, parenting an overweight child may produce added stress for the parent, making effective parenting more difficult. This stress may be exacerbated if parents subscribe to stereotypical beliefs about obesity, which may contribute to a withdrawal of both attention and effort. Such withdrawal may be rooted in the parents' own discomfort with obesity. Alternatively, some parents' may withhold investments of emotional and social energy because they believe their overweight children have more limited life chances, reducing the potential return to be gained from effective parenting (Crandall 1991; Crandall 1995).

Establishing the causal direction of this relationship is difficult because both weight status and parenting tend to be quite stable across adolescence. As a result, cross-lagged models produce insignificant results. Ideally, establishing the causal priority of these relationships will require data collection that begins when children are relatively young. In the interim, we considered other arguments that would indicate the direction of this relationship. Specifically, if the predominant causal priority is from parenting to child's weight status, the association should hold for all cultural groups. Conversely, if the direction is from weight status to parenting behaviors, the results should be strongest among groups with the greatest sensitivity to weight stigma.

This is the approach we took in establishing evidence for the direction of this relationship. Specifically, we expected that European American parents would show a decline in the quality of parenting they provided to their overweight children while African American parents would show little or no effect. This pattern would be consistent with the more moderate and less stigmatizing attitudes towards weight found among African Americans relative to European Americans (Lovejoy 2001; Nichter 2000).

We assessed this argument using community based samples of European American and African American early adolescents and their parents. Both hypotheses were supported. Our analysis indicated a robust association between weight status and parenting behaviors for European Americans but not for African Americans. These results were largely consistent across all four measures of quality of parenting (warmth, monitoring, inductive reasoning, and problem solving) and among both mothers and fathers. Altogether, these findings support for the argument that at least some portion of the causal effect goes from child weight status to parenting behaviors.

The most consistent patterns of association were those between child BMI and parental monitoring and inductive reasoning. Warmth and problem solving showed slightly more complex relationships; there was no association between child BMI and either of these constructs among mothers of European American sons. In addition, after controlling for a curvilinear effect, African American fathers were warmer toward their heavier daughters. On balance, however, the results provide substantial support for the argument that parents do respond to their children's weight status and that this response can influence the quality of parenting they provide.

In making these assertions, we do not rule out the potential that parenting influences children's weight. However, we suspect that primary pathways for that direction of causality move through the food parents serve, their communication about food and eating, and the degree to which they encourage and model physical activity. Of course, all of these arenas provide opportunities for the application of both positive and negative parenting behaviors. Consequently, the effectiveness of parental communication about eating and weight may also be conditioned by the extent to which it occurs in a context of high or low quality parenting.

There are limitations to this analysis that leave substantial room for future work. First, the measures used to calculate BMI were self report rather than objective. While this does pose some concern, the risk to validity for this study is likely to be quite small (Elgar, Roberts, Tudor-Smith, and Moore 2005). It is also possible that parents' weight status may be influencing responses to child weight. Overweight parents, for example, may be more attuned to the difficulties their overweight children will experience and this too could influence the quality and focus of their parenting. A data set in which height and weight were available for parents as well as children would make it possible to assess this potential; however, neither the IYFP nor the FACHS have such data.

It should be noted that the two samples used in our analyses differed in ways other than race/ ethnicity. All of the European American families lived in Iowa, whereas half of the African American families resided in Iowa and half in Georgia. Further, although our African American sample contained a number of middle and upper middle class families, it also contained a significant proportion of very poor individuals. Th us median family income for the African American sample was lower than that for the European American sample, most of whom were working or middle class. However, there was no evidence of an association between child's BMI and quality of parenting for African American families whether they lived in Iowa or Georgia. For both European American and African American families the association between child's BMI and parenting did not vary by family socioeconomic status. Th us, it is unlikely that regional and income differences between the samples account for the ethnic differences that we found regarding the association between childhood obesity and parental behavior.

Finally, the data used in these analyses was collected close to a decade ago and so it is worth considering whether these associations are still present today. Rates of obesity are higher today than they were when these data were collected. As any characteristic or phenomenon becomes more common, it is reasonable to expect stigmatizing responses to decline and for greater acceptance to occur. However, there is little evidence this occurring with respect to obesity. Rather, a series of recent reviews suggest discrimination and stigma directed towards obese people in general remains high (Puhl and Brownell 2001; Puhl and Brownell 2006).

While there is little evidence that stigma directed toward obesity is abating, public attention to obesity as a social phenomena with significant economic and social consequences is on the rise (Stein and Colditz 2004). Given the high levels of attention accorded to obesity and widely publicized statements about an "obesity epidemic," it is possible that the gap between African American and European American parents has narrowed over time because recent public discussion has increased the salience of the issue among African American parents. One factor suggesting this may not be the case, however, is that African American children continue to demonstrate weaker relationships between body size and psychological distress (e.g., low self esteem) than do European American children (Swallen, Reither, Haas, and Meier 2005). Th is suggests that the gap may not be narrowing. As new longitudinal data become available, however, it will be important to assess both trajectories of parental concern and to test for evidence that attitudes towards weight may be converging across racial groups.

Th e argument that obese children may receive lower quality parenting is important to consider because of the well documented relationship between quality of parenting and a child's emotional and social adjustment. Regardless of their weight status, children who are parented effectively are both physically and emotionally healthier and are less likely to engage in extreme dieting behaviors or other forms of disordered eating (Golan and Weizman 2001; Maccoby and Martin 1983; Mellin et al., 2002). In addition, there is growing evidence that genetic, biological, and environmental factors outside parents' control contribute substantially to the development of childhood obesity and these weight trajectories tend to begin when children are quite young (Berkowitz and Stunkard 2002; Davison and Birch 2001; Dounchis, Hayden, and Wilfl ey 2001). All of these factors contribute to obesity's relative intractability, even among young children, decreasing the likelihood it can be effectively altered and increasing the importance of social support for overweight children coping with the effects of obesity stigma. Focusing on quality of parenting behavior may be one avenue through which the physical and emotional health of overweight children can be improved even if their body size is not substantially altered.

REFERENCES

Adams, C., Smith, N., Wilbur, D., & Grady, K. (1993). Th e relationship of obesity to the frequency of pelvic examinations: Do physician and patient attitudes make a diff erence. *Women and Health, 20,* 45–57.

Adams, K., Sargent, R. G., Th ompson, S. H., & Richter, D., Corwin, S. J., & Rogan, T. J. (2000) A study of body weight concerns and weight control practices of 4th and 7th grade adolescents. *Ethnicity and Health, 5,* 79–94.

Ambert, A. (2001). *Th e Eff ect of Children on Parents (2nd ed.).* Binghamton, NY: Haworth Press.

Archibald, A. B., Graber, J. A., & Brooks-Gunn, J. (1999). Associations among parent-adolescent relationships, pubertal growth, dieting, and body image in young adolescent girls: A short-term longitudinal study. *Journal of Research on Adolescence 9,* 395–415.

Archibald, A., Bastini, M., Linver, R., Graber, J. A., & Brooks-Gunn, J. (2002). Parent-adolescent relationships and girls' unhealthy eating: Testing reciprocal eff ects. *Journal of Research on Adolescence, 12,* 451–461.

Baskin, M. L., Ard, J., Franklin, F., & Allison, D. B. (2005). Prevalence of obesity in the United States. *Obesity Reviews, 6,* 5–7.

Belsky, J. (1984). Th e determinants of parenting: A process model. *Child Development, 55,* 83–96.

Benson, P. L., Severs, D., Tatgenhorst, J. & Loddengaard, N. (1980). Th e social costs of obesity: A non-reactive fi eld study. *Social Behavior and Personality, 8,* 91–96.

Berkowitz, R. I., & Stunkard, A. J. (2002). Development of childhood obesity. In T. A. Wadden and A. J. Stunkard, (Eds.), *Handbook of Obesity Treatment* (pp. 515–531). New York: Guilford.

Braet, C., Mervielde. I., & Vandereycken, W. (1997). Psychological aspects of childhood obesity: A controlled study in a clinical and non-clinical sample. *Journal of Pediatric Psychology, 22,* 59–71.

Brener, N., McManus, T., Galluska, D. A., Lowry, R., & Wechsler, W. (2003). Reliability and validity of self-reported height and weight among high school students. *Journal of Adolescent Health. 32,* 281–287.

Byely, L., Archibald, A.B., Graber, J.A., & Brooks-Gunn, J. (2000). A prospective study of familial and social infl uences on girls' body image and dieting. *International Journal of Eating Disorders. 28,* 155–164.

Cash, T. F., & Henry, P. E. (1995). Women's body images: Th e results of a national survey in the U.S.A. *Sex Roles, 33,* 19–28.

Centers for Disease Control and Prevention. (2004). *BMI—Body Mass Index: BMI for Adults.* Retrieved February 12, 2007 from Department of Health and Human Services Web site: *http://www.cdc.gov/nccdphp/dnpa/bmi/ bmi-adult-formula.html*

Cole, T. J., Bellizzi, M C., Flegal, K. M., & Dietz, W. H. (2000). Establishing a standard defi nition of child overweight and obesity worldwide: International survey. *British Medical Journal. 320,* 1240–1243.

Conger, R. D., Conger, K., Elder Jr., G. H., Lorenz, F. O., Simons, R. L. & Whitback, L B. (1992). A family process model of economic hardship and infl uences on adjustment of early adolescent boys. *Child Development, 63,* 526–541.

Conger, R.D., & Elder Jr., E. H. (1994). *Families in Troubled Times: Adapting to Change in Rural America.* New York: Aldine.

Conger, R.D., Wallace, L. E., Sun, Y., Simons, R. L., McLoyd, V. C., & Brody, G H. (2002). Economic pressure in African American families: A replication and extension of the Family Stress Model. *Developmental Psychology, 38,* 179–193.

Conger, R. D., & Conger, K. J. (2002). Resilience in midwestern families: Selected fi ndings from the fi rst decade of a prospective, longitudinal study. *Journal of Marriage and the Family, 64,* 361–373.

Conger, R. D., Cui, M., Bryant, C. M., & Elder Jr., G. H. 2000. Competence in early adult romantic relationships: A developmental perspective on family infl uence. *Journal of Personality and Social Psychology, 79,* 224–237.

Crago, M., Shisslak, C. M., & Estes, L. S. (1996). Eating disturbances among American minority groups: A review. *International Journal of Eating Disorders, 19,* 239–248.

Crandall, C. S. (1991). Do heavy-weight students have more diffi culty paying for college? *Personality and Social Psychology Bulletin, 17,* 606–611.

Crandall, C. S. (1995). Do parents discriminate against their heavyweight daughters? *Personality and Social Psychology Bulletin, 21,* 724–735.

Davison, K. K., & Birch, L. L. (2001). Childhood overweight: A contextual model and recommendations for future research. *Obesity Reviews, 2,* 159–171.

DeJong, W. (1980). Th e stigma of obesity: Th e consequences of naive assumptions concerning the causes of physical deviance. *Journal of Health and Social Behavior, 21,* 75–87.

DeJong, W. (1993). Obesity as a characterological stigma: Th e issue of responsibility and judgments of task performance. *Psychological Reports, 73,* 963–970.

DeJong, W. & Kleck, R. E. (1986). Th e social psychological eff ects of overweight. In M. P. Zanna and E. T. Higgins, (Eds.), *Physical Appearance, Stigma, and Social Behavior: Th e Ontario Symposium, Volume 3,* (pp. 65–87). Hillsdale, NJ: Lawrence Erlbaum.

Dounchis, J. Z., Hayden, H. A., & Wilfl ey, D. E. (2001). Obesity, body image, and eating disorders in ethnically diverse children and adolescents. In J. K. Th ompson and L. Smolak, (Eds.), *Body Image, Eating Disorders, and Obesity in Youth: Assessment, Prevention, and Treatment* (pp.67–98). Washington, D.C.: American Psychological Association.

Elgar, F. J., Roberts, C., Tudor-Smith, C., & Moore L. (2005). Validity of self-reported height and weight and predictors of bias in adolescents. *Journal of Adolescent Health, 37,* 371–375.

Favaro, A. & Santonastaso, P. (1995). Eff ects of parents' psychological characteristics and eating behavior on childhood obesity and dietary compliance. *Journal of Psychosomatic Research, 39,* 145–151.

Fields, J. (2001). Normal queers: Straight parents respond to their children's "coming out." *Symbolic Interaction, 24,* 165–187.

Fulkerson, J. A., McGuire, M. T., Neumark-Sztainer, D., Story, M., French, S. A., & Perry, C. L. (2002). Weightrelated attitudes and behaviors of adolescent boys and girls who are encouraged to diet by their mothers. *International Journal of Obesity, 26,* 1579–1587.

Garn, S., Sullivan, T., & Hawthorne, V. (1989). Educational level, fatness, and fatness diff erences between husbands and wives. *American Journal of Clinical Nutrition, 50,* 740–745.

Goff man, E. (1963). *Stigma: Notes on the Management of Spoiled Identity.* Englewood Cliff s, NJ: Prentice-Hall.

Golan, M., & Weizman, A. (2001). Familial approach to the treatment of childhood obesity: Conceptual model. *Journal of Nutrition Education, 33,* 102–107.

Gortmaker, S. L., Must, A., Perrin, J., Sobal, A., & Dietz, W. (1993). Social and economic consequences of overweight in adolescence and young adulthood. *New England Journal of Medicine, 329* 1008–1012.

Gray, M. R., & Steinberg, L. (1999). Unpacking authoritative parenting: Reassessing a multidimensional construct. *Journal of Marriage and Family, 61,* 574–587.

Green, S. E. (2003). "What do you mean 'what's wrong with her?'": stigma and the lives of families of children with disabilities. *Social Science and Medicine, 57,* 1361–1374.

Hodges, E. L., Cochrane, C. E., & Brewerton, T. D. (1998). Family characteristics of binge-eating disorder patients. *International Journal of Eating Disorders, 23,* 145–151.

Jones, E. E., Farina, A., Hastorf, A. H., Markus, H., & Miller, D. T. & Scott, R. A. (1984). *Social Stigma: Th e Psychology of Marked Relationships.* New York: W.H. Freeman and Companhy.

Kinston, W., Loader, P., & Miller, L. (1987). Emotional health of families and their members where a child is obese. *Journal of Psychosomatic Research, 31,* 583–600.

Kumanyika, S., Wilson, J. F., & Guilford-Davenport, M. (1993). Weight-related attitudes and behaviors of black women. *Journal of the American Dietetics Association. 93,* 416–422.

Link, B. G., & Phelan, J. C. (2001). Conceptualizing stigma. *Annual Review of Sociology, 27,* 363–385.

Lovejoy, M. (2001). Disturbances in the social body: Diff erences in body image and eating problems among African American and white women. *Gender and Society, 15,* 239–261.

Lytton, H. (1990). Child and parent eff ects in boys' conduct disorder: A reinterpretation. *Developmental Psychology, 26,* 683–697.

Maccoby, E. E., Martin J., & Musser, P. H. (1983). Socialization in the context of the family: Parent-child interactions. In E. M. Heatherington, (Ed.), *Handbook of Child Psychology, Vol. 4* (pp. 1–101). New York: Wiley.

Maccoby, E. E. (1992). Trends in the study of socialization: Is there a Lewinian heritage? *Journal of Social Issues. 48*, 171–185.

Mellin, A. E., Neumark-Sztainer, D., Story, M., Ireland, M., & Resnick, M. D. (2002). Unhealthy behaviors and psychosocial diffi culties among overweight adolescents: Th e potential impact of familial factors. *Journal of Adolescent Health, 31*, 145–153.

Mendelson, B. K., White, D. R., & Schliecker, E. (1995). Adolescents' weight, sex, and family functioning. *International Journal of Eating Disorders, 17,* 73–79.

National Center for Health Statistics. (2000). Clinical Growth Charts, Vol. 2005. edited by National Center for Chronic Disease Prevention and Health Promotion. Atlanta: Department of Health and Human Services.

Neumark-Sztainer, D., Story, M., & Faibisch, L. (1998). Perceived stigmatization among overweight AfricanAmerican and Caucasian adolescent girls. *Journal of Adolescent Health, 23,* 264–270.

Nichter, M. (2000). *Fat Talk: What Girls and Th eir Parents Sax about Dieting.* Cambridge. MA: Harvard UP.

Puhl, R. M., & Brownell, K. D. (2001). Bias, discrimination and obesity. *Obesity Research 9* 788–805.

Puhl, R. M. (2006). Confronting and coping with weight stigma: An investigation of overweight and obese adults. *Obesity, 14,* 1802–1815.

Renman, C., Engstrom, I., Silfverdal, S-A., & Aman, J. (1999). Mental health and psychosocial characteristics in adolescent obesity: A population-based case-control study. *Acta Paediatrica, 88,* 998–1003.

Ritchey, P. N., & Fishbein, H. D. (2001). Th e lack of an association between adolescent friends' prejudices and stereotypes. *Merrill-Palmer Quarterly, 47,* 188–206.

Rucker, C. E., & Cash, T. F. (1992). Body images, body size perceptions and eating behaviors among African American and white college women. *International Journal of Eating Disorders, 12,* 291–299.

Sampson, R. J., & Laub, J. H. (1993). *Crime in the making: Pathways and turning points through life.* Cambridge: Harvard University Press.

Schneider, J., & Conrad, P. (1983). *Having Epilepsy.* Philadelphia: Temple University Press.

Schoenborn, C. A., Adams, P. F., & Barnes, P. M. (2002). Body weight status of adults in the United States, 1997–1998. *Advance Data:* 1–15.

Schwartz, H. (1986). *Never Satisfi ed: A Cultural History of Diets, Fantasies and Fat.* New York: Free Press.

Siegel, J. M. (2002). Body image change and adolescent depressive symptoms. *Journal of Adolescent Research, 17,* 27–41.

Simons, R. L., Johnson, C., Conger, R. D., & Elder Jr., G H. (1998). A test of latent trait versus life course perspectives on the stability of adolescent antisocial behavior. *Criminologv, 36,* 217–243.

Simons, R. L. (1996). *Understanding diff erences between divorced and intact families: Stress, interaction, and child outcome.* Th ousand Oaks, CA: Sage.

Simons, R. L., Chao, W., Conger, R. D., & Elder Jr., G H. (2001). Quality of parenting as mediator of the eff ect of childhood defi ance on adolescent friendship choices and delinquency: A growth curve analysis. *Journal of Marriage and the Family, 63,* 63–79.

Simons, R. L., Lin, K.H., Gordon, L. C., Brody, G. H., Murry, V. M., & Conger, R. D. (2002a). Community diff erences in the association between parenting practices and child conduct problems. *Journal of Marriage and Family, 64,* 331–345.

Simons, R. L., Murry, V. M., McLoyd, V., Lin, K.H., Cutrona, C. E. & Conger, R. D. (2002b). Discrimination, crime, ethnic identity, and parenting as correlates of depressive symptoms among African American children: A multilevel analysis. *Development and Psychopathology, 14,* 371–393.

Smolak, L. & Levine, M. P. (2001). Body image in children. In J. K. Th ompson and L. Smolak. (Eds.), *Body Image, Eating Disorders, and Obesity in Youth: Assessment, Prevention, and Treatment* (pp. 41–66). Washington, D.C.: American Psychological Association.

Sobal, J., Nicolopoulos, V., & Lee, J. (1995). Attitudes about overweight and dating among secondary school students. *International Journal of Obesity and Related Metabolic Disorders, 19,* 376–381.

Stearns, P. (1999). *Fat History: Bodies and Beauty in the Modern West.* New York: New York University Press.

Stein, C. J., & Colditz, G. A. (2004). Th e epidemic of obesity. *Th e Journal of Clinical Endocrinology & Metabolism, 89,* 2522–2525.

Steinberg, A. B., & Phares, V. (2001). Family functioning, body image, and eating disturbances. In J. K. Th ompson and L. Smolak, (Eds.), *Body Image, Eating Disorders, and Obesity in Youth: Assessment, Prevention, and Treatment* (pp. 127–147). Washington, DC: American Psychological Association.

Swallen, K. C., Reither, E. N., Haas, S., & Meier, A. M. (2005). Overweight, Obesity, and Health-Related Quality of Life Among Adolescents: Th e National Longitudinal Study of Adolescent Health. *Pediatrics, 115,* 340–347.

Th ompson, S. H., Sargent, R. G., & Kemper, K. (1996). Black and white adolescent males' perceptions of ideal body size. *Sex Roles: A Journal of Research, 34,* 391–406.

Vincent, M. A., & McCabe, M. P. (2000). Gender diff erences among adolescents in family, and peer infl uences on body dissatisfaction, weight loss, and binge eating behaviors. *Journal of Youth and Adolescence, 29,* 205–221.

Vondra, J., & Belsky, J. (1989). Infant play at one year: Characteristics and early antecedents. In J. J. Lockman and N. L. Hazen, (Eds.), *Action in social context: Perspectives on early development* (pp. 173–206). New York, NY: Plenum Press.

Racial and Ethnic-Related Stressors as Predictors of Perceived Stress and Academic Performance for African American Students at a Historically Black College and University

Tawanda M. Greer

Th e purpose of this investigation was to determine whether racial and ethnic-related stressors were associated with overall levels of perceived stress and academic performance among African American students at a historically Black college and university (HBCU). Hierarchical regression analyses were used to test racial and ethnic-related stressors and background variables as predictors of general levels of perceived stress and academic performance (i.e., grade point average). Th e results of the regression analyses revealed that gender, age, and Scholastic Aptitude Test (SAT) scores were signifi cant predictors of perceived stress. However, racial and ethnic-related stressors were the strongest predictors of perceived stress, over and above gender, age, and SAT scores. In predicting academic performance, SAT scores were the only signifi cant predictors, while racial and ethnic-related stressors were not signifi cant predictors of this outcome. Implications of these fi ndings and suggestions for future research are discussed.

Colleges and universities across the U.S. continue to experience increased diversity as a result of larger enrollments of racial and ethnic minority students (National Center for Education Statistics, 2003). Although the numbers of racial and ethnic minorities enrolling in college has increased over the years, considerable research attention has been given to the plight of African Americans in higher education (see Allen, 1992; D'Augelli & Hershberger, 1993; Fleming, 1984). Existing literature suggested that the attainment of a college degree for African Americans is replete with various fi nancial, social, emotional, and psychological challenges. In particular, it has been demonstrated that the college adjustment and academic outcomes of African American students are, at least, in part, associated with whether they attend a predominantly White college and university (PWCU) or an HBCU (Allen, 1992; Fleming, 1984; Greer & Chwalisz, 2007).

Tawanda M. Greer, "Racial and Ethnic-related Stressors as Predictors of Perceived Stress and Academic Performance for African American Students at a Historically Black College and University," *Th e Journal of Negro Education*, vol. 77, no. 1, pp. 60–71. Copyright © 2008 by Howard University. Reprinted with permission. Provided by ProQuest LLC. All rights reserved.

Psychosocial and Academic Outcomes at PWCUs and HBCUs

Most studies on academic and psychosocial outcomes for African American college students have been comparative in nature, in which differences in outcomes at HBCUs and PWCUs have been investigated (see Allen, 1992; Cokley, 2000; Fleming, 1984; Greer & Chwalisz, 2007). Regarding academic achievement, cognitive factors and issues associated with readiness for college have been proven to yield some infl uences on academic outcomes for African American students at both types of universities (Fleming & Garcia, 1998). However, non-cognitive factors such as campus racial climate, quality of student–faculty relationships, and peer relationships have been shown to disproportionately impact the college adjustment of African Americans attending PWCUs (Allen, 1992; Fleming, 1984; Greer & Chwalisz, 2007). Studies consistently showed that African American students at PWCUs report experiences of racism and discrimination in their interactions with White peers, faculty, and staff (Feagin, Vera, & Imani, 1996). Other commonly reported experiences at these institutions include feelings of isolation, lack of racial and ethnic representation among peers and faculty members, low social support, and lack of mentoring (Fries-Britt & Turner, 2001). Not surprisingly, the results of several research investigations revealed poor academic and psychosocial outcomes for many African American students attending PWCUs (Allen, 1992; Fleming, 1984; Prillerman, Myers, & Smedley, 1989; Smedley, Myers, & Harrell, 1993).

In contrast, African American students at HBCUs have been found to feel more accepted and supported in their academic pursuits, and are heavily involved in campus social activities compared to their counterparts at PWCUs (Allen, 1992; Fleming, 1984). Th ese students also displayed high levels of academic achievement (Greer & Chwalisz, 2007), with some researchers attributing these outcomes to positive student-faculty relationships and mentoring on HBCU campuses (Fleming, 1984). However, while a large volume of research has been conducted on factors aff ecting the psychosocial and academic development of African American students at PWCUs, insuffi cient empirical attention has been given to understanding these issues among African American students at HBCUs. Perhaps one underlying reason for this dearth in literature might be African American students at HBCUs have generally been included in research studies as mere comparisons to their counterparts at PWCUs, with little purpose to derive contextual understandings of their unique challenges faced within their HBCU environments. As a result, limited information exists in literature regarding the myriad of factors that contribute to their overall college outcomes at these institutions.

Stressful Experiences at HBCUs and PWCUs

Several factors have been linked to diff erential outcomes for African American students at PWCUs and HBCUs. Among these factors, persistent experiences of stress have been found to contribute to poor college adjustment and to academic outcomes for students at both types of institutions (Fleming, 1981; Greer & Chwalisz, 2007). While a number of theories exist regarding the concept of stress, Lazarus and Folkman's (1984) transactional theory is perhaps the most widely used theory of stress processes. In the transactional theory, it is postulated that stress is the product of transactions occurring between the person and the environment which are appraised by individuals as a threat to well-being, or as exceeding available resources to eff ectively address problems (Lazarus & Folkman, 1984). Th erefore, a poor fi t between the person and the environment is likely to produce high levels of stress. In applying this conceptualization of stress to African American students, students at PWCUs should be more susceptible to high levels of distress than their counterparts at HBCUs, given that PWCU campus environments have demonstrated to be replete with forms of racial hostility (Feagin, Vera, & Imani, 1996; Greer, 2003). However, the few studies that have been conducted in which the stress levels of African American students at both types of universities were compared have yielded mixed results. For instance, Greer and Chwalisz (2007) found no signifi cant diff erences in overall levels of perceived stress for African American students attending a PWCU and an HBCU. Similar fi ndings have been reported in another study (Fleming, 1981). Still another study reported diff erent fi ndings, with African American students at HBCUs displaying higher levels of positive stress compared to their PWCU counterparts (Nottingham, Rosen, & Parks, 1992).

In spite of inconsistent results regarding global stress levels, existing literature revealed some diff erences in the types of stress experienced that are uniquely associated with whether one attends an HBCU or a PWCU. For example, Nottingham and colleagues (1992) reported signifi cant diff erences in the types of stress experienced among African American students at an HBCU and a PWCU, with students at the PWCU reporting stress associated with experiences such as racism and few dating opportunities. Conversely, students at the HBCU reported stressful experiences associated with environmental concerns, such as poor living conditions and facilities (Nottingham, Rosen, & Parks, 1992). Similarly, Watkins, Guidry, Green, Stanley, and Goodson (2007), in a qualitative investigation of stressful life events of African American male college students, reported that African American men at a PWCU commonly discussed stressful experiences associated with their race and ethnicity (e.g., cultural confl ict, mistrust of the university, racial discrimination). In contrast, African American men at the HBCU in this study commonly discussed stress associated with lack of resources for advancement and the African American male image in society (Watkins, Guidry, Green, Stanley, & Goodson, 2007). Similar results have been reported in other investigations on stress and African American college students (Greer, 2003; Greer & Chwalisz, 2007). Overall, the results of these studies imply that the sources of stress for African American students at HBCUs are not overwhelmingly associated with racial and ethnic-related diffi culties within their campus environments, unlike their counterparts on PWCU campuses.

Th e diffi culties experienced by African American students at PWCUs have been conceptualized as emanating largely from their social positions as minorities in these environments. Minority status has been deemed a unique source of stress for African American students at PWCUs (Prillerman, Myers, & Smedley, 1989). Minority status stress is broadly conceptualized as chronic exposure to diffi culties that are associated with racial and ethnic group membership, especially within predominantly White environments (Smedley, Myers, & Harrell, 1993). Among African American students at PWCUs, such stressors included being the only African American student in a classroom, having few African American professors on campus, having few courses refl ecting one's racial and cultural heritage, as well as experiencing racial discrimination (Prillerman, Myers, & Smedley, 1989). Minority status stressors also included intragroup confl icts, such as feeling pressure to show loyalty to one's racial and ethnic group (Prillerman, Myers, & Smedley, 1989). As noted by Prillerman and colleagues, African American students at PWCUs contended with broad sources of stress, comprising general college pressures (e.g., studying) and stressors associated with minority status. Th ese sources of stress collectively posed tremendous challenges to college adjustment and academic success for African American students at PWCUs.

African American students at HBCUs generally comprised the numerical majority in enrollment at these institutions. Perhaps it is for this reason that negative racial and ethnic-related experiences on HBCU campuses have not been widely investigated among this population of students. HBCU campuses have consistently been proven in research studies to be supportive environments in which many African American students experience positive outcomes (Allen, 1992; Davis, 1995; Greer, 2003). However, the supportive atmosphere of HBCU environments does not inherently imply little or no exposure to racerelated diffi culties for African American students on these campuses. It is quite possible that, in ways similar to their PWCU counterparts, African American students at HBCUs experience some degree of racial and ethnic-related stressors that also contribute to their overall experience of stress and other college outcomes.

However, this author could not locate any published research investigations in which racial and ethnic-related diffi culties were investigated among African American students at HBCUs. Th is gap in literature evokes the question of whether African American students at HBCUs are truly not exposed to racial diffi culties and confl ict on their campuses, or whether they are exposed to such, however, researchers generally have failed to focus on these issues among this population of college students?

Th e purpose of the current investigation was to determine whether experiences of racial and ethnicrelated stressors predict overall levels of perceived stress and academic performance among a sample of African American students at an HBCU. Since, to this author's knowledge, no other research studies have been conducted to examine these specifi c issues, this research study was exploratory in nature. Guided, in part, by research evidence from studies conducted with African American students at PWCUs, it was anticipated that racial and ethnic-related stressors would signifi cantly predict overall levels of perceived stress, and yield signifi cant, negative impacts on academic performance (i.e., grade point average). Furthermore, gender and other background variables (e.g., age, college entrance examination scores, educational class status, and college aspirations) were also considered given previous research fi ndings which suggest that these variables were associated with perceptions of stress and academic outcomes for African American college students (Baldwin, Chambliss, & Towler, 2003; Fleming, 1981). In essence, there were two primary research questions to be answered through the current investigation: (a) do racial and ethnic-related stressors predict overall levels of perceived stress for African American students at an HBCU?, and (b) do racial and ethnic-related stressors predict academic performance among this sample of college students?

Method

Participants

Th e participants for this study consisted of 102 self-identifi ed African American college students from an HBCU located in the northeastern U.S. Participants were recruited from courses in introductory psychology, African American studies, and honors courses in English. Students in honors courses were required to maintain a grade point average of 3.0 on a 4.0 scale at this institution. Th erefore, some students in honors courses were included in order to facilitate an adequate representation of the full range of grade point averages in the sample. Of the 102 participants in the sample, 72 were female (70%) and 30 were male (30%). Th e representation of undergraduate class levels was relatively equal in this sample and consisted of freshmen (29%), sophomores (28%), juniors (19%), and seniors (24%).

Materials

General Perceived Stress. Th e Perceived Stress Scale (PSS; Cohen, Kamarck, & Mermelstein, 1983) was used to measure participant subjective appraisal of experiences of stress. Th e PSS is a 14-item scale which captures the extent to which individuals globally appraise their lives stressful. Th e items are answered in Likert-type format, with response options ranging from zero to four (never to very oft en). Respondents are asked to indicate the degree to which they perceive themselves as having experienced stress in the past month. Scores are obtained by reverse scoring positively worded items and then adding across all items to produce a total sum score. For this study, respondents were asked to consider their experiences of stress in academic pursuits as well as in their interactions with others in the campus environment. Th e original sample for the PSS was comprised largely of White European Americans (85.5%), with 7.8% of African Americans in the sample (Cohen & Williamson, 1988). Psychometric properties of the PSS were gathered from a smoking cessation sample and samples of college students (Cohen, Kamarck, & Mermelstein, 1983). Cronbach's alpha (a) reliabilities for each administration ranged from .84 to .86 (Cohen, Kamarck, & Mermelstein, 1983). Th e obtained Cronbach's a coeffi cient for the PSS in the current study was .75.

Racial and Ethnic-Related Stress. Th e Minority Student Stress Scale (MSS; Prillerman, Myers, Smedley, 1989; Smedley, Myers, Harrell, 1993) was used to assess racial and ethnic-related stressors experienced in the campus environment. Although the participants in this study represented the numerical majority in terms of race and ethnicity at their institution, minority status stress is a broad construct that encompasses both unique stressors associated with racial and ethnic group membership (e.g., racial discrimination), and also general college stressors that are exacerbated by one's racial and ethnic group membership (e.g., being the fi rst in one's family to attend college). Th erefore, this measure was deemed appropriate to capture racial and ethnic-related stressors for the participants in this study. Th e MSS is a 37-item questionnaire designed to measure fi ve areas of stress that students experience and attribute to their racial and ethnic background. Smedley, Myers, and Harrell (1993) and Prillerman and colleagues (1989) reported using the principal components factor analytic procedure to derive fi ve factors. Th ese factors representing accounted for 53% of variance. Th e measure consisted of fi ve subscales: (a) environmental stressors associated with campus climate (e.g., few faculty and peers of one's racial and ethnic group), (b) interracial stressors such as managing relationships both within and outside of one's racial and ethnic group, (c) intragroup stressors such as racial and ethnic group conformity, (d) racism and discrimination stressors (e.g., overt and subtle forms of racism-related experiences), and (e) achievement-related stressors (e.g., uncertainty about one's college achievement). MSS items are answered on a six point Likert scale, ranging from zero "does not apply" to fi ve "extremely stressful for me" (Prillerman, Myers, & Smedley, 1989; Smedley, Myers, & Harrell, 1993). Th e MSS is scored by summing across items for each subscale. Th e two research groups also reported adequate internal consistency for the MSS, with Cronbach's a reliabilities for each subscale ranging from .76 to .93. Cronbach's a coeffi cients for the environmental, interracial, intragroup, racism and discrimination, and achievementrelated subscales for the current study were .78, .84, .70, .70, and .77, respectively.

Demographic Information. A demographic questionnaire was created for this study. Information gathered included age, gender, educational class level, SAT scores, cumulative grade point average, and educational aspirations. SAT scores and cumulative grade point averages were gathered from self-report only, as some evidence suggests that African American college students are generally accurate in reporting such information (Greer & Chwalisz, 2007).

Procedure

Th e instruments were administered to participants in psychology research laboratories or in classroom settings. All measures were completed by participants anonymously. Participants received informed consent and were advised of their right to withdraw from the study situation without penalty. Most participants received course credit or research credit for their participation in the study. In cases in which participants did not receive course credit or research credit, their names were entered into a lottery to receive monetary compensation. Th e instruments were administered using a paper-pencil format, with an average completion time of 17 minutes.

Results

Descriptive Analyses

Th e mean age for participants in this study was 21.50, with a standard deviation of 4.9. Th e mean for college aspirations (M = 2.69, SD = 1.21) indicated that participants generally aspired to achieve a professional college degree at the Master's level. Th e mean class status for this sample was at the sophomore level (M = 2.37, SD = 1.13). Chi-square analyses were used to determine whether any potential gender diff erences existed among the participants in terms of educational class status and college aspirations. However, these analyses did not reveal any signifi cant gender diff erences for these variables. A t test also did not reveal any signifi cant gender diff erence in age for the participants.

Means and standard deviations of participant scores for the SAT, grade point average, perceived stress, and minority status stress are displayed in Table 1. Th e cumulative grade point averages for this sample ranged from 1.30 to 3.85 (M= 3.07, SD = .53). Th e mean for participant SAT scores was 900, with a standard deviation of 250. Multivariate analysis of variance (MANOVA) was used to test for the eff ect of gender on SAT scores and cumulative grade point average. Th e overall F value for the eff ect of gender on SAT scores and grade point average was insignifi cant. However, follow-up univariate tests showed that the participants signifi cantly diff ered by gender in regards to grade point average, F (1,100) = 3.76, p < .05, with women yielding a higher mean grade point average (M= 3.13, SD = .54) than men (M= 2.97, SD = .48).

Regarding stress levels, the participants reported experiencing a moderate level of perceived stress (M= 26.76, SD = 6.99), in addition to relatively mild levels of minority status stressors. Th e highest subscale means for minority status stress were seen for interracial (M= 9.10, SD 4.85) and environmental stressors (M= 9.14, SD = 5.61). MANOVA was used to test for the eff ect of gender for all minority status stress subscales. Th e overall F value for this analysis was not signifi cant, nor did follow-up univariate tests demonstrate any signifi cant eff ect for gender on minority status stress subscales. A t test was used to determine any gender diff erences in mean scores for the perceived stress measure. Th e t value was signifi cant, t = 2.01, p < .05, with women yielding a slightly higher mean perceived stress score (M = 28.01, SD = 6.92) than men (M= 25.07, SD = 6.87).

Table 1

Means and Standard Deviations for Minority Status Stressors, Perceived Stress, Grade Point Average[a], and SAT[b] scores (N = 102)

Variable	M (SD)
Perceived stress	26.76 (6.99)
Minority status stressors	
Environmental stressors	9.14 (5.61)
Racism/discrimination stressors	7.37 (4.63)
Intragroup stressors	7.14 (3.85)
Achievement-related stressors	7.75 (4.04)
Interracial stressors	9.10 (4.85)
Grade point average	3.07 (.53)
SAT scores	900 (250)

Note. [a]Self-reported cumulative grade point average; [b]Self-reported SAT scores.

Pearson's *r* correlations were performed on all variables for this study (see Table 2). Most notable were the moderate correlations seen among all of the minority status stress scales, with the highest correlation occurring between the interracial and intragroup subscales (r = .51). Perceived stress scores were positively correlated with all minority status stress subscales, with the exception of the racism and discrimination subscale of the MSS. Th ese correlations suggest that aspects of minority status stress are positively related to one's overall subjective appraisal of stress. Also, signifi cant, positive correlations were found between perceived stress and gender (r = .19), and with perceived stress and SAT scores (r = .26). A signifi cant, inverse relationship was seen between perceived stress and age (r = -.32). Th ese correlations were relatively low; however, they indicate that perhaps background variables or characteristics of individuals are also associated with subjective appraisal of stress.

Regression Analyses

Hierarchical regression analyses were conducted to determine whether minority status stressors would predict perceived stress and academic performance (i.e., grade point average), aft er accounting for the eff ects of all background variables. Prior to conducting the regression analyses, MSS subscales were composited to produce a total sum score, given previous fi ndings of high correlations among the subscales, and the potential threat of multicollinearity of these scales in regression analyses (Greer & Chwalisz, 2007). In addition, some background variables were recoded prior to inclusion in the analyses. Specifi cally, the variable gender was dummy coded (i.e., coded values as zero and 1), with males as the reference category. Th e background variables of educational class level and educational aspirations were eff ect-coded (i.e., values coded as -1 and 1) to allow for a comparison of underclassmen (i.e., freshmen and sophomores) and upperclassmen (i.e., juniors and seniors) students on outcome variables, and to allow for a comparison of those aspiring to achieve a college degree and those desiring to achieve a professional degree. Th e reference categories for educational aspirations and educational class level variables were those aspiring to achieve a professional degree and underclass students, respectively.

In the regression analyses, gender was entered fi rst, followed by age, SAT scores, college aspirations, and educational class level on the second step, and then, the minority status stress total score on the third step. One person was dropped from these analyses due to consistently missing data on some variables. A total of 1% of missing data existed for this sample aft er dropping the one participant. Th ese data were replaced with the overall mean for specifi c variables given the small amount of missing data. Th e results of the regression analyses are displayed in Table 3.

As can be seen in Table 3, gender was a signifi cant predictor of perceived stress, F (1,99) = 3.51, $p <$ .05, however, this variable accounted for only 4% of variance (R^2 = .04). Nonetheless, this result confi rmed that female participants experienced a signifi cantly higher level of perceived stress than their male counterparts. Th e inclusion of the other background variables on the second step increased the amount of variance accounted for in perceived stress at 18% (R^2 = .18), F (5,95) = 4.25, $p <$ .01. Both age (β = -.20) and SAT scores (β = .21) were signifi cant background predictors. Th e entry of minority status stress on the third step indicated that this variable was the strongest predictor of perceived stress, over and above background variables, (β = .32), F (6,94) = 6.09, $p <$ .001, and accounted for 28% of variance (R^2 = .28). In predicting academic performance, none of the background variables of gender, age, educational class level, or college aspirations were signifi cant. Minority status stress also did not signifi cantly predict this outcome. Participant scores on the SAT were the only signifi cant predictors of academic performance (β = .25), F (5, 95) = 2.86, $p <$ .05, and accounted for 13% of variance in grade point average (R^2 = . 13).

Table 2

Intercorrelations for Age, Educational Class Level, College Aspirations, Perceived Stress, Minority Status Stressors, Grade Point Average[a] and SAT[b] Scores (N = 102)

	1	2	3	4	5	6	7	8	9	10	11
1. Age	—	.46**	.14	-.32**	-.16	-.06	-.09	-.11	-.16	-.07	.17
2. Educational class level		—	.04	-.14	-.10	-.04	-.09	-.11	-.16	-.07	.17
3. Aspirations			—	-.10	-.14	-.03	.04	.01	.09	.01	.13
4. Perceived stress				—	.24*	.06	.41**	.31**	.36**	.26**	-.07
5. Environmental stressors					—	.50**	.43**	.40**	.30**	-.06	-.06
6. Racism/discrimination						—	.40**	.50**	.31**	.01	-.17
7. Intragroup stressors							—	.51**	.43**	.16	-.06
8. Interracial stressors								—	.41**	.19	-.10
9. Achievement stressors									—	.08	-.11
10. SAT scores										—	.20
11. Grade point average											—

Note. [a]Self-reported cumulative grade point averages; [b]Self-reported SAT scores; * $p < .05$, ** $p < .01$

Table 3

Summary of Hierarchical Regression Analyses Predicting Perceived Stress and Academic Performance[a] from Gender, Age, SAT Scores[b], College Aspirations, Educational Class Level, and Minority Status Stress[c] (N = 101)

Step	Variables Entered	β	R^2	ΔR^2	F	df	Significance of F
Predicting Perceived Stress							
1	Gender	.18*	.04	.03	3.51	1, 99	.051
2	Age	-.19*	.18	.14	4.25	5, 95	.002
	SAT scores	.21*					
	College aspirations	.04					
	Educational class level	-.03					
3	Minority status stress	.32**	.28	.10	6.09	6, 94	.000
Predicting Academic Performance							
1	Gender	.15	.03	.02	2.76	1, 99	.100
2	Age	.11	.13	.10	2.86	5, 95	.019
	SAT scores	.25*					
	College aspirations	-.09					
	Educational class level	.16					
3	Minority status stress	-.13	.15	.02	2.69	6, 94	.019

Note. [a]Self-reported cumulative grade point average; [b]Self-reported SAT scores; [c]Total sum score for minority status stress; *$p < .05$, **$p < .001$.

Discussion

Th e purpose of the current investigation was to determine whether racial and ethnic-related stressors predicted overall levels of perceived stress and academic performance among a sample of African American students at an HBCU. Hierarchical regression analyses revealed that gender, age, and SAT scores were signifi cant predictors of overall levels of perceived stress. However, racial and ethnic-related stressors were the strongest predictors of perceived stress, over and above gender, age, and SAT scores. Additionally, in predicting academic performance, SAT scores were signifi cant, and racial and ethnicrelated stressors were insignifi cant. Th e fi ndings hold implications for college personnel working with African American students at HBCUs, and for future research investigations with this population of college students.

Initial descriptive analyses indicated that the participants in this study reported experiencing a variety of racial and ethnic-related stressors, with the highest subscale means on the MSS seen for problems with campus climate, as well as with interracial relationships. No signifi cant gender diff erences were found regarding experiences of racial and ethnic-related stressors for this sample. However, the fact that students in this study perceived themselves as experiencing diffi culties associated with race and ethnicity within their HBCU environment is an important fi nding, given that, as previously mentioned, most research investigations on African American students have failed to focus on these issues among students at HBCUs.

Th e students in the current investigation reported relatively low levels of racial and ethnic-related stressors. However, in spite of their low levels of racial and ethnic-related stress, these stressors were found to contribute to the students' global level of perceived stress. Th is fi nding is of particular importance since it implies that African American students at HBCUs are not only experiencing racial and ethnic-related struggles in their campus environments, but that also these diffi culties may pose challenges to their mental health and well-being.

Although racial and ethnic-related stressors were the strongest predictors of perceived stress for this sample, some background variables were also signifi cant. Age was a signifi cant predictor of perceived stress. Th ere was an inverse direction of this relationship which suggests that students may manage stress eff ectively as they increase in age. Most notable was the fi nding that SAT scores signifi cantly predicted perceived stress. Th is result suggested an important relationship between cognitive test scores and mental health. Previous research investigations in which cognitive test scores of African Americans and White Americans were compared generally suggest that African Americans score lower than their White counterparts (Jensen, 1980). Stereotype threat has been pinpointed as one among many factors contributing to the gap in cognitive test scores between White Americans and African Americans (Steele & Aronson, 1995). Stereotype threat refers to the fear of fulfi lling existing negative stereotypes associated with one's race, and thereby contributing to anxiety and poor performance on cognitive tests (e.g., Steele & Aronson, 1995). Th e issue of stereotype threat was not explored, however, the direction of the relationship between SAT scores and perceived stress in this study was positive, and therefore revealed perhaps an additional function of stereotype threat. In other words, this particular fi nding suggests that students with favorable scores on cognitive tests such as the SAT are predisposed to high levels of stress in college, which may be associated with undue pressure to succeed. Similar fi ndings regarding the relationship between college entrance examination scores and stress were reported by Greer and Chwalisz (2007). Such results suggest that additional investigations are necessary to determine the degree to which scores on college entrance examinations are associated with self-worth and other aspects of mental health for African American students.

Gender was also a signifi cant predictor of perceived stress, which indicated that female participants in this study experienced higher levels of stress than their male counterparts. In general, African American females yield higher rates of degree completion than their same-race male counterparts at HBCUs and PWCUs (National Center for Education Statistics, 2003; 2004). However, in spite of high academic achievement, African American women in college are faced with obstacles that are linked to the intersections of racism, sexism, heterosexism, and classism in their campus environments (Bonner, 2002). For instance, it has been reported that many African American females experience anxiety in competitive situations, and may also make eff orts to appear less intellectually competent in interactions with their male counterparts on HBCU campuses (Allan, Epps, & Haniff, 1989; Fleming, 1984). Some research evidence suggested that African American women are making great gains in social engagement on HBCU campuses (Harper, Carini, Bridges, & Hayek, 2004), however, the results of the current study suggest that African American women are in need of continued mentoring and support on these campuses.

SAT scores were demonstrated to be the strongest predictors of cumulative grade point average for this sample. Th is fi nding suggests that African American students at HBCUs may engage in coping strategies to manage the stress that they experience. Eff ective coping eff orts may enable African American students to continue to strive for academic excellence in spite of encountering negative racial and ethnic-related experiences on campus.

Implications

Th e results of this study imply that additional eff orts are needed within HBCU environments to enhance cultural sensitivity among students, faculty, and staff . Specifi cally, college personnel should engage in eff orts to create educational opportunities in which students are constantly engaged in activities and intellectual growth regarding multiculturalism and diversity. Such eff orts should involve opportunities for students, faculty, and staff to challenge their own biases and assumptions about individuals both within and outside of their own racial and ethnic group. Th e need for HBCUs to embark on additional eff orts to improve diversity awareness is imminent given the increasing number of White American undergraduate students enrolling at institutions, which undoubtedly poses challenges to race relations on HBCU campuses (Greer, 2003). In spite of the increase in racial and ethnic diversity among students enrolling at HBCUs, African Americans still represent the majority of the student body at many schools; however, this does not inherently imply that students appreciate or value diff erences in cultural identities and lifestyles. Th erefore, it is further recommended that the implementation of diversity-related programs and courses incorporate the intersectionality of identities (e.g., race, class, gender, and sexuality) to enhance awareness of cultural similarities and diff erences among students and personnel at HBCUs.

Limitations

Two primary limitations should be considered when interpreting the results of this study. Firstly, the sample for this investigation was comprised of African American students from only one HBCU, located in the northeastern region of the U.S. It is possible that African American students' experiences of racial and ethnic stressors vary by the HBCU institution and the geographic location of the institution. Future research on this topic should include samples of African American students from several HBCUs to determine whether the same or similar results would be found. Secondly, the use of a composite score for the MSS, as opposed to using the fi ve subscales, limited the data analyses in that the predictive value of each subscale could not be tested.

Conclusion

HBCU campuses, like all college campuses, are social microcosms in which the values of the larger society, including the biases and prejudices, are refl ected among students, faculty, and staff . Th is study highlighted the general racial and ethnic-related diffi culties experienced by African American students at HBCUs. College personnel and future research studies should focus on underlying reasons associated with these diffi culties. Doing so will likely improve the college life and overall well-being of students on HBCU campuses.

References

Allen, W. R. (1992). Th e color of success: African American college student outcomes at predominantly White and historically Black public colleges and universities. *Harvard Educational Review, 62*, 26-44.

Allen, W. R., Epps, E. G., & Haniff , N. Z. (1989). Determining Black student academic performance in U.S. higher education: Institutional versus interpersonal eff ects. *International Perspectives on Education and Society, 1*, 115-136.

Baldwin, D. R., Chambliss, L. N., & Towler, K. (2003). Optimism and stress: An African-American college student perspective. *College Student Journal, 37*, 276-285.

Bonner, F. B. (2002). Addressing gender issues in the historically Black college and university community: A challenge and call to action. *Th e Journal of Negro Education, 70*, 176-191.

Cohen, S., Kamarck, T., & Mermelstein, R. (1983). A global measure of perceived stress. *Journal of Health and Social Behavior, 24*, 385-396.

Cohen, S., & Williamson, G. M. (1988). Perceived stress in a probability sample of the United States. In S. Spacapan & S. Oskamp (Eds.), *Th e social psychology of health*, (pp. 31-67). Newbury Park: Sage.

Cokley, K. (2000). An investigation of academic self-concept and its relationship to academic achievement in African American college students. *Journal of Black Psychology, 26*, 148- 164.

Davis, J. E. (1995). College in Black and White: Campus environment and academic achievement for African American males. *Th e Journal of Negro Education, 63*, 620-633.

D'Augelli, A. R., & Hershberger, S. L. (1993). African American undergraduates on a predominantly White campus: Academic factors, social networks, and campus climate. *Th e Journal of Negro Education, 62*, 67-81.

Feagin, J. R., Vera, H., & Imani, N. (1996). *Th e agony of education: Black students at White colleges and universities.* New York: Routledge.

Fleming, J., & Garcia, N. (1998). Are standardized tests fair to African Americans? Predictive validity of the SAT in Black and White institutions. *Th e Journal of Higher Education, 69*, 471-495.

Fleming, J. (1981). Stress and satisfaction in college years of Black students. *Th e Journal of Negro Education, 50*, 307-318.

Fleming, J. (1984). *Blacks in college.* San Francisco: Jossey-Bass.

Fries-Britt, S. L., & Turner, B. (2001). Facing stereotypes: A case study of Black students on a White campus. *Journal of College Student Development, 42*, 420-429.

Greer, T. M., & Chwalisz, K. (2007). Minority-related stressors and coping processes among African American college students. *Journal of College Student Development, 48*, 388-404.

Greer, T. M. (2003). *Predominantly White and predominantly Black institutions: A qualitative examination of student issues and problems.* Unpublished doctoral dissertation, Southern Illinois University, Carbondale.

Harper, S. R., Carini, R. M., Bridges, B. K., & Hayek, J. C. (2004). Gender diff erences in student engagement among African American undergraduates at historically Black colleges and universities. *Journal of College Student Development, 45*, 271- 284.

Jensen, A. R. (1980). *Bias in mental testing.* New York: Free Press.

Lazarus, R. S., & Folkman, S. (1984). *Stress, appraisal, and coping.* New York: Springer.

National Center for Education Statistics (2003). *Higher education general information survey.* Retrieved February 17, 2006, from http://nces.ed.gov/program/digest/d03/tables/dt264.asp.

National Center for Education Statistics (2004). *Historically Black colleges and universities, 1976 to 2001.* Retrieved July 24, 2007, from http://nces.ed.gov/pubsearch/pubsinfo.asp?pubid= 2004062.

Nottingham, C. R., Rosen, D. H., & Parks, C. (1992). Psychological well-being among African American university students. *Journal of College Student Development, 33*, 356-362.

Prillerman, S. L., Myers, H. F., & Smedley, B. D. (1989). Stress, well-being, and academic achievement in college. In G. L. Berry & J. K. Asaman (Eds.). *Black students* (pp. 198–217). New York: Sage.

Smedley, B. D., Myers, H. F., & Harrell, S. P. (1993). Minority-status stresses and the college adjustment of ethnic minority freshmen. *Journal of Higher Education, 64*, 434–451.

Steele, C. M. & Aronson, J. A. (1995). Stereotype threat and intellectual test perfonnance of African Americans. *Journal of Personality and Social Psychology, 69*, 797–811.

Watkins, D. C., Guidry, J., Green, B. L., Stanley, C., & Goodson, P. (2007). Using focus groups to explore stressful life events of Black college men. *Journal of College Student Development, 48*, 105–118.

AUTHOR

TAWANDA M. GREER is Assistant Professor, Department of Psychology at the University of South Carolina, Columbia.